W 30

Unclassified

Unclassified

Nigel Kennedy in Chapters & Verse

for David —
evidence of what goes on next door!
with love & best wishes —

Paul

Paul Munden

RECENT
WORK
PRESS

Unclassified: Nigel Kennedy in Chapters & Verse
Recent Work Press
Canberra, Australia

ISBN: 9780645651386 (hardback)

A CIP catalogue record for this book is available from the British Library

Cover image: © Adrian Borda
Cover design: Recent Work Press and Paul Munden
Set by Recent Work Press

recentworkpress.com

Limited edition hardback, 200 copies printed

Contents

Acknowledgements

Some of the material in this book was first published in the form of academic essays, in *TEXT, Axon: Creative Explorations*, and in *Migration and Mutation: New Perspectives on the Sonnet in Translation* (Bloomsbury, 2023). An article reflecting on the writing process, 'Unclassified Writing', was commissioned by The Royal Literary Fund and published on their website in December 2023.

'Summer' from 'The Four Seasons' appeared in *Axon: Creative Explorations* (Capsule 2), and the full poem in the Australian Book Review's *States of Poetry* Anthology (ACT, Series Three). 'The Memory of an Angel' was included in *Dancing About Architecture and Other Ekphrastic Manoeuvres* (MadHat Press, 2024), together with an accompanying commentary. 'Shuffle' was first shared as 'Fractious', within the University of Canberra staff exhibition 2018. Versions of other poems first appeared in books and chapbooks published by Recent Work Press.

A number of readers offered me invaluable advice: Simon Sweeney, Clare Taylor, Lyn Wait, Jen Webb, and Anouska Zummo. For other help, thanks are due to Caitlin Morgan, Julia Palmer-Price, and Beata Urbanek-Kalinowska.

Thanks beyond measure go to Shane Strange, whose initial mission as a publisher was the production of ultra-slim poetry books. To have taken on this monster and delivered it in such style was an act of exceptional creative faith, friendship and generosity.

For permission to reprint previously published material, grateful acknowledgement is made to:

Nigel Kennedy; the Yehudi Menuhin Estate; the Nick Drake Estate; the Pete Morgan Estate; John Baxter; Colin Bell; Stephen Duffy; Norman Lebrecht; David Owen Norris; Phill Brown and Tape Op Books;

Faber and Faber for the lines from poems by TS Eliot, Thom Gunn, Ted Hughes, Philip Larkin, Seamus Heaney, and for extracts from books by Humphrey Burton, John Haffenden, Paul Muldoon and Brix Smith Start; LiNQ journal for the lines by Michael Horovitz; London Magazine Editions for the lines by Christopher Hope; Oxford University Press for quotations from *Sudden Genius? The Gradual Path to Creative Breakthroughs* by Andrew Robinson; Little Brown Book Group Limited for the extract from *Great Lost Albums* by Mark Billingham et al (both of the above reproduced with permission of the Licensor through PLSclear).

Extracts from reviews and commentaries by other critics, musicians and writers cited is included under the Australian terms of fair dealing. In the case of other material acknowledged but not encompassed by the above, every attempt was made to contact the copyright holder.

'If you are a novice, start anywhere you like and read backwards or forwards, as you will, much as the connoisseur reads "Tristram Shandy".'

—AL Bacharach, *The New Musical Companion*

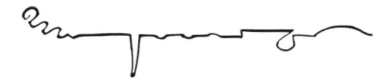

List of Illustrations

Timeline

1956   Nigel Paul Kennedy (NK) born in Brighton, 28
        December
1964   NK attends Yehudi Menuhin School
        NK's mother, Scylla Stoner, remarries to Duncan
        Forbes and moves to Solihull
        NK featured on the BBC's *Town and Around*
        Labour party wins UK General Election
1966   England win the FIFA World Cup
1970   Conservative party wins General Election
        James Marshall Hendrix dies
1973   NK appears in BBC Gala Performance (broadcast
        Christmas Day), leading to a five-year documentary
        project
1974   Labour party wins General Election
        NK wins scholarship to the Juilliard School of Music,
        New York
1976   Aston Villa beat Liverpool ('best team in the world')
        NK performs with Stéphane Grappelli at Carnegie Hall
1977   NK's London debut at the Royal Festival Hall
1978   BBC documentary about NK, *Coming Along Nicely*,
        broadcast
1979   Conservative party wins General Election
1980   NK's natural father, John Kennedy, dies of liver failure
        NK's debut with the Berlin Philharmonic
1981   Aston Villa win 1st Division League title
        NK's debut at the BBC Proms
1982   Aston Villa win the European Cup (vs Bayern Munich)
        Aston Villa win European Super Cup (vs Barcelona)
1984   NK: *Salut d'Amour & other Elgar favourites*, Chandos
        Records
        NK: *Nigel Kennedy Plays Jazz*, Chandos Records
        NK: *Elgar Violin Concerto*, EMI
1985   NK: *Tchaikovsky Violin Concerto & Chausson Poème*,
        EMI
        NK wins Gramophone Recording of the Year Award
        (Elgar Concerto)
1986   NK on *Desert Island Discs*, with Michael Parkinson

NK: *Music by Ellington and Bartok*, EMI
NK featured on Kate Bush, 'Experiment IV', EMI (and
on *Wogan*)

1987   Aston Villa relegated to 2nd division
NK: *Let Loose*, with Dave Heath, EMI
NK: *Walton Violin and Viola Concertos*, EMI
NK featured on *Tchaikovsky Piano Concerto No. 2*,
EMI
NK featured on Paul McCartney, 'Once Upon a Long
Ago', MPL/Parlophone

1988   Aston Villa promoted to 1st division
NK: *Sibelius Violin Concerto*, EMI
NK: *Mendelssohn and Bruch Violin Concertos*, EMI
NK featured on *Talk Talk*, Spirit of Eden, EMI

1989   NK: *Vivaldi, The Four Seasons*, EMI
NK featured on Kate Bush, *The Sensual World*,
Columbia Records
NK featured on Judie Tzuke, *Turning Stones*,
Parlophone

1990   NK: *Vivaldi, The Four Seasons*, VHS tape, EMI
NK plays the Berg concerto at the 'BBC Symphony at
60' concert
NK on *This Is Your Life*, with Michael Aspel
NK wins Golden Rose of Montreux
NK acquires the 'Lafont' Guarneri violin
NK elected a senior vice-president of Aston Villa
England lose to Germany in the FIFA World Cup semi-
finals in Italy

1991   John Drummond makes public criticism of NK
NK: *Brahms Violin Concerto*, EMI
NK has cyst removed from his neck
NK: *Always Playing*, autobiography published
NK awarded honorary doctorate (DLitt) by the
University of Bath
NK awarded Variety Club Showbusiness Personality of
the Year

1992   England Premiership football division founded
NK: *Brahms Violin Concerto*, VHS tape, EMI;
Laserdisc, Pioneer Artists (US)

NK: *Beethoven Violin Concerto*, EMI

NK withdraws completely from public performance

NK featured on Judie Tzuke, *Wonderland*, Essential Music

NK featured (with Brix E Smith) on *Donovan: Island of Circles*, Nettwerk

NK records *Music in Colors* with Stephen Duffy, EMI (released 2004)

1993   NK featured on Robert Plant, *Fate of Nations*, Es Paranza

NK featured on Kate Bush, *The Red Shoes*, Columbia Records

NK featured on Penguin Café Orchestra, *Union Café*, Zopf

NK's version of 'Fire' featured on *Stone Free: A Tribute to Jimi Hendrix*, Reprise Records

NK premieres *Alone at the Frontier*, composed by Dave Heath, with the Minnesota Orchestra

NK wins BRIT Award for Best Classical Recording (Beethoven Concerto)

1994   Aston Villa win League Cup

NK featured on Assorted Artists, *Arcane*, Real World Records

NK: *Vivaldi, The Four Seasons*, Video, EMI

1995   NK featured on The Stranglers, *About Time*, When!/Castle Comms

NK featured on U Srinivas, *Dream*, Real World

1996   NK's son, Sark Yves Amadeus, born to Eve Westmore

NK: *Kafka*, EMI

NK featured on Donovan, *Sutras*, American Recordings

Aston Villa win League Cup

1997   Labour party wins General Election

NK's 'comeback' Harold Holte Solo Recital at the Royal Festival Hall

NK: *Elgar Violin Concerto & Vaughan Williams, The Lark Ascending*, EMI

1998   NK: *Kreisler*, EMI

1999   NK: *Classic Kennedy*, EMI

NK: *The Kennedy Experience*, Sony

NK featured on Lukan, *Face Down*, Depth Records
NK featured on *British Rock Symphony*, Point Music
NK marries Agnieszka Chowaniec

2000   NK: *Riders on the Storm: The Doors Concerto*, Decca
NK: *Kennedy Plays Bach*, EMI
NK & Lynn Harrell: *Duos for Violin and Cello*, EMI
NK performs with The Who at the Royal Albert Hall
NK wins BRIT Award for Outstanding Contribution to British Music

2001   Aston Villa win Intertoto Cup
NK wins Male Artist of the Year BRIT Award
NK featured on Jane Siberry, *City*, Sheeba Records

2002   NK: *Nigel Kennedy's Greatest Hits*, EMI
NK becomes artistic director of the Polish Chamber Orchestra (until 2008)

2003   NK and Kroke: *East Meets East*, EMI
NK featured on Sarah Brightman, *Harem*, EMI
NK featured on *Bach, Lieder Ohne Worte* (with Albrecht Mayer), Deutsche Grammophon
NK: *Vivaldi*, EMI

2004   NK: *Vivaldi II*, EMI
NK appears at WOMAD with Kroke
NK/Kroke featured (remixed) on Chris Coco & Sacha Puttnam, *Remasterpiece*, EMI
NK featured on *Spirits of Music Part I* (2002 Leipzig concert) DVD, EuroArts

2005   NK: *Nigel Kennedy Plays Bach*, DVD, EMI
NK featured on *Spirits of Music Part II* (2002 Leipzig concert) DVD, EuroArts

2006   NK: *Blue Note Sessions*, EMI
NK: *Kennedy Live/Vivaldi Live à La Citadelle*, DVD, EMI
NK featured on Jarek Śmietana, *Autumn Suite*, JSR
NK breaks wrist falling off bicycle

2007   NK: *Polish Spirit*, CD/DVD, EMI
NK: *Blue Note Sessions*, DVD, EMI

2008   NK: *Beethoven and Mozart Violin Concertos*, EMI
NK: *A Very Nice Album*, EMI
NK supports David Davis's civil liberties campaign

NK returns to the Proms after 21-year absence

2009 NK's mother, Scylla Stoner, dies

NK featured on Jarek Śmietana Band, *Psychedelic: Music of Jimi Hendrix*, JSR

2010 Conservative party wins General Election

NK: *SHHH!*, EMI

NK curates Polish Weekend at the Southbank Centre

2011 NK: *The Four Elements*, Sony

NK featured on Clara Ponty, *Into the Light*, Eden Records/Le Chant du Monde

2013 NK: *Recital*, Sony

NK's comments about apartheid in Israel censored by the BBC Proms broadcast

NK accused of voting fraud in the 2010 General Election

2014 NK: *Vivaldi, The New Four Seasons*, Sony

2015 London premiere of Agnieszka Kennedy's production of Chekhov's *The Three Sisters*, with NK's incidental music

2016 Aston Villa relegated to the Championship

British Referendum decides, marginally, in favour of Brexit

NK: *My World*, Neue Meister

2017 NK performs at the Australian Tennis Open

NK 'and friends' at the Royal Albert Hall includes Robert Plant and Jean Luc Ponty

2018 NK: *Kennedy Meets Gershwin*, Warner Classics

2019 Aston Villa promoted to the Premiership

Brexit postponed

2020 NK schedules Beethoven anniversary concerts with a new work of his own, *Für Ludwig Van*

Coronavirus pandemic causes widespread lockdown

UK withdraws from European Union

2021 NK: *Uncensored!* published by Fonthill Books, together with 3-CD set of the same name from Warner Classics

'Nigel Kennedy & The Four Seasons', Episode of *Magic Moments of Music*, dir. Silvia Palmigiano, Isabel Hahn, ZDF/ARTE

2022 Russia invades Ukraine

NK releases film in support of Ukrainian refugees and
the 'Violins Not Violence' charity

NK featured on Donovan, *Gaelia*, Donovan Discs Ltd

2023   NK resumes performing in the UK

'Greatness remains a mystery. There can be supreme technical skill, originality, intelligence, and yet an absence of genius. Initially the word signified an attendant spirit, an animate power that gives to a very few human beings the secret of radiance. The ordinary ... casts a shadow. In a way we do not quite understand, ... genius casts light.

'Instinctively, we flinch from this light. We assure ourselves that genius must pay a terrible price. Often history bears us out: the creator, the supreme artist, the master of politics carries the scars of his greatness. Either in some twist of personality or through private and public desolation and the dramas of rejection that seem to characterize famous lives.' —George Steiner

Chapter 1: Overture

Nigel Kennedy's radically unorthodox approach to performing classical music didn't so much break the rules in its day but re-wrote the entire book.—Trevor Gager

You can't break down barriers without doing some damage.
   —Greg Lake

In 1989, the violinist Nigel Kennedy released a version of Vivaldi's *Four Seasons* that took the classical world by storm. It brought classical music to millions of people who hadn't engaged with it before, but some of the self-appointed guardians of the establishment were aghast at the brazenly commercial approach. Opinion about Kennedy has been divided ever since. BBC Controller John Drummond chastised him for vulgarity and never once booked him to play at the Proms during his 21-year tenure. Others have relished Kennedy's unconventional behaviour and his ability, both as performer and composer, to move across and blend an extraordinary range of musical styles, resisting any notion of classification.

As soon as I heard him play live I was a fan, and resolved to write a book about the nature of his talent and the strange controversy surrounding his fame. I began with *The Four Seasons* furore, going back to the score and discovering the lines of poetry generally attributed to Vivaldi himself. As a poet, I was intrigued. I decided to try my hand at new translations, working out how to make them new in a way that might parallel – and possibly complement – Kennedy's example. I hoped it might provide some useful insight into his own interpretative world.

Suddenly poetry was at the heart of my book. I decided to include poems between each of the eleven prose chapters I'd planned, once again taking my cue from Kennedy, who writes and performs what he calls 'transitoires' between the movements of Vivaldi's concertos. But even with this poetic impulse established, my overall intention languished. Then, during the Covid-19 pandemic and subsequent lockdown days of 2020, Kennedy wrote a book of his own, *Uncensored!*. Reviewing it, Richard Morrison wrote:

> I had to put on Kennedy's sublime recording of Elgar's Violin Concerto to remind myself why I had wasted six hours reading this stuff, but that only raised another question. How can a musical genius capable of touching the soul in so many different styles be such a prat in daily life?[1]

That was the spur I needed, the urge to delve in detail into Morrison's question: to justify the 'wasted' six hours, indeed to beg a further six or more in reading this, my own take on Kennedy's extraordinary achievements.

A host of other questions flooded into the frame: questions about how we nurture exceptional talent; the relationship between so-called genius and unconventional behaviour; the relationship between music and sport; and what it means to be a fan. Above all, I wanted to explore why it matters that everyone should, as the eighteenth-century writer Laurence Sterne puts it, 'tell their stories their own way':[2] tell stories, or write poems, play music, and indeed live life with truly individual purpose. Sterne's great book, the utterly unclassifiable *Life and Opinions of Tristram Shandy*, revels in eccentricity. And as my book became increasingly eccentric, I thought 'yes, that's as it should be'. How else to do justice to a maverick musician, described by his one-time girlfriend Brix Smith as 'a cross between Mozart and Keith Moon'?[3]

Sterne, godfather of eccentric art, became a presiding influence in my creative explorations. His notorious digressions became instrumental to my musings on where the mind roams when we listen to music. I decided to borrow his non-textual interventions: the black page, marbled page, blank page and the 'flourish of liberty' – his various incitements for the reader to bring their own imagination to the artistic adventure.

Uncensored! is Kennedy's story, his life and opinions 'Written in His Own Way and Words', its subtitle closely echoing Sterne's dictum. My aim here is to offer something complementary – in *my* own way and words, as a listener. Kennedy published his book in the run-up to his 64th birthday, a milestone he calls an 'amusing age ... in a position to be associated with a song by the most famous band in history'.[4] When I embarked on mine, my

64th birthday was ten weeks away; I decided to treat that as an amusing deadline, little suspecting that my whole life would be taken over by an ever more complex quest.

I first heard Nigel Kennedy in his debut recital at the Royal Festival Hall, 1997. I had somehow (how?!) missed the initial emergence of the Kennedy phenomenon and couldn't wait to see him play live. It followed a period in which he had withdrawn from the concert stage for several years. I had precious little money, but took the whole family to London from Yorkshire. It was a truly remarkable concert – and *event*. It was the same Richard Morrison who wrote:

> Nige is back! But hang on, is this really the same man? The Festival Hall posters proclaim the two words – Nigel Kennedy – that have chilled the hearts of classical music purists for years. The haircut is the same or worse. And the sound emerging from the figure standing alone with his violin in the spotlight last night is unmistakeable. It is the Bach Chaconne, played with surging passion and almost reckless freedom. Only one British violinist in my lifetime has produced anything as bold or as exhilarating as that.[5]

Morrison went on to praise the diversity of the programme and the extraordinary integrity with which it was delivered:

> No other violinist on earth could manage the astonishing stylistic transition presented here: Bartók's Sonata for Solo Violin (one of the most fiendish challenges in the 20th century repertoire) interlaced with Kennedy's own atmospheric arrangements of Jimi Hendrix numbers. True, few other violinists would want to. But at a time when musical 'crossovers' have acquired a bad name (fat operatic tenors warbling Lennon and McCartney) the audacity of Kennedy's scheme, to say nothing of its dazzling execution – by turns playful, intensely melancholic, or fiercely virtuosic – held a packed Festival Hall spellbound.

Morrison's comments are sincere and I can vouch for the 'spellbound'.

The logic of the programme, baffling to some, was highly considered. As Kennedy has said, 'There are intriguing musical parallels to be drawn between Bartók's adoption of folk, Hendrix's

absorption of the blues, and Bach's "universal freedom of spirit".[6] The fluidity of Kennedy's transitions was reflected in the
single-page programme sheet (as below), which offered a subtle
yet clear plan of the evening, and indeed the philosophy behind
it. As for further programme notes, there were almost none. It
echoed the sentiment of Kennedy's Tchaikovsky and Sibelius
album packaging: 'just listen'. At the end of the recital, having
welcomed Donovan onstage as a guest, he 'finished' the concert
by wandering quietly offstage still playing. More troubadour than
superstar. It felt like a statement – that the music always continues. The concert is not the end of the evening's entertainment.
He'd no doubt be playing on, with friends, at some other location.

Structures, Not Strictures

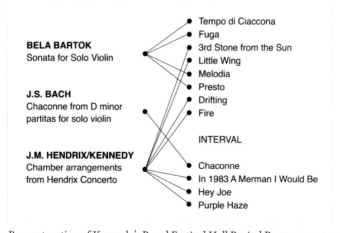

Reconstruction of Kennedy's Royal Festival Hall Recital Programme, 1997

There were two other statements, offered as a 'PS' in the minimal
programme notes. Kennedy wanted people to know that both
the Bartók and Bach renditions were based on the original manuscripts, also that the Hendrix pieces were from a composition
of his own, a work still in progress. The comments, looking both
forwards and back, underlined the serious nature of the whole
undertaking as research and creative practice. The violinist in
the spotlight had frequently been viewed as a flippant brat (and
John Drummond had dismissed Kennedy's success as a 'triumph

of philistinism',[7] more of which in Chapter 3) but here he was to be recognized as a musical authority – and composer.

Morrison was not the only critic to lavish praise on Kennedy's playing. Michael Church was initially wary of Kennedy's foot-stomping, but commented, 'I soon realised, however, that I was watching a great violinist... I was enormously impressed, particularly with the Bach, which was of the highest calibre.'[8]

Morrison's review of the recital appeared, remarkably, on the front page of *The Times*, together with a photo. That seems almost unimaginable now. Google 'Nigel Kennedy' and you'll find *people also ask*, 'What happened to Nigel Kennedy?' It's a reality, of course, that the public gaze eventually drifts away from even the most controversial figures, but the controversy surrounding Kennedy was not the usual celebrity nonsense; it shook the whole edifice of the classical music establishment, and introduced millions hitherto outside that establishment to classical music's joys. Have we forgotten the revolution that brought that much needed change? Or has there in fact been a slump back to 'normal'?

Shortly before his book was published, Nigel Kennedy was indeed in the news again, in a way that typifies the seriousness of his intent, indeed his high standards, and his battle with the new wave of musical segregationists. The villain this time was Classic FM, or 'Jurassic FM' as Kennedy amusingly dubbed the station that at one time had his support as representing a more popular approach to classical music, in contrast to the perceived failings of Radio 3. Classic FM was staging a concert at the Royal Albert Hall, and Kennedy was due to play with Chineke!, an orchestra of young black and ethnically diverse musicians. He wanted to play arrangements of Hendrix, but the sponsors wanted Vivaldi's *Four Seasons* yet again. The further detail is particularly interesting: Kennedy didn't just want to bang out some more Hendrix, regardless of what the audience might want. He planned to perform 'Little Wing' as if conceived by Vaughan Williams, the Celtic-style melody of Hendrix's song lending itself to such an interpretation. (You can hear very clearly what he had in mind in his playing on Jarek Śmietana's recording of the song.) It would have been both musically serious and of popular appeal. Moreover, Kennedy intended to spend rehearsal time over and above what was expected – and to waive his own fee. Instead, he was asked to run out *The Four Seasons* with – shock horror – a conductor, and minimal rehearsal time. It's actually hard to imagine how Jurassic FM thought that would possibly be acceptable, as every part of the equation seems calculated to appal Kennedy's artistic sensibility; it's far too easy to call him 'difficult', making him out to be a spoilt brat. Kennedy was actually standing up for all of us, as listeners with a right to be presented with imaginative, well-prepared musical performances that are not confined to what a radio station deems fit for our tastes. Of rehearsal time, he has said:

> It's slightly incongruous that a group like Girls Aloud is going to be better rehearsed than a symphony orchestra called the royal something or the London something ... It's morally incorrect that people might be paying £50 or £60 a ticket and they're listening to unrehearsed musicians supposedly playing the most sophisticated music in the world. You know, to me that doesn't really hack it.[9]

Clara Schumann might well have agreed: 'They call it a rehearsal here if a piece is played through once', she commented on her first tour to England in 1856.[10]

Kennedy's fall-out with Classic FM is the most recent in a long trail of justified grumps, but it's particularly ironic that the station pretty much owes its existence to Kennedy's success in the late 80s. It launched in 1992, with a mission that mirrored what Kennedy had just achieved – bringing classical music to a much wider public. Both memory and loyalty can be short-lived, with narrow-minded commercial priorities dominant.

It's not just the Drummonds and the Jurassic FMs that would limit our horizons. We are now surrounded by technology that thinks it knows best: you've *listened to that,* so you *might like this.* Such algorithms are unlikely to say that of Bartók and Hendrix; it's too complicated. The re-establishment of musical boxes now drives the whole business. The crusading spirit of Nigel Kennedy is needed now more than ever.

Richard Morrison's comment about Kennedy's debut recital, that 'no other violinist on earth' could have managed the combination of material, might be applied to almost every appearance since. At the Proms in 2008, Kennedy performed not only the Elgar Violin Concerto, a 'monster' (to use his own terminology at the time), enough to drain any violinist of the highest calibre;

he returned later in the evening with his jazz quintet (and guest Jeff Beck) to perform a full set of his own compositions. It's not only the versatility that amazed; it was the musical – and physical – stamina. Some like to suggest that Kennedy has somehow drifted away both from technical excellence and serious purpose: perhaps they find such things incompatible with his sense of fun; perhaps there's a bewildered jealousy in the mix – that an individual should accomplish what he does in a way that goes against the grain of their more traditional, conservative approach to their art. Kennedy would no doubt say they confuse 'serious' with 'boring', and that may indeed be part of it. It's also probably the case that many in the classical world (and no doubt other spheres too) who strive for perfection but don't receive the public reception that Kennedy did at the peak of his fame feel aggrieved by what they see as naïve public opinion, adulation from a vast audience with little knowledge of what else classical music might have to offer. It's true that terms such as 'great' and 'genius' need qualifying if bestowed without benchmarks or comparisons of any sort. Put simply, you have little right to call someone the greatest violinist that ever lived if you've only heard the one. But this brings me yet again to Morrison's comments about Kennedy that I have quoted: it's actually in the latter review, in some respects so scathing, that he uses the word 'genius'. This is not the praise of an ill-informed fan. George Martin used the word too:

> Every few decades or so, mankind delivers a prodigy in one or other of the arts or sciences, and the world is the better for it. In the difficult art of the violin, there have been many extraordinarily fine players but true genius comes along rarely. Only a few stand head and shoulders above the rest. Nigel Kennedy is one such violinist and musician.[11]

How hard it must be for the 'many extraordinarily fine players' to live with that 'head and shoulders above the rest' comment.

Menuhin recognized something exceptional when he created a scholarship for Kennedy at the Yehudi Menuhin School of Music, and Kennedy went on to achieve a perfect score in his ARCM diploma, and a place at the famous Juilliard School in New York. And yet that's somehow further grist to the mill of the detractors, Kennedy viewed as the child prodigy who turned his back on all that lavished attention and support, and somehow wasted his talent. It's hard, of course, to see someone dismissive of opportunities that for you would represent a dream come true, but two things should be mentioned here.

Firstly, Kennedy might come across as dismissive (and it's hard to forgive him for standing up Menuhin in favour of the pub when they were scheduled to perform Bach's double violin concerto, hilarious as the story might be) but he had great respect both for Menuhin, as a man and mentor, and for Dorothy DeLay at Juilliard. He remains appreciative of the support they offered, but not without reservations. Part of my impulse in writing this book is to explore how exceptional ability thrives in response to – or in reaction against – the education it receives, and may confound expectations. (As a writer, and for twenty-five years Director of the National Association of Writers in Education, I have sought, both with some success and considerable frustration, means of allowing creativity to flourish within an educational system that is fundamentally geared against it.) I will discuss in Chapter 2 how Kennedy's mentors and their institutions were mixed blessings for him, but their influence was undeniable. And whoever can take the credit, Kennedy has never turned his back on the hard work of developing his particular gift, practising Bach every day as a baseline from which to explore new musical ideas, never content with past achievement.

Secondly, though, it's necessary to investigate the very notion of genius and its accompanying traits. Drive and determination are often matched by idiosyncrasy that borders on the disturbing or reprehensible; an attraction to chaos. This brings us back to Mozart, whose behaviour was notoriously flippant, even obscene. As Ian Christians writes, 'The musical establishment hated [the film] *Amadeus* and its portrayal of Mozart as lightweight, vulgar and adolescent but blessed by God with enormous gifts.'[12] However authoritative that depiction may or may not be, Mozart was certainly a figure of contradictions, such as characterize other individuals of exceptional talent in a variety of fields. Kennedy's frequent references to football point to revealing examples: George Best, Paul Gascoigne, supremely gifted players with wayward tendencies. Alex Ferguson, former manager of Manchester United, regrets having failed to sign Paul Gascoigne, believing that he could have nurtured his talent more effectively (than Terry Venables et al), saving him from his own worst tendencies. We'll never know if that would have been the case, but I suspect that Kennedy would have been less than impressed by a tamed Gazza, as might we all. One almost feels that Kennedy has consciously followed the dangerous examples, individuals whose talent has thrived despite or just possibly *because of* their demons. The poet Rainer Maria Rilke once said, 'If my devils are to leave me, I'm afraid my angels will take flight as well.'[13] Such a fear may be well founded, or mere superstition – also, of course, a convenient justification for a hellraising lifestyle with or without talent.

In the world of rock music hellraising behaviour goes with the territory, at least it used to. Kennedy's affinity with 'rock royalty', as he refers to the likes of Pete Townshend and Robert Plant, has embraced the hellraising tendency, but people find it harder to accept a violinist behaving with such abandon. Keith Moon's rampages did (almost) no harm to his reputation as a drummer, but for Kennedy the equivalent mayhem has been viewed as damning evidence of a juvenile sensibility utterly at odds with the business of interpreting classical masterpieces. Trashing a Berlin hotel room admittedly looks rather like copycat behaviour, with an element of posturing, but it mostly derives from a 'work hard, party even harder' attitude to life. Kennedy has a natural, irrepressible sense of fun, which isn't actually that unusual for classical musicians, but it's probably not the norm for them to act as party animals with his level of intensity.

In the early years of his success, Kennedy had a connection with real royalty, playing at private and gala concerts, and finding favour with Princess Diana in particular. It's interesting to consider how both were outsiders in their respective arenas, gaining huge popularity – iconic status, even – in the face of tradition. In 1989, Kennedy gained a royal seal of approval, of sorts, when he was chosen as one of The Magnificent Seven, whose mission was to make more people aware of the Duke of Edinburgh's Award (DofE). He was joined by what now sounds like a truly unlikely bunch of inspiring individuals: Chris Bonington, mountaineer; Frank Bruno, boxer; Ronnie Corbett, comedian; Virginia Leng, three-day eventer; Gary Lineker, footballer; and Sue Lawley, broadcaster. (In those days, Sue Lawley was such a household name that it was natural to imagine one was hearing it as Sting belted out 'So Lonely', the Police song of 1978.) Dressed in cowboy gear, the Seven were photographed travelling to London's Ritz Club in a stagecoach. Ronnie Corbett wasn't available on the launch day, so appears in the publicity shot as a cardboard cut-out.

This is daffiness of the highest order, but it's also how Kennedy's lasting friendship with Lineker came about. It's rather appropriate, too, that Frank Bruno should be included, given Kennedy's fondness for boxing (more of which below). There they all were, national treasures in the making. Some of them delivered on that promise, while Kennedy, naturally, chose a different path. Like Diana, he was never going to fit the available mould. Rather bizarrely, he was asked, in the next century, if he was 'in danger of becoming part of the establishment' after all. Would he, for instance, accept a knighthood? His reply was unequivocal: 'I'd never accept a knighthood, because the Queen knows nothing about music, man. How can she say I'm good or bad?'[14]

There was something curiously British – eccentric – about the Magnificent Seven, but Kennedy was the only eccentric *individual* in the gang. They were largely safe choices; you couldn't imagine a Gazza having made the selection. Nor, for that matter, would any other violinist of the day have been in the running. Kennedy was that rare thing, a well-known classical musician who was also an ordinary, Bruno/Lineker kind of bloke. The DofE's embrace of artistic pursuits was never as prominent as its focus on sport and physical adventuring. Kennedy was the perfect figure to make a difference, and his own obsession with sport was a help.

Kennedy's connection with Aston Villa football club is widely known, and I'll say more about it in Chapter 8, noting aspects of sport and music that are more closely related than many might think. (I won't though, as some will be pleased to hear, be delving that deeply into particular Villa matches like Kennedy has done in *Uncensored!*.) While Kennedy's connection is a somewhat unusual obsession, it's surprising how many musicians do hold similar sporting interests – both as fans and athletes. Kennedy's friend and colleague, the cellist Lynn Harrell, was a USTA-rated tennis player, and golfer. Duke Ellington started out more interested in baseball than the piano. The violinist Vanessa Mae has competed as an Olympic skier.

Kennedy also plays golf (and, um, kitchen golf, more of which later). He follows cricket as well as football, and when interviewed on *Desert Island Discs* by Michael Parkinson in 1986, he opted for the latest *Wisden Cricketers' Almanack* as his castaway reading material (the Bible and Shakespeare deemed to be of better use in building a raft). But perhaps the most surprising of his sporting interests is boxing. His long monologues on the subject have bemused many an interviewer over the years, and I may be risking similar bafflement here.

Kennedy chose to take up boxing when he moved to New York to study at the Juilliard School, as something to do, other than prepare for his violin lessons. It's the most unlikely pursuit imaginable for a violinist, who needs to take care of their hands at all costs. He seems to have taken his cue from Miles Davis, who, although he never boxed as such (though his son did), remained a lifelong fan of the sport. For Davis and his friends, 'it occupied their thoughts and shaped their images of themselves ... it was a stance, a way of moving in your clothes, a way of being a man'.[15] Davis liked the 'brutal discipline'. Intriguingly, he 'worked the speedbag with bebop phrasing and triple-tongue rhythms, and for breath and endurance he threw himself into the heavy bag with bass drum explosions'.[16] He made a direct connection with the boxing world in writing music for a documentary film, *Breaking Barriers*, about the boxer Jack Johnson. His work on it was obsessive, 'reading everything he could about Johnson and boxing history, watching films of classic matches and sleeping with a photo of Johnson near his bed'.[17]

Perhaps it shouldn't have come as such a surprise to me when, on opening the Jarek Śmietana Band album, *Psychedelic*, on which Kennedy plays, I removed the CD to reveal a photo of Muhammad Ali. It's the famous image captured just after he knocked out Sonny Liston in the first round of their second title fight, in 1965. Ali towers over Liston, taunting him, demanding that he gets up to carry on the fight. Was this a Kennedy suggestion, or is there in fact a whole culture of boxing fanaticism within the jazz fraternity?

Even Menuhin, of all people, refers to boxing, saying 'Diligent pummelling of the punchball may improve a prize-fighter's performance'. He maintains, however, that 'strength in art can be gained

only through subtlety ... though for all I know the trade of slug-
ging one's fellow man has its refinements of feint and cunning'.[18]

Kennedy realized the folly of his choice pretty quickly, but
it didn't stop his interest in the sport, or following Miles Davis's
example in some fairly explicit ways. He talks about boxing, as
Davis did, with passion and intensity. He draws connections
between boxing and music in terms of the dedication needed and,
crucially, the nerve to go into the ring or the concert stage putting
your neck on the line. Davis's biographer John Szwed writes:

> Boxers and musicians are both itinerant workers in the arena
> of individualism, both pay the dues of a brutal meritocracy,
> and though public figures, both are embedded in a shadowy
> elite with its own code of values under the spotlights.[19]

As Szwed goes on to say, though, Davis makes a crucial distinction: 'Miles understood that the boxer must finally lose his title,
by either retirement or defeat, while the musician can remain
king forever.'[20] Kennedy takes a rather different angle, commenting: 'one rarely sees the boxer's courage, dedication and
commitment reflected in a musician.'[21]

One of my poetry heroes, Pete Morgan, was also a boxer.
He regarded it as a gentleman's sport and encouraged his son
to take it up too. He wrote a particularly fine poem, 'The Meat
Work Saga',[22] that when read seems to dance on the air just as a
boxer does in the ring, while offering philosophical assertions as
its point-winning blows. Boxing and poetry: the pairing defies
our stereotyped views, but there it is. The shattered stereotype is
invariably enlightening. Many poets cite their debt to Pete Morgan's lyrical and performance skills, just as many violinists today
owe much to Kennedy's innovative work as a musician.

I've already mentioned the problematic concept of 'greatness',
but it's something I'll be returning to many times. In the field of
boxing, there's surely an undisputed claim to greatness in the
figure of Muhammad Ali, who was voted Sports Personality of the
Century by BBC viewers in 1999. For Bruno, Ali was on another
level, just as Messi is for Lineker. And his opponent in the famous
'Rumble in the Jungle' match of 1974, George Foreman, who had
himself been World Champion, pointed not only to Ali's boxing
prowess, but the fact that he elevated the sport to an artform:

'to be honest with you, he belonged to the arts because he had ... poetry. He had it all.'[23] The 'poetry' was not only metaphorical. Ali shared his own poems at every opportunity, and their light-footed wit was sometimes matched by a heavyweight humanitarian punch. He was (allegedly) a candidate to become Oxford University's Professor of Poetry. His poetic 'trash-talk' album, *I am the Greatest!* (1963), on which the tracks are labelled 'rounds', had a Foreword by the distinguished American poet Marianne Moore.

At times, certainly in America, Ali was a controversial figure, but Kennedy is in no doubt as to his greatness as a man, let alone a boxer. 'Against far greater odds than we will ever face (whatever colour or creed) and at far greater cost to himself, he established a better world for future generations and for everybody around him.' Kennedy was introduced to Ali personally, at a British title fight where Kennedy had played the national anthem 'in a way which disturbed and upset some of the more mentally fragile and limited members of the British public'. Ali showed Kennedy respect: 'he treated a fukkin' violinist as being just as important as anyone else.'[24]

All the above goes some way to explaining why *Uncensored!* should sport Kennedy in boxing pose on its cover. It's a book with pugnacious attitude, with the Arts Council, the BBC, and the whole classical music establishment taking the biggest hits. But it's not a pose or attitude adopted for the book. If the boxing moves which characterize Kennedy's arrival or departure from the stage or interview are in any way an affectation, it's one that runs deep, just as it did for Miles Davis and friends. He's had to fight his own corner ever since he was small, becoming increasingly at ease with difficult, even dangerous situations; relishing the edginess, even the physical threat of street fights in the build up to matches at Villa Park. He's not a violent man, quite the opposite. But in the words of Pete Morgan's boxing poem, he 'can turn the tables', he 'can get up and win', he 'can dream'.[25]

The final bell is approaching, I promise, but I need to say: I've never been interested in boxing *per se*, but I caught Ali's various fights on TV in my parents' house, and was utterly entranced. He remains unique as a boxer who caught my imagination. And that, I am sure, is also true of Kennedy as violinist for the thousands, maybe millions, who have no great interest in classical music but have nevertheless found Kennedy enthralling. That, of course, is no definition of greatness, though it may be an indicative factor – if accompanied by substantial expert opinion and endorsement from peers. Rankings, however, simply don't exist as they do in sport. As a violinist, you don't have opponents as such (although Kennedy effectively took on Sebastian Karpiel-Bulecka as part of his England vs Poland event, described in Chapter 8). There may be music competitions (the least said about which the better), but there's never a world title contest. We'll never be treated to a violin face-off like the drum battle played out by Dave Grohl and Animal on the Muppets in 2015. (Drum kits destroyed, they each concluded that the other won.)

And so it is that I reluctantly resist calling Kennedy 'Britain's greatest violinist', as Jools Holland did when introducing Kennedy on his show in 1996; it's too simplistic, but similar lazy hyperbole abounds. The blurb for *Grumpy Old Rock Star* describes Rick Wakeman as 'the most gifted keyboardist of his generation'. What about Keith Emerson? Jon Lord? Wakeman himself, wonderful as he is, may well have been embarrassed by that. And although I personally agree with it, the statement on the promotional leaflet for Paul McCartney's two volume publication, *The Lyrics* (2021), that it's 'a unique self-portrait by our greatest living songwriter' is also unnecessarily adamant. As I write, in January 2022, plaudits have been flooding in for Jeff Beck, who has died at the age of 78: 'legendary' has been a frequent term in the headlines, rather than 'the greatest', and that feels right, even though none of his contemporaries did anything but look up to him. But then Alice Cooper on facebook had to come out with 'the greatest guitarist, PERIOD – The greatest of all time.'

The fact that Kennedy is, I fully admit, my *favourite* violinist doesn't mean that I've paid no attention to his critics, or indeed the wealth of other violin playing past and present. Part of the pleasure in researching this book has been the discovery of many other musical marvels. And Kennedy's own writing, despite its primary focus on his own life, offers generous and illuminating pointers to many other musicians. The process of writing has also helped me to understand what exactly it means to be a 'fan'. It's not, as one might think, an uncritical position. Just think of football fans, and their need, on occasions, to vent fury at their players, manager, or board. Ian Hamilton's wonderful book *Gazza Agonistes* (1993) was a particularly helpful model in how to write thoughtfully as a fan. It also encouraged my belief that mere words could do some justice to a non-verbal field of artistry, be that football or music.

Kennedy refers to *Uncensored!* as his first book, which probably comes as a surprise to those who have read the 1991 book, *Always Playing*, which also bears his name. Written as a first person account, it turns out to have been ghost-written by John Stanley, his manager at the time, Kennedy dictating his thoughts over the phone while in Florida.[26] Reading the two books, it's clear that two very different voices are at work. There is some overlap, in terms of the stories covered, but the emphasis is very different. The early book takes stock of Kennedy's initial success in challenging the staid traditions of the classical music establishment, and broadening classical music's appeal. And even though there is plentiful rebelliousness in evidence, the book was clearly aiming to consolidate Kennedy's reputation, to cash in on a big wave of public interest. But written, as we now know, by his manager, at a time when Kennedy had only just recorded the Brahms concerto, and only two years after his *Four Seasons* breakthrough, the book didn't take any undue risks; it didn't burn any bridges. Yes, it described the problems in dealing with record company executives. There was even a mild cockiness that the battle had been won, given the *Four Seasons'* success. But Stanley (if not Kennedy) was no doubt thinking ahead, knowing that new deals would need to be struck. In actual fact, Kennedy would only release one more classical recording before taking a major break (the focus of Chapter 6).

Written thirty years later, *Uncensored!* is altogether less guarded. I'm tempted to say the gloves are off, but the cover shows them on. Gone is the need for any diplomacy – with the music industry, or indeed the audience. It's 'take it or leave it' stuff, though the chapter in which he lists his recordings (chaotically, and incompletely), towards the end, is rather touchingly peppered with pleas to 'check it out!' or 'buy it!'. The book presents things that would have been unthinkable – even for Kennedy – when still building a career, but he's now at ease in being utterly true to himself, to spend pages talking about his escapades with Villa fans, and the police of various countries, and to ignore whole swathes of his musical success. But while on one level he may not care, the publication of *Uncensored!* still presented a clear risk that Kennedy's own reputation, rather than that of the BBC, Arts Council etc, might be the biggest casualty.

I'm put in mind of Ken Russell's *Lisztomania*, a film many found unwatchable, just as some will find *Uncensored!* unreadable. There was widespread feeling that dear old Ken – one of our alternative national treasures – had finally lost it (producer David Puttnam said 'frankly, he just seemed to go off his rocker'[27]), and that his reputation couldn't possibly recover. But if *Lisztomania* was Russell's silliest venture by far, it was nevertheless a curiously personal film, and a bravura example of having a truly crazy idea and seeing it through in a way that has remarkable logic within the context of its own madcap rules. There's a further parallel to be drawn with Kennedy in the way Russell sides with rock royalty, when expectations were for a more faithful treatment of a classical composer. The director, fresh from filming The Who's rock opera, *Tommy*, cast Roger Daltrey as Liszt, Ringo Starr as the Pope, and brought in Rick Wakeman to render Liszt's compositions as rock fodder for the soundtrack.[28] Thirteen years later, in 1988, Russell included Kennedy in his South Bank Show episode for London Weekend Television: *Ken Russell's ABC of British Music*, a clip of which can be found in what remains online of the Kennedy episode of *This Is Your Life* (1990). There's something inevitable about the fact that Kennedy and Russell should be linked, twin followers of William Blake's maxim that 'The road of excess leads to the palace of wisdom.'[29]

Lisztomania was a box-office disaster, but it has its fans; I guess I'm one of them, along with broadcaster Tom Service, and that doyen of film critics, Roger Ebert, who called it 'a berserk exercise of demented genius'[30] (yes, genius). For Tom Service, Liszt himself was 'someone who dared to face the world head on, who lived the contradictions of his character'. He suggests that Liszt's 'fearlessness' and 'wildly imaginative universe of music' has been a gift to us all. 'We're all Lisztomaniacs now', he claims.[31] Well, possibly. The wildly imaginative, and the fearless, poses a threat to those who don't want their expectations confounded. And there are those who would sideline Liszt for his so-called showmanship, just as they wash their hands of Russell or Kennedy. But it's true that such figures alter our imaginative landscape. Liszt turned the piano sideways on to the audience in order to *present* his playing more powerfully to his listeners. That in itself changed concerts forever. But his music was always more about poetry than virtuosity, despite so much received opinion. And Kennedy – as I hope to portray in this book – has confounded expectations not only with sensational musical ventures, but also with remarkably subtle, restrained and moving interpretations and compositions. Who knows, maybe Russell's Gershwin film, had it ever been made, might have pulled back from excess, and like Kennedy's Gershwin album, enabled us to hear the music afresh, without 'abrasive pseudo-cultural singing and two dimensional acting'.[32]

Those fearless and wildly imaginative qualities mentioned above may always steal the headlines, as indeed they have with Kennedy, but the contrasting, complementary qualities we group under the title of 'poetry' are equally vital. Contrasts and contradictions are themselves a crucial part of what is *marvellous*. Kennedy's performances have been characterized by extraordinary contrasts, just as his own character seems full of contradictions. There's been a common but blinkered perception that his playing is aggressive, frenetic; that his personality is brash. Yes, there's plentiful, almost unrivalled attack in his playing – where the music needs it; elsewhere however it is astonishingly tender. He makes those contrasts dramatic in themselves. It's part of what he loves in much of the music he has played and admired. He talks of it when discussing Vivaldi, comparing that mastery of chiaroscuro to the shifts within a Peter Gabriel concert – the comparison startling in itself. In his playing of concertos from later eras, the contrasting speeds and dynamics of the various movements are often accentuated well beyond what most of his peers would dare. Anyone who has paid close attention to his work knows this well, but for others – perhaps a majority – the predominant Kennedy image has obscured the complexity. 'Image' itself has been part of the issue, something I discuss in Chapter 5. Kennedy has benefited from some effective marketing and management, notably handled by John Stanley and later Terri Robson (who was also Pavarotti's manager), but sometimes a simplistic image, even a caricature, is what remains of a successful marketing campaign in the public imagination.

The 'punk violinist' persona was to some extent cultivated by Kennedy himself, and having a Spitting Image puppet in one's name, however grotesque, was pretty good going for a violinist. When, in 2019, Warner released *Nigel Kennedy: The Early Years (1984-1989)*, a box set of seven CDs, the punk image was still firmly in place. The cover instantly brings to mind The Sex Pistols, whose album *Never Mind the Bollocks, Here's the Sex Pistols*, used the same lurid yellow. There's a black band covering Kennedy's eyes, reminiscent of the defaced image of the Queen that appears on the Sex Pistols' 'God Save the Queen' single. On one level, it's all understandable, relevant in a way to the early years in question, but it also risks a denial of the complex, subtle musical riches on offer in the seven CDs. Thankfully, John Fordham's excellent essay in the accompanying booklet does the opposite.

The broadcaster Trevor McDonald offers a recollection that, while highlighting Kennedy's unconventional appearance, playing the Beethoven Concerto, makes a more interesting observation – about the event as a whole: 'He [Kennedy] stood there, in long boots, very un-Festival Hall-like garb. Klaus Tennstedt was the conductor, and they looked so different, so odd, but they created this marvellous harmony, this marvellous atmosphere, and it was quite wonderful.'[33] It's not just Kennedy who is odd; it's the pairing with Tennstedt, and the fact that a sublime musical performance emerged is yet more oddity – in a thoroughly good way. There was also, for McDonald, an element of edginess, of worry – that the violinist's headscarf would get entangled in his bow. He made it his top choice on *Desert Island Discs*.

Can such precarious oddity really deliver? That seems to have been the initial question for some, partly a matter of sheer intrigue. When oddity triumphs, the question changes. Is it, perhaps, fundamental? And does it remain interesting in itself? Samuel Johnson famously commented, 'Nothing odd will do long. Tristram Shandy did not last.'[34] But his opinion of Laurence Sterne's groundbreaking book has proved to be wrong. Written not so long after Vivaldi wrote *The Four Seasons,* it still stands as a monument to the triumph of odd; one could call it a textbook for the fearless imagination, for every artist determined to do things differently.

Sterne's wish, 'to let people tell their stories their own way',[35] is for all of us, whatever our talents. It's a clarion call for non-conformity. I suspect we warm to that, as amateurs, with modest or little talent in whatever fields we may nevertheless be interested in, as it suggests that distinctive achievement of some sort is still possible. There's no absolute, perfect example of how anything should be done, despite frequent educational claims to the contrary. This isn't, as some might be quick to conclude, anti-excellence. On the muddy local football pitch, during a Sunday morning kickaround, we might just score an astonishing goal. And while that doesn't make us Gazza, or Messi, we've still achieved a little bit of greatness, *our own way*, which in turn allows us to grasp even more the artistry of our heroes. Those who excel at football have most likely emerged from ordinary backgrounds; there's no mystical domain from which we see them suddenly appear as fully-fledged superstars. The same is true of rock and other popular music. Punk, in particular, encouraged the idea that anyone could make effective music by just getting on with it, just as earlier skiffle bands made the most of homemade or improvised instruments. But classical music has often presented a more baffling and potentially off-putting scenario. Who are these exotic creatures in their tailcoats and bow ties? From what strange land do they come? And what, even, are these instruments they play? (Kennedy, in *Uncensored!*, claims his muggers in New York had no idea what his violin was.) Weirdest of all, what is this person doing, going through such strange physical and facial contortions, on a podium, with no instrument at all, just a white stick?

When Kennedy burst onto the scene, television screens in particular, with his *Four Seasons* recording of 1989, there was a new surge of interest in classical music and, I believe, a new perception of who those exotic creatures described above might actually be. They might be football fans. They might speak with a less than posh accent, and share jokes. They might, after all, be on a mission to have fun, and communicate with an audience not privy to the rules and rituals of their exclusive world. Here was someone prepared to step forward from that world and do things their own way.

Such boldness wouldn't have worked, or had any lasting impact, if the level of skill involved hadn't been so very high. This wasn't a case of 'Eddie the Eagle', brilliant as Michael Edwards' story as a determined ski-jumper may be.[36] But Kennedy's punk association was interesting, carrying as it did that suggestion of 'anything's possible'. There were undoubtedly many failed or dormant violinists who once again took up their instruments. At the same time, other top-level players were given reason to believe that there wasn't one single, traditional *modus operandi*. Naturally this wasn't necessarily good news for the conservatoire system. Kennedy had famously dropped out of Juilliard, and many other star names – some of them quoted in this book – have done the same. The conformative model of success had been exploded.

Kennedy's success, selling over two million copies of a single abum (*The Four Seasons*), was that extraordinary, contradictory thing: an achievement of the highest order (regardless of whether or not you like his interpretation of Vivaldi), and a message to the world that such achievement – and indeed access to it – is not the preserve of a particular elite.[37] As I discuss in Chapter 5, however, the success was not without problems. It threatened to typecast Kennedy as Mr Four Seasons. And the purists were still at large, those who believe that popularity is a sign of mediocrity, and that boundaries need to be preserved at all costs. Kennedy has had to contend with considerable criticism alongside the effusive praise. He may treat most of the criticism with disdain, and it may even have urged him to follow his own path with even greater resolution, but it's wrong to assume he has pursued his own projects with total freedom. As later chapters here reveal, there have been many frustrations.

I began this introduction with Richard's Morrison's conflicted comments. There have been two other critical encounters over the years that have acted as prompts to me writing this book. The first was in 2006, as I settled into my seat on a train from York to London with the BBC *Music* magazine, which featured Kennedy on the cover. 'That awful man!' said the passenger next to me. I couldn't let that go, of course, without brief reply, but the very idea that such prejudice was at large made me determined to organize my thoughts and be better prepared for any such argument in the future. A further, less confrontational but equally compelling encouragement followed two years later, reading Rob Cowan's review of Kennedy's Beethoven/Mozart album. While approving its boldness, Cowan wouldn't give it a general recommendation, considering it only for 'Kennedy fans, and the curious'.[38] I was outraged not only on Kennedy's behalf, but for all those who place proper value on curiosity; outraged for curiosity itself.

The list of 'whys', as to the purpose of this book, continued to grow, even as I was writing. I realized how many interesting things had been written about Kennedy over the years, and what interesting comments Kennedy himself had made in countless interviews, but I realized, too, how ephemeral such comments can be. It's ironic, in our internet age, when commentary of all sorts is captured seemingly forever, online, that certain material should still be so hard to find, or vanishes completely. If digitized, older print material may still be hidden behind a paywall. Other things, such as concert programmes – even CD booklets, as I discuss in Chapter 9 – are discarded. In the new world of music streaming, for all its undoubted benefits, certain things are lost. I figured I would be doing a general service in bringing together some of the most informative, intriguing and revealing Kennedy literature and broadcast material from the past five decades or so, and placing it within the context of other writing about music and art in general – including poetry.

How often we hear music, at its best – either as composition or performance – compared to poetry. It works the other way too, poetry described as musical. Vivaldi's *Four Seasons* provides an example of a work approached through both arts; Vivaldi may well have been the poet, the writer of the sonnets inscribed in the score, as well as the composer of the music. Kennedy's interpretations of Vivaldi have taken considerable note of the poetry, and the poetry of his performances – of repertoire of all sorts – has been widely applauded. I have therefore used poetry as a significant touchstone in my prose chapters here, but have also included new poems of my own (including new translations of the Four Seasons sonnets). It seemed appropriate to add a creative element to my writings; hence chapters *and verse*. I have two models for this approach. One is the work of Paul Hyland, who uses poems as preludes to the chapters of two books: *Purbeck: The Ingrained*

Island (1978) and *Wight: Biography of an Island* (1984). The second model is from Kennedy himself, who inserts his own transitional passages – 'transitoires' – between movements of other works. My poems included here are therefore titled 'transitoires' in recognition of Kennedy's prior use of the device.

I had moments of doubt, moments of thinking the whole enterprise was a ridiculous endeavour, but like Richard Morrison, I only had to play a CD or watch one of the relatively rare DVDs of Kennedy in performance, and I knew exactly why his music mattered to me so much, and why I should attempt to understand and explain my reaction.

I became more methodical, collecting and listening to every recorded Kennedy work that I could find. I have made at least some passing comment on all of them, and sometimes considered them at much greater length. I have, inevitably, made a few comparisons with other violinists' performances of certain works, and noted some comparisons made by others, but I haven't been tempted into some kind of Record Review. More significantly, I hope, I delved back into my own musical memory – two decades and more of attending Kennedy concerts. Following the Harold Holt Solo Recital at the Southbank Centre, I've caught a Kennedy concert whenever I could: Greatest Hits in Sheffield; the marathon Polish Weekend, again at the Southbank; I've heard him play the Beethoven, Brahms, Elgar, and various Bach concertos, three utterly different versions of *The Four Seasons*, and three Proms performances – not to mention others on television. His own compositions have also featured in those concerts: *The Four Elements*, pieces from *Kafka, Recital, My World*, and *Kennedy Meets Gershwin*, plus many from the two Nigel Kennedy Quintet albums. I hope this is a reasonably representative experience, even though I know that his live performances all around the world have encompassed so much more.

With my head full of music, and poetry, and a slowly amassing bulk of written notes, there remained a question of audience and style. I wanted the book to speak not only to musicians, both professional and amateur, but also to the general (curious) reader, and to fans and detractors alike. I felt nervous initially, writing about music, not least because it's often done so very badly, in a way that bears no relation whatsoever to what we hear. Kennedy has referred to 'the mountain of intellectually self-satisfied crap already written about all kinds of music',[39] and I didn't want to add to it. I wanted to find a less precious style than experts and academics tend to adopt when talking to each other. So although I've made use of some classic texts, and a handful of pretty obscure monographs, I was more attracted and influenced by eloquent writers such as pianist Jeremy Denk, and the more colloquial storytelling of Dave Grohl. But most of all, Tom Service and his weekly broadcast on Radio 3, *The Listening Service*, has been particularly inspiring.

All of the above might sound strange, given my long association with various universities, but just as Kennedy reacted against the conventions of the classical music world, I too have struggled with certain expectations of academia, not least the standard prose style of academic publications. There's an appalling, mangled variety of prose that's become not only acceptable but required, and the sooner it's rumbled the better. Somewhat perversely, you might think, I undertook a professional doctorate, but the intention was specifically to find a way of writing that was academically rigorous while cutting through the crap. Above all, it needed to remain personal, an aspect of writing that's still widely denied within scholarly circles. Kennedy, who had the good fortune to be given an honorary doctorate by the University of Bath, has been outspoken about 'degrees' and 'toilet paper diplomas',[40] and yes – why did he need one from Juilliard, when the concert stage beckoned? But you can no longer gain a university position, even as a poet, without a PhD. Sometimes you have to take on the system at its own game.

Armed with a DProf, I found a university on the other side of the world where, despite – or I like to think *because of* – their high standards, they embraced a creative approach to pretty much everything. The University of Canberra has, to my knowledge, the only Centre for Creative and Cultural Research, and it has International Poetry Studies as a prime focus. I was given considerable freedom to write and to *think*, though setting up and running Canberra's first ever poetry festival was part of the bargain. I owe my colleagues there a debt of gratitude for supporting my eccentric mission; for including my various Nigel Kennedy poems in staff projects and exhibitions; for listening to me talk at academic seminars on the England v Poland football match of 1973, and how Kennedy rendered its high drama as an improvised musical event.

A possible structure for the book developed in my head. I've already mentioned the transitoires, and I felt the sequence of prose chapters should in some way correlate with a programme of music; hence this 'Overture', the midway 'Interval' and the final 'Encore'. The sequence is also largely biographical, even though the book is definitely not a biography as such. Despite my liking of non-linear narrative, it was simply convenient here to use a largely chronological framework. Since the chapters are also thematic, the chronology isn't always precise, but a Timeline is provided to show where my musings have wandered.

Reference to structure is a frequent feature of Kennedy's comments about music. Menuhin also stresses its importance: 'Leonardo da Vinci felt he could not paint a body unless he knew its skeleton, and the skeleton of a piece of music is the structure around which the notes, the flesh, develop and take shape.'[41] This makes sense for the painter, or composer, but it's sometimes less clear what is meant by a sense of structure in reference to a musical performance. It's all too easy to think of musical structure as something that's simply *there*, not requiring attention in the same way that other aspects of a work require interpretation. But structure, of course, is a feature not only of the overall piece but also of its smallest phrases, and the way in which those parts are voiced – dynamically shaping the whole – is essential to our sense of the larger structure that might for the average listener seem an abstract concept. It's easier to grasp the composition of a painting, or the architectural whole of a cathedral, at a single glance, than it is to take in the structure of a long musical work. But the best performances enable us to view the whole cathedral, as it were, within a span of time.

A poetry recital offers a useful example of what I mean. I was involved in a project, Poetry by Heart (which I mention further in Chapter 3), in which teachers and students were encouraged to perform poems from memory. In one preparatory session, poet Mario Petrucci asked the audience to react if they sensed any loss of trajectory, a moment when the projected structure of the poem had shown a fault, or collapsed. This didn't mean a pause; a poem is full of them, and they can even be sustained. There's a subtle but crucial difference between a long, purposeful pause and a moment when the sense – the flow, the *structure* – is lost. The same goes for music. And it's not only a performer's memory failure that may cause a problematic hiatus. The listener's attention may be lost even in the midst of a frantically paced passage if the sense of the whole has gone astray.

Contradictory as it may seem, structure affords freedom. This is the essence of jazz, and musicians who play with the greatest (truest) freedom are also the structuralists at heart. When Jeff Beck said, 'I don't care about the rules' it's because the rules were in his bloodstream. He went on to say, 'if I don't break the rules at least 10 times in every song, then I'm not doing my job properly'.[42] You can't break them if you don't grasp them.

Sometimes, with free jazz, free verse, a seemingly wild cadenza, or (heaven help us) with Kennedy's self-styled hands-off free-wheel driving, the plot may seem to be lost. As audience (or passenger) you need faith, which may or may not be justified. I hope you'll keep faith with my own, eccentric free-roaming train of thought in these pages, and I do at least have the backing of a fellow poet and friend, Philip Gross, who writes:

> What gives poetry life is often the spread – the apparent randomness, even – of its references ... the unexpectedness of what gets connected with what, for example in the knight's move of a startling simile, is the thing that makes us *see it new*. It's hard to imagine how to advise a writer to prepare for this activity except by recommending the worst sort of academic practice – to read widely, by chance and whim and serendipity, picking up snippets of this and that.[43]

Gross's wish for us to 'see it new' connects with Ezra Pound's 'make it new' statement that I discuss in Chapter 4, with particular reference to Vivaldi, and what Kennedy has done to make those familiar concertos – and so many other musical works – new. Poets, myself included, have always known the importance of seeing it new, and the value of that 'spread' in forming poems, but I hadn't previously conceived of an equivalent strategy in research, what Gross goes on to call '*free-search*, reading way beyond your field, with no method or purpose in mind ... This isn't sloppy or lazy, but a particular tool – the discipline of deliberate indiscipline, you might say.' I realized how a maverick approach to research and academic writing was exactly what was needed in order to do justice to my maverick subject, and the startling connections he makes – in music as in life. It occurs to me, now that I've finished, that my approach to writing this book has had something in common with a musician's approach to playing free jazz.

Almost as my first exercise in free-search, I took a book from my shelves that I'd never even opened before: *The New Musical Companion* edited by AL Bacharach. I think it must have been given to me as some school prize. Delving into it, I was stunned by some of the antiquated views about music and performance, but I've included in these chapters some choice quotations, partly as amusing asides, but also to demonstrate how our musical culture has changed over my lifetime, with the Kennedy Effect a significant part of the revolution. I then wondered: was this book of mine some kind of *companion*? A Nigel Kennedy Companion? A Poetic Companion – to Nigel Kennedy? Or was that actually the wrong way round? After all, Kennedy has been my musical companion for years.

Titles were tried out, and some seemed briefly appealing, like interesting clothes that nevertheless weren't right for the occasion, or quite *me*. They were put aside, just like the books that were so helpful, initially: 'poetic biographies' written, for instance, by Jessica Wilkinson (*Suite for Percy Grainger*, and *Music Made Visible, A Biography of George Balanchine*). Jonathan Coe's biography of BS Johnson, *Like a Fiery Elephant*, had also been at hand, Johnson widely considered to be an heir to Laurence Sterne. Structured unlike a conventional biography, it is highly personal in its approach, and asks questions about 'the fundamental motives and contradictions at the heart of all literary activity'.[44] That much I certainly held onto. But I wasn't writing a biography, or even a critical study of however unconventional a sort. I realized I was writing something unclassifiable, and how that was actually appropriate. Classification of music has always been anathema to Kennedy, and any classification as a musician is something that he continues to resist. As author of this book, I'm resistant too. I take my lead instead from Sterne, and his unclassifiable Shandean adventures.

I've mentioned the various visual inventions that Sterne makes in his text. One, the marbled page, Sterne describes as the 'motley emblem of my work'.[45] As originally produced (an example of which appears at the end of this chapter), no two marbled pages were ever the same, thereby ensuring that each copy of the work is unique, emblematic of its endlessly varied readership. It struck me that the symbol of the marbled page, pointing to the one-to-one relationship between writer and reader, was also expressive of what I and so many others have experienced listening to Nigel Kennedy perform: his ability – even within a massive, packed concert hall, where you're sitting at the very back – to communicate the music directly to you, an individual. No one else in the auditorium can know precisely how you are affected, but they'll have similarly unique experiences of their own. And if anyone were to go to the next night's performance too, it would be different again.

So here it is, a test of my own curiosity, boldness, and eccentricity; an object lesson in the fanatical; hopefully, too, an informative and thought-provoking book about its primary subject, a musician who has inspired many more fans than me. I gave myself ten weeks, but it took well over ten months, and probably had a ten-year gestation.

The poet Ian McMillan, in his Foreword to a book on performance poetry that I once edited, amusingly wrote that 'of course we have to accept that a book about performance poetry is a bit like a photograph of a bag of chips or a drawing of a piano concerto'.[46] He's absolutely right, but remembering that remark has made me realize that this new book is not so much trying to capture the music of Nigel Kennedy as relating my experience in listening to him play; where my mind roams under the spell of his musicianship, and in contemplating his uncompromising approach to life. Picture Kennedy on his desert island, reading the *Wisden Almanack*, mere statistics enabling him to travel into mesmerizing realms of cricketing artistry. Treat this as an invitation to *free-search* your own particular memories and horizons.

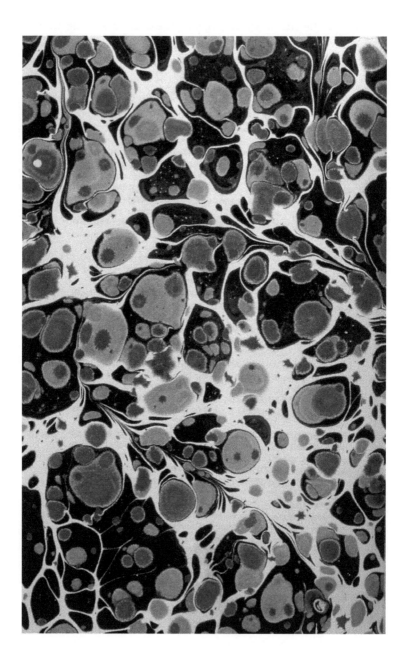

Outlaw

During her lessons, a small boy sits
under the grand piano, an outlaw
hiding in the shade of a dark tree,
happily doing nothing but watch
the girl's bare legs with their white
ankle socks and buckled blue shoes.

He listens to the tentative, repetitive
mistakes, and then – when his mother
takes charge – the full power
of the music in the canopy overhead:
the boom of the tingling strings;
the sheriff's posse on the gallop.

Chapter 2: Coming Along Nigely

I have never let my schooling interfere with my education.
—Mark Twain

In 1978, the BBC broadcast a documentary account of the young Kennedy's progress: *Coming Along Nicely*. 'Nicely'? What on earth were they thinking? The title smacks of a pre-conceived notion of compliant development, everything that Kennedy's story contradicts. As a pupil he was by turns dormant, recalcitrant – and eventually outrageously successful.

The main focus of this chapter is on schooling, but education begins before school. We can generally talk before attending even a nursery school, learning by example. For those who are in some sense destined for musical accomplishment, an equivalent introduction of some sort to music is also likely to have taken place. And since his mother was teaching piano while pregnant, Kennedy goes so far as to say that 'even from before being born, there was music going on'.[1]

Some introductions are pretty commonplace: the gift of a toy drum, or whistle, things intended primarily for play, but nevertheless leading a child into experiment with rhythm and melody. With electronic toys more the norm, more children probably have little electric keyboards to play with, but few will do much more than bash them – a drum and whistle in one. Venezuelan pianist Gabrielle Montero is a notable exception: given a keyboard in her playpen, when only seven months old, she quickly played tunes – before she could even speak. Montero's great skill is at improvisation, clearly a *gift* in the rather different sense of the word.

It is far beyond the scope of this book to analyze the occurrence of inborn talent, though there is evidence, as with Montero, that it may exist without obvious genetic precedent. Yehudi Menuhin was of the firm opinion that violinists, in particular, are born, saying 'I don't think you can become a violinist unless the skill is born in you'.[2] He qualified this by saying 'and even then you need one of the few right teachers to develop it'; more of that anon. Whatever innate gifts we may be born with, the way in which they are nurtured – or go unrecognized – is crucial. I wonder, for instance, how Montero might have developed had that toy keyboard not been presented. Many people don't come across a piano keyboard of any sort until much later, if at all.

In Kennedy's case, instruments, example and encouragement were all there. My poem preceding this chapter pictures the young Kennedy under his mother's piano, a scene he has himself described, and which mirrors the image from a poem by DH Lawrence, 'Piano':

> Softly, in the dusk, a woman is singing to me;
> Taking me back down the vista of years, till I see
> A child sitting under the piano, in the boom of the tingling
>   strings
> And pressing the small, poised feet of a mother who smiles
>   as she sings.[3]

Lawrence's poem captures the potency of that childhood experience by viewing it as an adult recollection. The phrase 'the boom of the tingling strings' was the inspiration for Jon Lord's composition of the same name. Lord is a musician much admired by Kennedy, indeed the two have worked together. He is probably best known as part of the rock band Deep Purple, but here he gives us a piano concerto; a musical boundary crossing as big as anything Kennedy has done, and in the opposite direction. Unlike those who like to prove their alternative credentials with tortuous or ineffectual products, both Kennedy and Lord work with natural ability in multiple spheres.

For Lord, the highly personal nature of Lawrence's poem was compelling. He writes: 'The "I" of the poem seemed to be me.'[4] The other key factor is the mother – or rather the relationship of mother and child. As in my own poem, and in Kennedy's early memory, the mother is not *teaching* the child; that is for later. The child is simply *there*, listening – and in a particularly intense way, positioned within the 'boom' and the 'tingling' of an actual instrument, not just listening to the radio or a record player. This is how we first learn a language, by listening, not to a lesson, but absorbing the speech of those close to us, in action.

So far so good, then, for Kennedy: the source of his first musical nourishment was his mother (and grandmother, who also taught piano). It's natural for a child to copy, especially if the impetus comes from within. The model of children learning to play music themselves was right in front of him, without being forced on him personally. Mis-timed encouragement or worse, coercion, is not necessarily effective. As Kennedy himself says, 'Being just a "small person" doesn't stop you forming opinions.'[5] It was only when Kennedy started showing active interest in the piano that his mother started teaching him, for fifteen minutes a day, before he set off to his Montessori school in Brighton, The Fold, together with his imaginary friend, Bertie.

The circumstances may have been propitious, but such scenarios may still prove insufficient – if not for natural talent, and we can only assume that Kennedy was at an advantage, both his parents and grandparents being musicians. His grandfather was the renowned cellist, Lauri Kennedy, who played with Kreisler. His father, John, also a cellist, had left before he was born, and was therefore a negative role model in other ways. His mother wanted Nigel to learn a stringed instrument, but the cello's associations made it *persona non grata*; hence the violin.

There are gifts, and there are poisoned chalices; and gifts, in the more ordinary sense, can also impress us in different ways.

Gifts

He can still hear his mother's
muffled ground floor piano
as he whiles away hours
in his attic bedroom. On tiptoe
he can see the blank
horizon beyond the pier.
A platypus and koala keep
company in the corner – gifts
from the father he has never met,
who plays the cello,
and is drinking himself to death
under a harsh southern sun
on the far side of the world.

This year's train set is more
compelling and takes no time
to assemble – the track

articulating the confines
of his life. It takes longer to pull
the wings and all but two legs
from a fly – an improvised driver
poked inside the engine cab.
He watches the ensemble glide
around the room, resting his chin
on the waxed pine boards,
his eyes level with the empty
carriages reflecting in the gleam.

It was little more than a year after he started piano lessons that Kennedy took up the violin too, and within a further year that he gained his place at the Menuhin School. In a BBC film, *Town and Around* (1964), the diminutive, seven-year-old Kennedy is interviewed at his home, after being awarded the £4000 scholarship created specially by Menuhin to enable Kennedy to attend. He's asked to stand on the piano stool in order to come up to the interviewer's height. He gives careful replies to every question, sometimes pausing to think. He's been learning the piano for 'two years', the violin for 'eight months'; he prefers 'violin' (though he would later claim he didn't like it much at all, saying that the piano was his favourite); he practises each day for 'quarter of an hour, on both'. Does he like practising? A mischievous smile and a pause, before 'quite!' At school he plays 'quite a lot' of sport: 'football and cricket'. 'I like cricket best', definitely the most surprising answer of all – even the interviewer sounds taken aback – though later, returning from America, he would wax lyrical about England, as 'the most pleasant place to live; you've got cricket matches here, and that's quite important really, not just cricket in itself, but the sense of tradition'.[6] Then the crucial question: 'What sort of music do you like best?' 'Don't mind which sort.' His favourite piece? Very definitely 'Tchaikovsky's music', all of it.

Kennedy goes to fetch his violin while the interviewer turns to his mother, Scylla Stoner. She talks about his education being assured 'for the next eight or nine years, and in the best way possible for *him*' – she appears to be absolutely certain about that. Asked if she has always wanted him to go to a musical school, she replies, 'well since I've known he really has some talent, I thought he ought to go to one'. As for the musical family background, 'I think in this case he's probably inherited talent'. She had in fact already lined up a place for him at Arundel School, again as a music scholar, but the Menuhin scholarship trumped that.

Alan Yentob, in an episode of *Imagine* focusing on Kennedy, states: 'His mother had agonised before sending Nigel, her only child, to the Menuhin School.'[7] Her reservations intensified, though with a mother's natural pride in the mix: 'From the age of seven, his life was under intense scrutiny. His precocious gifts made him a constant source of fascination for the media.'

Before he attended the Menuhin School, Kennedy was happily being taught by a teacher in Brighton, Amina Luchesi. As Kennedy says, she was clearly an excellent teacher, as two more of her pupils also gained places at the Menuhin School. This begs the question, would Kennedy have been happier, less conflicted, if he had made more 'normal' progress with a good teacher at home? He might, of course, have dropped the instrument that he has on occasions said he disliked; 'drop', not as he did as a game at the Menuhin School, (until a Gagliano violin in his care came a cropper), but in the sense of 'giving up'. 'I did get a bit sick of being subservient to the instrument because it takes so much work to actually become good at it, to be able to express yourself.'[8] Other statements put it even more bluntly:

> As a kid, I really hated the violin ... a really difficult challenge ... You have to hold your hand in a different position than normal people ... I couldn't find a way to like say 'hello' to somebody on my instrument, or just to introduce a concept and to try to share it.[9]

Compare this with, for instance, Itzhak Perlman, who, aged three, and 'too small' to be accepted into the Shulamit Conservatory in Israel, was already so keen on the violin that he taught himself on a toy fiddle. Menuhin, too, had been desperate to learn the violin from age three, though he too spoke of finding it hard initially: 'At the outset merely holding the violin, at arm's length, very tightly, lest it fall (or recoil), seemed problem enough; where did one find a second pair of arms to play it?'[10] Rachel Barton Pine, yet another who begged to learn the violin aged three, having fallen in love with the sound of the instrument at her local church, also mentions the struggle: 'It's definitely not an easy instrument. There were some things that came quite quickly. There were other techniques that I really struggled with for years to be able to master.'[11]

Without the Menuhin School regime, having to practise every day for four hours, even as a seven-year-old, Kennedy might well have given more time to football, and been happy enough persisting with both the piano and violin in a more casual manner. The 'difficult years' at the Menuhin School took things in a different direction – the boy who supposedly liked the violin best developing a love/hate relationship with the instrument for some time. Those of us who have witnessed and applauded his concerts are likely to say the direction was good, worthwhile, but who speaks for the young boy? In her book *Class, Control, & Classical Music* (2019), Anna Bull cites the story of 'Owen', who, through classical music training, moved 'between two worlds', from a 'working-class, lower middle-class' environment, focused on football, to 'the institutional ecology' of 'a conservatoire which he hoped would lead to an orchestral career'.[12] But why was that assumed to be a wholly positive trajectory? In a totally opposite story recently in the news, Christopher Guerin, deemed to be 'Britain's brainiest kid', was rewarded with a VIP ticket to watch his beloved football team, (it had to be) Aston Villa.[13]

*

Kennedy has expressed ambivalence towards his teachers. His attitude towards teachers generally – and to any form of 'standard' or 'syllabus' teaching – is pretty ruthless, but both Yehudi Menuhin and Dorothy DeLay escape the worst of his scorn. They were the individuals that made his education tolerable – and in one sense at least rewarding. It's interesting to consider their own backgrounds in working out why their particular type of encouragement proved fruitful for Kennedy.

Menuhin showed extraordinary talent from a very early age. Having started the violin aged four (as a remarkable number of children do), he was performing as soloist with the Francisco Symphony orchestra when only seven; a child prodigy by any definition. (Kennedy, incidentally, rejects the term being applied to himself; he won't associate with the 'droves of pre-pubescent supertots crowding the world's stages'.[14]) Menuhin became one of the foremost violinists in the world, but his musical life was far from typical. He was born into a Lithuanian Jewish family that changed their name from Mnuchin when settling in America. But his mother defiantly called him Yehudi (meaning Jew in Hebrew) when experiencing discrimination in renting an apartment.

Menuhin's most influential teacher had been Georges Enescu, whose initial impact on the boy was dramatic:

> He came to San Francisco when I was seven or eight, to ... play the Brahms Concerto, and before a note was sounded he had me in thrall. His countenance, his stance, his wonderful mane of black hair—everything about him proclaimed the free man, the man who is strong with the freedom of gypsies, of spontaneity, of creative genius, of fire. And the music he then began to play had an incandescence surpassing anything in my experience.[15]

The attraction of the wild-man image evoked here is fascinating in light of the furore surrounding Kennedy's own brand of wild; the old-school romantic version is perhaps more easily embraced. And yet much of Menuhin's recollection (leaving aside the specifics of hair) might well be a description of Kennedy. It's as if Menuhin somehow channelled the influence of his own mentor in fostering a new incarnation. Another teacher at the Menuhin school, Jacqueline Gazelle, had also been taught by Enescu, and Menuhin expresses pleasure 'that double lines of descent place Enescu in indisputable grandfatherhood to at least the violinists, and in some measure all the children, in my charge'.[16]

Menuhin performed both during and after World War II, notably for concentration camp survivors. Controversially, he performed in Germany, believing that music had an important role in the reconciliation process, though he later questioned how effective any of his actions had been. He became a friend of Ravi Shankar, collaborating with the sitarist well before the Beatles did. He worked extensively with jazz violinist Stéphane Grappelli, who became an even more significant mentor to Kennedy. When awarded the Wolf Prize by the Israeli government, Menuhin took the opportunity to criticize Israel's occupation of the West Bank, an issue that Kennedy would later also take very much to heart.

He wasn't above popular stunts: he performed at the Eurovision Song Contest in 1978, along with Grappelli and Oscar Peterson. Some would say that, in his later years, his performances declined, which is hardly surprising, if one keeps playing into old age (his final recording was made aged 83, shortly before his death). But he was, at the same time, generously helping the next generations of musicians to thrive. He formed the Yehudi Menuhin School at Stoke d'Abernon in Surrey, where Kennedy would spend ten years.

The Yehudi Menuhin School

The Menuhin School was established in 1963, initially as an annexe of The Arts Educational Trust set up for drama and ballet and run by Grace Cone. The permanent base at Stoke d'Abernon was found the following year. The school's aim was to foster general musicianship, teaching harmony and composition alongside instrumental instruction. That principle still remains: the school is not, as one might think, a hot-house for soloists, though many of its pupils, Kennedy included, have brought their own single-mindedness to their studies. Part of Menuhin's thinking concerned musical culture generally, specifically teaching. His belief was that, if new generations could be taught to the highest standard, and if even a proportion pursued teaching as their own career, then excellence in teaching would broaden its base throughout the country.

One of the pupils from the early intake, Katherine Stevens, interviewed by Eric Fenby, echoes Menuhin's concept: 'I feel, apart from anything else, it's my duty to hand it on to the next generation because it would be terrible if we just left it there and didn't carry it on.'[17]

Menuhin's idea for the school derived from his visit to the Central School for Young Musicians in Moscow in 1962, but there were many aspects of that institution – and the young musicians it produced – that he found disturbing:

> Dear little monsters aged four or five or six, their pigtails pinned to the crowns of their heads, whipped their way through Chopin and Liszt and all the showy composers with a cool competence that was at once admirable though alarming.[18]

Older pupils tackled more serious works 'with a skill and perfection of execution that also left one baffled'. For Menuhin they
were 'well-tooled machines'.

Menuhin's rather different model was ground-breaking for
young musicians in England. Its ethos, and something of its early
atmosphere, is captured in *Menuhin's House of Music*, published
in 1969. The numerous photographs, by Nicholas Fisk, are accompanied by text by the composer Eric Fenby, famously a friend
of Delius, as hauntingly portrayed in Ken Russell's film, *Song of
Summer*.[19]

As Fenby mentions, the closest equivalent to Menuhin's school
was 'the traditional English Cathedral Choir School where a seven-year-old boy may receive an excellent musical training along
with his normal school curriculum until his voice breaks',[20] the
type of school I myself attended. But Menuhin was acutely aware
of the unusual nature of his particular venture. In a very strange
Foreword to Fenby's book, he writes:

> 'The violinist is born': so, however is the criminal. But neither
> would exist without the special circumstances and oppor-
> tunities conducive to their development. Nor do I deny the
> originality and gusto—yes, even the defiance—necessary to
> both pursuits. Some people could feel, in fact, that a school for
> young musicians might prove only the thin end of the wedge
> to a school for young criminals, furnished with full degrees.[21]

For all its humour, there's an intriguing echo here of the wild-
man persona presented by Enescu. There's scant evidence of little
criminals in Fenby's book, however. The interviews and photographs portray an environment of relative gentility – democratic,
relaxed, with neither prefects nor school uniform – though the
culture of practice, as well as mutual cooperation, is emphasized.
'This is no soft-option school. Group activities for all children
begin at seven o'clock each morning: for those of twelve and
over—once or twice a week—as early as half-past six.'[22]

The need to nurture string players in particular is highlighted by Fenby, who is probably correct in his assertion that
other instruments 'are essentially easier to play in the physical
co-ordination requisite'.[23] His argument goes further, claiming
that, while other instruments can be taken up later in life, 'it is
unheard of on the violin'.

> Sustained progress to an advanced degree on the violin, viola
> or violoncello is as much a matter of muscular development
> of the child—in the same way as Olympic swimmers and cen-
> tre-court tennis players are coached to develop the correct
> muscles from early childhood. The hammer-like precision in
> flexibility of left-hand fingers stopping the strings in accurate
> spacings of perfect intonation; the subtle nuances of tone in
> every conceivable pattern of sound; these are not won without
> sweat and tears and the daily grind of hours of practice no
> matter how naturally gifted the player. The violin is the most
> cruel tyrant of all and exacts a lifetime's servitude.

This certainly chimes with Kennedy's comments. It's at once an
endorsement of the school and an acknowledgement of the cru-
elties involved.

Fenby's interviews with pupils provide a variety of insights as
to why anyone would endure the necessary cruelty or tyranny.
They speak eloquently about their undertakings and challenges.
Unsurprisingly, Kennedy is not amongst them. Two years earlier
a school report had termed him a 'dormouse', and even in 1969, the
year of the book's publication, the headmaster Antony Brackenbury wrote that Kennedy was 'not sure enough of himself in some
funny way to look me square in the eye'.[24] It's unlikely that he
would have mustered the confidence to talk about his ambitions
at that stage.[25] There is also the possibility that he might, instead,
have offered the sort of comment that the school would not have
wished to publicize.

It would be three whole years later that Brackenbury would
write, 'His strongly individual personality is beginning to
emerge'.[26] It's good to know that individuality was welcomed,
and Fenby's book ends with emphasis on this aspect of Menuhin's
vision: 'Of course it is understood that technical mastery is only a
means towards gaining the interpretive imagination.'[27]

Kennedy's audition for the Menuhin school included some
tests where musical phrases were played to him, and the task was
to respond with a further succession of notes. This was what he
did best, he recalls, rather than perform his prepared pieces on
violin and piano.[28] Menuhin's recollection was slightly different:

> When he came for the very first time, with his violin,
> he played a composition of his own, and he played with

intelligence ... on the piano ... when he did play on the violin, he played perfectly in tune ... with the mark of strong rhythmic personality ... a perfect ear ... I knew I was dealing with one who would inevitably become the musician he was destined to be.[29]

Menuhin doesn't mention the call-and-response test, but he does acknowledge Kennedy's creativity as well as the crucial performative skills. Fenby also quotes him as saying, 'Children should be stimulated to express themselves in music—music of their own making. We must reinstate the various ancient disciplines of improvisation, one of which survives on the organ today, others in jazz.'[30] One might imagine, from this, that the school was a perfect fit for Kennedy, but he claims that jazz was discouraged. That must have been highly frustrating, given that his ability to improvise was the very skill that helped gain him a place. The whole picture is rather contradictory, in that the grand vision for the school was matched by a degree of disorganization. 'I think at the time some of the good things about it were almost by mistake, you know, the fact that it was a new school and they didn't really have a whole degree of structure to it.'[31] If the school had been further advanced at the time, Kennedy might well have had an even more difficult time.

Menuhin writes frankly about the early challenges, albeit in a manner that claims to have avoided them, thanks to the annexe plan:

> how nerve-wracking it would have been if, from day one to the next, one had found oneself in sole and total control of eleven youngsters, responsible for housing and feeding them, instructing them in the three Rs and other, more arcane disciplines, in charge of their health and digestions, their physical exercise and their emotions, with a little matter of intensive musical education to be fitted in somewhere![32]

Nerve-wracking indeed – also a terrifying prospect for any guinea-pig child.

There's a remarkable contrast here, between the child learning from the most experienced tutor, and having to take pot luck with other aspects of their nurture; equally, the incongruity of adults supremely qualified in one arena simply 'having a go' at something else. And yet, there is something very human about this – the desire to shrug off the need for a full skillset or blueprint, in order to try something *other*. And it may well be that exposure to such a high-risk strategy is in itself an inspiration of sorts, nurturing a 'why-not' mentality. It's relevant to note here that Menuhin wasn't trained as a conductor, but took the leap, believing that his knowledge as a player and general musician would prove sufficient. There are of course a multitude of more questionable examples, for instance those who believe they can step into politics or, even more deludedly, run a country with no real credentials (though Volodymyr Zelensky is a magnificent exception). Reality television shows offer a less consequential demonstration of how things can go well or very wrong.

Menuhin's why-not attitude was kept in check by his entourage, and the school took developmental precautions, as it were, enough at least for its reputation to steadily rise, despite some emerging issues.

Kennedy pokes fun at Menuhin, not least for his obsession with yoga and vegetarian cuisine, but he is generally appreciative. 'Without Yehudi I might be just another classical musician on the circuit … In his school we were never taught that anything was impossible. We were taught there was this beautiful music and we could be a part of it.'[33] It is also fascinating to see pictures of the very small boy Kennedy looking up at Menuhin; they present the very image of absorbed admiration. Referring to his own mentor, Menuhin comments, 'Enescu accorded my ten-year-old self the serious respect due to an equal', and he's quick to apply the same principle:

> In my turn I too respect the individual's way of doing things and would not spoil it by imposing my own. That pedagogy which insists on one conception or one technical means of expressing a conception seems to me constricting. I have my preferences, but I tolerate other visions and believe that someone who plays with conviction should be encouraged in it.[34]

Sometimes, of course, we all fail in our best intentions, and there would come a time when Menuhin did indeed try to impose his way on Kennedy, notably in performing the Elgar concerto, but that's a later story.

Kennedy acknowledges that Menuhin was an exception to other teachers' disapproval of jazz. It was Menuhin himself, making occasional visits to the school, whom Kennedy found inspiring, not least for bringing Grappelli to the stage, and Menuhin's own attitude to jazz needs some discussion. Perhaps the most revealing comment – almost a confession – is in his autobiography:

> Perhaps because I was by temperament or training inclined, even at the crest of a wave, to calculate its amplitude and momentum, I have always thirsted for abandon ... improvisation promised abandon to musical impulse. Thus, Ravi Shankar followed the gypsies and, in course of time, Stéphane Grappelli, the great jazz violinist, followed Ravi Shankar, successive mentors on a journey to spontaneity.[35]

For Menuhin, 'the desire to travel that path was always latent; as probably it is for other violinists'.[36]

Menuhin first discovered Grappelli through his recordings, and eventually took the plunge of joining him in a BBC Christmas broadcast, playing the gypsy tango 'Jealousy', by Jacob Glade. The title of the chosen piece seems somewhat ironic, since Menuhin owns up to the fact that, for his recordings with Grappelli, his part was pre-written, by Max Harris, while Grappelli, true to form, improvised everything, playing differently from one take to another. 'He is a man I envy almost as much as I love him, who off the cuff can use any theme to express any nuance – wistfulness, brilliance, aggression, scorn – with a speed and accuracy that stretch credulity.'[37]

As quoted earlier, Menuhin also mentions the art of improvisation surviving on the organ, something I witnessed at Winchester Cathedral in Clement McWilliam's astonishing playing. At the end of a cathedral service, he would take the tune of the final hymn and improvise a fugue. It was so magnificently done that the majority of the congregation – if they were staying to listen – no doubt assumed it was 'written'. Intriguingly, McWilliam would come out with sudden chants of 'Arbroath!' (his favoured Scottish football team); Kennedy is not alone in championing football in the midst of his sophisticated musical endeavours. The top two musicians I have encountered have demonstrated a similar attraction to the same/disparate spheres of creative passion.

Menuhin felt that he might one day learn the knack of improvisation, but he knew it would be a difficult path for him personally. He took pride in his own considerable qualities, but also knew his limitations. Comparing himself with Enescu, he writes, 'I am a smaller man', 'I don't play the piano, or compose, or have his breadth of musical knowledge'.[38] Was this self-awareness (one might even call it regret) perhaps part of the reason he took an almost father-like attitude towards Kennedy? Did he see the gift that he knew he lacked and want to nurture it at all costs? Is this why he *indulged* Kennedy, as some no doubt saw it?

Whatever conscious or subconscious attitude was at work, Menuhin only introduced jazz as something extracurricular. Kennedy mainly nourished his own passion by listening to jazz on the radio, secretly, in bed. But there was another teacher whom Kennedy found sympathetic. Nadia Boulanger was by all accounts an exceptional figure within music education. Eric Fenby quotes American students waxing lyrical about her:

> Her lessons are quite original; different and full of surprises. She quotes Valéry, and draws on painting and philosophy ... most of all, she knows how to concentrate one's *deepest atten-tion* on music; and how to awake in *others* a similar response to what one is playing oneself.[39]

It was Boulanger who, when George Gershwin came to Paris in the mid-1920s seeking expertise in classical composition, turned him down, claiming that 'rigorous classical study would ruin his jazz-influenced style'.[40] Ravel, similarly, 'did not relish spoiling Gershwin's musical voice'.[41] Gershwin's ambition was essentially in the opposite direction to Kennedy's: a jazz musician and song-writer, he wanted to join the European classical fraternity. With *An American in Paris* and subsequent works he partly succeeded, but was still widely shunned.

Put in front of the loved but feared 'demigod' Boulanger, Kennedy thought she 'seemed really pleased that I wasn't playing something she'd heard before'.[42] It's a small anecdote, yet somehow important. As with mutual appreciation between those with great talent, so it is when someone of strong personal conviction encounters a similar force. Menuhin's own comments also seem in favour of cultivating *attitude*, wanting students 'not only to do but to understand and be able to defend [their] position against alternatives', aiming to instil 'violinistic and musical security'.[43]

Menuhin's philosophy was to encourage not only technical expertise but the ability to use it in order to express something meaningful, whether from a written score, within oneself as interpreter, or in mercurial combination of the two. At the heart of this is a deep understanding of the complexity of interpretation and performance, something that I will discuss further in later chapters. In seeking to enable students to be meaningfully expressive in that way, Menuhin aimed for breadth of musical encounter (hence Grappelli's and Shankar's appearances in amongst those of classical guests). This breadth seems wise; after all, how else do you help young musicians identify their own musical soul? I doubt Kennedy would have liked the school to be *teaching him jazz*, and such specialized teaching would not necessarily have served him well. A BBC journalist once said to me that courses in Journalism were not as valuable as Literature or History degrees. And much as I would personally defend (good) creative writing classes, I would have to agree that the breadth of a Literature course is invaluable to any writer. Musicians benefit from a similar scope of knowledge, even if their sights are set on a specific career.

The Menuhin School's focus on musical fundamentals, including its approach to understanding harmony and counterpoint, is particularly relevant here. Fenby, appreciative of the approach, writes: 'It is my strong conviction that harmony is best taught ... creatively through the vertical soundings from the free movement of parts which is counterpoint, rather than from blocks of sound.'[44] This seems very well put, and the approach was surely beneficial for a musician such as Kennedy who would be working not only as a classical soloist pitched against an orchestra, but also as a jazz musician – and composer – attending to the simultaneous emergence of individual musical lines. Crucially, Fenby reinforces this by stating, 'teaching harmony is creative rather than imitative'.[45] This strikes a chord with me, having worked to introduce creative writing teaching in UK schools. (A six-year process resulted, briefly, in an approved A-Level; a

Conservative government review, driven by ideology, rooted it out a mere couple of years later.) The 'creative' label, absurdly, was always contentious. Faced with those preferring 'rhetoric', I spoke out against a pupil experience that was exclusively focused on imitative practice. That was already present in English Language studies, where the object was to write in the manner of an established writer. There is of course plenty to be gained by such practice. Ultimately, however, the writing style of, say, Henry James or Sylvia Plath, is something that was uniquely useful to those artists, developed over time in order to express their individual visions and ideas. The postponement of that quest, for any budding writer, is potentially wasteful, not least because it risks enjoyment being sidelined. The same is surely true of music.

There is much to applaud, then, about the Menuhin School's ethos and practical strategies, and it quickly established a significant reputation, the profile of its founder matched by the achievements of its alumni: not only Kennedy but Nicola Benedetti, Tasmin Little (who remembers Kennedy pulling her hair) and Daniel Hope. In Menuhin's autobiography, Kennedy is singled out with a slightly back-handed compliment:

> I am pleased to be able to say that along with well-disciplined musicians the school has produced a number of unconventional, even eccentric performers in the noblest British tradition. One is the well-known and very gifted Nigel Kennedy...[46]

The fact is that the school did somehow, perhaps against the odds, allow for the development of the eccentric, the true maverick musician. Much of what Kennedy says and does would seem to derive from Menuhin's own thinking, albeit delivered in very different terms. And yet Kennedy has been outspoken in his criticism of the school. He states, 'I haven't spoken with any alumni who remembered it as a wonderful place.'[47] Worse still, some pupils were 'traumatised', and allegations of abuse within such institutions continue to emerge. In 2003, a *Guardian* article quoted Kennedy as saying, 'There were strange things going on with some of the girls and the older teachers that would have been illegal, definitely.'[48] In his new book, he states that, 'instead of trying to fix things, the school threatened a lawsuit against me'.[49] In 2023, a police enquiry was launched, investigating 22 allegations of abuse made by pupils who had attended between 1964 and 2007. This, however, was with the full co-operation of the school, which now has strict safeguarding measures in place.

One can but hope that abusive behaviour has now been eradicated, not just in the select music schools but in boarding schools generally, and yet questions remain about the level of risk in entrusting children to any such 'closed' institution, away from their parents. I myself went through the boarding experience; it was a requirement of attending the cathedral choir school into which I was accepted. There were many wonderful things about that experience, including music lessons from Clement McWilliam, and the opportunity to play much more sport than Kennedy was able to at Stoke d'Abernon, but I would still question the overall virtue of being sent away from home during one's formative years.

Intriguingly, given Kennedy's strong football connection, and my own support of Southampton FC – there has recently been some interaction between the Menuhin School and the Southampton club's academy. As mentioned earlier, we shouldn't be too surprised about connections between sport and the arts, and yet this particular liaison still seems highly original. Staff at the Southampton academy, which is highly regarded for developing the likes of Theo Walcott, Alex Oxlade-Chamberlain, Luke Shaw, Adam Lallana, Gareth Bale and James Ward Prowse, approached the Menuhin School in order to refine aspects of their 'elite training' even further. As Edd Vahid, Southampton's head of academy coaching (and now employed in a similar role by the Premier League itself), comments, 'The opportunity to get out of your own environment, where you're sometimes over-immersed, and go to other high-performing organisations, helps you grow.'[50]

There were several identified areas of overlapping interest, such as 'the integration of academic and professional training'. Other matters emerged only as a result of the academy's first visit to the school, including, for Vahid, a new understanding of what solo practice was all about.

> And that was one of the things we took from visiting [the school], the amount of practice we observed. So on the tour there was a lad in the middle of a corridor practising, and

he was almost oblivious to this party of six or seven people walking past him. And that was one of my take-home messages, actually, do our lads know how to practise? Because that's really hard. Rather than just the concept of it, do they know how to practise, do we create enough opportunities for them to practise, do they understand what possibilities exist when they're not with us, and what that looks like?

Practice is something that Fenby highlights: 'the child must first learn *how* to practise and, this achieved, become established securely in the habit of *purposeful* practice.'[51] What this actually means varies 'in practice' from one individual to another, something I explore later in this chapter.

Crucial for any elite establishment is the complex business of ongoing assessment. Richard Hillier, headmaster at the Menuhin School, recalls: '[the Southampton academy] were very interested in the idea of assessment, of how you judge potential. How can you tell whether young people are meeting their potential, what do you do if they don't?'[52] That last point is particularly important. A criticism levelled at such institutions – whether focused on the arts or on sport – is of a certain ruthlessness. What happens to those young people who find they're not the next Nigel Kennedy or Gareth Bale?

The Menuhin principle was always to equip young people for whatever they might choose to do with their emerging talent, be that as soloist, teacher, or creative practitioner in some other field. Hillier maintains the same attitude, saying, 'if they discover at 17, 18, they would rather be studying English Literature – much as they love music and want to continue playing, they want to study something different – that's fine for us as a school, that's not a problem.' Vahid embraces this concept, placing the emphasis on learning – whatever the focus: 'The best players are going to be the best learners, is our view', he says. 'Whether that's in the classroom or on the pitch, if they've got the ability to learn they're going to progress and develop.'[53] With an attitude similar to Menuhin's he's happy if his young charges become international stars, coaches, referees, or minor-league players – whatever represents fulfilment for the individual.

The attention to detail extends to the relationship of brain and body, the growth spurts that young people have to cope with, whether footballers or violinists, and how coaches need to take that into account. Patience is key in enabling the individual to progress in a natural, comfortable way, whatever the general expectations of discipline and dedication.

What impresses me most about this exchange is the shared understanding about so-called mistakes, and indeed perceived failure. Vahid mentions a concert he witnessed:

> When that young girl – I mean, we didn't know, but apparently she made an error in the first 20 seconds of her performance. And she just got on with it. She has to park it there, rather than emotionally kill the rest of the performance.

Shortly after reading that, I was watching football on TV. The Spurs and England captain Harry Kane missed an open goal but had the temperament to put that behind him and play superbly for the rest of the match. Such temperament is indeed an important quality, and one that can be nurtured.

Historically, the high achievers have not always been well looked after. One only has to think of George Best, the supremely gifted Belfast boy suddenly finding himself in the spotlight at Manchester United, and not entirely coping with the attendant fame and fortune. Paul Gascoigne also suffered, notably at the hands of the tabloid press, which first adored him, then decided he was fair game for destruction. A club can play an important role in addressing those problems. As the Southampton academy project suggests, the issue can perhaps be addressed much earlier, nurturing the development not only of the footballer but of the human being; instilling strengths of character that may weather future storms. That's an entirely admirable aim, and I'm possibly either cynical or perverse in feeling that we don't want our heroes to be perfect. A Paul Gascoigne that never played the clown? A Kennedy that never spoke out of order – what would actually be *perfect* about that?

The nurturing Kennedy received at the Menuhin School remains difficult to gauge, a strange mixture of repression and enlightenment. Perhaps, by chance, that was the ideal combination for the emergence of the Kennedy we know: the musician who has taken such risks; the man who, by his own admission shows little interest in 'growing up' in the traditional sense. 'ALL

IMMATURE PEOPLE OF THE WORLD, UNITE' he writes in *Uncensored!*.[54] If exceptional talent develops ahead of 'normal' maturity, then this is perhaps to be expected. It's also, perhaps, what the Southampton academy, with all its psychological and physiological attention to detail, is trying to avoid – for better or worse.

One thing is for sure: seven-year-olds don't know what they're getting into. The child who is a gifted footballer is unlikely to resist the opportunity of attending a football academy, but are they expecting psychology to be involved? Likewise, the young musician may already harbour a sense of ambition, but the reality of a closed, elite institution is going to spring innumerable surprises. Parents' expectations create a further complication. Malcolm Singer, Director of Music at the Menuhin School, is clear on this, and the parallel situation at Southampton: 'parents' expectations, and how you should be auditioning the parents as well as the child sometimes, they apply to both fields.'[55] That seems slightly at odds with Fenby's claim that Menuhin would always ask 'Does the child want to come to the school of its own accord? Or is it solely at the parents' wish?'[56]

It would not have been Scylla Stoner's expectation that her son would fall under the spell of the visiting Stéphane Grappelli, or that his time at school would then be disrupted by trips with Grappelli to Ronnie Scott's. But that, for Kennedy, was the unexpected inspiration amongst the quotidian demands and frustrations.

Juilliard

Once you're in a certain system, it tends to keep hold of you (and it's interesting that Kennedy should have been happy for his son Sark to go to a boarding school). In my own comparison, as above, I left the choir school aged thirteen, only to move to another private boarding school so close to home that the boarding was really a nonsense. I'll own up to the fact that it was the school John Drummond also attended, though well before me. I'll also say without any qualification that the school during my time there was a good environment for creative development, not least in its sympathetic handling of rebellious behaviour. And although

I found it at first a tough environment in which to settle, I eventually loved my time there, made many friends for life, and was able to develop my own interests, notably poetry, to the full. A surprising number of poets and other writers emerged from the school – albeit together with the man whom Kennedy calls 'the most futile over-educated toff I have ever had to deal with'.[57] More of that later.

In Kennedy's case, the logical move was to the Juilliard School in New York, a much more dramatic adventure. Menuhin pointed him either to New York or Moscow, and the New York jazz scene of course swung it for Kennedy.

Money was limited, so he lived for the first year in cheap accommodation near Harlem. I don't suppose that's the standard Juilliard student experience, and it was tough, even for someone already used to the street fights surrounding Villa Park on match days. In *Uncensored!* he tells the story of being repeatedly mugged, but with a touching conclusion: his muggers (he claims) had never previously seen a violin, and once he showed them how it was played, and told them how there were many more valuable for the taking at the school, they let him go. In Kennedy's story it's a formative moment, *contra* Juilliard, where priceless violins were all around, the standard accoutrements of a privileged world. Playing to his muggers was more interesting than playing to his peers, certainly more dangerous. Kennedy pursued danger further, in frequenting the clubs where he must have appeared thoroughly out of place.

> First of all I was white, second I was English, third I was a teenager – and I played a violin. It was like I was at the bottom of the class spectrum for what I wanted to do, which made it much more satisfying once I finally got accepted.[58]

He would play with Jimmy Rowles in Bradley's (now gone) in Greenwich Village, or with Ellis Larkins at the Cookery. Kennedy may joke about being bottom of the class spectrum (or saying 'how many things can you have wrong with you?'[59]), and it's easy to gloss over this episode with a 'wow'. But this was Kennedy who, just a few years earlier, had been a 'dormouse'. Yes, his London experience with Grappelli had paved the way, but it's still astonishing that someone with that capability to be withdrawn, unforthcoming, should suddenly feel able to breeze into clubs of that sort, uninvited, and share the stage with the jazz legends of America. The requisite confidence in one's talent is considerable, let alone the social daring to make it happen.

As Jed Rasula states, 'Jazz as music is inseparable from the African-American experience',[60] and Langston Hughes expands that further:

> jazz to me is one of the inherent expressions of Negro life in America; the eternal tom-tom beating in the Negro soul—the tom-tom of revolt against weariness in a white world, a world of subway trains, and work, work, work; the tom-tom of joy and laughter, and pain swallowed in a smile.[61]

There's no way Kennedy can lay claim to an African-American experience; and his is not that same struggle. But he was nevertheless a stranger in a strange land, fighting to gain a path to joy and laughter, against considerable odds.

Studies were bound to suffer. When not in the jazz clubs, Kennedy preferred to hang out with the Europeans playing football against Puerto Ricans in Central Park, or busking outside Tiffany's, earning $200 in two hours – not bad in the 70s. Many of us have known the tug of war between tertiary study and social life. Here the stakes were high on both fronts. There would only be one real winner, and yet Kennedy still has kind words to say about his Juilliard tutor Dorothy DeLay (while also taking time to joke on her name). It was she who, like Menuhin, was the saving grace for Kennedy. She herself was a Juilliard graduate, and returned there to teach, in preference to a performing career. She famously fell out with her colleague Ivan Galamian, whose focus was primarily on technique. DeLay had the particular gift to identify the unique qualities of an individual, and aimed to help them thrive accordingly. As one of her pupils, Nadja Salerno-Sonnenberg, puts it, DeLay 'was teaching me to teach myself—and that's why she is a great teacher'.[62] This was a controversial approach, though I'm not entirely sure why. As Menuhin says, 'Even though the teacher is important, most of what every violinist has to learn he discovers for himself'.[63] The value of her approach has been proven by the number of pupils, Kennedy included, whom she helped to become stars. Her process was akin to what we might now call coaching rather than teaching, but it was rigorous as well as friendly. She encouraged the practice of solo Bach as a daily routine, something to which Kennedy still adheres.

Despite his recent references to a culture of 'artistic mediocrity', Kennedy has tended to acknowledge some benefits of his Juilliard attendance, with DeLay the central figure.

> Lots of teachers say 'Play this way,' which coincidentally is their way. She didn't. She would wait for you to formulate your own, intelligent questions and find your own approach. My greatest gift in music was what I got from her. The school was actually a bit right-wing in many ways, but my time there was really helpful.[64]

Both Menuhin and DeLay, then, in their approach to education, clearly believed in *educere* (to lead out) rather than *educare* (to train or mould). There is little doubt that Kennedy would not have stomached the latter.

Other aspects of Juilliard experience proved irritating to Kennedy: 'there were so many ambitious people who were thinking only about career and not about music.'[65]

> It was strange to me when people asked if I had got any gigs through knowing Yehudi Menuhin. It was all to do with that, rather than asking about his insights into Bach or Beethoven. It was depressing to see young people so hardened and ambitious in such a narrow way.[66]

Kennedy isn't alone in his criticism of Juilliard (though he's the only one to call it 'The Juilliard School of Boredom'[67]). Anne-Sophie Mutter has also spoken out, saying:

> there are no longer great violin-playing schools – we have this kind of machinery, as at the Juilliard, which brings forward great generations of players, but they all come with a metaphorical stamp on their foreheads. It's hard to escape from that machinery.[68]

DeLay's individual approach, that made Juilliard worthwhile to Kennedy and others, would seem to have been lost. It's remarkable how a single individual can almost define the character of an institution, with the consequence that the character changes when they're gone.

Kennedy is generous in his comments about DeLay, but there were nevertheless 'issues'. When asked, by Alan Yentob, if she encouraged Kennedy's interest in jazz, Delay replied, somewhat evasively:

> It's very difficult for a young person who's preparing for a concert career to get enough time to do the practising he needs to do, and of course to be in school at the same time, and then carry the practising load and then do jazz on top of it seems to me a very difficult thing.[69]

Kennedy argues back:

> they thought that playing jazz would be bad for your technique as opposed to the actual truth which is it helps you listen, and you can work with harmony in a much more substantial way than if you don't know anything about harmony, so it obviously makes you better as a musician to be playing jazz.[70]

During Kennedy's time in New York, it was Grappelli, again, who sparked the ultimate showdown. The story has been told in countless articles, and most recently in *Uncensored!*. It's a pivotal moment in Kennedy's life that in a sense changed nothing – except that most crucial aspect of his psyche: the resolution to trust his own instincts, even against the advice of those he respected, such as DeLay. To give the brief version, Grappelli was appearing at Carnegie Hall, and Kennedy was invited to join him on stage. A&R representatives from CBS (later to become Sony) who had an interest in signing Kennedy as a classical soloist were in the audience, and DeLay warned her pupil against presenting himself in the 'wrong' field. Backstage, Kennedy agonized – drinking a third, a half, or two-thirds of a bottle of scotch in the process, according to which version of the anecdote you read. He eventually gained clarity: there was no way he would pass up the opportunity to perform with the man who was, in his opinion, 'the greatest violinist'. It was by all accounts, a terrific evening, and I find it touching that DeLay herself said of the CBS men, 'they thought it was very good'.[71] She did of course continue to inform Kennedy that the potential recording contract was now off.

'Dottie', as he calls her, was actually very supportive after Kennedy had left the Juilliard without graduating and struggled to feel happy with his initial career development. A good mentor never deserts you.

The Long Childhood

It's interesting to consider a certain set of words we use to put people down: 'childish', 'puerile', 'infantile', 'immature', 'impetuous'. They have close relations that represent, if not the very opposite, then something much more valued: 'childlike', 'boyish', 'innocent', 'unaffected', 'spontaneous'. Sometimes 'childlike' and 'childish' are confused. Kennedy is a classic example of someone caught in the crossfire of all this. Brix Smith, who was dating Kennedy around the time of his *Four Seasons* success, describes him in her memoir:

> What became clear was that Nigel was like a child. He was totally in touch with the childlike wonder of the world. And soon I was seeing the world through his joyful eyes. He seemed free from most adult constraints and behaviour. If he didn't like a mouthful of food, he'd spit it out. If he wanted to play with mud, he'd smear it on his face, and if he didn't want to tidy his house or his car, he simply wouldn't.[72]

Both 'childlike' and 'childish' are in the mix here. The first half of what we are told is laudable, especially the transference of joy that is so true of Kennedy's musical performances. But the freedom from 'adult constraints and behaviour' – that's the twist that heralds the further comments about behaviour that's harder to approve. How is it that we both revere and deplore the nature of youth? As Jacob Bronowski states, 'our civilisation ... adores above all the image of the child, ever since the Renaissance: the Christ child painted by Raphael ... the young Mozart and Gauss', but this already points towards a major confusion. The revering of Mozart as *child prodigy* actually contradicts the essential importance of human childhood that Bronowski explains so well:

> we are concerned in our early education actually with the postponement of decisions. ... We have to put off the decision-making process, in order to accumulate enough

> knowledge as a preparation for the future ... That is what
> childhood is about, that is what puberty is about, that is what
> youth is about.[73]

Bronowski cites Shakespeare's Hamlet as example. Too much is asked of a character too young to make momentous decisions. When Hamlet finally dies, the tragedy 'is that he dies exactly when he is ready to become a great king'.

Why, then, should we have an obsession with the child who seems to bypass that crucial aspect of human development? The internet shows countless examples of small children whose show-pony performances of classical repertoire (always classical) seem to proclaim 'I am a virtuoso', as if no decision-making process (or understanding of musicianship) needs nurturing at all. In many cases, their decision has not been their own, but that of their parents. For instance, Ruth Slenczynska, who in the 1920s was 'heralded as one of the greatest child prodigies since Mozart',[74] has stated: 'The reason that people were startled at what I could do at the piano was quite simple ... Father was now making me practice nine hours a day, every single day of the week.'[75] The further detail is even more disturbing:

> If I showed signs of wanting to be just an ordinary little girl,
> like wanting to cuddle my sisters' dolls or make a little noise
> or jump up and down and run with the neighbourhood kids,
> father would come down on me with his pail of ice-cold water:
> 'That's all baby stuff! You're not a baby. You're a musician. Stay
> away from those kids and their stupid games. It's all a waste of
> time! You've got to act like a grown-up young lady.'[76]

If she made so much as a single mistake, she would be slapped, 'very methodically, without a word'.[77] Slapping a child for hitting a wrong note is an abominable practice on every level: the worst kind of parenting; the worst kind of teaching. Alarmingly, such abusive practice is still at large, notably in the arena of gymnastics, where the pursuit of so-called excellence has consumed some coaches to the absolute neglect of the welfare of the child.

Leaving aside the worst cases of abuse, what we have here is a seeming determination to override what Bronowski calls 'The Long Childhood', with crucial, formative time to play. His belief in its importance is matched by a recognition of how often it is ignored.

> Think of the investment that evolution has made in the child's brain ... when I was born, my body was a mere appendage to the head; it weighed only five or six times as much as my brain. For most of history, civilisations have crudely ignored that enormous potential ... children have been asked simply to conform to the image of the adult.[78]

Bronowski describes how, in various ancient civilisations, 'the ascent of the talented, the ascent of the imaginative' has been repressed, to the detriment of the society itself: 'by one test they all fail: they limit the freedom of the imagination of the young. They are static ... because the son does what the father does, and the father what the grandfather did.'[79]

Here we have yet another complication. After all, Kennedy's mother was a pianist. His father and grandfather were both cellists. It is not necessarily 'unimaginative' to pursue a similar career – if the choice is self-made, and the particular trajectory properly individual. As Andrew Robinson states, 'Mozart owed his childhood success to his violinist father's formidable tutelage—yet he was compelled to break with his father in his mid-twenties before he could compose his greatest works.'[80] Ruth Slenczynska, on the other hand, needed to abandon her father in order to have an ordinary, fulfilling life. In both examples, however, the child grew wise, having taken their time to grasp what was best for their personal future.

In recent times, our society – in England at least – has put great store in supporting children of exceptional promise. There was a phase (towards the end of the twentieth century) when the moniker was 'gifted and talented', though I have yet to come across a meaningful distinction between the two. G&T, amusingly, was the common abbreviation, as if some serious drinking might be involved; unsurprisingly, the phrase and its abbreviation have been dropped. Whatever the label, pupils identified as the 'most able' typically demonstrate certain characteristics, including strong curiosity, a high level of energy, a sense of humour, and a vivid imagination. They 'persevere when interested', are likely to be highly creative and, intriguingly, they also tend to question authority.[81]

There is a political issue here, and a question: is it more important to nurture a 'solo' talent, or provide opportunities for all? And are those priorities really mutually exclusive? Eric Fenby, who acknowledges that 'ideally *all* children should receive some musical education', suggests that 'the professional level must be reserved for the gifted and determined'.[82] That alternative label seems a useful one, putting the emphasis on the inner motivation of the child, not on the talent-spotting ambition of the teacher or coach, but it still begs the question about educational opportunity. As Menuhin himself says, 'All children are gifted; nearly all are denied the chance to develop their gifts. The children who come to my school are ordinary, good, musically gifted children who have been given a chance.'[83] Understandably, Menuhin champions his own 'special' school, but fine musicians have thrived in very different circumstances.

One prominent family of high-fliers, the Kanneh-Mason siblings, thrived at a school in Nottingham where 'music was something that everyone did. It made a real community out of the school, and people were so encouraged and it was a wonderful experience'.[84] They were then able to gain specialist music tuition at the Royal Academy while still benefiting from a relatively 'normal' schooling. Given the level of their achievement, their educational trajectory would seem to have been thoroughly sufficient to their talent, while also fitting the 'long childhood' model that gives individual human potential full rein. Key to their progress was of course the determination specified by Fenby, manifested in a dedication to practice, something that needs discussing here in greater depth.

'If I skip practice for one day, I notice. If I skip practice for two days, my wife notices. If I skip for three days, the world notices.' So says Vladimir Horowitz.[85] There is, thankfully, hard evidence to show exactly *why* we should practise. 'The brain is plastic, and it alters through practice' writes Andrew Robinson,[86] making clear how this applies as much to taxi drivers memorizing maps as to musicians developing the aural and visual/spatial skills required to read and play music while interacting with other musicians. Bizarrely, Kennedy has joked about taxi driving as his alternative career. But as a performing musician his visual/spatial skills would seem exceptional, almost defying the laws of physics. I have witnessed him offering comic verbal asides to members of his orchestra while playing fiendishly difficult passages. It reminded me of how birds, like flies, lizards and even human children, are said to apprehend the detail of their surroundings within a different timeframe to other mortals, as if, for them, time passes at a slower, more easily assimilated rate.[87]

Both grey matter and white matter are affected. Fredrik Ullen, who is both pianist and neuroscientist, has found that myelin, 'the white fatty substance that sheaths the conducting axons (thread-like nerve fibres) of the adult brain like plastic insulation around a wire', thickens with practice, thereby improving the essential function of the brain.[88] So far, so good, but what about the specifics?

There is a theory, promulgated by Malcolm Gladwell, that 10,000 hours are required to master any art. That's equivalent to about ten years of your learning life, an uncanny match for Andrew Robinson's reckoning of how the great creative breakthroughs in history, far from being moments of 'sudden genius', have come about as the result of ten years' work.[89] Gladwell's theory has however come under scrutiny. Brooke Macnamara points out that the 10,000-hour figure was only ever identified as an *average*, accumulated 'in the best group of student violinists ... by age 20'. Many had accumulated fewer hours, others more. She also highlights the error in assuming that practice is 'the only predictor of expertise'. In her own research she has found that only 23% of variance in achievement was attributable to practice. 77% was more directly attributable to genetic factors; intriguingly, these also affected the *inclination* to practice.[90]

The importance of inclination is backed up by Gary McPherson's research, which shows that it's not all about the hours; inclination to practice makes every hour of application more worthwhile.[91] Even so, as the Southampton academy observed, you still have to know – or rather learn – exactly *how* and *what* to practise, whatever the hours put in.

Pianist James Rhodes reckons that, for professional musicians, practice should be immensely 'finickety', with an 'attention to detail that drives you round the bend'.[92] But should artistic endeavour sound so much like dangerous drudgery? Who can forget the terrifying scene in Stanley Kubrick's film *The Shining*, in which Jack (Torrence/Nicholson) is found to have typed, end-lessly, the same phrase, 'All work and no play makes Jack a dull boy'? He has quite literally gone out of his mind. The repeated lines are full of typographical *errors*, a vital part of the effect achieved.

According to Rhodes, the focus for amateurs should be differ-ent – on enjoyment rather than perfection. I find Rhodes's opinion logical, but at the same time bewildering. Is there really such a division? Kennedy, for one, believes not. If anything he believes that amateurs (in the true sense of the word) are the true musi-cians, with jazz players in that category. It is also worth noting that perfection is, in any case, an illusory goal. There is no such thing. We all have 'imperfect fingers, bodies and feelings', says Tom Service.[93] That's what actually makes the music we make wonderful, even when playing a digital synthesizer. 'We are all gloriously imperfect, which is exactly as it should be', he contin-ues. Indeed, but then he says:

> There's no such thing as a mistake. The notes aren't wrong, because they can't be. You can't say that time you spent trying to play this passage was a mistake, because that's like saying that part of your life was a mistake, which it wasn't.

I still can't work out if this is philosophical genius, or claptrap, but it certainly tallies with Kennedy's belief that playing with pas-sionate purpose, soul, is far more important than merely playing without mistakes.

However (im)perfect our practice, it is the content that makes it meaningful. Key to this are pieces that take away the drudgery by virtue of their high artistic merit, pieces specifically written to cover particular skills while also providing deeper musical satisfaction, notably studies or études by those with real flair for that kind of twin musical offering. For the pianist, there are works by Chopin and Debussy, which, as Tom Service says, 'turn the pursuit of technical excellence into a poetic pleasure'. In the case of Debussy, he claims 'the poetry is in the technique'. Sets of such works extend the realm of musical competence and wonder, sometimes in a graded progression. Bartók's *Mikrokosmos* offers 153 pieces, a sequence both to delight the beginner and put one's level of commitment or inclination fully to the test.

These and other studies are by some of the greatest composers for the piano. Turning to the violin, things are rather different. Kreutzer, whose studies are popular and well regarded, is hardly in the same league as Bartók or Chopin. John Cage's *Freeman Etudes* put performability to the ultimate test, while hardly registering as popular repertoire. Why are there so few equivalents to the generous piano offerings? Menuhin perhaps puts his finger on it:

> Even though the teacher is important, most of what every violinist has to learn he discovers for himself. True, you can be taught a certain amount of technique, though not as much as on other instruments; but basically the fiddle is not a thing for which you can lay down a set of rules.[94]

His main point here is about teaching, but the comment about rules surely goes some way to explain the études void. Amy Barlowe, a former Juilliard student (of course) has composed a set of *12 Etudes Caprices in the Styles of the Great Composers* (2010). Pitched at the 'intermediate' player, I'm sure they have value, but the very concept strikes me as diminishing. How, in comparison to playing Liszt or Ligeti, are we to gain meaningful, poetic, almost philosophical rewards from what is more akin to homage or pastiche? There is a piece 'In the Style of Bach', complete with detailed practice guide. I am sure there are violin teachers and students all over the world lapping it up. I also believe that, by Menuhin's definition, the work is misguided. If you want to play Vivaldi, there are plentiful original works (which you can also interpret as you like). Why the need to downgrade? The 'intermediate' player could never become a *great* player by following such a slimline musical diet.

I have already mentioned the preferred alternative, as recommended to Kennedy at Juilliard by Dorothy DeLay: Bach, the maestro of musical imagining. Even at Grade V piano, we can grasp this, playing the C major prelude. Bringing one finger at a time into action, in a simple, regular rhythm, we can discover how melody describes a harmonic progression, shaped to perfection. Ok, Bach on the violin probably kicks in at a higher level, which is of course where the teacher can help, suggesting pathways to the sublime that are suited to the individual. For the serious violinist,

Bach offers almost endless rewards, and Kennedy's daily, long-term dedication to practising Bach is testament to that.

It may be stating the obvious, but Bach violin music, like any violin or stringed instrument music, presents a particular difficulty not faced by those tackling Bach on the piano: playing in tune. Menuhin's praise for the young Kennedy playing 'perfectly' in tune is significant, as it's no mean feat for a child (or anyone). As Fenby says, you have to start early, something backed up by research at the Laboratory of Developmental Neurobiology in the US. Its Director, R Douglas Fields, states that 'Children whose brains are still myelinating widely find it much easier to acquire new skills than their grandparents do.'

> You built the brain you have today by interacting with the environment while you were growing up and your neural connections were still myelinating. You can adapt those abilities in many ways, but neither you nor I will become a world-class pianist, chess player, or tennis pro unless we began our training when we were children.[95]

Fields here uses the word 'training', which is a term interestingly pitched somewhere between 'teaching' and 'practice'. As athletes we can, if we choose, train without a trainer, and some violinists have done the same. Kennedy has particular admiration for the self-taught, notably Grappelli, but also the British violinist Albert Sammons, who had only a few lessons before going it alone. He even made his own violin. These are violinists whose personal mission was a greater factor in their success than anything a teacher could have imparted.

Even when formal teaching takes control, the personal sense of mission remains perhaps the strongest factor of all. Daniel Coyle cites research that assigns considerable importance to how pupils first enter the whole arena of lessons, and practice.

> We instinctively think of each new student as a blank slate, but the ideas they bring to that first lesson are far more important than anything a teacher can do, or any amount of practice ... At some point very early on they had a crystallizing experience that brings the idea to the fore, that says, *I am a musician.*[96]

I find that a very different concept to the aforementioned supertot announcing 'I am a virtuoso'. It doesn't shout 'Look at me now!'; rather, it speaks quietly, perhaps only to itself, like a Kennedy dormouse, embracing – even if with misgivings or fears – the ten years of application ahead.

One thing certainly seems clear: forced practice is pointless, counter-productive, even destructive; 'child cruelty' rather than 'empowerment' says Tom Service. Pianist Stephen Hough says of those responsible for the coercion, primarily parents, 'I'd put all these people in prison'. He also speaks out against an emphasis on young students' careers, and the encouragement to outstrip their peers: 'It's all about the wrong things, and it's unhealthy for kids.'[97] And that tallies precisely with Kennedy's Juilliard reaction.

I have questioned the need to send children away to school, in the pursuit of excellence, but the home scenario may of course present problems of its own. Kennedy's father had disappeared before he was even born. As Kennedy tells the story, his mother even managed to leave him alone in his pram on a top floor balcony at the house in Brighton while she went off to teach piano in London. 'I recall screaming a lot and I was freezing, but no one came to rescue me. It's probably very telling that my first memory is one of abandonment.'[98] The family atmosphere of the Menuhin School seems truly benevolent by comparison. And worse was to come for Kennedy as a teenager, his stepfather prone to violence. Suffering difficult circumstances of any sort can sometimes be a motivating force for an individual to escape, to do better, to dig deep into their personal resources and thrive. Andrew Robinson highlights a particular statistic: 'One study of 400 eminent people of the twentieth century found that 85 per cent had come from highly troubled homes ... Moreover, a disproportionate number of creative achievers lose one or both parents in childhood.'[99]

It's a troubling concept, the idea that losing a parent might provide a greater creative stimulus than parental support. Philip Larkin puts it humorously, though still with disconcerting bite, in his poem 'This Be the Verse'.

> They fuck you up, your mum and dad.
> They may not mean to, but they do.
> They fill you with the faults they had
> And add some extra, just for you.[100]

Parents may be in pole position on this front, but teachers can be guilty too. I remember an art lesson in which the teacher looked over my shoulder at what I was painting, and simply said, 'oh dear'. I lost all courage and confidence in practising visual art after that. I wish WR Anderson could have swooped in with his forthright admonition from *The New Musical Companion*: 'above all, never suggest fear to a child. It is simple wickedness to do that.'[101]

I would hope that wickedness such as that is rare, but a bigger question mark hangs over educational systems. Educational guru Ken Robinson once produced a chart of how metaphorical thinking diminishes as we progress through education. He called it 'The Decline of Genius'.[102]

Age	Capability
3-5	98%
8-10	32%
13-15	10%
25+	2%

This remains one of the most alarming presentations of statistics I have ever seen. As we progress through formal education, we lose one of the very things it should be nurturing. It comes close to saying that education is a terrible waste of time.

Metaphorical thinking might seem to refer primarily to literary matters, and it's perhaps more useful here to talk of *divergent*, or *lateral* thinking. That way, we can see Kennedy's assemblage of Bach, Bartók and Hendrix in his South Bank recital as a perfect example. For Chick Corea, the keyboard player who worked with Miles Davis, such thinking is fundamental: 'it's a pretty common way of looking at life, you see one thing and you associate it with another.'[103] Corea attended the Juilliard but – wouldn't you know it – dropped out.

If education is indeed the enemy of creative thinking, artists are right to be wary of it, as Daniel Coyle identifies to be the case. 'With scientists, formal education at school and university tends to be accepted and welcomed, while with artists it is often resisted and even rejected.'[104] Kennedy has become increasingly vociferous in his questioning of educational systems, and certainly the need for the 'meaningless pieces of paper' that they hand out – or in his case, not; his absence from Juilliard classes in his final year was too persistent for the necessary credits to be granted, and he didn't really care. He is not alone in casting an element of scorn on the very relationship between academia and the arts. Peter J Martin writes, of jazz: 'Already there are dire warnings that the price of academic respectability – with its catalogue of canonic figures, standardised teaching methods and approved repertoire – may be the death of jazz as an individualistic, creative and spontaneous music.'[105] I am put in mind here of a comment made by the writer Philip Pullman, when asked how he would encourage creative writing in schools: 'ban it', he said, in serious jest.[106] That way it would be elevated to the status of smoking behind the bike sheds, something forbidden and enticing.

*

During the first Covid-19 lockdown in 2020, Ruth Slenczynska, at the age of 97, uploaded home recordings of Beethoven's Sonatas to YouTube, to celebrate the composer's 250th anniversary. (Kennedy marked the anniversary with a new concerto, *Für Ludwig Van*, but his tour went on hold.) Neither this nor her youthful performance is anything truly remarkable. It's just the age-related achievements (at both ends of the spectrum) that people seem to find so worthy of praise. Ironically, Slenczynska was probably a truly gifted musician, whose maturity went somewhat to waste. Her talent was recognized by both Enescu and Boulanger; Rachmaninov, too, offered her encouragement. But her father's controlling demands, together with the absurd expectation of the critics – that a child should demonstrate musical maturity – ended in her abandoning her career until such time as she could continue on her own modest terms. It's heartening that she did eventually find some stability, peace, and enjoyment in playing music, after those traumatic early years. Kennedy, reflecting on his own early years at school, would seem to echo this sentiment: 'I've found a normality and it's not bad.' By contrast, 'Five or six of the people who went to the Menuhin school ... have committed suicide. They've had nervous breakdowns. They don't love music. They don't love life.'[107] Nevertheless, the impression made on Kennedy by Menuhin himself was profound. 'When he died, I couldn't believe it. I didn't go to his funeral because I didn't want to believe the man was dead.'[108]

Kennedy's reaction is as heartfelt in grief as Menuhin's was in joy when witnessing what his pupils achieved. Their extraordinary self-confidence, their 'enjoyment' and 'dedication', and the level of their performance, 'exuberant yet structured, prepared yet spontaneous ... moves an audience almost to tears'.[109] From different perspectives, both comments speak of a meaningful relationship between teacher and student, whatever complications may exist.

It's so tempting to believe in exceptional talent being born, rather than bred, partly because so many 'great' artists react against the formative influences with which others are satisfied. And yet, as Andrew Robinson clarifies, 'No genes "for" domain-specific talents have yet been located',[110] despite hundreds of studies. Equally, as Fenby states: 'Profound ignorance exists at all levels as to what it takes to develop rare gifts, especially in the sphere of music.'[111] What we have is a wealth of examples, Kennedy included, that continue to beguile. Perhaps none is more intriguing than the comparison between Wolfgang Amadeus Mozart and his sister, Nannerl.

> It is extremely unlikely that Wolfgang Mozart's genius was simply a product of his training. Seldom has there been such a clear case of a creative individual and a close relative living in the same family and undergoing similar dedicated training in a particular domain of activity. There is a strong case for supposing that the differences between the capacities of the two people who emerged were the product of their personal biological endowments. On the other hand, it is indisputable that without the intense nurturance provided by Leopold, Wolfgang's creativity would not have blossomed.[112]

Nigel's own (half) siblings were fathered within John Kennedy's second marriage and further partnership in Australia; they share neither the exact same DNA, nor parenting or education, so no direct comparison can be made. It was simply a thrill to open the programme for the *New Four Seasons* concert in the Sydney Opera House, 2017, and see Nigel and Erica Kennedy were about to perform on the same stage; to know that wildly divergent paths can lead to the same place.

Bertie

You're only five years old
when you randomly decide
to smash a bottle
over another boy's head
in the playground at The Fold.
It's not you but your little
accomplice, Bertie,
who has nowhere to hide.

*

You leap from a chair
and deliver a powerful right
hook into thin air –
'punching God,' you claim
(surely above your weight).
Should God be seriously hurt
your invisible friend Bertie
may have to take the blame.

*

You drop your violin from
an ever greater height
as a bedtime game.
It's only a matter of time
until your skilful frivolity
is outdone by sheer gravity
and the violin breaks. Bertie
is absolved of the crime.

*

Bored with mediocrity
you skive off school,
busking on 57th street
to make ends meet.
The jazz clubs of Harlem
are irresistibly cool
and make you welcome.
You – or is that Bertie?

*

Still playing the fool
you rip out the tv and hurl
it from your roof
into the hotel pool,
narrowly missing Neil
Tennant but giving proof
that your old friend Bertie
is alive and well.

Chapter 3: Playing by Heart

The violin ... is in between your ear, your mind and your heart.
—Nigel Kennedy

Jazz is a heartbeat—its heartbeat is yours.—Langston Hughes

Dorothy DeLay might have been 'right' in saying that the CBS reps would lose interest in signing Kennedy having heard him play the 'wrong' music for their purposes, but it was surely only a matter of time until some kind of recording deal was offered. Kennedy's talent was obvious; well-connected sponsors had backed his Juilliard studies, and his exposure was already a positive factor, one would think, for any record company seeking success. The BBC had tracked his progress in the documentary, *Coming Along Nicely*, which culminated in his debut performance at the Royal Festival Hall in London, with Riccardo Muti and the Philharmonia orchestra, playing the Mendelssohn concerto. Further concert opportunities followed – and the attention of Menuhin's agent. Kennedy quit the Juilliard School and left the New York jazz clubs behind, on a mission to pursue a classical concert career despite his many misgivings.

It was never going to be a predictable process, however. One major problem was that record companies were a law unto themselves; the other was Kennedy's own wilfulness.

In *Coming Along Nicely* Kennedy, aged 16, was asked about his future career. It's an unusual question to put to someone that age, but then Kennedy had been facing interviewers' questions since he was six. His answer was remarkably measured, but ambitious. 'Well, it's difficult to say, just enjoying my music ... I would like to become a solo concert violinist if possible. Also a solo jazz violinist.' The combination was bold, and potentially fraught. Kennedy himself was already saying 'I hope I'll still be playing jazz and classical music, and more things, quite freely, hoping they won't get in the way of each other.'

These days, it's hard to grasp why the twin focus should have been quite so contentious. And even at the time, it was hardly unprecedented. Menuhin, alongside his numerous classical albums, recorded six with Grappelli. It was however unusual, not something that any single record company was likely to embrace. Menuhin got away with it, as he was so well established. As already discussed, he wasn't really comfortable playing jazz, despite his own yearnings, but his beliefs were strong.

> To reach our apogee, we have to subjugate our natures, then to free them. In the venture, each tradition, the extempore and the interpretative, can help the other, and those musicians who synthesize the two are the most complete, the worthiest of our admiration.[1]

Kennedy, certainly without any ambition to be *worthy*, was already entirely at ease in both modes, even if his synthesis of the two was to develop even further. Eventually, there would be many violinists and other musicians working across genres, if not always convincingly. It's become almost expected, which is probably unrealistic, given the special status Menuhin ascribes to the ability.

Some artists have ventured with a degree of caution. When Anne-Sophie Mutter finally recorded works by Gershwin, with André Previn, she worried that she didn't have the gene for swing, but Previn said, 'listening to you today, you sounded like you'd been out on the road with Count Basie. Your sense of time felt absolutely built-in, spot-on.' Mutter's reply was interesting, pointing out that 'all this has also to do with being a soloist. I can stretch things, be behind the beat, yet still be in time at the next junction-point.'[2]

Others have been less troubled by self-doubt. In 2022, Simon Rattle recorded *Nazareno*[3] with the London Symphony Orchestra, and reaction to the facebook promo was not kind. Comments included 'horrendous'; 'geeks grooving worse than dad dancing'; 'swings like a statue's cock'. Funniest of all was the question, 'Is he playing air orchestra?', something I will pick up on later, in connection with Kennedy's attitude toward conductors.

This of course raises questions about the essence of jazz, the difference between *jazzing something up* and exploring with the true jazz musician's sensibility. Recent research at the Max Planck Institute has found that 'the brain activity of jazz pianists differs from those of classical pianists, even when playing the same piece of music'. It goes on to suggest that musicians – even those exceptional individuals who are skilled in both 'disciplines' – are likely to find it hard to switch from one to another. The research report quotes Keith Jarrett, who was once asked 'if he would ever be interested in doing a concert where he would play both jazz and classical music: "No, that's hilarious ... practically impossible ... It's [because of] the circuitry. Your system demands different circuitry for either of those two things."'[4]

In light of this, Kennedy's sixteen-year-old hope that 'they won't get in the way of each other' might be considered wishful thinking, the brain fundamentally ill-equipped to accommodate the challenge. Menuhin may have collaborated with Grappelli, but their brains were not required to 'switch'. Grappelli was in his element, and Menuhin had his parts pre-written. As Gunther Schuller puts it, music in the mid twentieth century 'was still for the most part divided among sharply defined lines of musicians who, on the jazz side, could not (or preferred not to) read music ... while on the "classical side" musicians could not improvise, could not swing, could barely capture the unique rhythmic inflections and expanded sonorities of jazz'.[5] The Planck research seems to suggest that this status quo has a biological basis.

The research, however, makes another point, right at the start: 'A musician's brain is different to that of a non-musician. Making music requires a complex interplay of various abilities which are also reflected in more strongly developed brain structures.' The specific research delves into the further fine-tuning of those developed structures, making interesting distinctions (e.g. the classical brain deciding 'how' to play, the jazz brain deciding 'what') and leading to conclusions about 'how precisely the brain adapts to the demands of our surrounding environment'.[6] There is nothing to suggest that the human brain is limited in developing its structures to deal with alternative environments.

For some exceptional individuals – Keith Jarrett, Chick Corea, Keith Emerson, to name just a few – the brain would seem to develop alternative structures to reflect the diversity of environments in which they operate. Schuller remarked on this emerging trend and found, in the growing number of such individuals, 'proof of the advantageous intermingling of jazz and non-jazz influences'.[7]

To some extent, we all do this, musicians or not. A project at Princeton University brought poet Paul Muldoon together with chemist Warren S Warren. Brain scans were used to assess the physical response in a volunteer reading first a Muldoon poem, then an official university document. The results showed how 'The prefrontal cortex, the seat of reasoning and emotion, is visibly more engaged when dealing with the complexities of poetry than with straightforward bureaucratic prose.'[8] This is perhaps unsurprising, but underlines the potential for the human brain to 'switch'. Might it not be possible, after all, for the doubly exceptional brain not only to be capable of consummate performance in both the classical and jazz environments, but also, even when so far developed on both those individual paths, to switch like mere mortals do in less complex situations? Is this the type of thing, perhaps, that we mean by 'genius'? While studying at the Royal Academy, the virtuoso organist and harpsichord player, Francis Monkman, was deemed a genius by his tutor, and his subsequent contribution to diverse musical fields – often switching between them in performance – would seem to give credibility to such a theory.[9]

Putting the term genius aside again for now, the development of such ability is clearly not instant, and I refer again to Robinson's ten-year principle. Kennedy started mixing things up very young; even so, by the mid 80s he was recording Elgar, and jazz, but not together. They were separated, if only by an hour in the pub (more on which below). Ten years later, at his 'comeback' recital, he was moving effortlessly from Bach to Hendrix. In another ten he would put electrified jazz into a Mozart concerto.

In the 80s we see Kennedy performing classical music almost as if in a trance. Even in the Bach Prom of 2011, he hardly moves. As he turns to jazz, he becomes animated. As David Horn explains, jazz from the start was characterized by a 'display of those elements that history has often considered superficial or clichéd: energy, vitality and physicality, often exuberance'.[10] Kennedy slipped very happily into this mode, but became increasingly drawn to allowing the mode to infiltrate his classical concentrations. Moments of particular rhythmic drive or emphasis are marked by a physical, forward surge, or a stamp of the foot. It's not contrived, as some insist on seeing it (and are a conductor's sweeps of the arms and tossings of the head not far more exaggerated and distracting?); it is simply the musician being wholly absorbed in the music, in the same way we are drawn to dance to irresistible tunes. It is also, perhaps, a sign of how the brain has grown to accommodate supposedly conflicting impulses.

It's true that Kennedy's switches, his different modes of behaviour, tend to be pronounced. Indeed, it's the switches that seem to have proved irritating to some people, even while they tolerate a conductor's relentlessly overblown gestures. Consider, though, Robinson's observation, 'that the more creative a person is, the more multifarious is his or her personality ... To be exceptionally creative means to have a chameleon personality. Exceptionally creative individuals modify their personalities to suit their context.'[11] Given this statement, we might infer that a reaction against Kennedy's switches is a reaction against creativity itself. If a sublime performance is followed by a 'juvenile' comment to the press, is it perhaps the critic who lacks depth when dismissing the former on account of the latter? Satyajit Ray describes Mozart as 'a bundle of contradictions. In spite of being prodigiously gifted, he had a flippant side to him. He wrote letters which contained jokes in poor taste and in fact occasionally bordered on the obscene.'[12] The flippant side was however reined in when it mattered: 'the fact remains that he must have applied himself very seriously to the task of composing his masterpieces, and at these moments he must have undergone a complete change of personality.'

Of course, what annoys certain people most – whether with Mozart or Kennedy – is the *proximity* of different behaviours, the ultimate offence being a melding of two extremes; such 'irreverence' automatically relegates the artistic achievement, in their view. The artist is simply a brat, an *enfant terrible*, success leading someone to believe they can behave as they like, as with a spoiled child. In some respects, however, the Plank research points to such proximity or melding as the height of sophistication.

Behind these controversies is a complicating fact. As Bruce Johnson explains, jazz musicians are in fact 'heirs to a tradition of improvisation once practised by Frescobaldi, Handel, JS Bach,

Haydn, Mozart and Beethoven'.[13] For some, this is an inconvenient truth. For Kennedy it's a prime defence and a rallying cry.

The demise of improvisation within classical music is a complex story. The fact that nineteenth-century composers increasingly notated cadenzas in full certainly played its part, as did the split between composers and performers, another complexity in its own right. The composing performer is of course still alive and well – in the field of pop and rock music, and of course jazz, in fact in almost every musical arena other than the classical, where the combined role once flourished. With the demise at its peak, as it were, jazz emerges, as if the urge to improvise had gone underground and reappeared in a totally different place. For some, it proved unrecognisable. Eric Blom's scathing comments about jazz don't even acknowledge its extemporizing heart:

> Jazz, popularly supposed to be much the most rhythmic music, is not rhythmic at all, but rigidly metrical. True rhythm has the fundamental regularity, but also the quick, responsive variability, of the human pulse, not the mechanically precise beat of the metronome. It feels time and goes in time, but not dead in time. Yet the jazz fever—if anything so cold-blooded and machine-pulsed may be called fever—has been allowed to invade the concert room.[14]

One wonders if Blom ever listened, properly, to any jazz. He's not alone though in not *getting* jazz, which, Frank Tirro says, has generally been regarded as a 'somewhat mystical art'.[15] Even some of those who enjoy it would probably own up to not understanding how it is made; it's not as simple as Louis Armstrong makes out in *High Society*. And yet, perhaps partly *because* of its mysteries and technical demands, jazz has long been the alternative music of choice for many classical musicians: something to unwind to, as player or listener; perhaps a party trick; and occasionally, a genuinely equal passion and practice, as with Kennedy.

Bearing in mind the difficult situation with record companies, Kennedy was perhaps fortunate, making his debut as a recording artist, to keep both classical music and jazz in the frame, and it was partly as a matter of luck. Not that long after his debut recital, CBS had offered Kennedy a contract after all – to play Mozart. His agent fudged the deal, and it was half a decade later that Kennedy finally entered a recording studio, not to play Mozart, but much more appropriately, Elgar, for a recently formed independent label, Chandos. It was an inexpensive option, featuring only Kennedy and the pianist Peter Pettinger, playing the Sonata in E minor and other 'Elgar favourites' (cellist Steven Isserlis joining them for 'Salut d'Amour'). When the recording finished several hours ahead of schedule, Kennedy and Pettinger, kindred spirits in more ways than one, adjourned to the pub and cooked up a plan to go back into the studio (with a crate of beer), which their producer, Brian Couzens, agreed to. The result was an unrehearsed and unedited album of improvised jazz standards that was actually released before the Elgar. Almost by chance, then, Kennedy was able to present a balanced account of his musical personality on record, right from the start. But 'chance' is an interesting concept. Kennedy was with Pettinger, a musical ally. The classical recording proved quick and easy; there was time for 'more' – and a will to make it happen.

Chandos may have been a small, new label, but Kennedy was already proving a hit in the concert hall, so the releases got attention. Both were in a sense low-key offerings, and this did them no harm at all. There was no hint of Kennedy seeking virtuoso status. The Elgar disc gave the Sonata top billing, with Elgar, Kennedy and Pettinger all pictured. The improvised album was titled *Strad Jazz*, a nice reference to the fact that Kennedy was playing a Stradivarius violin. It was subsequently re-released as *Nigel Kennedy Plays Jazz*, which seems both less interesting and slightly wrong, in that Pettinger is somewhat removed from the equation; the original cartoon-like cover featured them both, and gave their names equal billing (though why on earth was Kennedy drawn with blonde hair?). The Elgar was also subsequently re-titled, as *Nigel Kennedy Plays Elgar*. Given the burgeoning Kennedy brand, it was an understandable marketing ploy, and did at least bracket the albums as a pair.

Gramophone's review of the Elgar found Kennedy's playing of the Sonata 'stunningly beautiful', and made the interesting point about the further works that 'light music usually lies outside the understanding of today's young players'. The album even included '6 Very Easy Pieces in the First Position', almost like an invitation for budding violinists to believe that they too could step up to such heights. The true heights, however, were about to be revealed, with chance again playing its part.

'Aquí está encerrada el alma de . . . . .'

The Elgar Violin Concerto, with its enigmatic inscription ('Herein is enshrined the soul of . . . . .') is considered one of the most difficult – and greatest – works in the repertoire. Elgar abandoned his early work on it in 1890, and it was twenty years later that the masterpiece emerged; sometimes works of art themselves have a long childhood. It's a concerto that is only ever performed by violinists of the highest calibre. Recordings, compared to those of other major concertos, are relatively few. In 1984, Kennedy had been playing the concerto in the concert hall, to considerable acclaim, firstly with Menuhin conducting. Menuhin had famously performed the work with Elgar himself conducting; not only were the two names strongly linked, but Menuhin's performance was long considered to be definitive. Kennedy was naturally on a mission to do something different – not for the sake of it, or simply to escape Menuhin's shadow, but to connect with the heart of the work to the very best of his ability. He visited Elgar's birthplace, The Firs, to study the original score, but learned most from the surrounding countryside, the Malvern Hills, experiencing the connectivity between landscape, music and emotion that Ken Russell captured so well in his BBC *Elgar* film of 1962. Kennedy would later choose to live in the same area.

A new interpretation of the work emerged, though somewhat aligned with that of Albert Sammons, for instance in the use of portamenti, but primarily in a shared, eloquent and coherent grasp of the work's vast structure. Kennedy performed it with a variety of conductors, including James Loughran, Sir Charles Groves, and finally Vernon 'Todd' Handley, and it was Handley whose quick thinking enabled them to make use of a cancellation within EMI's recording schedule. The result would win the Gramophone Record of the Year Award of 1985.

There was a wow factor, simply in the fact that a violinist should make Elgar their debut concerto recording; Mendelssohn or Bruch are the typical options. Menuhin admittedly recorded the Elgar at an even younger age (eighteen), but he had already

notched up the Bruch. An additional element of surprise was that
a British violinist was in the spotlight at all. Kennedy claims
that the prejudice against such a thing was endemic within
the industry, and his success in overcoming that – not only for
his own career but for those who would follow – remains one
of his cherished achievements. But none of that would have
come about, or counted for much, had the performance not
been of such astonishing maturity and communicative power.
It heralded a new era of classical music playing to a wide and
more diverse audience precisely because of the depth of personal
connection made between soloist and source material; a British
violinist and a British concerto in seemingly perfect understanding, driven by emotion yet holding that turbulence within
structural grace.

I mentioned the inscription, which has never been fully
decoded (nor the reason for its Spanish entirely justified), though
the evidence for believing the five dots to refer to Alice Stuart
Wortley, daughter of the painter Millais, is strong. Elgar referred
to her as 'Windflower', a spring flower he had known from childhood, and themes within the concerto are given the same name.
Moreover, Elgar repeatedly wrote to Alice with mention of 'our
own concerto'. The significance of this, as Michael Kennedy
points out, is the remarkable 'expressive personal intimacy'
within a work 'designed on a grand and opulent scale'.[16] As Ken
Russell suggests in his film, Elgar was 'the last great composer
to be in touch with the people'; even so, the concerto was the
only work he ever called 'personal'. He also, famously, called it
'awfully emotional! too emotional, but I love it'. Ernest Newman
writes:

> we are not listening to mere music-making, not witnessing a
> mere attempt to fill a conventional form, but following up a
> long and always interesting trail of human experience; all this
> music has been lived before it was put on paper.[17]

These comments are, in a way, slightly strange, in that Newman
is conflating the listener's experience and the written work. The
latter is something of an abstract until performed, and it is therefore the interpreting musicians – the soloist in particular, in such
a personal work – who enable us to follow that trail of human

experience through the empathy of their playing. Kennedy clearly had an intuitive understanding of the work, and we might well apply Newman's comments to his interpretation, as much as to the 'abstract' work. None of this human experience, it should be said, is in any sense explicit or programmatic, quite the contrary. It is deliberately opaque. The interpreter's task is, paradoxically, to communicate the mystery.

The unorthodox nature of the concerto is perhaps relevant to its particular appeal to Kennedy. The traditional concerto 'shape' is expanded; there are relentless changes of tempo. 'Melodic phrases are daringly drawn out, and curious digressions abound.'[18] These features (I'm tempted to say criticisms) might almost be labels for Kennedy's own musical mannerisms. Most significantly, there is no cadenza until the final movement, and even then, its arrival is not heralded in traditional fashion, with a cadential chord that acts like a colon in text. Instead, it's introduced by very quiet 'thrumming', as Elgar calls it, and then unfolds almost like a slow movement within a movement. HC Colles writes, 'Elgar dwells on his themes as though he could not bear to say good-bye to them, lest he should lose the soul enshrined therein'.[19] But of course he must, after the dream has been slowed and stretched to the limit, and the coda surges towards a dramatic conclusion, of which Elgar himself said, 'two souls merge and melt into one'.[20]

The inscription continues to intrigue. Why is it in Spanish? The quotation comes from an eighteenth-century French novel, *L'Histoire de Gil Blas de Santillane*, by Alain-René Lesage, which was translated into English by Tobias Smollett around the time Laurence Sterne was writing *Tristram Shandy*. The plot thickens, as the work may well have earlier Spanish origins, and has certainly found its way into a multitude of subsequent works, both literary and operatic. All this is likely to have appealed to Elgar with his fondness for enigma. The epitaph he quotes is indeed in Spanish within the *Gil Blas* text, but he then translates it, choosing the word 'enshrined', rather than 'entombed'. Why keep the Spanish?

There are so many far-fetched theories about the mystery Elgar created, that I have no qualms in putting forward my own, and it relates to a piece that Elgar never finished. *The Spanish Lady* was planned as an operatic adaptation of a Ben Jonson play, *The*

Devil Is an Ass. Elgar didn't complete much of the music, concentrating instead on the libretto. The story involves a character disguising himself as a Spanish woman, in order to liaise with someone else's wife. This immediately makes me think of the concerto's Spanish inscription, where not only the name but also the gender of the subject is deliberately concealed. It seems to me that not only five-dot 'Alice' (a married woman) but also five-dot 'Elgar' are enshrined (not entombed) in what he so deliberately called 'our concerto' in his letters.

If that's nonsense, so be it, but I feel there's an underlying truth in the concerto enshrining the very spirit of Elgar. And that raises the question: how does one give a *performance* of such a thing? 'Performance' seems an altogether insufficient word. As Michael Kennedy describes it, 'The soloist is called upon to be orator, singer, poet, conjurer and wizard, such is the expressive and technical range of the writing'.[21] But even that doesn't quite go far enough. The soloist, for the space of almost an hour – short in one sense, a lifetime in another – needs to enshrine everything that Elgar summoned in the writing: the long trail of human experience.

In 1921 Elgar wrote: 'I am still at heart the dreamy child who used to be found in the reeds by Severn side with a sheet of paper trying to fix the sounds and longing for something very great.'[22] In his recording of the concerto, I feel Kennedy has intuitively grasped and expressed this – both the original dreamy child, and the older man still holding to that dream. He does Elgar justice by daring to enshrine *himself* – his own dreamy childhood – in the music too.

I am not claiming that Kennedy is unique in his ability to achieve such mesmerizing affinity with a piece of music. It may however be the case that certain individuals make exceptional connection with particular works. Sammons clearly did so with Elgar too, though of course we can't hear it today with the same clarity. Both Sammons and Kennedy are British; is that a prerequisite? No, no more than it is necessary to be Russian to do justice to Tchaikovsky. But I have to say I have heard non-British orchestras perform Elgar, and it can sound very strange. Appreciation of Elgar amongst Americans, in particular, has been limited. Maybe they need to spend more time in the Malverns. Kennedy's sparkling performances with Leonard Slatkin may have changed some opinion, though Kennedy has also met some resistance in the States, not least because of a clash of opinion about encores. More (yes more!) of that later.

For Kennedy, somewhat in accord with Russell, the Elgar Concerto is 'the last great statement of real concertos in the world, let alone English music'.[23] When his recording received the Gramophone Recording of the Year Award, it was the first time that the honour had been bestowed on a concerto. It was a pinnacle of achievement, however you looked at it, right at the beginning of his recording career. Where do you then go, from such heights?

*

'Long and pretentious'
'An accumulation of discords, confused climaxes and dressed-up trivialities'
'Music run mad, a frenzy of notes of incomprehensible savagery'
'Music that stinks to the ear'

No – not reaction to Kennedy's debut album as composer, *Let Loose*, which was looming, or even Philip Larkin on Charlie Parker. These are just some of the comments hurled at Tchaikovsky's Violin Concerto after its premiere, notably by the Viennese critic Eduard Hanslick, seemingly intent on damaging Tchaikovsky every bit as much as the composer, in his view, had done harm to the violin. Critics should control themselves. The concerto quickly gained huge popularity, while Hanslick headed for ignominious irrelevance. The concert hall may seem like the epitome of civilized calm, but musical history is full of controversy and uproar, with the audience sometimes the savages. The premiere of Stravinsky's *Rite of Spring* was literally a riot.

Popularity can create further problems. As Kennedy says, the Tchaikovsky concerto 'has committed the crime of becoming phenomenally popular with classical audiences all around the world'.[24] This is archetypal Kennedy vs critics, but it's also true that a certain group of people – quite a large group, across all artistic genres – are dismissive of art that is too widely applauded. That's a nonsense, obviously, but it's a prevalent nonsense that

Kennedy is absolutely right to call out. It's absurd to dismiss the profundity of Monet's waterlilies just because there's a trail of people through the Paris Orangerie filming it on their phones.

Given how the six-year-old Kennedy expressed a love of Tchaikovsky's music – 'all of it' – it was only a matter of time until he would seek to put his own stamp on the much-loved concerto. It's where we might have expected to find Kennedy's soul enshrined, had Elgar not possessed him. We don't tend to lose our feeling for works that appealed to us at an early age. Knowing how best to approach them, however, with childhood passion blended with maturity, can be challenging. The notion that Tchaikovsky didn't really know 'what a violin can do to hold its own against an orchestra'[25] has been a red rag to many violin bulls who give overblown accounts of what is at heart a highly lyrical work. Kennedy, supremely able to give the violin a full starring role, decided to pull back, in favour of a more symphonic approach to the work. He has never favoured unnecessary virtuosity.

The fact that he admits to some disappointment with his rendition is at once understandable and regrettable. It should have been a landmark recording; instead, it's simply very good. When it was reissued, in combination with the Sibelius concerto, Kennedy made a point of dismissing the need to dwell on autobiographical background to musical works, the fact 'that Sibelius was an alcoholic or Tchaikovsky was homosexual'[26] (the sort of thing which Ken Russell dwells on in his films); but as he demonstrated with his Elgar recording, a deep personal connection with the scenario of a composition pays significant dividends. Tchaikovsky had been through a particularly turbulent, emotional period of his life when he wrote the concerto, and perhaps the performances that Kennedy himself rates above his own – those of Maxim Vengerov and David Oistrakh (both, yes, Russian) – are outstanding in the way they capture Tchaikovsky's personal sense of release and *rejoice* in emerging from darker days. I nevertheless find Kennedy's version highly engaging, and his cadenza refreshingly shorn of *me me me*.

Works can enter the popular imagination in surprising ways. Tchaikovsky's concerto is evident within John Williams's score to *Star Wars: The Empire Strikes Back*. One can also see a performance of part of the work within the 1947 film *Carnegie Hall*, directed by Edgar G Ulmer. Jascha Heifetz plays not only the music but a bit part in the drama, which revolves around a young woman whose story is inextricably entwined with the venue. This is the same Heifetz, revered as a classical purist, in the thick of a piece of Hollywood entertainment, and it's surely no bad thing that top quality playing should find alternative ways of reaching a wide audience. It's worth bearing in mind that classical music probably has its greatest exposure within the cinema. Millions will have listened to classical music without realizing it, either excerpts of established works, or original scores in a symphonic style very different to music they otherwise choose. It's one reason to dismiss any claim for classical music's demise. And Kennedy, returning to the stage in 2023 after a period of lockdown, chose to showcase a number of film themes, including Chaplin's 'Smile', adapted from the score to *Modern Times* (1936). For me, the highlight of that concert, at the Evesham Regal Cinema, was the exquisite rendition of 'A Nightingale Sang in Berkeley Square', a song featured in the film of the same name released in 1989.

In each of four releases, Kennedy's recording of Tchaikovsky's violin concerto has been accompanied by other works, firstly with Chausson's *Poème*, written just a couple of years earlier; it's French, but based on a Turgenev short story. Full of drama and lyrical reflection, it makes a fine prelude to the longer work, and the poetry of Kennedy's interpretation is more than enough to recommend the album as a whole. Curiously, the same pairing of works was re-released in reverse order the following year. Another release of 1986 incorporated the piano concertos, the second of which breaks the mould of the concerto by giving the main soloist the company of two others in the central movement. Cue Nigel Kennedy and Steven Isserlis joining Peter Donohoe. As already mentioned, and discussed later in this chapter, a further album brought together Tchaikovsky and Sibelius.

Bartók and the Duke

I'm sure many people couldn't wait for Kennedy to record the other big-hitters – Beethoven, Brahms – but they were in for a surprise. EMI agreed to Kennedy's idea – again unconventional – to record Bartók and Duke Ellington (middle name Kennedy) together; an imaginative pairing that furthered Kennedy's approach to programming generally. Both composers are close to his heart, and he describes here the logic to his choice of works:

> There are other great works by Bartók but none of them seem to match the mental strength of the Solo Sonata. Bartók has such a rich mixture of Hungarian folk-inspired melody integrated with great compositional architecture that most of the compositions by his contemporaries would have sounded second best alongside it on this disc.
>
> There was one obvious exception to this: Duke Ellington. He also used material inspired by his background and put it into bigger structures, one of the best examples being his *Black, Brown and Beige* Suite.[27]

It comes as a jolt. *Contemporaries*? Shurely shome mishtake. But of course he's right; it's just disconcerting, like seeing a motor car in a Peckinpah western. Kennedy spells out the dates:

> *Black, Brown, and Beige* received its premiere in Carnegie Hall, New York, performed by Duke Ellington and his big band in 1943, and selections from this work were recorded in 1944, the year in which Yehudi Menuhin gave the Bartók Solo Sonata its premiere in the same hall.[28]

It was Menuhin who commissioned the Sonata, a mere two years before Bartók's death, and it's a formidable piece. As Kennedy says of the 'Fuga' second movement, 'This is a barbaric four-part fugue ... It took me quite a few performances before I could play it!'[29] Menuhin called it 'without a doubt the greatest work for solo violin since Bach'.[30] The debt to Bach is apparent from the start, the first movement (Tempo di ciaccona) beginning almost with an homage, before swiftly veering into thoroughly different harmonic and rhythmic territory. But the intensity, dense texture, chords and polyphony are all redolent of Bach, while also startlingly fresh. Kennedy's playing is bright yet warm, rendering dissonance seductive, and in the contrapuntal passages you might believe you are listening to two violins, at subtly different volumes. It seems to redefine what the violin can *be*. The ferocious 'Fuga' (in which you can at times hear Kennedy's take on Hendrix in formation) is followed by 'Melodia', a movement so calm and spacious that you're drawn into its depth, as with a Rothko painting. It's the final movement where folk tune is most prominent, some of it almost bluesy, and the imminent Ellington is already making perfect sense.

The masterstroke in the pairing (and the consequent transition between the two works) is that Kennedy arranges Ellington's big-band composition primarily for solo violin, with only Alec Dankworth's double bass adding depth, and some useful friction.[31] The original had a violin part played by Ray Nance, which Kennedy much admires, and borrows, but he also uses the violin (again, almost reinventing it) to carry the full weight of a work that was originally advertised as 'Duke Ellington's first symphony'. It couldn't be done if not for his grasp of implied harmony learned from Bach and Bartók. 'Without doubt Bartók is the greatest composer I have known', wrote Menuhin,[32] and he surely passed on this strength of feeling to Kennedy.

Ellington is indeed Bartók's match, a colossus of black American culture, and of *Black, Brown and Beige* Claudia Roth Pierpoint says, 'It seems unlikely that any other musical début has carried such hope of repairing divisions: between jazz and classical, between black and white.'[33] The timid young Kennedy portrayed on the album seems an unlikely figure to carry the torch, but the image belies the boldness of his project. In the sleeve notes he writes, 'I haven't seen any albums like this in the record shops before.' Nor would he or anyone have encountered such programming on the radio, or in *proximity* in any other musical or social arena. It was – and remains – a genuinely important album. Strangely, in *Uncensored!*, where he plugs many of his other recordings, Bartók/Ellington is not even mentioned. That's a shame, since it probably needs plugging the most.

Despite his legendary status, there was a time – not so long after *Black Brown and Beige* – when Ellington's critics suggested he had to make a choice: 'the century's most important jazz composer could narrow his focus, concentrate, and compose—or lead the band and tour until he dropped. Not both.'

> For Ellington it would have been like choosing his heart over his lungs; the whole system by now worked together or not at all. The choice was apparently personal as well as musical: he

loved the life of the road, surrounded by people yet essentially
alone.[34]

The heart and lungs analogy would work for Kennedy too. *Mainly
Black* is an arrangement, not a composition as such, but it provides clear evidence of Kennedy's early intent and capability as a
composer, something he has developed in parallel to a relentless
touring schedule, following the Duke's example, writing in close
collaboration with his fellow musicians. As Ellington once commented, 'You can't write music right unless you know how the
man that'll play it plays poker.'[35] He would have smiled, perhaps,
if he'd witnessed Kennedy's virtuoso bluffing when faced with
his muggers in Harlem. The most extraordinary footnote to all
this is that Kennedy had once been approached by Ellington's
manager as a potential replacement when Ray Nance left the
Ellington band. Aged only fourteen, he wasn't able to override
the Menuhin/parental disapproval. In two years time, Ellington
would be dead, and Kennedy at Juilliard. It was a missed opportunity that Kennedy still cites as his biggest regret. It is hardly
surprising that he has never felt full allegiance to the classical
world.

In 2010 Kennedy opened the Latitude festival with a full Duke
Ellington set, which was apparently magnificent. My daughter
should have been there to give me a first hand account, but a
chronically delayed train meant she missed it. Bloody British
Rail. I could have wept.

Let Loose

When EMI agreed to an album of Kennedy's own compositions,
they were perhaps expecting jazz more akin to his Chandos
release. What they got was something pretty wild, which they
didn't really know what to do with. They clearly didn't have much
interest or belief in it. The design has a rather homemade feel,
as if it's been knocked together by a mate. The cover image is,
frankly, baffling; full of 'message' without the message really
coming across. Let loose to do his own thing, Kennedy is pictured
in a leather jacket, beneath which he's wearing an Elgar t-shirt,
but confusingly, he doesn't appear at all relaxed; he looks rather
stern. Cradling his violin with one hand, he holds the other like

a fist. And he's sitting on – what? A rubbish dump? What might be mistaken for an enormous dumb-bell is most likely the wheels and axle of a truck. Only inside do we find a much smaller image of Kennedy, smiling, a solitary figure on the edge of a dilapidated building by the water. There are no explanatory sleeve notes, just track information listing all artists involved. On which note, it was perhaps a mistake not to make more of this collaborative aspect of the album. The cover is all Kennedy, but his friend Dave Heath was a major part of the collaboration. The focus on Kennedy put him directly in the line of critical fire. In *Uncensored!* he takes umbrage at a reviewer suggesting that he was 'copying the innovations of Miles Davis's album *Tutu*'[36] (which was something of a pop fusion, using synthesized orchestral effects), though it's umbrage he turns into a brag, having never heard *Tutu* at the time. He also feels the negative review was driven by prejudice – against a classical musician performing such material.

Kennedy calls the album 'ill-fated', with some justification. There was no joined up thinking within EMI, no mechanism for promoting a contemporary album from a classical artist; and the problem was mirrored within the critical press. In the previous decade, the classical guitarist John Williams had success in straddling different musical domains, but his personal projects were released on a different label to his classical output, and the material was in any case less of a bold departure than Kennedy's. By the time he formed Sky, with Francis Monkman et al, his particular brand of fusion was highly popular, though not without adverse criticism. He was even criticized in his classical performances for wearing a polo-necked sweater.[37]

I've dared use the f word, and it is indeed controversial. There's a strange resistance to anything that isn't categorized, in many walks of life. With classical music, jazz, or rock, people know what they're dealing with (or think they do). As soon as the categories blur, there's trouble ahead. The reviewer of *Let Loose* reaches for something comparable: *Tutu*. It's a way of putting the music in a box, when in fact no box exists. The word 'fusion' itself is an attempt to categorize material that doesn't actually want to be labelled. Even within those categories that seem clear there are difficulties. 'Classical' music has a sub-section called – err – classical. How confusing is that? And what about the works that don't fit neatly into the 'classifications' (of Baroque, Classical, Romantic, etc)? We could perhaps call some of them works of fusion, except that would be ridiculous, as you can't, when you compose, fuse a style from the past with something yet to be defined.

Tom Service, talking about our definitions of style and period, suggests that 'we're scared of what might be between those categories, we're scared of the gap because it's an uncertain abyss in between two apparent certainties'. In his view, some of the most innovative composers are overlooked precisely because of 'their uncategorizable creative energy'; they don't 'fit'. Even a figure such as CPE Bach, son of JS, goes somewhat unacclaimed, and yet:

> not only [is he] the father of Mozart and Beethoven and Haydn, CPE Bach is the grand-daddy of Frank Zappa too, and he's the patron saint of any composer who dares to imagine what happens in the hybrid zones in between genres and styles and historical movements.[38]

Andrew Robinson's claim that a genius has yet to beget a genius is put to the test in the case of the Bachs.

I smile that Zappa is mentioned here, being a Kennedy favourite. You could call Zappa a master of fusion, synthesis, of a hybrid approach to art, but the resulting works have the further distinction of being utterly unlike anything else, truly 'odd' in the best sense: the controversial category of one. Some works are so highly original that classification seems defunct.

CPE Bach's circle of friends in Hamburg included philosophers and writers.[39] Remarkably, bearing in mind the Shandean connections I have been making, one of those friends, Johann Friedrich Zückert, was the first German translator of *Tristram Shandy*, perhaps the single most uncategorizable literary work of all time ('I imagine it will be like discovering Frank Zappa in 250 years', writes one blogger). Translation is further explored in the next chapter (my one reckless foray into the land of linguistic theory), but it's worth noting here that translation is itself an act of fusion, a hybrid of cultural and linguistic heritage. In his preface to the first six books of *Tristram Shandy*, Zückert expresses the challenges:

> Tristram's very peculiar ... manner of writing—since he
> moves from one thing to another without any connection,
> now uses disjointed sentences which, because they have not
> been completed, remain obscure, now uses provincialisms
> which are unfamiliar to a German, and lastly sometimes
> invents new words which can hardly be translated—and
> his long and involved sentences and his allusions to certain
> persons and events which cannot even be familiar to every
> Englishman, must suffice to excuse the translator for his
> imperfect work.[40]

I find Zückert's difficulties, experienced in the mid-eighteenth
century, expressive of what we all have to deal with in assimilat-
ing adventurous art in any era, any genre. And in his reference
to 'disjointed sentences' we can surely see an equivalence to jazz,
where 'a soloist's most salient experiences in the heat of performance involve poetic leaps of the imagination to phrases that are
unrelated, or only minimally related, to the storehouse'.[41]

With Kennedy, we're faced both with disjunctions *within*
works, for example the 'loose' material of his Dave Heath collaborations, and disjunctions *between* works, exemplified by *Let Loose*
being followed by Walton concertos. John Stanley (for it was he
not Kennedy writing *Always Playing*) describes the latter disjunc-
tion as a form of 'musical schizophrenia,'[42] and this has been a
prevalent attitude in the perception of Kennedy as a musician. His
concerts have sometimes been games of two halves – classical and
contemporary – and his audience in the 80s was not necessarily
ready for both. But for Kennedy there needed to be those two
halves, even at the risk of the match report saying that the early
dominance was frittered away.

The term 'schizophrenia' is misused here, as indeed it often
is. Yes, it derives from the two Greek works meaning 'split' and
'mind', but it refers to a serious mental disorder, not the divisions of interest that are in fact typical of many creative people.
Robinson gives examples of individuals whose widely divergent
interests appear to have been instrumental to their creative discoveries. And the all-important character of some popular figures
is in no small part owing to their range of expertise: Johnny Depp
and John McEnroe, for instance, the actor and tennis player both

guitarists. It may well be advantageous for an artist to have such a stereoscopic take on life.

By comparison, a twin interest in classical and contemporary music seems like no schism at all, merely the perfect qualification to make innovative, hybrid art. As Tom Service suggests, fusion of some sort is fundamental:

> Because when the truly creative composers let their imaginations fly, they're all working as hybrid artists, taking influences and ideas wherever they find them, from music, from the rest of the arts, from the rest of the world, fusing them into new shapes and ideas and sounds that haven't existed before.[43]

Equally, he sees it as our responsibility, if we have creative spirit of our own, to 'follow them down into the rabbit hole'.

Let Loose, which is far from my favourite Kennedy album, is important in that it makes a statement – not just about Kennedy being released from other expectations, but also about music being freed of classification. It's an uneven album, 'loose' in yet another sense. It has its mellow moments, but there's also enough savagery and dissonance to put a lot of people off. You could easily imagine Philip Larkin consigning it to his box of modernist horrors, with 'Parker, Pound and Picasso'.[44] We know Larkin's prejudice for what it is, but we need to keep putting our own to the test. As listeners, or readers, we need to match the adventurous daring of the artist. We need to be hybrid thinkers. As Homi Bhabha states,

> hybridity is precisely about the fact that when a new situation, a new alliance formulates itself, it may demand that you should translate your principles, rethink them, extend them ... [as against] a timid traditionalism – always trying to read a new situation in terms of some pre-given model or paradigm, which is a reactionary reflex, a conservative 'mindset'.[45]

Kennedy wouldn't revisit this territory, on record at least, for some years. The more reliable career was on the classical circuit, but even that was being transformed – Kennedy's spirit let loose within the concert hall, complete with jokes...

The Violinist Makes a Joke

Why
do
people
take
an
instant
dislike
to
viola
players
?

It
saves
time.

Having heard Kennedy make this joke onstage, I figured I could mimic his style of staccato verbal delivery on the page, in the form of the equally throwaway 'word sonnet'. This form, with the traditional fourteen lines but with only one word or character on each, is used extensively by the poet Seymour Maynes, and there's an example too by Paul Muldoon.[46] It's hardly a popular form, and I may now have added viola players to its detractors. All of which is highly unfair, as viola playing needs all the encouragement it can get. Yehudi Menuhin is honest about the difficulty experienced at his Stoke d'Abernon school: 'the beautiful, despised viola we have to encourage almost artificially.'[47] But he also writes, 'To play the viola is to endow oneself with another voice. It is like growing a beard and finding one's weak chin suddenly authoritative'; 'it gives a feeling of strength and thus strengthens violin playing'; 'To a violinist it offers a new repertoire and an extension of his experience without requiring of him in return an altogether new technique.'[48]

As Menuhin puts it, 'It is not an instrument for the vain violinist showing off his pyrotechnics, but for the serious musician who takes his part in the inner harmony or orchestra or string quartet'. Kennedy took to the viola within the school orchestra for exactly that reason, to avoid the violin section 'inhabited by wannabe soloists with their violins screeching acerbically like a Cat on a Hot Tin Spoof'.[49]

The German word for the viola, *Bratsche,* derives from the Italian *braccio,* meaning 'arm', and the viola is indeed a more conspicuous extension than the violin. It needs to be bigger, to achieve the required resonance, but intriguingly there's no set size. For acoustic purposes, it should actually be even bigger, but the 'correct' size would be impractical, hence the compromise. The viola is therefore a truly maverick instrument, and it seems fitting that Kennedy – for all his onstage jokes about viola players – should have embraced its possibilities – and one of the finest works written for the instrument, the Walton concerto. He regularly plays five string electric violins, which encompass the viola's range, but the acoustic viola makes very different demands: the finger spacing needs to be greater.

If the instrument is an extension of the human arm, it is also, like its unarmed relative the viola da gamba, a close match for the human voice, in range and expressive quality. Composers including Haydn and Mozart named it as their favourite instrument. Mozart gave it a starring role in his Sinfonia Concertante, a work that Kennedy admires, despite his misgivings about Mozart generally. Berlioz's use of the viola as the central unconventional 'character' in *Harold in Italy* is in close relation to Walton's use of the instrument as 'an introvert, a poet philosopher'.[50]

Menuhin played the viola only occasionally in public, more often for himself, 'as a practice instrument, especially on holidays',[51] but he did record the Walton concerto, as well as the later concerto for violin – a unique undertaking at the time. Kennedy went further in deciding to record both together – yet another adventurous pairing of works – and his mastery of the two is exceptional.[52] His recordings are with Walton's friend André Previn conducting (Mr Preview as Eric Morecambe famously introduced him), a musician for whom Kennedy has great respect, being not just a conductor, but composer (of Oscar-winning film scores, amongst so much else) and pianist – proficient at jazz as well as classical repertoire. The jazz connection is significant with Walton, who incorporated so many elements of jazz into his work. Kennedy's feel for Walton's music is more natural than, say, Menuhin's, as he's more adept at dealing with the jazz inflections – especially the bluesy drifts.

When first performed in 1929 the viola concerto gained instant acclaim, though Elgar didn't like it. (Apparently the two composers found themselves next to each other at the Hereford Cathedral urinals, and did little but grunt recognition; but what kind of sophisticated, critical conversation is expected in such a situation?) The work nevertheless established Walton's reputation. With the poet-philosopher soloist at the heart of it, the work is itself something of a tone-poem. Walton also wrote film music, something that Kennedy too has expressed interest in (and both, remarkably, have written music for versions of Chekhov's *Three Sisters*). Walton thought it an entirely different business to his other compositions, but scoring a film is surely, above all else, a matter of capturing mood. Some of his scores were for propaganda films (and written at a pace far removed from his usual painstaking approach to composition), and perhaps that led him to be somewhat dismissive of his achievements on that front. The fact that his score for *The Battle of Britain* was largely replaced with music by Ron Goodwin can't have helped.

By the time he wrote his violin concerto, in 1939, Walton was living on the Italian island of Ischia, and the work feels full of Mediterranean light. It was yet another violin concerto with love for an Alice (Lady Wimborne) at its heart. And yet, a World War was staring it in the face. Heifetz had commissioned it, and had exclusive rights to perform it for two years, but with war having broken out, and being unable to travel, he waived his right. A delayed British premiere took place in 1941, and Walton then revised the work in 1944.

The concerto is a formidable technical challenge. Julian Haylock, who worked with Kennedy on more than one occasion, was astonished at how Kennedy dealt with it:

> [he] turned up quite out of breath to the rehearsal, got his violin out, and willingly responded to the conductor's outrageous request to play the excruciatingly difficult opening section of the Scherzo.
>
> What happened next was simply jaw-dropping as, from cold, he got around the instrument with a facility that was

up in the Heifetz class. Everyone in the hall was awestruck by this display of virtuosity.[53]

If the work is virtuosic, it is also characterized by passages of sublime dreaminess, and Kennedy deals with those two elements superbly. As Christopher Palmer states, '*sognando* [dreaming] is a favourite Walton term',[54] just as *nobilmente* is for Elgar, and Kennedy gets to the heart of both. But as with Elgar, Walton has been viewed as slightly old-fashioned, not influential. Perhaps that's the fate of someone who assimilates so many diverse elements into a genuinely personal style. Walton was hurt by critical opinion, and commented, 'Today's white hope is tomorrow's black sheep ... I seriously advise all sensitive composers to die at the age of 37'.[55] He actually died in 1983, at the age of 80, just four years before Kennedy's recording. But how curious that Kennedy claims to have celebrated his own 50th birthday when he was, of all ages, 37.[56] More on that in Chapter 10.

Bearing in mind what Kennedy has said about the last/great/English status of the Elgar concerto, his embrace of the later Walton work is perhaps surprising, but this was a phase in which Kennedy was relentlessly extending his repertoire, and the challenge of tackling both concertos was unprecedented. It's perhaps ironic, given what I've said about the 'humble' viola, that the double act becomes a virtuosic feat in its own right.

It seems fitting that Walton should have incorporated a joke of sorts, albeit in the violin rather than the viola concerto. Having been bitten by a tarantula while composing, he allows the middle movement to break into a tarantella rhythm.

*

'Polonaise for polar bears'[57] – so wrote Donald Tovey, describing the final movement of the Sibelius violin concerto (a work he greatly admired). Critics can sometimes make good jokes too. Amusingly, composer Craig Alan has since used the phrase as title for a piece for tuba. Music historian Donald J Grout considers Sibelius's work of this period to be intensely emotional without being autobiographical; I take it, then, that the polar bears shouldn't be considered figments of the composer's inebriated imagination. You might wonder what you've been drinking, though, if you listen to 'Beach Baby', a song from the pop charts of 1974. It uses the big horn theme from Sibelius's 5th symphony (which is coupled with the violin concerto on the Kennedy/Rattle album). It's so prominent in the extended conclusion to the song (just as it is in the symphony) that the Sibelius estate took note, sued for copyright infringement, and gained 50% of the profit from sales. Kennedy's album notes, by William Mann, make a slight error in attributing the song to the Beach Boys, I guess because of the name of the song. So just for the record, it was per-formed by a hastily put together band, The First Class, having been written by John Carter and Gillian Shakespeare – plus Sibelius.

Weirdly, alcohol is mixed with my own earliest Sibelius mem-ories. My school organized concert trips to the Bournemouth Winter Gardens, where Paavo Berglund was conductor of the Bournemouth Symphony orchestra. I played with Berglund's son Juha ('Pokku') in our school orchestra, struggling to keep up. I led the way though in buying friends drinks in the interval, all of us under age, and therefore took most of the flak that followed. In my defence, I wanted to celebrate the magnificent music I'd heard, Berglund being a magisterial interpreter of Sibelius. The BSO was sometimes criticized for being seemingly adrift from their conductor's beat, but Berglund understood what Sibelius himself encouraged, the need to 'swim as in gravy'.[58] Accuracy and atmosphere had to be friends. Berglund was actually the most dedicated of conductors to long preparation and rehearsal time; Kennedy would undoubtedly have approved. And Rattle learned much from Berglund in his own approach to Sibelius.

Berglund, like Sibelius, was himself a violinist. He owned a Bergonzi violin (like Kennedy) previously played by Isaac Stern. And Stern's recording of the Sibelius concerto was one of Kenne-dy's chosen tracks on *Desert Island Discs*. I'm fascinated by these connections, which seem to tell us something about musical gravy; the way a whole range of musical influences past and present converge in the best of musical interpretations – with the listener's own imaginative hinterland part of the blend.

But wouldn't you know it, Kennedy, in his listings towards the end of *Uncensored!*, seems to have forgotten all about his recording of the Sibelius concerto. Maybe his falling out with the conductor Simon Rattle in later years was enough to have con-signed it to oblivion. (Kennedy's listings are actually a bit weird.

The classical albums are all listed under 'Concertos', despite the fact that some of them are not, while *The Doors Concerto* written by Jaz Coleman is listed under 'My Albums'.) As with his omission of Bartók/Ellington, it seems a shame, as it's similarly impressive. Kennedy as soloist was at one with Sibelius the violinist-turned-composer. Despite the virtuosic nature of much of the solo violin part, Kennedy is equally mindful of the symphonic texture. The extended cadenza in the first movement, which distinguishes the piece structurally, is explored with poetic purpose; it's still part of the overall symphonic poem, the fiendishly difficult technical challenges downplayed in favour of an ethereal, frosted haze. And yet he's also prepared to treat certain big moments with real force: at the very beginning, for instance, the melody – almost as soon as it's firmly established – slips into a dramatic dissonance, and Kennedy makes you feel as if a sudden crack has opened in the ice, and we might very well fall through, except that equilibrium (though still full of danger) is restored.

Critics of recordings make much of whether the soloist is sufficiently knowledgeable about the folk-tune origins of particular themes, but what is that about, apart from their own sense of 'expert' self-satisfaction? What matters much more, surely, is the degree to which all the musical material communicates in a coherent (if also interestingly contradictory) way to the audience.

As with the Tchaikovsky concerto, the premiere caused a storm. The violin part was basically too difficult for the chosen soloist, and was subsequently rewritten, as part of a general revision. The soloist originally chosen for both premieres was unavailable on each occasion, and threw a tantrum when replaced. (Of *course* the word 'diva' is of musical origin.) Leopold Auer took it up, and handed the baton to Jascha Heifetz, who was instrumental in gaining others' attention to the work. Kennedy's recording was made in the year that Heifetz died, 1987.

Sibelius wrote no other concerto. It remains much less well known, at least to the general public, than the sweeping landscape of *Finlandia*, the Beach Baby tune from the 5th symphony, or the *Karelia Suite*, the driving rhythm of which Keith Emerson turned so effectively into hard rock with The Nice, Keith 'Lee' Jackson at one point using a bow on his bass guitar. It's easy to think of that going down well in the Royal Albert Hall where

The Nice performed, but the band was banned from that venue after Emerson set fire to an American flag as accompaniment to his performance of Bernstein's 'America' from *West Side Story*. They were performing in an anti-apartheid concert, but chose to make a rather different type of protest in the wake of US Senator Robert Kennedy being shot. Bernstein never forgave them. But they had made their point, and made it well, also including an adapted line from one of their own compositions: 'Dawn America is pregnant with promises and anticipation, but is murdered by the hand of the inevitable.' The gesture is reminiscent of Hendrix, firstly his 'metaphorical' burning of the American flag at the Monterey Pop festival the year before, then his guitar-burning stunt, something that Kennedy would emulate at the London Palladium, attempting to burn a violin. Officials rushed on with a wet blanket (ok, it was actually asbestos; some gestures work better than others). Kennedy has made plenty of more powerful protests, as I'll mention later.

In choosing the Walton and Sibelius concertos, Kennedy was hardly opting for popular material, despite the fact that both works are of course well known amongst professional classical musicians. His next choice, however, was a very familiar pairing of two concert hall staples. He had played the Mendelssohn and Bruch concertos from an early age, and extensively on tour. Recording them together, at the suggestion of EMI, made perfect sense, and yet, following Kennedy's more adventurous choices so far, it seemed strangely predictable. As Kennedy himself puts it, 'every Tom, Dick, Harry and Yehudi'[59] had already done it. Joshua Bell recorded it as his debut album the very same year, aged 21. But if it looks a little like a CV requirement, it's one by which many violinists seek to show not only their technical expertise, but the fact that they have something interestingly different to offer. How realistic, though, is that aim, with a relatively lightweight work such as the Mendelssohn? It's not as if you can dig in deep to find new layers of understanding. That's not an issue in the concert hall, where there is always (hopefully) a new audience for well-loved classics, and habitual concert goers will happily go to hear old favourites performed by someone new. But how many people buy multiple recordings of the same music? Does it really makes sense to stack up more and more alternatives? How many of us sample different versions before making our choice? Record stores used to have booths where you could listen before buying. That way you could potentially make an informed decision; a short pre-purchase clip on iTunes isn't really going to help in the same way. But the uninitiated are in any case unlikely to be seeking comparisons at all. They'll be taking a shot in the dark, based perhaps on hearing a bit of something by chance. (I do that with pop music, hearing a song and buying a whole album on spec. And when, in 1990, Kennedy appeared on Michael Aspel's chat show, after *The Four Seasons* release, and chose to play Bruch rather than Vivaldi, the Bruch recording went straight to No. 2 in the classical charts.) There are no doubt those who attend to Radio 3's 'Building a Library' programme. It's a remarkable resource, but who's it really for? You need to be pretty well educated, musically, even to understand the conversation. Today, of course, there's a question that overrides all of this: who is even building a library at all?

I don't mean to be negative. Firstly, choice is a very good thing. I'm also glad that Kennedy recorded Mendelssohn and Bruch, as I didn't know either work at the time. I bought it as I imagine so many did, as a follower of Kennedy (just as Joshua Bell fans no doubt went a different way). We often then take that first purchase, that first recording, to heart, and find subsequent encounters lacking, despite their merits, because of that emotional or aesthetic loyalty. And if Kennedy's Mendelssohn/Bruch is not exceptional, in the way that some of his other recordings are, it's extremely good, worthy of its high recommendation by *Gramophone*. Interestingly, Kennedy's playing is described as 'masculine'. I'm not sure what to make of gendered terms in describing music. Anne-Sophie Mutter's Mendelssohn album has her pictured surrounded by pink flowers – to tell us what – that it's 'girly'?

Kennedy was frustrated that the conductor, Jeffrey Tate, fussed with orchestral details in the Mendelssohn to the extent that recording time for the Bruch was limited. But the Bruch, a greater work anyway, stands out on the album, and rightly comes first. It's followed by Schubert's Rondo for violin and strings, a piece that is actually longer than any of the concerto movements.

It acts as a substantial palate cleanser, and the Mendelssohn that follows feels richer as a result.

Neither Mendelssohn nor Bruch were revolutionary composers, and yet neither concerto is entirely conventional. Mendelssohn boldly introduces the soloist without the usual orchestral preamble. He also wrote his cadenza in full, breaking with the improvising tradition that Kennedy so admires. (Joshua Bell has actually gone against Mendelssohn in re-writing the cadenza himself.) He also linked the movements, to make the work play as a whole, avoiding the applause between movements that was perfectly acceptable at the time. Bruch followed suit. Unlike many today, Kennedy has no problem with such applause, but neither would he argue with Mendelssohn's concept of a single arc, the presentation of a structural whole.

I've possibly overstated the conservative aspect of this album. Kennedy has great respect for the classics that earn their popularity by virtue of memorable melody and unpretentious warmth, and he does full justice to those qualities. But he was inevitably heading for other challenges. And taking stock of the output so far, we as listeners might be wondering, where's the Baroque in this growing list of recordings? Why no Bach? Also the other Bs, as mentioned – Beethoven, Brahms – ? Kennedy had in fact recorded baroque concertos in October 1986, prior to the Walton: Vivaldi's *Four Seasons*. The fact that they languished in the dark for so long turned out to be fortuitous, as their eventual release, discussed in the next chapter, would benefit from entirely new thinking around the marketing of classical music. Skipping them for now, we find Kennedy turning to one of the lesser-known Bs: Alban Berg.

B is also for black.

The Black Page

What's going on? You might well ask, unless you're familiar with this gesture of dressing the page in a black pall. In 2014, the Sydney *Daily Telegraph* did so to mark the death of cricketer Phillip Hughes, repeating what Laurence Sterne had first done in 1759 to mark the death of his character Parson Yorick, in *Tristram Shandy*. And in 1990, Kennedy opted for a similar gesture, a black pall for his own figure, as he played the Berg Violin Concerto, a work that memorializes Manon Gropius (daughter of Alma Mahler), to whom Berg had been very close. The event was a concert for the 'BBC at 60'. It was sublime – and notorious, on account of the black. But the whole dark background to the concerto needs explaining.

Manon Gropius died having suffered infantile paralysis from polio, aged eighteen. Described by her mother as 'a creative energy, such as I have never seen',[60] Manon was a highly unconventional character, who wanted to be an actress. Her mother allowed her to go around naked. With waist-long hair, she was described by the conductor Bruno Walter as 'an unearthly apparition'.[61] Carl Zuckmayer, playwright, gave her snakes, for which she had a passion. After Manon's death, Berg wrote:

> I can no longer live without her. She was the closest to my heart ... I think only about the nature of my death. I want to travel to Venice – put myself in her poor bed and open the gas tap.[62]

Somehow turning such desperation to more creative resolve, he asked Alma's permission to write a requiem in the form of a violin concerto, a highly unusual combination, but one that shows the composer's intention to put a personal voice at the heart of the work.[63] The violin part is stripped of all showmanship, despite its technical difficulty (triple stops etc); an almost ever-present voice, it sings within and above the flux of unfolding tragedy.

The concerto was written at the Waldhaus, Berg's summer cottage beside the Wörthersee in Carinthia, between May and August 1935. While there, Berg suffered a serious insect bite and died of blood poisoning a few months later. As Alma Mahler commented, the requiem for her child effectively became his own.

It's a particularly complex concerto in its construction. It uses the twelve-tone system of composition developed by Schoenberg, a somewhat mathematical, cerebral method (though the same might be said of fugue). It has scope for producing extreme dissonance, but Berg's approach is to use the twelve-tone method in fusion with more traditional harmonic elements; the music is still imbued with Romantic warmth. The violin concerto incorporates two elements seemingly at odds with the tone-row concept, but blended to perfection: a Carinthian folk song, and a Bach chorale ('Es ist genug'). The chorale is one that Kennedy was familiar with from his Sunday singing sessions at the Menuhin School, and one of his favourites. Berg's chosen twelve-note tone-row concludes with four rising whole tones precisely matching the opening of the chorale, so the introduction of the latter is seamless, almost mystical in its unfolding, weightless yet profound. It is exactly the type of musical melding for Kennedy to admire. Berg includes textual descriptions in the score – 'groans', 'cries', 'Lähmungsakkord' (chord of paralysis) – indications of how the music relates to its 'story' (not dissimilar to Vivaldi's textual annotations in *The Four Seasons*, discussed in the next chapter). The unsung words of the chorale are also written in the score with the solo violin part, suggestive of the violin's role as 'narrator'. It's a programmatic tone poem as much as a concerto.

Berg, like his mentor, Schoenberg, is considered an expressionist, a term explained here by Donald J Grout:

> By virtue of its subjective starting point expressionism is an outgrowth of Romanticism; it differs from Romanticism in the kind of inner experience it aims to portray and the means chosen to portray it. The subject matter of expressionism is man as he exists in the modern world ... isolated ... prey to inner conflict ... and all the elemental irrational drives of the subconscious, and in irritated rebellion against established order and accepted forms.[64]

This description bears an uncanny resemblance to Kennedy himself, performing the Berg concerto. But instead of marvelling at such an embodiment of the music, a certain BBC controller – representing of course the 'established order' – chose to publically denounce it. If he had ever read *Tristram Shandy*, it clearly didn't come to mind that day.

In 2009, to celebrate the 250th anniversary of *Tristram Shandy*'s publication, the Laurence Sterne Trust invited 73 artists of all sorts to produce their own versions of the memorial gesture – page 73 in the famous work. I was privileged to be amongst them, together with other poets, visual artists, and composers, including Harrison Birtwhistle and Michael Nyman.[65] Perhaps, if John Drummond (for yes, the Controller was he) had encountered such a thought-provoking project, he might have reserved judgement on Kennedy. If he wasn't familiar with *Tristram Shandy*, he might at least have remembered how, for the first performance of Haydn's *Seven Last Words of Christ*, in an underground church in Cádiz, the walls were draped in black.

Drummond even suggested that the red patch of skin on Kennedy's neck, a common affliction among violinists, was some kind of Dracula allusion. Like 'a misplaced extra for the *Rocky Horror Show*',[66] wrote Stephen Johnson, and to be fair, Kennedy did offset the black cloak with 'ghostly' make-up, and perhaps that accentuated the love-bite look, but the idea of the visual effect trivializing the music – the same type of accusation levelled against Ken Russell's films – is too *easy*. Russel's *Mahler* of 1974 may seem 'over the top' – Gustav has visions of himself in a glass coffin; Cosima Wagner appears in pseudo Nazi dress – but its dramatic purpose is sincere. As Jonathan Dakss comments, it's a film where 'historical content matters less than metaphors, feelings, emotions, and interpretations';[67] the style of the film is scrupulously honest about those priorities. And 'sensational', lurid imagery is not always far-fetched. There can be genuine grounds for its relevance. Consider Manon's extreme theatricality – and Berg's, envisioning himself committing suicide *in Manon's bed*. Some have identified an even darker side to the composer, speaking of a 'demon'.[68] Chris Walton describes Berg's drawings as 'what one might expect to see scribbled by a thirteen-year-old boy on the back of a school toilet door, not by a grown man in his late forties on the back of a letter'. One of them

> depicts a naked woman with flowing hair down to her heels, heavily pregnant, with a distended navel, prominent nipples and hairy pudenda striding with open legs toward a man in soldier's uniform with a dagger at his belt, who is holding

toward her what is either the hilt of a knobbly-ended sword or a highly elongated, erect, black penis.[69]

And Ken Russell is 'over the top'? Kennedy 'inappropriate'? Berg's concerto may be dedicated 'Dem Andenken eines Engels' ('to the memory of an angel') but Berg was also a sexual obsessive, with some Nazi sympathies. If, as rumoured, Kennedy really wanted to have a blood capsule in his mouth, only persuaded against that at the last minute, I for one am tempted to forgive him.

As Kennedy puts it, the concerto 'is all about redemption after the destruction of the body':[70] redemption of a sort for Manon; but redemption too for Berg the miscreant.

Kennedy has recorded the Bach chorale, a performance of exquisite subtlety that I chose as one piece of music for my wife's funeral. It appears on his Greatest Hits album, but nowhere else, and the concerto itself he has never recorded. Why? Was the Drummond business all too tedious? Did Berg's twelve-tone credentials not quite fit with Kennedy's broad assertions of what music mattered to him? On the sleeve notes to his Bartók/Ellington album he writes: 'He [Bartók] was the only significant one of his generation who could continue along the lines of the great tradition set by Bach, Beethoven and Brahms, instead of resorting to mathematical formulae.'[71] Whatever the reason, it seems a great shame. It's a personal cause for regret that I have never heard my favourite violinist perform my favourite violin concerto. How I wish that could be corrected. Brushing aside Drummond's jibes (surely every bit as childish as anything Kennedy may have done), the performance was by all other accounts superb. George Martin was there and was captivated, 'delighted to see that the audience was, in the main, composed of people under the age of thirty'.[72] But given how the performance was overshadowed by controversy, wouldn't a recording be the perfect way to put matters straight? There again, suggesting what Nigel Kennedy should do – a sure-fire way of guaranteeing it won't happen. And since Berg never heard his own concerto performed, I shouldn't feel hard done by.

Kennedy did say, in an interview in 1996: 'I'd love to do an album of spiritual music, and put something like [Hendrix's] "Little Wing" alongside the Alban Berg concerto.'[73] The Berg concerto is 'only' 30 minutes long, so a recording would indeed need complementary material. Daniel Hope (another Menuhin School pupil) pairs it with the Britten concerto of roughly the same length, and from much the same era.

Am I perverse to ask why, with the Hope recording, no-one raised eyebrows about its visual presentation? Hope (who plays the work well) is pictured on the cover with an expression that's pretty close to Jack Nicholson's manic look in *The Shining*, eyes menacingly half concealed beneath their brows, plus incongruous grin. On the sleeve notes, Hope's red hair flares out behind his violin in what comes across as a pastiche of Kennedy's violin on fire on the front of *The Kennedy Experience*. On the back of the CD case, Hope tosses his violin in the air. I struggle to see how these images relate to a serious interpretation of the concerto. Kennedy's sombre black cloak and pale make-up seem positively reserved by comparison. And yet we have furore around Kennedy, silence around Hope; dual standards at work.

In 1976, Frank Zappa wrote a composition titled 'The Black Page', a reference to the visual density of his typical written notation. Berg's score, for all its complexity, doesn't really rival the visual density of what Zappa packs into a page (though it has a good attempt, at the 'Höhepunkt'); instead, it conjures an emotional density, a metaphorical black. When attending a concert hall performance, we witness one type of black translated into the other – with the myriad colours that also emerge.[74] The curious thing is how that process seems to happen in two different ways – at the very same time: off the page (orchestra), and by heart (soloist).

Getting to the heart of it

There's a degree of mystery around the classical concert. It tends to be a one-off occasion, an exceptional opportunity to see certain musicians come together; quite how, we often don't know. A soloist may be on tour, performing with different orchestras in different parts of the world, repeating the same work; the orchestra may be playing entirely different repertoire the next day. Or vice versa. A related mystery is there in plain view: the orchestra has printed music; the soloist plays from memory.

Mark Lawson once asked Kennedy about the time required to achieve this seemingly supernatural feat. His reply makes it seem, if anything, even more astonishing:

> I think it was a week on the Berg, and Walton was about two or three weeks, because it was the first viola gig I'd played. I mean, you learn all through your life from playing the music over but, in terms of getting it technically together and from memory, it probably takes a week to get a concerto sorted.[75]

Is this for real? As Tom Service says, 'It's not really like memorizing a novel, it's like memorizing the complete works of Marcel Proust or Jane Austen'.[76] He takes this comparison further, in a different way, explaining the process: how, in memorizing text, we don't focus on individual letters, or even words so much as phrases – the 'meaning and the flow'. This is also the musician's prime technique, 'thinking ahead, seeing ahead, feeling ahead, to where the music might take you ... it becomes a series of physical and emotional feelings, not a constellation of randomly assembled notes in precise order that they have to remember'.

In 2013 the Poet Laureate Andrew Motion set up an annual poetry recitation competition for students age 14-18. I was involved in evaluating the project, and later in the adjudication process. Memorizing poetry was something that had largely gone out of fashion, having associations with learning by *rote*. The reasons for the tradition's demise are well chronicled by Catherine Robson in her book *Heart Beats*. But Robson also investigates why the practice remains compelling, discussing the fundamental alliance between poetry and memory. Witnessing the initial Poetry by Heart competition, I was struck by something remarkable, a sense of the reciter *becoming the poet*, somehow enacting the poet's own tussle with content and form, melody and cadence. I worked with other poets in helping teachers to assist their students in the process, and they frequently referred to verbal clusterings, rather than individual words, as the units on which to focus; clusterings, and of course poetic lines (and their attendant breaks). But a grasp of the poetic *whole* was crucial. Learning a poem in its entirely was part of the solution to remembering its parts.

An intriguing question emerged: could an 'imperfect' recitation, for instance with misremembered or forgotten words,
outperform one with everything in its right place? To some
extent, not *caring* too much about absolute precision, coping with
mistakes, is an important part of the process – even a necessary
risk in the quest for an exceptional recital. Of course, 'not caring'
can be a pitfall. 'You're playing all the wrong notes' said André
Previn to Eric Morecambe, to which the comedian replied with
perfect blasé timing, 'I'm playing all the *right* notes, but not necessarily in the right order.'

Interestingly, Robson states that the art of memorizing a poem
won't necessarily help the memory in other tasks, and this corresponds with what the violinist Eva Thorarinsdottir says: she
confesses to being hopeless at remembering anything but music.
Pianist Richard Sisson agrees: 'my memorizing skills are only
available to music, and no other aspect of my life'.[77] Kennedy says
he forgets his wife's birthday, but that's perhaps another matter.

The concept of memorizing a *whole* goes some way to explain
the fabled story of the young Mozart hearing Allegri's 'Miserere'
in the Sistine Chapel, and later writing out the score. (The music
was considered so sacred that printed copies were not in circu-
lation.) The structural relationship of all the notes in each of the
five voices was not so much daunting as the ultimate mnemonic.
We lesser mortals can probably best grasp that by thinking about
melody: how we remember a tune – the sum of its parts – with
remarkable ease. Poetry is memorable in a similar way. Don Pat-
erson describes the poem as 'a little machine for remembering
itself'.[78]

The question remains: why should this feat of memory be
required (or not)? And what is the effect on the audience?

Imagine, for a moment, Mozart eagerly sharing his latest concerto with an orchestra. He's the soloist; he knows the entire piece
by heart, naturally, so needs no music. Being Mozart, he will also,
of course, improvise some passages. The orchestra, on the other
hand, has never seen or heard the music before, but the members
are all proficient musicians, and can sight-read the music. Here we
have the model for years to come: the soloist appearing to produce
the music from within, while the orchestra works from the score.

The 'model' is in a sense corrupted when it becomes 'tradition'. If the soloist is not composer but 'merely' interpreter, adhering to the tradition could be seen as an act of appropriation. In the days when Franz Liszt would perform, from memory, a mix of his own compositions and those by his contemporaries, such as Chopin, the audience might well have assumed all the works were his, a fact that Chopin, for one, was none too happy about. Today, that's much less likely to be a problem, but the soloist is still perhaps open to the charge of *pretence*. And this, I believe, is where the soloist is most exposed – in their ability to take ownership of the music, honestly, and without presumptuousness. To put it another way, the player who is fully inhabited by the music, without striking any false note of authority, is the one who communicates the music most powerfully. For me, Kennedy is more successful in this most difficult of tasks than any other violinist I have seen.

Not everyone, however, agrees that playing from memory is the best way to play from the heart. Violinist Patricia Kopatchinskaja asks:

> why pretend that you can know everything there is to know about a piece as a performer by going out there with no music in front of you? That knowledge only truly belongs to the composer, and each performance instead should be an exploration of possibilities, rather than a rehearsal of what's already known.[79]

It's an interesting point, but I don't buy it. Think of the sophisticated performances in the arena of jazz or rock, where for several hours a number of musicians are performing a communal act of music-making, some of them playing an instrument and singing at the same time. Not for a moment are any of them concentrating on remembering the music; it's 100% inside them and their fingers/vocal chords. Not even a fraction of their attention is distracted, either by the labours of memory or by attending to a score.

Why, then, do we accept an orchestra 'reading the notes'? When watching Kennedy play with a small band, we would find it very strange if some of the musicians were playing from memory and not others. Paul McCartney puts it bluntly: 'If someone is just reading off the notes ... I always feel as if they don't enjoy it as much. It's just a job.'[80] It's strange enough when Kennedy is joined by another soloist on stage, say for the Bach Double Violin Concerto, or the concerto for violin and oboe, and the guest soloist uses sheet music. The guest, of course, may be drawn from the orchestra; they may not be required, or have asked it of themselves, to be a master of musical memory. They could probably 'do it' but are happier with the prop, the safety net. Kennedy is clearly happy with the arrangement, and he would certainly not revel in any perceived hierarchy. But the scenario begs several questions.

What would we make of Kennedy (or Vengerov, etc) performing sitting down, or behind a music desk? Of course, at the Menuhin School and at Juilliard concerts Kennedy was indeed doing precisely that. I've personally seen him play from sheet music just the once – during his Chopin Super Group concert at the Festival Hall (see Chapter 8), for which preparations had been somewhat fraught.

Is the urge to step away from those music desks part of the soloist's particular drive? Is the risk of the high-wire act part of the attraction? A high-wire act is definitely less compelling with a safety net in plain view. You can of course come a cropper. Kennedy recalls playing Indian music in Westminster Hall: 'We reached a point in the raga where it doubled time and I just couldn't remember the next bit ... So we were playing on and on. People were walking out, and not walking back in!'[81] Sometimes such *longeurs* happen for other reasons. McCartney at Live Aid in 1985 had to just keep playing the opening chords of 'Let It Be' until the microphone/amplification system was restored. If anything, it added to the occasion. But you need extraordinary musical and personal confidence to get through such situations.

McCartney was sitting at a grand piano, and it's the nature of that instrument that sitting is required. The physical presence of the concert grand itself makes a soloistic statement. But players of electric keyboards often stand, especially when they need to be shifting from one instrument to another. There is some basic, practical logic for most musicians to stand when projecting their performance; the body has a greater physical freedom when standing, and my earlier comments about Kennedy's movements are relevant here. Some solo violinists though don't have the luxury of choice. Itzhak Perlman performs seated (though on a podium to raise him slightly above the orchestra), having contracted polio aged four. I suspect people stumble on YouTube clips without knowing the story, and find it a strange sight. Rachel Barton Pine, who suffered a horrific train accident aged twenty, has also, recently, had to accept being seated. She makes a point of saying 'my ability to fulfil my life's purpose as an artist remains unaffected'.[82] The astonishing thing is that for years she persisted in standing, even with a prosthetic limb. Such adherence to convention seems on one level absurd, however much we may admire the will to do it. And I find myself outraged by the convention that forces Perlman on and offstage for repeated curtain calls, on crutches.

There's a parallel question: what would we make of an orchestra standing up, with no sheet music in sight? In this case, we have an answer. The Aurora Orchestra has made a point of performing in exactly that way, notably at the Proms. Aurora player Eva Thorarinsdottir has spoken about the experience – and the challenges involved. As a member of the second violins, her task is arguably harder than memorizing a soloist's part, or even that of the first violins, which involves more 'melody'. She says of the second violin part, 'the writing can be very non-sensical', 'non-melodic ... you're learning very complicated sequences'. But she equally states that the rewards are immense. She finds it 'so liberating to be onstage and have everyone's undivided attention'.[83] In this scenario, every musician is equally exposed – both to risk and its rewards. It's certainly refreshing for the audience to see a whole orchestra without their heads down in the score.

There is no better example of Kennedy playing *by heart* than in the video accompanying his Brahms recording of 1991. Not only is he playing the music from memory, he appears to be playing the *violin* from memory too, with eyes closed for much of the performance, or if open, focused on some abstract distance. This is a feature of his playing generally, especially in quiet reflective passages, though it's usually balanced by plentiful eye contact with conductor and/or fellow musicians. What's slightly strange about the Brahms video is the fact that Kennedy inhabits a totally different space to the orchestra, who occasionally appear projected onto a screen behind him.

Brahms wrote his violin concerto in 1878 on the other side of the same lake where Berg, half a century later, wrote his. It is one of the most loved and respected works in the repertoire, though Tchaikovsky apparently hated it, and there were initially other dissenting voices, calling it a work not 'for' but 'against the violin'.[84]

Kennedy first studied the concerto aged fifteen, and takes pride in having gained 100% in his performing diploma playing 'probably the greatest violin concerto of them all'.[85] And yet, as seems to be a familiar story in the works that Kennedy has chosen to record, the emphasis is not on technical virtuosity, difficult as much of it is to play, and performances that go for virtuosic speed are misguided. Menuhin refers to a disappointing trend to 'sacrifice style for speed ... You want to move an audience. You do not always want to impress only by superficial brilliance, which finally becomes boring because the performance lacks human content.'[86]

The first thing one notices about Kennedy's recording is the very slow pace of the first movement. Some have found this bizarre, even annoying. But while the orchestral introduction does feel surprisingly ponderous, it makes perfect sense once the soloist enters, and the full gravitas of the performance becomes apparent. It demonstrates how energy is not reliant on high speed. Far from losing the structural shape, as some would suggest, the approach is an expansive embrace, allowing for moments of almost total calm – as well as the final headlong surge to a conclusion.

Kennedy provides his own cadenza 'in the allotted space at the end of the first movement';[87] those are Kennedy's words underlining his *traditional* approach. As already mentioned, the cadenza in a concerto was originally conceived as an improvisation, but as RO Morris wrote in 1935:

> the cadenza actually played at a modern performance is almost certain to be one specially written beforehand. Few performers in these days would trust themselves to improvise a cadenza for one of the great classical concertos, and such mistrust is doubtless well grounded.[88]

Morris's comment is almost universally true. Kennedy, in improvising a cadenza for this concerto, as he would also do for the

Beethoven, is following a 'more orthodox route', as he bullishly puts it, but also a brave one. Some critics have failed to acknowledge Kennedy's right to create his own cadenzas. They are used to hearing a particular cadenza, and anything different is therefore an assault on their expectations. In this respect, Morris is correct in a way that he didn't necessarily foresee: the violinist should be wary of improvising the cadenza not because they can't deliver it, but on account of the blinkers of certain critics.

Morris goes on to quote CHH Parry, who writes in *Groves Dictionary of Music* about cadenzas: 'With regard to their form there is absolutely no rule at all. They should contain manifold allusions to the chief themes of the movement, and to be successful should be either brilliant or very ingenious.'[89] Somewhere along the line, this concept seems to have been buried, as Kennedy's cadenzas, sometimes brilliant, sometimes ingenious, sometimes both, and always highly inventive, have been much maligned. On the Brahms recording, he works meticulously from the musical material we have heard. In later performances he has chosen to introduce other elements that he feels are relevant, though some have felt that his sense of relevance is over-stretched. For a 2012 concert (in which he was reunited with Andrew Litton from the Juilliard School of Boredom) he wrote:

> During this, you might detect my belief that Brahms loved gypsy music and that, therefore, if he had had the same access as we do to, say, Indian music or the blues, he would probably have incorporated these equally important types of community music into his work as well.[90]

I was present at that performance, and can vouch for the sense of relevance – and excitement. It was also interesting that Kennedy, for his second half of the event, got the orchestra into their shirtsleeves.

The video of 1991 presents us with a very different type of adventure, using 'relevant' visual imagery to accompany the music. Some of it is presented full-screen; other parts are used as visual backdrop to Kennedy. It's a bold, yet somehow underwhelming combination of sound and image, the latter running through the full gamut of cliché: sunrise, sunset, waterfalls, crashing waves, boiling clouds, lightning, erupting volcanoes.

But there are moments that work well: low flying geese in slow motion, matching the speed of the music; the camera gaining pace to swoop across countryside and coast for the more upbeat passages. Lingering shots of a lake bring the Wörthersee to mind.

If the imagery is naïve, it is nevertheless revealing of how Kennedy finds parallels between the power of music and the forces of nature. Patricia Kopatchinskaja, writing about her formative musical education, makes an even more explicit connection:

> My first teacher was the rain. I listened to the drops. They were the first short, round notes in my childhood imagination. Then came the sun. The notes became longer and more transparent, beginning in the clouds and disappearing into infinity. Wind taught me momentum, the night taught me silence and the suddenness of the morning.[91]

This is poetically put, perhaps more convincing than the Kennedy video, but it also helps in understanding the motivation of the video, even if the latter doesn't reach poetic heights of its own. Certainly superfluous are the interjected stills of Klaus Tennstedt conducting, moments of visual inertia that belie the conductor's grace. The best parts of the film are those focusing on Kennedy's own intense performance. It just doesn't seem right for him to be at such a remove from the orchestra.

The Brahms video was released on VHS tape, and a DVD of the first movement only was included on the CD *Legend*, packaged with the Bruch and Beethoven concertos in 2005. It remains a charming curiosity, rather than a truly compelling artwork. One can feel, though, what Kennedy was after, and might have achieved with later technological capabilities. McCartney's multimedia ambitions were only fully realized around the turn of the millennium, when the technology had caught up with his Beatles-day imaginings.

I find it hard, now, to listen to the work without Kennedy's video playing in my head. But while the imagery is limiting, the vision of Kennedy playing is not something I would want to be without.

Kennedy's Brahms recording with Tennstedt had come about (yet again) by chance. The conductor had fallen out with Kyung

Wha Chung, and Kennedy stepped in with a single morning to prepare. The following year he made a second recording with Tennstedt, this time of Beethoven's violin concerto (like so many others, he only wrote the one). An uncontested masterpiece, it had one of the most disastrous premieres of all, with the soloist, Franz Clement, not playing the work by heart but instead having to sight-read some of it, and interjecting a piece of his own.[92] It was Mendelssohn who helped to reboot its reputation almost 40 years later.

On the album, it's performed by Kennedy at the peak of his powers (one of many peaks, he will later joke). In reviewing it for *Gramophone*, Edward Greenfield commented: 'Repeatedly one is caught by the magic of a phrase as one has never heard it before.' But just as Mark Berry remarked on the 'wonderful "old school" approach' to the 2012 Brahms performance, 'sounding almost midway between Heifetz and Menuhin',[93] the grandeur of the Beethoven recording also seems to derive from a stylistic past; pre-Kennedy as we now think of him, if that's not a contradiction in terms. And that's (almost) true of the cadenzas too.

Beethoven's concerto is a prime focal point for cadenza controversy, and Kennedy actually treads a pretty diplomatic path through the minefield. In the first movement he plays the popular cadenza established by Fritz Kreisler, but improvises his own material in the passage between the further movements, and the cadenza in the third. This, for Kennedy, is following 'a more orthodox route' than playing Kreisler's inventions. If some have found Kennedy's cadenza curiously 'atonal', a historical view reveals its wanderings as remarkably restrained, certainly adhering to the traditional *concept* of the cadenza more faithfully than Alfred Schnittke's radical cadenzas of 1977. Schnittke, who was commissioned by Mark Lubotsky, incorporates material from later concertos (by Brahms, Bartók, Shostakovich and Berg). The cadenzas feature on a 2021 recording by Vadim Gluzman, who writes: 'By connecting all these great pieces to Beethoven, Schnittke is showing: Here, this is the root of everything. In one way or another, Beethoven is a predecessor to all of them.'[94] This seems a thoroughly valid point, but it demands a certain erudition of its audience, which, for Kennedy, goes against the grain. Kennedy, like Gluzman, had been exposed to Gidon Kremer's recording of the Schnittke cadenza while at Juilliard, but rejected it outright, considering it fit only 'for a few nerdy students'.[95] As his comments about his own Brahms cadenza make clear, it's not that he's averse to travelling through musical time; he simply has no interest in limiting his audience, preferring to appeal to the thousands of interested listeners who might even be called – e.g. by Eric Fenby – 'musically illiterate, a state which Frederick Delius preferred in a listener to that of technical knowledge'.[96]

It should be said that Kennedy does occasionally throw in musical references: Vivaldi, Beethoven and Led Zeppelin in his Proms performance of Monti's Csárdás in 2013; Duke Ellington in *The Four Seasons*. But they are arguably more generally known – and joyously interjected. The only people he risks alienating are those who probably, in his opinion, deserve it.

For all their deliberation, Schnittke's cadenzas are unconvincingly shaped, though I do find elements to admire, notably the final episode, in which the soloist is pitched against the other violinists who randomly (and therefore dissonantly) trill and slide upwards, a quarter-tone at a time. 'A "swarm of bees" is a good way to describe it', says Gluzman; 'Schnittke often talked about society against the individual.'[97] Both Schnittke and his commissioner Lubotsky were fighting against the Soviet authorities, and the way in which the solo violin escapes the 'swarm' seems emblematic of their struggle and triumph. This, at least, might have appealed to Kennedy: the whole business of taking musical risks in pursuit of one's vision. And there is, perhaps, the faintest trace of acknowledgement in his own cadenza: the 'curious atonal passage with quarter-tones', as described by Edward Greenfield in his review.

Ultimately, however, the Schnittke cadenza is surely a contradiction in terms. On the one hand it attempts to be fiercely individual in its approach, and project Beethoven's influence into the future; on the other it is prescriptive – a written cadenza that is only prepared to take the future so far. An indicative structure, in which the soloist might travel to the here-and-now, on their own terms, would surely be more persuasive. That, after all, is the full implication of that *fermata* mark in the score where time is suspended, and the compass of the composer's work is stretched: it says 'stop' or 'stay' to those behind their music desks, reading the score, and beckons the jazz soul of the soloist to the fore; it welcomes all-comers, present and future, their diverse personalities, and their manifold abilities to communicate to new listeners, not just the initiated, or musical historians.

Kennedy would record another performance of the Beethoven concerto fourteen years later, and cadenzas were once again in the spotlight. That recording, which is discussed in Chapter 8, offers a fascinating example of how a single work can be presented to such different effect.

For his recording with Tennstedt, Kennedy won the 1993 BRIT Award for Best Classical Recording. Presented with the award by Meatloaf, he made a point of requesting that the background 'muzak' should be turned off, before thanking Chelsea and all the other teams in the first division that helped Villa do so well. He then suggested the Award statue was up for sale (£2000) and that the money would go to the miners' appeal.

There's a video on YouTube that corresponds to the Kennedy/Tennstedt Beethoven album. In contrast to the Brahms video with its Tennstedt stills, here you can see how the conductor does his job, and it's an example to the world. No histrionics. Kennedy feels that Tennstedt really endorsed what he was doing, and found that incredibly important as a young musician. Peter Alward comments on there being 'a mischievous quality to both of them' but also the way 'they both dedicated themselves to the music ... when the red light goes on'.[98] The recording would nevertheless be the last time Kennedy would record with Tennstedt, and indeed with any conductor for some while. The classical circuit was starting to feel like playing by rote, rather than by heart.

Kennedy always likes to make a point, which is perhaps why some react against him, but the point is often correct. With the Beethoven recording, he was at pains to point out that it was a 'Real, Live' recording (complete with solo Bach encores).[99] It's a depressingly infrequent scenario, some recordings that make the claim being sewn together like Frankenstein's monster from various performances. There is also applause left in (much to the annoyance of some critics), and Kennedy is particularly pleased that there was applause after the first movement – another case of honouring a healthy tradition that is now mostly frowned upon: heartfelt spontaneity; the audience rising to the performer's example.

In *Tristram Shandy*, Sterne famously includes a blank page (p147 of Volume VI). Rather than describe the beauty of a particular character, he asks the reader to 'paint her to your own mind ... please but your own fancy in it'.[100] It strikes me that the fermata heralding a cadenza is a similar blank space, and invitation, hence this alternative version of Sterne's gesture.

The Memory of an Angel

We've only just settled
when we're appalled

by the curious apparition
that shambles onstage

in long black cloak
and ghostly make-up

that accentuates the rough
love-bite on his neck –

kiss or curse
of the wooden appendage

now clamped between
collarbone and chin –

as our applause
for who knows what dies

down and he starts tuning up,
or so it seems – the open

strings so commonplace,
so quiet – but it's the pulse

of haunting, musical life
from which a masterpiece

will emerge, and what we hear
comes not from a score

but flowing from the soul
via the muscular

chambers of the heart
like spontaneous

pleasure – and pain, unforeseen
by both the child in the story

and the childlike violin-man
who bears witness

to her tragic paralysis
and premature demise,

the composer's grief
a long moment of almost

deafening dissonance,
our empathy intense

as each solemn accomplice
seated behind the soloist

follows their part like fate
and with unerring belief.

A Carinthian folk tune
drifts in as if from afar

or that other country, the past,
like lost innocence.

Equally distant is the ethereal
chorale, the premonition

of every funeral
we will ever have to bear.

What is memory without
loss? And what would we make

of loss without memory?
How else would we create

such immaculate silence
as follows this performance,

every member of the audience
held in thrall?

The black cloak is both pall
and the dress of a dark angel.

As he bows out, he taps his fist
against his pounding chest.

Chapter 4: Harmony vs Invention

Some works are so familiar that it is almost impossible to hear them afresh.—Nick Kimberley

I have a memory – vivid but also unverifiable – of watching a particular wildlife documentary on television in the 1970s. Parched land, and from nowhere – a rainstorm. What I remember best is the music that interpreted and dramatized the images so powerfully. I didn't know then that the driving rhythms I was listening to were from the final movement of Vivaldi's 'Summer'. While the date of my memory is vague, it was undoubtedly before Nigel Kennedy released his *Four Seasons* recording in 1989. The work was already popular enough to find its way off the shelf into a television soundtrack, but its rise to popularity had been relatively recent. In the early twentieth century it was almost unknown.

Vivaldi, born in Venice in 1678, wrote *The Four Seasons* in the years around 1720; the exact date is as vague as my memory. It may have coincided with the three years he spent in Mantua, taking a break from the Ospedale della Pietà, the orphanage in Venice where he was *maestro di violino* and later *maestro de' concerti*.[1] The Mantua connection would seem to fit the rural focus of *The Four Seasons*, though as with so many creative works, there was most likely a fusion of influences. Vivaldi would have been in Venice when the lagoon froze over some ten years earlier; the account of such a scenario in the 'Winter' concerto seems every bit as first-hand as the trials of a rural Italian summer.

In thinking about Vivaldi, I have leapt into talking about associated images; such is the dominance of *The Four Seasons* in our twenty-first-century consciousness of his work, but those particular concertos are just four of approximately five hundred. Vivaldi also wrote almost a hundred operas, as well as sacred music; it was highly unusual in the eighteenth century to cover such a diverse range (but perhaps highly beneficial in the cross-fertilization that resulted). What was commonplace, however, was to write in bulk. A work might be well received, but there'd be another hot on its heels, as with pop music today. Therein lay the money. There was no 'classic' status as such for a new work to aspire to. It was all too possible for works to accumulate in the realm of the forgotten, rather than a canon. Vivaldi's music, though highly popular through much of his life, fell out of fashion in his later years. An ill-fated relocation to Vienna, and the death of the Emperor Charles VI, left Vivaldi without the patronage he sought, and he died in poverty.

That might well have been the end of the story, Vivaldi's work largely ignored through the following two centuries. But in the 1920s interest was revitalized, like a desert after summer rain. First came the discovery of long-lost manuscripts in a monastery; then Fritz Kreisler's concerto 'in the style of Vivaldi', and Vivaldi concerts staged in Rapallo and Siena – with the poet Ezra Pound a vociferous champion. Pound was also a composer – notably for the violin, working closely with violinist Olga Rudge. He not only made transcriptions of Vivaldi's works, but also new arrangements, taking his cue from JS Bach, who had been quick to seize on Vivaldi's *L'estro armonico* concertos and arrange them for organ or harpsichord. Pound wanted to make the music (indeed all cultural heritage) accessible, *usable*, not locked away in libraries. 'Bach had a perfect right to reset Vivaldi for his organ. He wanted a USABLE version of magnificent compositions', he wrote, in his *Guide to Kulchur* of 1938.[2] In making new transcriptions of Vivaldi, Pound was 'transforming the music—interpreting it, reimagining it for a new context, making it into a modern composition'.[3]

Pound's mission to promote Vivaldi and Italian music generally was partly political, aligned with his support for Italian nationalism. That's an uncomfortable association, but music, not Fascism, was the long-term winner, with the Vivaldi resurgence continuing throughout the century and beyond. *The Four Seasons* in particular became popular, with a few recordings in the 40s and 50s, and a recording by the Academy of St Martins in the Fields in 1969 selling over half a million copies. There are now over a thousand versions on record, and in Venice there's a performance almost every night.

Viva Vivaldi!

Five hundred concerti,
maybe more, or –
as a certain critic claims –

just the one,
re-written
five hundred times.

Poems within the score
consign a choice four
to ubiquitous immortality.

Rescuing Vivaldi from obscurity may be a thing of the past, but with familiarity comes a different, though related issue. Can a work be over-exposed? How does it remain fresh? There's a very real danger that its popularity may be its downfall – especially when it gets abused as musical filler, in hotel lifts or phone calls on hold. How has Vivaldi survived?

'Make it new', said Ezra Pound in his 1934 book of the same name, insisting that art should be innovative above all else. Vivaldi's *Four Seasons* not only epitomizes that concept as an original work; it also seems to bestow on its interpreters a similar function. Innovation is at its heart; innovation and repurposing. The opening theme of 'Spring' reappears in another of Vivaldi's works, the opera *Dorilla in Tempe*, just as operatic thinking informs the drama of the *Four Seasons* throughout. Of *course* it made sense for Bach to repurpose Vivaldi; repurposing is in the music's DNA.

Pound's mantra came with interesting complications, as Eric Bledsoe explains:

> The artist must break with the formal and contextual standards of their contemporaries in making works fundamentally individual. These 'new' modern works cannot be wholly autonomous, however, as they must consider the aesthetics of the past in the context of the present moment.[4]

This refers, primarily, to the original creation, but it applies equally well to subsequent interpretation, almost more so. The interpreting artist must also 'make it new', and an understanding of the original work's novelty – and inherent freedoms – is part of the solution. For instance, as Pound points out, Vivaldi 'often had the self-assurance to leave his lines blank and unembellished wherever he or a contemporary would have immediately understood which notes needed to be added to his meagre indications'.[5] Today, a performer needs to be bold in embracing this 'tradition' – not only to honour the true spirit of the work, but by inhabiting that spirit, to make the work new all over again. Eyebrows have been raised at Kennedy's embellishments, but those violinists (and there are many) who choose a less inventive path often sound downright dull by comparison. They're missing the creative imperative within the work.

It is also instructive to read how Vivaldi himself played the violin. The son of a leading violinist at St Mark's, he was the only one amongst six siblings to inherit his father's talent, and took it to new heights. He seems to have introduced a new type of soloist persona, capitalizing on his fiery red hair and virtuoso skills, and drawing his audience into a matching frenzy. Johann van Uffenbach witnessed him playing 'a cadenza that really frightened me'.[6] Not simply a gifted member of the ensemble, this is the soloist 'as rock guitarist', or so Rick Wakeman puts it.[7] And many have found further resemblances between rock and the baroque. Hugo Ticciati points to the recurring bass lines, the driving rhythms, and ritornelli.[8] Kennedy writes, of the 'Summer' Presto:

> The inspiration of this movement seems to be a precursor for subsequent similar styles of music including, for instance, the guitar playing found in heavy metal. For an audience member, it must have almost been shocking in Vivaldi's day to hear this type of music played, live, in front of you![9]

In 1971, the band Curved Air (again with Francis Monkman, pre-Sky) made the explicit connection with their single, 'Vivaldi', written by Darryl Way. The title is significant: the piece is not a version of any particular work, rather an exposition of Vivaldi's rock credentials. In plundering Vivaldi's seam of rock, it perhaps eschews the more subtle strata. At the time, it undoubtedly appealed more to prog rock fans than to conservative classical musicians. It now comes across as a strange curiosity – a good thing, in my terms, though maybe more of a period piece than any Vivaldi original. (Such has been the fate of 'prog', though who knows, it may enjoy a revival.) It does, of course, use electronic instruments as well as Way's violin, a fusion of technologies that has since been pursued by other Vivaldi enthusiasts. It is, in that respect, the polar opposite of what the 'historically informed' brigade have done, returning to what we might well call 'antiquated' instruments. The 'authentic' use of period technology is of course a thoroughly valid experiment, but it has to be remembered that you cannot acquire an eighteenth-century sensibility to go with it, in the light of which, the strategy of limiting one's resources has to be questioned. Robert Layton, writing in *Gramophone* put it particularly strongly: 'We need a revival of period strings as much as we need a revival of period dentistry.'[10] Kennedy's recording of *The Four Seasons* was a deliberate stance against the revivalists:

> It's like they were saying there was only one way to play a composer. But you can't diss Casals's or Gould's Bach just because it's not on the instruments of the period. I don't care if it says 'authentic' or 'jazz' on the label if the players have a line to the composer's soul.[11]

Vivaldi drew on all available musical technologies, but he also made use, as Tom Service says, of 'that ready-made laboratory, his orchestra and choir at the Ospedale della Pietà, to create this massive output of music that's still being discovered. Vivaldi is our present tense.'[12] Curved Air place Vivaldi in the laboratory of *now*, with new instruments and technology at their disposal. If the result is odd, that's maybe appropriate (and of Shandean credit), given the derivation of baroque: 'odd', or 'irregular', originally referring most frequently to pearls. It also puts Kennedy's radical Vivaldi into perspective. In choosing to record his *Four Seasons* in a church (St John-at-Hackney, London, in 1986), Kennedy was also, in his own way, taking the music back into the lab of the Ospedale. Kennedy even revisited the same lab/church to make it new once again before the album's release, three years later. The physicality of his performance – which we can see, thanks to the accompanying film – taps directly into what we know of Vivaldi the violinist.

Kennedy has continued to explore *The Four Seasons* through-out his career, making it new every time. That, for him, is an absolute pre-requisite of performance. He made a second recording with members of the Berlin Philharmonic in 2003, and re-fitted the whole lab for his *New Four Seasons* of 2014, bringing in piano, rather than harpsichord, and a range of electric instruments including Hammond organ, together with drums programmed by Damon Reece of Massive Attack fame. The first recording was Kennedy's commercial breakthrough, and it remains a delight, fully worthy of its iconic status. But although it blew away innumerable cobwebs within the industry, it comes across now as strangely conservative. The logic, however, is impeccable. The embellishments within the 'Spring' slow movement are perfectly attuned to the flowering meadow it depicts. And even the so-called idiosyncrasies are thoughtfully matched to the narrative: the sliding harmonies that take us from second to third movement of 'Autumn' effectively drag the semi-comatose peasants into the saddle for their morning hunt. And with Kennedy, like Vivaldi, an asthma sufferer, you can almost imagine an inhaler being brought into play. Ok that's a bit fanciful, but essentially, it all makes perfect sense. The controversy was perhaps more to do with the film (more of which later), and other aspects of its presentation. Critics warmed to the second version, perhaps because they steeled themselves for a bigger shock, and were surprised instead by the way Kennedy controlled every thrill with playing of the highest order. But it's the most recent version, for all its variation from the written score, through which I feel I know *The Four Seasons* – and Nigel Kennedy best. It has full confidence in being abrasive as well as extensively lyrical. Contrast is all. The work is expanded: it has grown in Kennedy's imagination, as indeed it has in ours, over the years. The whole idea of 'making it new' has been tackled from the ground up.

In all three recordings (and in every performance), Kennedy is the leader; there's no conductor. He comments: 'when I was an eighteen-year-old, starting off in the profession, how many times – I can't count them – that the orchestra come up to me and said "don't worry, we're not watching him, we're listening to you".'[13] It has the additional benefit, in the 1989 film, or in live performance, of not distracting us, the audience, by the conductor's abstract encouragements. Our attention is wholly focused on the instrumental playing, the seemingly spontaneous emergence of the melodies, the intimate dialogue between soloist and ensemble, the sense of freedom with which the soloist takes off on virtuosic flights of fancy – all of which brings us even closer to the visceral nature of the music. As Hugo Ticciati puts it, we are 'imbibing, living, experiencing and reacting to the moment'.[14] We're participants in the interpretative process. And it's the business of translation, and its attendant conflicts, on which I want to concentrate – from a highly personal perspective – in this chapter.

Il cimento dell'armonia e dell'inventione

'The contest between harmony and invention' might well be the strapline for Pound's notion of 'making it new'. Equally, it's a fitting description of Kennedy's take on interpreting the classics; but also the challenge that Vivaldi rose to in his pioneering rendition of verbal poetry in purely musical sound: the twin poetry of *The Four Seasons*.

Il cimento dell' armonia e dell' inventione is a set of twelve concertos, published in 1725, of which *The Four Seasons*, as they are commonly called, are the most famous. They are distinguished, musically, above the other eight works, but also on account of the words included within the score, which make clear the concertos' programmatic intent. These Italian phrases assemble into sonnets, 'generally thought to be written by Vivaldi himself – based on comments he made in the margins of his sheet music, but there is some question over the attribution'.[15] Each explanatory sonnet (*sonetto dimostrativo*) includes a set of letters to show where the phrases fit the corresponding marks in the score. Sometimes, the phrases themselves are written in (see illustration above).

A mere five years after Vivaldi's famous work, James Thomson would write a more lengthy poetic work called *The Seasons*. Interestingly, it begins with Winter, after which we are given Summer, Spring and Autumn, Each is approximately 70 pages. Fresh from his success with *The Creation*, Haydn set the Thomson poem (in adapted form) as an oratorio, first performed in 1801. There are aspects of the work that reflect Vivaldi's. There's a hunting song, carousing and dancing peasants, and a loud thunderstorm such as Beethoven would later feature in his 6th symphony, the 'Pastoral'. There is even an early example of what we now call 'sampling', when Haydn requires a peasant to whistle a tune from *The Creation* (his own work, so no potential lawsuit there). The libretto was by Baron Gottfried van Swieten, who had also provided the text for *The Creation*, and worked with Mozart too. Haydn wasn't altogether happy with the libretto, referring to it as 'Frenchified trash'.[16] Most of Thomson's real *poetry* was lost (and Swieten's further translation of the work into English made matters even worse). Particularly offensive to Haydn was the idea of imitating croaking frogs – something that the French composer

André Grétry had also used as musical tone-painting, explaining, perhaps, Haydn's seemingly xenophobic comment.

Intriguingly, the four elements were also being developed as musical matter at this time, something I discuss in Chapter 9 in relation to Kennedy's *The Four Elements*.

The astonishing thing about all of this is how, in the twentieth century, Julius Harrison, contributing to *The New Musical Companion*, could possibly have ignored this major development of what we now call 'programme music', music descriptive of particular scenes. Harrison refers to Purcell's Masque, *Venus and Adonis*, where 'we hear on violins a reiterated figure meant to illustrate the baying of the hounds when Adonis goes a-hunting'. But there is no mention of Vivaldi, nothing indeed, until the 'pictorialism' of Beethoven's Pastoral Symphony.[17] And opera, being a stage drama set to music, was in a different artform box. The eighteenth-century combination of poetry and music somehow went unrecognized or unacknowledged. András Schiff manages to echo this oversight when referring to Bach's 'Echo' movement that concludes the French Overture, in which melodic fragments 'are repeated very quietly, like an echo ... it's music that mimics nature, and that's very rare with Bach. Otherwise we find these natural elements only with Beethoven and Schubert and much later.'[18] That Vivaldi's musical mimicry should be way off Shiff's radar makes it less surprising that he responds with such little understanding to Nigel Kennedy, more of which in Chapter 5.

As a poet, discovering the 'Vivaldi' sonnets from Kennedy's sleeve notes, I became intrigued by their origin and relationship to the music. It struck me that the process of translating them afresh might provide a means of understanding Kennedy's own interpretative process as musician.

I was already convinced that my writing about Kennedy should follow his own example: that 'interpretation' should be deeply attuned to the source material; that knowledge and disciplined technique should underpin departures from artistic convention; but that creative expression and, most importantly, the power to communicate should hold sway. To this end, addressing the Four Seasons sonnets as a poet and (amateur) musician but with little knowledge of Italian, I recruited the expertise of my daughter, Anouska Zummo, who provided me with literal translations from the original Italian.

The inclusion of the poems makes clear the music's deliberate depiction of particular scenes. If attributed to Vivaldi, it would mark a significant, early instance of what is called inter-semiotic translation, the act of re-creation across different sign systems, in this case words and music. This notion is further enriched by the work's ekphrastic origins, being 'based on four paintings of the seasons by Marco Ricci'.[19]

We don't know which came first, words or music. Rita Williams states that 'Vivaldi attempted to convey in sound what was written on the page about birds, zephyr winds and storms that break with thunder and lightning', suggesting that the music was in reaction to the words, but her following statement is contradictory: 'So engrossed in the challenge was Vivaldi that he included supplementary "captions" throughout the music, directing the musician's attention to the barking dogs, chattering teeth and other striking effects.'[20] The confusion here is perhaps a mark of just how intertwined the words and music are.

One thing is certain: the literary merit of the sonnets is insubstantial compared to the stature of the music. Translations tend to reflect their archaic language. And not even those (unattributed) translations in the booklet accompanying Kennedy's *New Four Seasons* recording rise above the banal. Here is the first stanza of 'Spring' together with the original Italian:

> Giunt' è la Primavera e festosetti
> La Salutan gl' Augei con lieto canto,
> E i fonti allo Spirar de' Zeffiretti
> Con dolce mormorio Scorrono intanto
>
> Spring has arrived and festively
> the birds greet it with happy song,
> and the streams, blown by the West Wind,
> flow past with gentle murmur.

There is little, poetically, to champion here, certainly in the English version. The original is at least prettified (and dignified) by the easy Italian rhymes, and some might claim that the Italian language is more intrinsically musical. The line 'Con dolce mormorio Scorrono intanto' has a rhythmic sonority that achieves a delightful onomatopoeic effect even for those with no grasp of Italian. The flow of soft, open vowel sounds corresponds to Vivaldi's groups of semi-quavers alternating between two notes (see C in illustration).

Whatever their poetic merits, the place of the poems in the broader history of art is of considerable significance, yet translations that do them justice are few. Those by WD Snodgrass are notable exceptions, accomplished sonnets in their own right, and Snodgrass is at pains to match the original segmentation, so that 'the English phrases could be inserted into the score at the same place as their Italian counterparts'.[21] He suggests (though his justification is unclear) that Vivaldi 'meant these sonnets to be read aloud with the performance'. At the first of Menuhin's Gstaad festivals in Switzerland, in 1956, with Benjamin Britten and Peter Pears involved, Pears 'narrated Vivaldi's descriptions of the musical goings on'.[22] And in 1995, Arnie Roth's recording included Patrick Stewart (of *Star Trek* fame) reading the poems before each movement. More recently, Vladimir Jablokov has staged performances that involve not only the words but also visual accompaniments. Aged ten, Jablokov witnessed his father reciting the words, and decided to go further. It's a logical enough experiment, although the marketing banner, 'Four Seasons Explained', is unfortunate. The very word 'explained' is of course anathema to Kennedy, and the idea of seeing a barking dog at the very moment the viola is offering its musical bark, seems simplistic, even reductive. The same pitfall lurks when matching poetry and photography; a supposedly exact correlation detracts from the poetic resonance of both elements.

Juliette Pochin, on her 2006 album *Venezia*, sings lines from the Italian sonnets over the concertos, selectively replacing the solo violin. In early performances of his *New Four Seasons*, Kennedy used four vocalists drawn from popular rather than classical spheres; 'vocalists' rather than 'singers', and I say more about that in Chapter 9. Accomplished as the singing was, the overall effect was pretty strange, as if the Parisian Swingle Singers from the 1970s (now the 'Swingles') had crashed Kennedy's Vivaldi party. Three of the singers – Xantoné Blacq, Z-Star and Lucy Potterton – are still credited on the recorded disc, but in the two-year gap between tour and recording, the original idea was clearly scaled back and it's quite hard to detect the voices in the mix; you might catch the odd 'tweet, tweet' amongst the actual chirping violins/birds.

Unlike Snodgrass, I wasn't aiming for a translation that would 'fit' in that way, either in the score or a performance, and I resisted a linear or sequential approach; I wanted to write new poems that were adventurous, like Kennedy's musical rewrite, and my specific idea was this: I would not be matching my words to the score; I would match them to Kennedy's live *interpretation* of the score; even the physical attributes of performance were to be brought into play – Kennedy in his customary Aston Villa football shirt, bumping fists with his fellow musicians.

In *Uncensored!* Kennedy mentions his disappointment that the record company (Sony) refused to let him include new poems, rather than the customary bland English versions of the Italian originals that were in the end preferred.[23] He calls the originals 'rather mediocre', though touring programmes feature him talking them up somewhat as 'beautiful poetry'. Perhaps, if there is ever a re-release of the CD (or even a 'fourth recording', as Kennedy pitches it) then perhaps my poems, included at the end of the chapter, might be candidates for inclusion. Kennedy probably had in mind something more radical. He mentions Murakumi, Kureishi and Zephaniah as examples of a 'relevant living writer'; any of those would no doubt take a very different approach to mine. In one sense I've been quite conservative, maintaining the original structure, whatever the new colours and texture.

I hope these new poems are of interest for anyone who has heard Kennedy's 'Rewrite', as it was called when it first toured in 2012, but also for anyone interested in the concertos themselves, their relationship to poetry, and the complexities of any interpretative process, either as translator or musical performer. I offer here some further discussion of this interpretative process, quoting various translation theorists. As Kennedy might say, you might want to skip this bit, but who knows, it might just be useful in convincing a record company of why Kennedy was right to want new poetry published in the CD booklet.

Poetic Licence

Deep inside us all there is something that speaks to us and drives us, almost unconsciously, and that may emerge at times sounding as poetry or music.—Johannes Brahms

I was provided with very useful literal translations, following the Italian syntax, but it was the notion of *The Four Seasons* as an existing work of intersemiotic translation that took precedence in the further drafting. The overall, multi-dimensional quality of what we engage with, witnessing a Kennedy/Vivaldi performance, mattered as much as the Italian words on the page. This approach is endorsed by Michael Edwards, who remarks of the translator:

> he can and should be concerned for what we call, out of sad necessity, poetry's aesthetic element, for what the Anglo-Saxons called *songcræft*, a term which expresses the work and study of poetry more strikingly than *poetics* or *the art of poetry*, which underlines the relation between poetry and the voice, and which affirms jubilantly the poem's desire to be fully achieved in all dimensions.[24]

A further underlying principle – close to Kennedy's heart, and as previously mentioned – was already prevalent during the baroque: the practice of treating scores as the basis for improvisation.[25] Kennedy might well call it irresponsible *not* to improvise in any way when playing Vivaldi. Such practice is less common in poetry, though Liam Guilar describes his approach to Old English poems varying 'from literal translation, via adaptation, to appropriation, to something more like a musical improvisation on a theme'.[26] He also mentions Carol Braun Pasternack's claim 'that the Old English poems we know are made up of "movements" and that these movements were interchangeable between poems':

> the movement structure means a text is open 'to a certain amount of play, giving the reader the choice of leaving the ambiguities open, at play, or resolving them through interpretation' ... Pasternack's point is that, in use, any Old English text could have been reassembled to produce a very different 'poem'.[27]

'The poem' is thus made manifest by performance – and with considerable scope for variety. Paul Muldoon takes this notion further when he writes of translation that 'both original poem and poetic translation are manifestations of some ur-poem'.[28] It is fascinating to relate such comment to *The Four Seasons*, of which we simply do not know whether the poems or the music came first. Future scholarship may yet establish the chronology but we are currently presented with two parallel attempts at the very same task; each addresses the same fundamental source of inspiration with a matching – or at least intimately related – creative and communicative purpose. And as readers or listeners, we too have a sense of the elemental seasons that speak to us each year in a sequence that is both repetitive and endlessly varied, making the familiar new.

At this point, one might wonder that Kennedy has not taken even greater liberties in presenting the multiple movements of *The Four Seasons*. Why the conventional order? Astor Piazzolla's *The Four Seasons of Buenos Aires* (1970) were first performed (and recorded) in the seemingly random order of Winter, Summer, Autumn, Spring.[29] And in an era when climate change seems to have run amok with our seasonal expectations, one might reasonably be confronted with some radical re-ordering. In his Foreword to *Uncensored!*, however, Kennedy makes it clear that he doesn't believe in man-made global warming, so that perhaps explains it. He has though occasionally broken off mid-sequence, to perform something else: in his 2010 Vivaldi tour, 'Summer' was interrupted by Duke Ellington's 'It don't mean a thing if it ain't got that swing', which worked for me, and the whole audience seemed hugely amused. Kennedy pitched popular tunes into his take on *The Four Seasons* as early as 1989, when his original recording was promoted with CD singles, 'Summer' with Gershwin's 'Summertime' as a bonus track, performed by Kennedy 'and the London Wasp Factory', his band of the time. At the Proms in 2013, his performance with young Palestinian musicians featured improvised Arabic melodies from the guests, and as Richard Morrison wrote, 'Sometimes whole movements were turned into exhilarating jam sessions, with all the players doing their own thing over held chords'.[30] In *The New Four Seasons*, Kennedy makes extensive use of his trademark *transitoires*, improvised linking passages between Vivaldi's movements. They account for over 17 minutes of the work, and improvisation time overall is rather more. (Kennedy's version with the Berlin Philharmonic in 2003 came in at 33.36; here the main movements *sans* transitoires take 43.48. The more 'hidden' transitoires in Kennedy's original recording make it 40.13.) The original calendar sequence is intact, but Kennedy adds a guitar introduction that makes 'Spring' seem to emerge from an existing musical environment, rather than start from scratch. This, together with an additional 'End' track in a similar vein, is suggestive of an ongoing music, even a cycle. Electronic devices may of course make the cycle a reality.

Compilation albums present isolated seasons, though it is interesting that on Kennedy's own *Greatest Hits* CD 'Spring' and 'Summer' bookend the first disc – in the 'correct' order. Kennedy is remarkably faithful to structural imperatives, however much he stretches their compass. In *The New Four Seasons*, his introduction of jazz trumpet in 'Autumn' may seem radical, but it opens up the party atmosphere of the harvest celebrations precisely in accordance with the accompanying poem, without distorting Vivaldi's musical progression, further evidence that the sonnets are crucial to Kennedy's overall interpretation. Max Richter's *Recomposed* version of *The Four Seasons* (2012) makes far more radical departures. Richter himself has said 'I've probably thrown away … three quarters of the notes'.[31] The poetic structure to which Kennedy adheres, indeed any connection with the Four Seasons sonnets is not evident in Richter's version.

Kennedy's approach, from which I take my own cue, shares much with Walter Benjamin's concept of translation as a balancing act between capturing the original spirit and making it new. Kennedy is outspoken about so-called 'authentic', 'historically informed' performance, 'which, although reviving one set of historical skills, shows … disrespect for the past by ignoring the skills developed by musical communication over the last 150 years'.[32] In his view, such performances are fundamentally misconceived, a view that chimes with Benjamin when he states:

> no translation would be possible if in its ultimate essence it strove for likeness to the original. For in its afterlife – which could not be called that if it were not a transformation and

a renewal of something living – the original undergoes a change.[33]

A useful term for the 'transformation and renewal' involved in both literary translation and musical performance is 'transcreation', made popular by Brazilian poet Haroldo de Campos, who considered that 'every translation of a creative text will always be a "re-creation", a parallel and autonomous, although reciprocal, translation—"transcreation".'[34] For me, the 'transcreation' of the Four Seasons sonnets was in part a means to understanding something of Kennedy's own processes. Bringing my own creativity to the task of interpretation was fundamental. I was already involved in a sonnet-writing project with Paul Hetherington at the University of Canberra, exploring how the traditional form might be treated with a degree of freedom. That same spirit of experiment informed the Four Seasons writing more than any conscious engagement with translation theory, though it is interesting, in retrospect, to consider how the instinctive experiments fit with such theory, and where the poems sit on the spectrum between 'translations' and 'versions'.[35] In terms of Roman Jakobson's tripartite distinction – between 'intralingusitic (rewording), interlinguistic (translation proper) and intersemiotic (transmutation)'[36] – the intersemiotic or transmutation category clearly applies best.

Perhaps most relevant, though, is Eugene Nida's distinction between formal and dynamic equivalence: 'A translation of dynamic equivalence aims at complete naturalness of expression, and tries to relate the receptor to modes of behavior relevant within the context of his own culture.'[37] Considering various degrees of equivalence within translation, Nida's dynamic equivalence hints at a transference of the spirit or sense of the original, whilst accepting that this may retain faithfulness beyond literal transfer. 'Thus a translation can express an evident "deep" sense of a text even by violating both lexical and referential faithfulness.'[38]

In these new Four Seasons sonnets, the culture (to use Nida's term) is partly that of baroque concertos, partly that of the Munden and Hetherington 'untidy sonnets' project, and partly the maverick musical world of Nigel Kennedy. The new sonnets aim to include all key images from the originals, while adhering more insistently to the vitality of Vivaldi's music – and Kennedy's rendition. Where he takes the greatest liberties – as with a crushing electric violin in the summer storm – so do the new sonnets.

The original Four Seasons sonnets, once the individual lines are gathered from their positions in the score, are habitually presented in stanzas corresponding to the three movements of each concerto, rather than a more traditional sonnet form. My new poems follow suit, though varying the allocation of lines. The middle stanza/movement (typically a slow movement, adagio or largo) is indented, to accentuate the shift; sometimes, however, the syntax straddles the divide, reflecting the fluidity between movements mentioned earlier. There is a flexible rhyme scheme (including half-rhyme), typical of my rhyming poetry generally. Some rhymes operate at a distance across stanzas, not an unusual poetic strategy, but relating here to Kennedy's tendency to echo ideas between movements. A ten-syllable line (the typical English equivalent of the longer Italian line) is maintained throughout.

Each of my sonnets is titled like its equivalent concerto (e.g. 'Sonnet in E major'), signaling the inter-semiotic nature of the work. The titling (and reference to musical tempi, e.g. *allegro – largo – allegro*) is partly a conceit, a tribute to Vivaldi's own dual thinking, and it reflects Kennedy's titling of the movements on his *New Four Seasons* CD, e.g. 'The Peasant Celebrates the Rich Harvest' and 'Pleasure of Sweet Slumber'. It is also suggestive of how music and poetry, despite fundamental differences, can operate alike. As Burton Raffel states:

> Both music and poetry are, in a sense, languages within languages. Organized sound – perhaps the broadest definition of music – is scarcely ever a communication system in the way that words are: music speaks, to be sure, but if its message is to be translated into verbal terms only the most elementary expressions are recognizable. But in the manipulation of its proper component parts – pitch, rhythm, instrumental color, dynamics, and the like – music is closely analogous to speech.[39]

In 'Winter' there are some notable departures from the original text that actually align the words even more closely with the music. The '*brrrrr*', for instance, is nowhere in sight within the original text; it's taken from the shivering low trill on the solo violin at the related moment in the music; a direct if unusual form of onomatopoeia. Likewise, the 'pizzicato rain' mirrors the music as much as the Italian text, with the quality of verbal/musical sound the priority, yet with the introduced word (pizzicato) acting as a bond with the original language.

I have reflected Kennedy's more extreme departures – the unexpected improvisation at the start of the harvest celebrations, for instance – building in some justification for us both: 'Jazz trumpet? It's a party!' Those who frown at Kennedy's liberties will no doubt disapprove of mine too, but I would nevertheless maintain the integrity of the approach. Vivaldi's *Four Seasons* exists as a rich set of printed instructions for performative interpretation, and the unusual addition of poetic text adds complexity to the interpretative task. It is perhaps unsurprising that performances vary so widely: two different semiotic systems are in play, making it doubly unlikely that any two performers will react in the same way. In writing my sonnets, I have in effect attempted an imaginative account of how Nigel Kennedy might be reading the whole score – musical notation *and words* – when preparing a performance. Consider, for instance, the dog mentioned in the second movement of 'Spring'. Kennedy has always (and increasingly) tended to emphasize the barking, with the violas producing a particularly gruff, almost unmusical sound. In *The New Four Seasons* he takes this even further; in the third movement he leads the orchestra into vocalized barks before each reprise of the main theme, pretty wild barking, it has to be said, or as I convey it, 'revelry that breaks into yelps and whoops'. 'The dogs are out', I continue, alluding to the deliberately uncouth sonic intervention, the sense of mayhem. But it is not the case that 'anything goes'; on the contrary, it is a serious (though boisterous) re-imagining of Vivaldi's 'Spring' – just as my 'fly-infested lull, a fractious growl / itching for a livewire scare' and Kennedy's extended silences mixed with distorted electronica attempt to depict the oppressive reality of his Italian 'Summer'. And I have yet to encounter another recording that captures the gallop of the hunt in 'Autumn' so vividly. It inspired me to transfer that rhythmic urgency to the carousing that kicks the whole thing off: 'they drink at the gallop, drink till they drop'.

There is a deliberate conflation here of music and poetry, which accords with what Ray Jackendoff has argued:

poetry is the result of superimposing musical principles to
some degree on linguistic utterances. Thus to the extent that
poetic form conveys affect, it is precisely because it invokes
principles of musical perception that are not normally associated with language.[40]

That music and poetry relate in this way holds particular significance for the translator and yet, as Şebnem Susam-Sarajeva
comments, 'the topic of translation and music has remained on
the periphery of translation studies'. She goes on to say:

> Few of us with a background in translation studies can effec-
> tively deal with meanings derived not only from text, but also
> from melody, pitch, duration, loudness, timbre, dynamics,
> rhythm, tempo, expression, harmony, pause, stress or artic-
> ulation in music. If we consider that research in translation
> and music may also require a background in media studies,
> cultural studies and/or semiotics, we can begin to appreciate
> the difficulties encountered by anyone who ventures into this
> field. [41]

Throughout this chapter I have referred to 'my' poems, partly
for convenience, but the work of translating the original sonnets
(and indeed the writing of this chapter) was a collaborative
undertaking, with Anouska Zummo, informed by our different
but complementary backgrounds. In Susam-Sarajeva's words,
we experienced how 'The intersection of translation and music
... can enrich our understanding of what translation might entail,
how far its boundaries can be extended and how it relates to other
forms of expression.'[42]

Translating the sonnets was not part of my original plan in
writing about Kennedy, but the process has proved hugely informative, highlighting a general virtue of translation as a practice
for writers. As Raffel comments:

> Surely no one will deny that the immense facility with which
> musicians can cross-fertilize each other is a blessing to the
> art. It would seem to be largely poets, however – and only a
> minority even among poets – who are aware of how much
> translation can do to cross-fertilize them [as writers].[43]

Our collaboration has served a valuable purpose not only in translating the sonnets but also in approaching my larger subject – a

musician for whom collaboration is an essential, driving force. Unlike music, poetry is often viewed as a predominantly solitary art, and the viability of poetry in translation is ever questioned. Perhaps a model of collaborative, inter-semiotic, poetic translation may usefully unsettle both views.

Post-Kennedy Vivaldi

> We shall not cease from exploration
> And the end of all our exploring
> Will be to arrive where we started
> And know the place for the first time.
> —TS Eliot, 'Little Gidding'

Kennedy's Four Seasons #1 sold over three million copies, and gave Vivaldi another useful Pounding. A whole range of re-explorations have since been made, some worthy of Pound's imperative, some not. Hot on Kennedy's heels came Vanessa Mae, whose version of 'Summer', retitled as 'Storm', makes no acknowledgement of Vivaldi whatsoever. Effectively claiming it as her own composition seems a bit much, just as Chopin might have felt about Liszt. 'Storm' also excludes one of Vivaldi's most dramatic ideas, the sudden silence between each of the opening, thunderous riffs – the very means by which such intensity is created. Mae fills the silence with an ongoing beat. It's a shame, since other parts of the album are good.

Darryl Way, writer of Curved Air's 'Vivaldi', has recently revisited the composer's work with *Vivaldi's Four Seasons in Rock* (2018). The notes, he says, are all Vivaldi's 'except in some of the slow movements where it is generally accepted that the written notes can be embellished'. He has added 'rock instrumentation and rhythms, synth textures and in the slow movements, some chill out beats'.[44] Way performs the whole lot. I applaud his desire to do it, and the accomplishment, but don't find anything significantly new in the result. Uli Jon Roth has rather more edge. He first tackled Vivaldi's 'Spring' on electric guitar in 1993, and ten years later recorded the full *Four Seasons* with orchestra, adding a further 'Cadenza' movement of his own, which is possibly the best part of the whole album. His Sky guitar was developed specifically for the purpose. It's able to tackle violin repertoire by virtue of its increased number of frets (35 half-tone frets, with later models using either whole-tone frets at the top end, or no frets at all). The 7-string models have a range of over five and a half octaves. Roth wrote his own work, *Metamorphosis*, to complement his Vivaldi – complete with new poems. The accompanying artwork, like the poems, is more New Age than avant-garde, but it's clearly sincere. Patrick Rondat's 'Vivaldi tribute', a version of 'Summer', on his album *Amphibia* of 1997 is also notable, and full-blooded. Since then, it's become almost a badge of honour for rock guitarists to cover Vivaldi. I just wish their efforts were more *electrifying*. The sight of Sinfonity – some 14 earnest electric guitarists sitting in a semicircle giving a restrained performance that seems to bore even themselves – is rather depressing.

For all its promise, the same was true of Joshua Bell's 2021 Prom concert, interleaving Vivaldi's *Four Seasons* with Astor Piazzolla's *Four Seasons of Buenos Aires*. The Argentine work was originally for a small band, including violin but also electric guitar and, most importantly, bandoneón (concertina). Its four tango movements were originally separate pieces, but Leonid Desyatnikov arranged the four pieces for orchestra, adding references to Vivaldi. It must have seemed a clever idea to apply those references to the polar opposite season, given the seasonal differences between Italy and Argentina, but poetically it makes no sense. Imagine throwing Vivaldi's Winter sonnet into a southern hemisphere Summer. The whole mix was made worse by Bell's programming – and stylistic approach, a blending of the overall content, which, now that I'm writing about it, makes me want to form a new word: *blanding*. A similar interleaving version was recorded in 2014 by Yury Revich, but with the interesting addition of the Italian sonnets, and lyrics from other Piazzolla songs, to match.

At the 2023 Proms, Finnish violinist and conductor Pekka Kuusisto delivered a version of *The Four Seasons* (played with pristine precision) that owed everything to Kennedy – without any acknowledgement. I was frankly flabbergasted by the fact that the BBC commentators made no mention of the connection. There were heavily divergent transitoires, and yet the very clear precedent received no mention. Worse was the fact that the transitoires, while so heavily indebted to Kennedy on one level, held no relation to the associated poetry; they were a travesty. The commentary talked of *The Four Seasons* as being 'an open space to manoeuvre in'. Shame that Tom Service was not the commentator on the day, as he would no doubt have added some historical perspective.

Also misguided, in my opinion, is Paul Carr's *Four New Seasons* (2021).[45] Musically, it owes much to Vivaldi, and yet it's chosen not to bother with any baroque crackle. The interest lies in the addition of a choir, singing not Vivaldi's words but those of other poets, mainly nineteenth-century. Carr explains his Vivaldi transfer process:

> I have taken the harmonic structure of each movement and formed new material of my own, adding in direct quotes here and there from the more popular and instantly recognisable sections of the Vivaldi; for example ... the lyrical theme he uses in the 2nd movement of Winter to describe a day by the fireside, I've given to the oboe in accompanying Rossetti's popular poem 'In the Bleak Midwinter'.[46]

Other poems featured are by AE Housman, Walt Whitman, Emily Dickinson (x3), William Shakespeare ('Shall I compare thee to a Summer's Day?'), Sara Teasdale, Robert Louis Stevenson, Emily Brontë, Sarojini Naidu, and Lucy Maud Montgomery. It's a pleasant choral work, but nothing *new*, more like architecture approved by King Charles. The grasp of what Vivaldi was doing seems slim, and the transfer of music to new words is sometimes downright bizarre: 'the hunting motif Vivaldi uses in the 3rd movement of Autumn, I've used to evoke the fluttering of leaves as they fall to the ground.' That's blanding taken to a whole new level. It also drifts into pure comedy: 'Thou art more lovely and more temperate' is actually very funny when pitched against the fly-infested summer Vivaldi experienced in Italy.

More convincing (though obviously no use for a choir) is Oliver Davis's *Seasons* (2015), a new work *sans* Vivaldi musical references but using the Vivaldi sonnets, set for soprano voice. Nothing ground-breaking, it's nevertheless a minor delight, with Kerenza Peacock leading on violin, and the recording benefits hugely from soprano Grace Davidson's purity of tone.

Swedish composer Stefan Thorsson has made use of the words to Spring as the basis for his single *Sonetto Dimostrativo*, a work for string ensemble, though as with Vivaldi, the words are there only by association, not sung.

The idea of packaging Vivaldi with other works – seeing where the baroque can go – has been done with great imagination by Patricia Kopatchinskaja on her album *What Next Vivaldi?*, which 'invites Vivaldi into a time laboratory'. Five contemporary Italian composers are brought into the experiment. Giovanni Antonini, who collaborated with Kopatchinskaja on the recording, makes a distinction between the questionable 'historically informed' approach to performance and the properly 'philological' approach, which delves into original sources, practices (and yes, instruments themselves) with the purpose of finding new ways to make 'early' music speak most powerfully to contemporary audiences.

> One of the results of this Baroque 'New Wave' was a style of playing ... with sharper contrasts of colour, much greater emphasis on the rhythmic aspect and, in general, with a 'rhetorical', discursive and 'dramatic' approach to the scores of the seventeenth and eighteenth centuries. ... [it] also demonstrated similarities between Baroque music and artistic expressions of the twentieth century – such as jazz, where, as in early music, improvisation is of fundamental importance – and also helped us to review the concept of 'classical music' in relation to other genres.[47]

The use of 'period' instruments, then, can be for a creative purpose rather than a hollow pageant, 'ghostly speech before ghosts', as Friedrich Nietzsche referred to the historical rendition of music in his vociferous agreement with 'our Schiller', that 'the living are always in the right'.[48] We raid the past not for its irrelevant trimmings, but for that which truly inspires us. Thus Kopatchinskaja, who according to Antonini is 'anti-academic', 'aphilological', uses a baroque bow to perform Vivaldi's 'La Tempesta di Mare' – complete with her own cadenza 'inspired by the ghosts from *Pirates of the Caribbean*'.[49] Other cadenzas on the album are Vivaldi's, and these are equally astonishing in their modernity, conveying that sense of danger reported by Uffenbach. Elsewhere on the album, in a Vivaldi-inspired piece by Marco Stroppa, a violin is set apart from the main duet, interjecting 'like a referee in the boxing ring'. Yes, who would have thought that boxing would make yet another appearance in this book.

Kopatchinskaja's belief is that the juxtaposition of old and new encourages the listener's close attention; that innovative programming encourages innovative listening. That's something embraced very effectively by Hugo Ticciati and the O/Modernt chamber orchestra. The Swedish 'O/Modernt' translates as 'Un/Modern'. 'In practice, this means celebrating the act of looking back to find something innovative and original: using imaginative programming to explore vital connections between old and new', says Ticciati. He interleaves works by Metallica and Muse between various Vivaldi movements; the aim is to make connections:

> For example, the pedal points, bass lines and instrumental character of Metallica's Orion forge links with Vivaldi's Concerto for Two Cellos, performed on bassoon and double bass. In Vivaldi's La Folia (which appropriately means 'madness'), each soloist improvises a rock-inspired 'cadenza'. The music is performed as one continuous sequence, with smooth transitions achieved by juxtaposing related harmonic areas, or exploiting rhythmic motifs and improvisations. As the concert progresses, one becomes increasingly aware of the emotional affinities between Vivaldi's music, heard 300 years ago in Venice, and the global phenomenon that is modern rock.[50]

This points to the fact that Curved Air's 'Vivaldi' wasn't just a curious aberration, but an early marker of what could be done. And who knows what might yet come of Kennedy's collaboration with Uli Jon Roth, an event originally scheduled for 2022 on the Insel Grafenwerth, an island in the middle of the Rhine.

The rock connection even informs Max Richter's *Recomposed* version of *The Four Seasons*, by far the most popular of all the re-imaginings to date. For Richter, passages in the first movement of 'Summer' are 'heavy music for the orchestra. It's a relentless pulsed music, which is a quality that contemporary dance music has; and perhaps I was also thinking about John Bonham's drumming.'[51] Somewhere along the line the poetry went missing, which is why, I think, the final movement of 'Autumn' falls flat; lacking narrative, it's too abstract, one-dimensional. Overall though, it works because, as Nick Kimberley says, 'Richter has absorbed Vivaldi's *Four Seasons* into his own musical bloodstream'.[52] It's disconcerting, yet beguiling. It puts me in mind of what Richard

Ginell says about the 'other', generally forgotten version of the Sibelius Violin Concerto: 'it is like seeing a familiar friend through the warped prism of a dream.'[53] And I think once more (with new understanding) of Muldoon's captivating comment about the ur-poem to which both the so-called original and subsequent translation are related.

In 2022, Vivaldi's *Four Seasons* was once again cropping up in various new guises. Vladimir Jablokov played it 'straight' but with visual accompaniment. Max Richter re-recorded his 2014 *Recomposed* album, using period instruments. *The New Four Seasons: Vivaldi Recomposed* borrows Kennedy's 'New' tag from 2014 (the same vintage as Richter's version #1); it also features Chineke! Orchestra, the very musicians that Kennedy was lined up to work with, before the Jurassic FM fiasco.

You might be forgiven for thinking all this is a kick in Kennedy's teeth, but it's more a case of genuinely shared territory, however radically different the approaches. Richter, writing about his project in *The Guardian*, was quick to acknowledge Kennedy's role in sending *The Four Seasons* into 'stratospheric' popularity: 'No classical work before or since has reached such a huge audience', he writes, before adding that 'the recording's popularity made Vivaldi's piece ubiquitous'.[54] That consequence was what drove him to rather hate the work as a 'sonic irritant'. It's somewhat ironic that it's now Richter's piece that is everywhere, not just on the radio, but used within Netflix productions, notably *Bridgerton* and *The Crown*. So far, it has been streamed over 450 million times, which somewhat dwarfs Kennedy's record sales.

Richter's use of period instruments has challenged my own prejudice, as his purpose is very different to that of the historically informed brigade. The strategy is altogether more complex, using gut strings and short bows to perform what is in essence a 21st century piece of music. He also introduces a 1970s analogue Moog synthesizer, the equivalent early instrument within the electronic keyboard field. He clearly does so with a sense of humour, but he's also serious about the niceties of electronic sound.

> Nowadays, you can do all this inside a machine ... But to me, the screen and the computer can have a flattening effect on anything that goes on inside them. These old synthesisers, by

contrast, are a bit wild and unpredictable. They have personalities. They feel alive.[55]

If we allow for pulsed Vivaldi with Moog, or the power-driving
Sky guitar, then we should perhaps also accept soft-core alternatives. As Laurence Sterne would have it: 'let people tell their
stories their own way.' But that mantra also puts the onus on the
storyteller, or performer, to enthrall us; otherwise we walk away.
Why should we accept the banal, the violinist who goes through
the motions, playing all the notes without making them new, or
worse, adds meaningless, emoting gestures with the bow, like the
worst ham actor? As Patricia Kopatchinskaja states, 'regardless
of period and style, the essential thing is to pay the music back in
its own coin, to experience it truly and dangerously, with all your
senses'.[56] That, for me, is what Kennedy sets out to do, every time
he plays Vivaldi, and he has probably played it more often than
anyone on the planet.

Not long after Kennedy's original *Four Seasons* was released, a
filmed version was broadcast during the Christmas holiday – a
prime time TV slot if ever there was one. How I managed to miss
it I'll never know. But the film was also released on VHS tape, and
later included on DVD in a twentieth anniversary edition of the
recording. It was the film that startled people most, particularly
those who had never witnessed a classical concert before. Was
this what it was like, this level of *excitement*? Regular concert-goers were equally surprised, because no, it wasn't usually like this at
all. All of which was controversial. *Should* it be like this?

Even viewed today, it's not hard to see why opinion was
divided. Those of us who watch the BBC coverage of the Proms are
now accustomed to the cameras' scripted attention to individual
instruments, as if taking their cue from the conductor. It's very
smoothly done, its own sense of purpose unobtrusive. Kennedy's
film had a very different approach: the editing was as dynamic as
the music; it wanted to be expressive of the musical drama – shock
horror! In the pre-concert chat with Mariella Frostrup, he refers
to the music as an 'animal', and in performance he does indeed
prowl across the stage like a feral beast; Vivaldi uncaged. The
camera homes in on his outrageous boots and the glittering violin
jewellery pinned to his clothes.

In other respects, the visuals are pretty restrained. There are changing lighting effects to match the season, together with projected seasonal imagery, but that's very much in the background, unlike the Brahms presentation. The focus is always on the musicians, who are clearly having a ball. Yes, the orchestra donning dark glasses for 'Summer' (doh!) might be questionable, but it simply raises a smile while we become freshly absorbed in the new concerto. For the most part, the stage dressing is simply that, an appropriate backdrop.

When Uli Jon Roth dresses his orchestra in eighteenth-century costume, he is perhaps doing something similar, simply colouring the stage. It also, of course, makes an interesting point about the musical time travel we are witnessing; the costumes are the backdrop to Roth performing on his electric Sky guitar. This music originated in the eighteenth century. It's also here and now, alive and kicking.

The Four Seasons
after Vivaldi, Nigel Kennedy and the Orchestra of Life

Sonnet in E Major (La Primavera/Spring)
allegro – largo – allegro

Ushered in by a noodling guitarist,
the birds are in full swing; for the soloist,
with this music in his veins, it's a lark.
In his Villa shirt he chirps and chirrups
while tight, bright buds unfurl to improvise
a canopy of leaves. His supple wrist
whips up a storm then settles for reprise.

> A trance... he drifts off, sprawled under the trees
> among daisies and meadow buttercups,
> with a sampled, softly murmuring breeze
> and the viola's monotonous bark.

Bring on the cheerleaders, goat skins and pipes,
revelry that breaks into yelps and whoops...
The dogs are out – *Yeah!* A bump of the fist.

Sonnet in G Minor (L'Estate/Summer)
allegro non molto – adagio – presto

Scorched pines. A sweltering stasis. The heat
has pressed the air almost to silence. Note
follows note like stuttering beads of sweat
but there – in the bow's quick tilt – the cuckoo,
followed by a warbling dove and the trill
of the finch, those fingers thrillingly close.
Breezing triplets flutter against a beat
the north wind blasts to hell – and there'll be more.

      A fly-infested lull, a fractious growl
      itching for a livewire scare. So why not –
      with a stack of Marshalls to hand – let loose

the thunder and lightning for real? ... *One ... two*
mississippi three mississippi four ...
The cornfields are all trashed by golf-ball hail.

Sonnet in F Major (L'Autunno/Autumn)
allegro – adagio molto – allegro

Jazz trumpet? It's a party! – the harvest
gathered in. The drinking is in earnest
with flagons of claret and ale on tap;
they drink at the gallop, drink till they drop,
nod off ... only to get that second wind
and party on full pelt into the night.

       Passed out, they enter a parallel realm –
       a kaleidoscopic haze in which time
       is an elasticated, weightless dream
       in the autumnal cool – sleeping till dawn

when it's hip flask, hunting horn, horse and hound.
One poor terrified animal must run
for its life – their sport. It gives up the fight.
Sling it over a saddle and trot home.

Sonnet in F Minor (L'Inverno/Winter)
allegro non molto – largo – allegro

Frost... snow... layers of ice. The wind has bite.
We're shivering in its grip, a cold snap
like nothing we've known... *brrrrrr...* We run, and thump
our numbed, gloved hands together, stop and stamp
our snow-deep frozen boots on frozen earth.

      Later, feet up, in a chair by the hearth,
      I hear the pizzicato rain outside,
      a soporific, intimate reprieve

before we're back on the shifting ice, slide
and slip with skittering strings that believe
they can negotiate the cracks. The slap-
stick of our fall is what hurries our flight,
and if the wind howls through the house despite
battening it down, it's a shrill delight.

See Appendix for the original Italian.

Chapter 5: Furore

Nigel Kennedy became a sensation because the world of classical music had not before experienced a musician of that type.
   —Yehudi Menuhin

Those to whom the gods give their largesse are envied, even hated, by their peers and contemporaries.—George Steiner

Furore: *a wave of enthusiastic admiration; a craze; an outbreak of public anger or excitement.* How strange it is that a single thing can cause such opposite reactions. We certainly see it in politics: an election victory causing both jubilation and despair. Even a VAR penalty decision in a football match can produce the same effect. But how come art falls prey to similar wild divergence of opinion? Do we choose what type of art we support, as we choose a football team? Are there similar tribal forces at work? Different people side with particular athletes: Agassi or Sampras; Ovett or Coe; all super-talented, but we tend to know who we think deserves to win (I was always with Agassi and Ovett). Do we divide into those who embrace or resist the maverick? If so, is it possible for an exceptional talent to overthrow our natural allegiance? Might that just be a useful indication of genius?

Back in 1957, Eric Blom was urging audiences to 'hear everything with an open mind, to accept nothing too gushingly and dismiss nothing hastily',[1] but such advice seems to go unheeded. Critics, like fools, rush in where angels fear to tread, to borrow from the poet Alexander Pope, writing around Vivaldi's time. Strong opinions make more noise than nuanced discussion, and critics want to be heard. There are of course brilliant critics, often occupying quiet corners of the press, while the more tabloid breed grab all the attention. But across the whole spectrum there's been a tendency, in writing about Kennedy, to reach for the easy epithets, the ones people recognize straight away. They mainly fall into two categories, negative and positive, though there are some that sit on the fence, opinionated without quite giving away a sense of *for* or *against*. Thus we have:

outrageous
anti-establishment
bad boy of classical music
renegade violinist
classical rebel
hell-raiser
enfant terrible
scourge of the classical music world
immature violinist
blokeish joker
unshaven British iconoclast
the world's most hyped classical violinist
a Liberace for the '90s
prat

plummy-voiced child prodigy
fragile violin prodigy turned classical punk rocker
the Sid Vicious of the classical fiddle
eternal teenager
53-year-old wild-child
school joker, black sheep and Peter Pan all in one
Britain's most publicised, notorious and controversial musician
a persistent enigma
Britain's meanest fiddler
maverick
Our Nige

brilliant/stunning/consummate musician
marvellously inspiring
mesmerizingly musical jazz lover
brilliant/wonderful classical fiddler
one of the most important violinists Britain has ever produced
everyone's favourite 'geezer with strad'
genius

These are journalists' comments. Bloggers are more extreme in both directions. If someone is seen to have uncompromising opinions, that's also negative, unless of course those opinions are yours too.

With the success of *The Four Seasons* recording and film, Kennedy was touring extensively. His concert halls were packed, but there was also a knock-on effect for classical music generally. And wouldn't you just know it, there were dissenters. The barbarians were at the gate, and they shouldn't be let in. Audiences might not know how to behave; they might start to applaud between movements! That would be taking classical concerts back to how they once were, before classical *manners* were put in place by the self-appointed guardians of all things elitist. They suspected that Kennedy was 'cheapening his music by encouraging the wrong kind of people to buy it for the wrong reasons'.[2] The idea of 'wrong people' is astounding; 'wrong reasons' slightly more plausible. Paul Fernandez, working in a Piccadilly record store commented at the time: 'People come into the store asking for anything by Nigel Kennedy. If there was a record of him tuning up, they'd probably buy that.'[3]

Not only did his *Four Seasons* top the classical charts; it also reached No. 3 on the pop LP charts and remained in the chart for eighteen months. That was a level of success that sat uncomfortably with the classical music industry's expectations. 'Second-rate. One of the worst on the market'[4] wrote Nicholas Kenyon in *The Observer* about Kennedy's recording. That is surely the comment of someone riled by the seemingly cocky newcomer trumping the efforts of so many previous contenders. Both of Kenyon's phrases are unworthy; he was aiming to bring Kennedy down, and should have known better – not least because that wasn't going to happen. For Ivan March the recording was 'physically thrilling', 'highly communicative', 'atmospherically expressive',[5] and in a round-up of various versions, Stuart Nickless called it 'the most imaginative recording of the last few years', commending the 'passion, energy and strong ideas', the 'huge range of tonal colours and shades'; 'the articulation is crisp, and there is no doubt that the overall effect is genuinely exciting'.[6] How bizarre that Kenyon should find those rare qualities second-rate.

Even Julian Haylock, who was hugely impressed by other Kennedy recordings, comments: 'Oddly enough, that best-selling *Four Seasons* is his least satisfying album to date.'[7] That probably says more about Vivaldi as crowd-pleaser (compared with Elgar, Bartók, Walton, Sibelius) than Kennedy's delivery of the music. It's as if doing justice to Vivaldi were itself a second-rate activity.

It is of course the critic's instinct to compare recordings. They react to Kennedy's *Four Seasons* primarily in relation to their previous encounters with the work. The vast majority of those *buying* the album had never heard it before. It's unlikely that they would have been aware of any controversial elements, although anything that seemed unusual might just have been what drew them to try it out.

One thing to remember, in regard to negative armchair critics, is that they are listening to what Kennedy calls, at best, a 'replica' of a live performance. They cannot witness what Norman Lebrecht has called Kennedy's 'unique ability to reach the furthest seats in the gallery with the blazing urgency of his music'.[8] Even so, the replicas are rather fine ones, and it seems wilful to miss the blazing urgency within. Unsurprisingly, Kennedy made no appearance at the Proms while Kenyon was in charge.

The live performances that followed the album release were reconceived along the lines of the film: 'seasonal' lighting changes, and also 'subtle sound reinforcement to lift and equalise the dynamic levels very slightly'.[9] I have some reservations about that, having heard some truly awful examples of such 'lifting', the excruciating amplification of Nick Cave's solo grand piano being the worst, but Kennedy (Stanley) stresses that it was done 'without detracting from the natural sound emanating from the concert platform'. The more recent *New Four Seasons* performance I heard in the Sydney Opera House was undoubtedly 'lifted', and both the warmth and brightness felt right.

It seems extraordinary now, but one of the other significant innovations to the concert staging was the lowering of the house lights. I have to think hard to remember my trips to the Bournemouth Winter Gardens in the 70s, but it's true: stage and auditorium were equally lit; that was the tradition. As Blom comments, 'In the concert room, as in life, far too much is accepted simply because it is among the "things that are done".'[10] One possible reason was to help those following the printed score, but no one, surely, does that anymore. Dimming the house lights, as in a theatre, has become the new norm, though Chick Corea for one doesn't like it; he started to request the reverse, unhappy with being spotlit while the audience was in the dark.

> It's not a very conducive atmosphere to communicate. It's like if you were in the room with a couple of friends and you put them in the dark and you put a spotlight on yourself, and you were the only one talking. That's the sense I would get. So more and more, I started to ask that the lighting is even between the stage and the audience, so we're in the same light.[11]

It's an interesting view. Even a theatre production might conceivably have reason to request the same thing. The important thing is to create the most conducive environment – flexibly – according to performers' particular aims.

Those that flocked to Kennedy's live concerts were unlikely to quibble. There was, however, a larger, barely veiled reason for dissent in certain quarters. According to the cynics, Kennedy's popularity was all down to marketing.

Always Playing tells how John Stanley arrives in the Kennedy story, and tells it in a very positive light – hardly surprising, given that Stanley himself wrote the book. Stanley was indeed instrumental in changing the way EMI put Kennedy in the spotlight, but the story is more complex. It was Kennedy's own way of working that set the whole thing in motion. As he clarified in an interview with Mark Lawson, the process starts at home, and proceeds to the larger laboratory of the auditorium. 'I'd start something because I like it and have some identification with it. Work at it, play it at a few gigs, see how it goes, if it's worth recording.'[12] He put his *Four Seasons* to the test in Spain, and felt that a recorded 'replica' would have the unusual benefit, for a classical album, of being showcased in its smaller parts, just like pop singles.

It was Rupert Perry at EMI who brought Stanley to the task of delivering Kennedy's vision, and a marketing budget of £175,000 was agreed; not an unusual sum in the pop world, but unheard of for a classical promotion. It was a big risk, the sort you only take if you have absolute confidence in the work. Stanley had in fact made earlier overtures to Perry, with a 'private thesis'[13] alerting him to how the music industry would need to change.

An easy-fit epithet was there for Stanley too: 'ex-manager of the Bay City Rollers'. Repeated ad nauseam, it wasn't even true. He had simply helped promote them in America (which actually sounds like quite a tough challenge). He was simply good at that 'breakthrough' type of role, 'handling', as he called it; he was good at his job. But the 'Rollers' image (helped perhaps by the fact that Stanley drove a blue Rolls Royce) was sufficient to raise hackles. In a new film charting his *Four Seasons'* success (an episode of *Magic Moments of Music*), Kennedy recalls Stanley saying 'Everyone's going to try to destroy you afterwards', to which Kennedy replies, 'Look, I don't give a shit'.[14]

Stanley's warning was as logical as Kennedy's reaction was indifferent. Kenyon & Co went on the offensive, but Kennedy had the armour against their critical knives. It might have been more painful had fellow musicians been hostile, something that Stanley may well have been predicting too. There's nothing like exceptional success to invoke the resentment of one's peers. And as with scientists working in the same field, approaches to any art can be so differently conceived as to blind the recognition of achievement. Tchaikovsky hated Brahms's violin concerto, and the German's music generally, writing in his diary that it even angered him they shared a birthday, 7 May; lesser talents would have enjoyed such a coincidence, as indeed I smiled when realizing I shared my birthday with JS Bach. Maybe there were some private sour grape thoughts amongst violin soloists, but Maxim Vengerov puts it perfectly when he recalls his reaction to Kennedy's *Four Seasons*: 'I hate you man! This is so ridiculously cool!'[15] Any sense of professional jealousy is put in its place by sheer marvel.

I say violinists; other notable concert soloists have indeed been less generous, with marketing the bugbear. András Schiff hates marketing with a passion. 'I cannot imagine Furtwängler appearing on a talk show; he would just say we do our art, our music, on our own terms and you are welcome to join.'[16] But does this mean that art that benefits from marketing is tainted? Schiff's further comments suggest that he thinks so. 'It seems to me today that we don't want to accept the fact that classical music will always be for a minority.' That seems to me a very strange attitude, one that wants to preserve the limitations of what should surely be a communicative art with no boundaries.

There is of course another side to marketing: the commercial opportunities that are presented to someone in the public gaze. Young British tennis star, Emma Raducanu, has notched up sponsorship deals from Nike, Tiffany and Co, HSBC, Evian, Dior, British Airways and more. It's one of those curious things, where major companies give money to the rich, while at the same time asking the less well-off to pay to walk around in their branded t-shirts, etc. Kennedy has received offers 'from a world-famous Italian fashion house through to manufacturers of ultra-thin rubber gloves, from cars and drinking chocolate to office equipment'.[17] He does, even today, on their website at least, promote Venta, the manufacturer of air purifiers and humidifiers. There's obviously logic there, as Kennedy has used Venta machines to keep his violins in good condition. 'Wherever I perform in the world: my agents are required to provide Venta-Airwasher because my priceless violin needs the best possible environment. Only Venta gives me the peace of mind that the air humidification will be perfect.'[18] Hardly typical Kennedy speak and even a video on the site shows him unusually scripted, though his point about being 'just the custodian of the instrument' is nicely put.

It's surely more shocking to know that Elgar, asked to endorse Du Maurier cigarettes in 1931, accepted wholeheartedly and received 200 cigarettes every month.

With or without sponsorship, Kennedy was now making serious money – money that would enable him finally to buy his own violin, the Guarneri 'Lafont'. That seems quite a modest thing for one of the world's top violinists. But money is always a contentious issue, and it had been for Kennedy right from the start. He says, 'I was subject to the most racist financial and artistic prejudice which meant a Vengerov or a Rostropovich could come over and perform for major fees and a British artist couldn't come anywhere near those fees.' He believes that the careers of earlier British violinists, such as Albert Sammons, were similarly hampered. 'Sammons's playing was so poetic and so honest and technically refined, he deserved much more recognition.'

> If I hadn't put my head above the parapet, and had the help of John Stanley, I would still be languishing there in the shadows earning a pittance. I remember one prominent promoter spreading it about that I should be paid £250 a night.[19]

Other British violinists might still be suffering too. As Kennedy sees it, he did the likes of Tasmin Little, Clio Gould and Daniel Hope a big favour.

£250 only just rivalled what Kennedy had earned by busking in New York. While at Juilliard, he used to makes ends meet by playing outside Tiffany's, making $200 in a couple of hours. He reckoned that he could always go back to busking, if necessary, to make a living, and you sense that he might even have preferred that to being part of a system he viewed as unjust.

A rather different perspective on this made news in 2007 when, as an experiment organized by a journalist, Gene Weingarten, Joshua Bell busked in the Washington DC subway, playing pieces similar to those that he was playing in the concert hall by night. Out of 1097 people who passed by, only 27 gave any money, amounting to a total of $52.17. Apparently, only 7 people stopped to listen for any time. (There are rather a lot of 7s in the story, but it seems to be true.) Bell went back to the subway 7(!) years later, announcing the plan, and his audience was huge.

Try as I may, I still can't quite see the point of the experiment, especially the reprise. It tells us – what? That people will flock to a free performance by a famous musician, but only if they know it's happening? [Obviously] That there's little overlap between concert-goers and commuters? [Concert-goers constitute a small fraction of any general social group] That commuters tend to be in a hurry? That Bell's is not a well-known face? That his choice of busking location was not the best?

One thing it did reveal is that Bell was making $1000 a minute from playing at Boston's Symphony Hall three days earlier, with seats at $100. Somewhat disingenuously, Bell commented afterwards that $52 was 'not so bad, considering. That's 40 bucks an hour. I could make an okay living doing this, and I wouldn't have to pay an agent.'[20] That was I assume a joke, but it's also nonsense: he probably paid $40 each way for the taxi he booked in order to take care of his $3.5m Stradivarius. It's easy to joke when you haven't actually experienced either the need to be busking or a regime of insulting fees.

Bell's performance fee in 2007 was around £75,000. Almost a decade earlier, Norman Lebrecht had written a column in *The Telegraph,* bemoaning soloists' fees: Maxim Vengerov, £14,000; Itzhak Perlman £27,000; Anne-Sophie Mutter £35,000. The 'Three Tenors' (Pavarotti, Domingo and Carreras) were earning $1 million *each*, with a vast additional income from television rights and distribution deals. Kennedy came in at a mere £12,000, but was nevertheless the main target for outrage about riders, the further conditions attached to a performance contract. These included: three first-class return airfares; a two-bedroom suite in a five-star hotel, the bedrooms to be separated by a lounge; the suite to have humidifiers and satellite or cable television in every room; a piano for stays longer than three nights; the suite to be furnished with thick curtains; a chauffeur-driven Mercedes with sun-roof or, at worst, a convertible Rolls-Royce; a bodyguard or minder to be provided at all times; 35 complimentary top-price tickets for the event. Specifications for the dressing room included 'two bottles of Veuve Clicquot in an ice bucket, along with tea-making facilities (Earl Grey and PG Tips) and a tray of vegetarian and meat sandwiches, with pitta bread and dips'; and for the stage, a large 'rubber-soled' square of carpet. Stipulations for rehearsal were that 'Kennedy must be called first. If delayed for more than 10 minutes, "he reserves the right to cancel the engagement". Any change of conductor and he can also quit.' The headline for all this picked out the fact that 'All UK venues must be prepared to accept Kennedy's dog'.

> So this is what it has come to. At a time when classical music is being squeezed out of schools, when the Festival Hall stands empty for the whole of August, when record sales have dried up and orchestral musicians are living on the poverty line – the leading lights of a fading art are concerned that there is champagne in their dressing-room, a king's ransom in their wallet and a pair of free tickets to hear the three tenors demolish our last delusions.[21]

At Glastonbury in 2005, Kennedy was in trouble with the organizer, Michael Eavis, who thought it unreasonable that special air-conditioned accommodation should be provided for Deadly,

Kennedy's dog. Eavis even trotted out the story on *Desert Island Discs*. The conditions were in fact for the violin, but there's a sense that Kennedy plays up to the confusion.

It's easy to be disparaging about demands of this sort. Some of the stipulations do look a bit absurd, but the 'needs' of the violin (as opposed to the dog) are genuine. Take out the other pretty reasonable requests, and you are only left with a handful of indulgences, and if that's the 'norm' then why not? To put them in perspective, Van Halen has required a bowl of M&Ms with all the chocolate ones removed, Eminem (no relation) a koi pond, Cher a whole room for her wigs. Others need a full police escort, or a framed photograph of Princess Diana. Joe Jonas asks for twelve puppies. As these examples suggest, there's almost a tradition of mixing essentials with absurdities. It's way of having a bit of fun at the money-men's expense (though ultimately, of course, at our expense too).

The way artists are charged – almost as with a crime – of making money (and having associated fun into the bargain) seems strangely vindictive, considering how sports stars' earnings go comparatively unquestioned. Lionel Messi earns $345,000 per day. There is almost an inbuilt assumption within some quarters of society that art is made for free. The apogee of this attitude was surely the advertisement placed by a London branch of Sainsbury's, in 2016, for 'a creative and ambitious artist to voluntarily refurbish our canteen'. The backlash, thankfully, was rather splendid, including a suggestion from artist Conor Collins that Sainsbury's might like to feed all his artist friends in Manchester on a similarly free basis.[22]

The notion that serious art, money and fun should all be mutually incompatible was put nicely in perspective by the 'jazz poet' Langston Hughes, writing about Armstrong et al: 'They were communicating for money. For fun, too—because they had fun. But the money helped the fun along.'[23] Yet the money issue still rumbles on. Gary Tomlinson writes about the 'snobbish distortion of history by jazz purists attempting to insulate their cherished classics from the messy marketplace in which culture has always been negotiated'.[24]

Kennedy has spoken out against the culture – both classical and pop – that involves stars in limos, protected from the public at all costs. In his Blue Note DVD commentary he contrasts this with the jazz world, where people are, in his view, more ready (indeed keen) to have real contact with their audience. He's surely right. And his own superstardom is balanced by a thoroughly modest ambition, simply to get together with yet another interesting group of musicians and make a connection with an audience. The DVD commentary shows him busking by the Seine; it's the least self-important presentation you could imagine.

And yet, the money-making image took hold. In their book, *Great Lost Albums* (2014), Mark Billingham et al include *We Hurt Too,* a work by Bruce Springsteen and the Wall-Street Band, for Banker Aid.

> The financial crisis of 2008 affected many people, none more so than Bruce Springsteen, who subsequently spent three months visiting some of the hardest hit areas – Beverley Hills, Palm Beach, Malibu – before settling down at his ranch (otherwise known as Colorado) to record what would become the holy grail for Springsteen collectors – *We Hurt Too.* ... Springsteen daringly decides to eschew his trademark acoustic guitar for a full orchestra and classical soloists. (A rough mix circulates of 'Born to Run a Multinational' with Nigel Kennedy's violin clearly audible as Springsteen sings: 'Just strap your hands cross my financial instruments/Together we can break this bank.')[25]

It's such a wonderful spoof that I completely forgive them for including Kennedy. In reality, not only does Kennedy support humanitarian causes with donations from his own concerts, he has also pursued thoroughly uncommercial projects and been prepared to turn his back on the treadmill of lucrative concert-hall engagements.

The 'taint of personality'

Norman Lebrecht's depiction of a classical world in crisis puts the 'leading lights' at the heart of the problem; those that are not just musicians but personalities, celebrities. Back in 1957, Eric Blom was already warning: 'Much of the emptiest and artistically most meaningless applause comes from the ... habit of personality-worship. Indeed this amounts to a positive vice, which the lover of music cannot be strongly enough urged to shun.'[26] Blom also points to an insidious collusion between the celebrity and the press:

> distrust virtuosi about whom the more popular newspapers go out of their way to print what they call 'stories', in other words interviews by which they tell the world through the medium of a reporter exactly what they want it to know about themselves.[27]

In Kennedy's case, the press has been a two-edged sword. Newspapers have put a spotlight on his eccentric behaviour, and given him a platform for his strong opinions; they have then given him more coverage if he plays up to the bad boy image. They did the same with Paul Gascoigne. Blom's term 'notoriety' seems appropriate here, in speaking of 'spontaneous eccentricity', 'which soon enough loses its spontaneity and grows into a pose'. We might say the spontaneity is childlike, while the pose is childish, but the press must take part of the blame in that mutation.

Kennedy's chameleon quality, which I have praised, can seem to lapse into something more questionable. Julian Haylock comments that 'his behaviour became increasingly eccentric as the desire to shock and create a fresh impact each time became all-consuming and in the end self-defeating'.[28] The culmination of this phase was perhaps the wrecking of a hotel room in Berlin, although it's something that Kennedy still seems proud of, part of his rock star credentials.

All this, however, still skirts the main issue. How does such behaviour affect our listening experience? John Stanley comments, 'The image thing causes as many problems as it solves, but without it he wouldn't be Nigel Kennedy.'[29] True, but to what extent should that impinge on the music?

In 'The Lark Ascending', the poem by George Meredith quoted by Vaughan Williams in his piece of the same name, which Kennedy has often played, there are two lines in particular that fascinate in connection to this issue:

> The song seraphically free
> Of taint of personality[30]

It's an astonishing phrase, and yet the word 'seraphically' seems (to echo John Stanley) to cause as many problems as it solves. It's simply bursting with personality – but not *tainted*.

The poet Geoffrey Hill was once asked by John Haffenden, 'do you disavow that poetry has anything to do with the personality of the writer?' He answered, 'No, I don't. I deny that it has anything to do with the display of the personality of the writer.'[31] Hill's distinction is a good one, more useful, surely, than TS Eliot's belief in the *subjugation* of a poet's personality, 'a continual surrender of himself as he is at the moment to something which is more valuable. The progress of an artist is a continual self-sacrifice, a continual extinction of personality.'[32] That notion of 'extinction' feels utterly wrong to me, as a tactic or even a consequence, whether in composition or interpretation. As Blom writes, 'An artist of strong personal convictions can read much more into a work without danger of warping it than one who is content to mirror the music as he sees it without holding very strong views of it.'[33] His comment suggests that, far from 'tainting' the song, a strong personality can best set it free.

This conundrum is reflected in what Kennedy says about his *Four Seasons* recording: 'It's a bit ironic that quite a personality cult grew out of my album even though the other guys' albums were more about their personalities and my album was more about Vivaldi's.'[34] His attitude here is pretty humble, even though it acknowledges the 'cult'. It's a fascinating comment, with humility that still verges on a brag. But in Blom's terms, the brag is probably justified: 'Thus does the great interpretative artist, in superimposing another individuality on that of the composer, often illuminate rather than obscure the latter's work.' He makes a distinction between 'good' and 'great':

> the first test should be whether the artist delivers something that impresses one as being the truth—one of the many possible truths—about a composer and his work. If he does, the performance must be called a good one ... Greatness comes in, I think it may be said, where the performer adds an imaginative quality that is quite his own and could not be reproduced just like that by anyone else, but does so—please remember—without in the least warping the aforesaid truth, but on the contrary enlarging and clarifying it.[35]

Matei Calinescu endorses this with his statements about the interpretative art of translation:

> Interpretation is always part of a dialogue: the interpreter listens, tries to understand, then speaks. When his response is adequate, the interpreted work is enriched, and so is the interpreter. Should I add that by 'adequacy' in this context I mean a faithfulness which can only result from imagination?[36]

'Dialogue' suggests a meeting of equals, but András Schiff, for one, disagrees with this equation. 'Performers are second class citizens to composers', he says, admitting that 'They're important citizens because the music will not be listened to without us', but insisting on their limited scope: 'To me a musical masterpiece has a number of possibilities of approach, and there is a certain frame in which performers have liberty to move around. It's like the law in life. If there is anarchy, then chaos breaks out.'[37] Schiff here is running scared. He wants to limit the imagination – the very thing that Calinescu views as essential to faithfulness. And by Blom's definition, he is in danger of ruling out the truly *great* performance.

'Anarchy' is a strong, divisive concept. Even The Sex Pistols rhymed 'anarchist' with 'anti-Christ'. And the classical conservatives no doubt saw Kennedy's gift to their world as a Trojan horse full of infidels. But Schiff is not entirely wrong in bringing it to mind. Gerald Bruns makes the link between anarchy and poetry, 'of the sort Antonin Artaud imagined when he said that whenever "the poetic spirit is exercised, it always moves toward a kind of seething anarchy, a total breakdown of reality by poetry"'.[38] Is it perhaps the case that full anarchic rein should be given to the imagination in order for it to fulfil its faithful role? The alternative, according to Bruns, is grim. He quotes Bernard Waldenfels – 'If we should one day succeed in taming all that resists, in ruling out the unruly and in filling in all the blanks, the game would be up' – before adding, 'This is also the moral of Tristram Shandy'.[39]

These philosophers' comments derive from their discussion of hermeneutics. Is that of relevance here? I believe so, and may even have Jimi Hendrix to back me up.

Hermeneuts, in the original sense, were interpreters of scriptures, helping people to know how to *act* in accordance with sacred, authoritative texts. But they are also, as Kate Maguire points out, 'derivatives of Thoth'[40] and his later incarnation Hermes Trismegistus: messengers, storytellers – and tricksters. (The christening of Tristram Shandy, an increasingly prominent figure here, was a comic translation error, his father's choice being Trismegistus.) Maguire makes explicit that active, personal involvement is inherent to effective interpretation:

> The hermeneut is also the anthropologist evolving from the 'observer', trying to bracket off their own experience, to the 'participant observer' recognising the reflexivity required to fully comprehend human impact on each other and the world, to the 'advocate' who can no longer separate themselves from what they have encountered once they have uncovered the internal connection which Bruns believes is a prerequisite for understanding.[41]

András Schiff might well relate to the idea of the performing musician as messenger, but wouldn't seem to admit the full importance of the messenger's personality, subjectivity, or indeed the playful innocence of the trickster. The latter is surely personified by Mozart – the ultimate trickster, conjuring playful yet utterly profound music from thin air, messenger of his own unbounded imagination to the world, the very image of what Hendrix describes in his famous comment: 'A musician, if he's a messenger, is like a child who hasn't been handled too many times by man, hasn't had too many fingerprints across his brain. That's why music is so much heavier than anything you've ever felt.'[42]

Here, again, is where Schiff's hierarchy is misfounded. In his comments quoted earlier, he completely ignores the concept of the performer who is also a composer: not only Mozart, but also Vivaldi, Chopin, Liszt – and of course Kennedy, and many more before the typical modern classical soloist became cut off from this duality. The idea that Mozart should preferably have tamed his imagination in performing his own works is clearly a nonsense. More plausible, it must be said, is that composers performing the works of others may potentially drag a work from its original realm into their own. As Octavio Paz says of translation, 'In theory, only poets should translate poetry; in practice, poets are rarely good translators. They almost invariably use the foreign poem as a point of departure toward their own.'[43] Unsurprisingly, I disagree with Paz, while acknowledging his point. The result may be wonderful, but it might also need relabelling.

The hermeneut, the messenger, takes music or poetry to new audiences, across boundaries and barriers. Those that do so risk the wrath of border control, but their champions are many. As Blom says of Liszt, 'In spite of the disconcertingly vulgar streak of the showman in his oddly contradictory personality, he made a vast amount of great piano music accessible to an almost limitless public.'[44] More recently, Clemency Burton-Hill has said, 'I will defend to the end my conviction that opening up classical music does not dumb it down.'[45]

Critics, of course, are interpreters too, as are conductors, though in Kennedy's view both are inferior breeds. On rare occasions, critics break down barriers themselves. Theirs is the power to point us to a Hendrix or a Kennedy, a musician who disrupts our assumptions, and astonishes in new ways. Sometimes being lost for words can do the job. Trevor Gager says of Kennedy, 'It's impossible to write a review when you are left completely speechless at the end of a concert.'[46] Such a description seems to match Patricia Kopatchinskaja's highest accolade: 'A really good interpretation has me sitting on the edge of my seat in rapt attention and full of astonishment.'[47]

Is it possible for someone to be in that rapt, edge of seat mode, while another person is left unmoved? András Schiff, if indeed he has ever witnessed Kennedy play live, might say yes: 'A concert is not an entertainment. It should be a deep emotional and intellectual experience from which the listener takes something home to feel and to think about.'[48] He sounds as though he doesn't *want* to be on the edge of his seat, but to go home and contemplate. Surely the two attitudes can co-exist. Eric Fenby says of watching Menuhin, 'the impression is one of fulfilling a high and noble function as a musician, and not performing merely to give pleasure to the listener. He never allows us to forget that the role of music is to transport.'[49] That captures both elements; he seems to side with Schiff over the marketing that gives us 'Classics for Pleasure' like a brand of 'easy listening', but he goes on to quote Menuhin himself, who states, 'I do not wish to stress the solemn at the expense of the earthy, the buoyant or even the vulgar.'

I'm in danger of casting Schiff, a marvellous musician, as villain within my argument. His dismissal of Kennedy – and entertainment – makes him fair game, but much of what he says is less perverse and indeed enlightening. In several ways, he and Kennedy are in accord: both hate computers, and they agree about 'authentic instrument' recordings:

> [They] don't resemble a live performance, and most of the things they play they never do in concert. They sight read them in the studio and I oppose that. A recording must be a document of when you have reached a phase in your life. You don't have the right to record a piece sight reading in the studio. It's not serious.[50]

Like Kennedy, Schiff criticizes conformity:

> The middle level is very strong today – there are very many people in the conservatoires who play an instrument very well. But they are not necessarily very musical or very talented. There should be more vérité: the whole system of the production of musicians is not right.[51]

This also tallies with what Anne-Sophie Mutter says about the Juilliard 'machinery'. As for Schiff's thoughts about record companies, they begin to sound like Kennedy himself:

> The record companies have overproduced, and misused their power and their great opportunities. I don't think they will survive and I don't think that's necessarily a bad thing. They have become too powerful, they have overspent on huge offices and overheads, and pandered to the egos of conductors who want to conduct their third or fourth Beethoven symphony cycle despite the fact that nobody wants to hear it because all their versions are basically identical.[52]

It seems that experts can agree after all.

Schiff also makes interesting comments about 'play'. In reference to Bach's French Suites, he says:

> This is playful music in the best sense. Let's not forget that in [almost] every language we talk about 'playing' an instrument ... only the Italians say 'suonare', in other words they 'create a sound'. But this playful element, when we play an instrument, must always be present.[53]

So far so good. Then he continues, saying how Bach, 'endowed with a certain wisdom, looks back as it were, on his own childhood and writes playful pieces for his own children too but on the highest level. There's nothing cheap here.' Ouch. 'Nothing cheap' is another classic Schiff defence against play that isn't *serious*. He doesn't want 'play' to have the ambiguity it does in the Kennedy/Stanley book title, *Always Playing*, which accommodates the idea of playing the fool.

'Cheap' is of course frequently partnered with that even stronger word, 'vulgar'. And though Menuhin might defend it, John Drummond used it as a scourge when he said of Kennedy, 'That kind of vulgarity is quite unnecessary.'[54]

Banging on about Drummond

Helen Wallace, herself an admirer of Kennedy, wrote an obituary for John Drummond, Controller of BBC Radio 3, describing him as a 'visionary but dictatorial impresario', who made 'public criticisms of Alan Yentob and Melvyn Bragg'; Kennedy was not alone in suffering his 'impatience'. The biggest irony seems to be how Drummond's great aim 'was to throw out the academic atmosphere and replace it with that of a lively artists' café'.[55] One cannot but conclude that he resented the artists and impresarios that could do the job without him.

What sort of title, in this day and age, is *Controller*? The Fat Controller of the Reverend Awdrey's railway comes to mind, in charge of 'Troublesome Engines' such as Thomas and friends. In 2020 it was announced that the BBC would be doing away with Controllers from April 2021. 'Instead, portfolio editors will be appointed to handpick shows commissioned largely for iPlayer by genre heads with supercharged powers.'[56] 'Supercharged powers' sounds every bit as disturbing, but Controllers actually remain – in radio.

I know first-hand what a grievance such as Kennedy's feels like. Alan Davey, who became Radio 3 *Controller* in 2015, was previously Chief Executive at Arts Council England, and was responsible for the introduction of a new portfolio system of funding. Davey claimed, despite a few sleepless nights, to be totally comfortable with his decisions that threw arts funding into chaos. The organization I ran at the time, the National Association of Writers in Education, had its entire Arts Council funding withdrawn, an act that felt perilously close to Baron Beeching's cuts to Britain's rail network in the 1960s, this time ripping up the lines of communication and support for writers working in schools and community. A petition against the decision gained substantial support and coverage in the press, and we made a formal complaint – to no avail. The 'independent' review did however acknowledge that the Arts Council's process made no provision for national organizations that were based outside London. A moral victory then, of a sort. And we survived, thanks to the enormous commitment of our members. It took me years though to get over Davey's behaviour and, as you can tell, I'm still not entirely done. It's remarkably easy to cultivate a lifetime grudge. Forty-three years after 'Bohemian Rhapsody' was released, and the surviving members of Queen produced a film of the same name, they flagged up all the negative comments that the song had received. Mercury's biographer Lesley-Ann Jones thinks that's sad, as she does of Roger Daltrey's behaviour when he published his memoir in 2018, including a lifetime's grudge in the title: *Thanks a lot Mr Kibblewhite*; his headteacher had told him he would never make anything of his life, as he expelled him from school. I understand Jones's take on that, but I'm right behind Daltrey, Taylor/May, and Kennedy.

When Davey, in 2015, took control of the classical and speech output on BBC Radio 3, leadership of the BBC Proms and overall leadership of the BBC Orchestras and Choirs, I feared the worst. He has now stepped down, and I'll be the first to admit that the worst didn't happen, though Kennedy didn't feature once at the Proms under Davey's control.

During the Arts Council showdown, NAWE Patron Alan Bennett wrote to me, saying, 'How do you measure the quickening of a child's imagination? The Arts Council answer seems to be "You can't" and so why bother? ... impotent rage is what one feels as one does about the closing down of libraries.' I feel something of the same rage that a violinist so gifted in awakening musical delight should have been kept from the UK's prime classical stage.

When Kennedy did return to the Proms in 2008, between 'bans', at the invitation of Roger Wright, he played the Elgar concerto. It was scheduled to be conducted by Vernon Handley. Sadly, Handley was unwell (he died two months later), and was replaced by Paul Daniel. There was comic interplay ahead of the performance, Kennedy claiming to have 'found' some British music to play, but Daniel wasn't so amusing when he chose to beat the Drummond Drum. Drummond had died just two years earlier and, according to Daniel's introductory homage, didn't even know the meaning of 'dumbing down' – the accusation frequently levelled at every Controller. Thinking back to that moment, I'm somewhat surprised that Kennedy remained onstage to play. Nothing could possibly have irritated him more. He was back at the Proms after *an absence of 21 years*, a period that coincided with Drummond's controllership, then Kenyon's. But he was somehow able to subjugate any anger to the requirements of the moment.

To borrow from Oscar Wilde, to lose favour with one controller may be regarded as a misfortune; to be outcast by his successor too looks less like carelessness than unfair dismissal.

'****'

Where Laurence Sterne uses asterisks to bleep out certain words, Nigel Kennedy rarely holds back. It's got him into trouble in situations where parents have young children in tow, and 'foul-mouthed' has of course been added to the easy epithet list.

Mind Your Language, the sitcom that ran on British television in the 70s and 80s, was actually about a variety of characters studying English as a foreign language, but its title played on our sensitivity about swearing. Another sitcom of the same era, *Sorry!*, is remembered primarily for its catchphrase, 'Language, Timothy', the reprimand given to The Magnificent Seven's Ronnie Corbett's character whenever he was suspected of a *double entendre*. (The use of 'language' as an abbreviation for *bad* language can have thoroughly amusing consequences. Our current poet laureate Simon Armitage was once called in to see the Headmaster at a school he was visiting. 'I'm told your poems have *language* in them' was the prelude to a warning to behave.) EMI dropped The Sex Pistols after their swearing on the Bill Grundy show as last-minute replacements for Queen in 1976. *The Daily Mail* used the headline, 'The Filth and the Fury', happy to be outraged and sell newspapers into the bargain; this the same *Mail* that would promote *The Four Seasons* with free CDs.

A low tolerance for swearing has even plagued the cinema. *Four Weddings and a Funeral*, the film that was a massive hit in 1994, begins with repeated use of the word 'fuck'. It's wonderfully startling, also completely grounded in the characters' panic. But in the light of Kennedy's *Four Seasons* controversy, it should come as no surprise that *Four Weddings* – a film of such appeal that audiences stood to applaud in the cinema – was also deemed by some to be the worst film they had ever seen. The swearing, which is so fundamental to the opening scenes in particular, came in for criticism. Audiences in Salt Lake City walked out. And on American television the language was censored: 'fuck' was changed to 'bugger', and I'm still looking for any explanation of why that makes any sense. (In the uncensored film, the occasional shift from one word to the other is highly deliberate, and effective.) It reminds me of the South American censors running shy of the nude wrestling scene in Ken Russell's *Women in Love*, a cut that left the audience with a single shot of 'two men lying naked on the carpet, side by side, panting'.[57]

That was 1969. Two years later, with the release of *The Devils*, things had changed, but only so far. Russell recalled:

> Of all the dozens of hours I spent arguing the pros and cons of this and that with John only one moment still sticks in my mind. 'I'm afraid we can't have Vanessa saying "cunt,"' he said. 'It's taken me ten years of fighting just to get "fuck" accepted. I'm afraid the British public isn't yet ready for "cunt".'[58]

When the film *Amadeus*, scripted by the brilliant Peter Shaffer, put bad language into Mozart's mouth, there was of course uproar. And even those who appreciated its basis in historical fact weren't entirely comfortable with the point of the portrayal, described well by Peter Culshaw: 'Mozart as a barely housetrained lout, the scruffiness and swearing being a kind of guarantor of his authenticity and unconventional genius.'[59]

There's the rub: the cause for divided opinion both about *Amadeus* and Kennedy. John Drummond's words about the latter continue to boom. Vulgarity is unnecessary – if you have no interest, that is, in understanding the nature of creativity, or the complexities of character that bless us with their creative works. But Drummond wasn't alone in his comments. Others to lay into Kennedy included his own former agent, Jasper Parrott, Lady Barbirolli and, most surprisingly, Melvyn Bragg. It's telling, however, that fellow musicians tended to take Kennedy's side. When asked if Kennedy's image affected his playing, a loaded question if ever there was one, Christopher Warren-Greene, leader of the London Chamber Orchestra, replied, 'Yes ... but in a positive way. If he feels free, he'll probably play that way.'[60] The furore raged on in the press, on *Newsnight*, and even in parliament. As Kennedy says with some pride, 'The discussions ended with my beloved Labour Party (the real one, that is) passing a motion that what I was doing was good for classical music.'[61]

The discussions didn't really end though, and the publication of *Uncensored!* has put the swearing, in particular, back into the spotlight. For the lingering Drummond brigade, the language is no doubt sufficient to prevent them reading the book, but they should take note of the research now available. 'Think swearing isn't big or clever? Think again' writes Richard Stephens in a piece for *The Conversation*. 'Studies have shown ... that swearing may in fact display a more, rather than less, intelligent use of language.'

> a study by psychologists from Marist College in the US found links between how fluent a person is in the English language and how fluent they are in swearing ... the size of your vocabulary of swear words is linked with your overall vocabulary, and swearing is inextricably linked to the experience and expression of feelings and emotions.[62]

Stephens' article quotes Timothy Jay, who states, 'Swearing is positively correlated with extraversion and is a defining feature of a Type A personality.' An article by Jay, with Kristin Janschewitz, goes further, and with reference to a number of other studies. They make connections between swearing and honesty, and with general intelligence: a 'swearing vocabulary' is indicative of *good* language skills, rather than a paucity.[63] This is certainly backed up by reading Kennedy's book in full: some chapters may be crammed with profanities but they are also highly descriptive, with imaginative and sometimes hilarious digressions. Moreover, as Tully Potter observes, the chapter 'written from beyond the grave by his grandfather' shows Kennedy writing 'perfectly decent prose when he wants to'.[64] This connects with the 'chameleon' aspect of the creative personality that I've already mentioned. Jay and Janschewitz also mention 'social intelligence', the ability to use swearing in a way that is appropriate to the setting and the timing, and it's this that's so problematic in relation to Kennedy. The ability to 'switch' between vocabularies is clearly there, but so is the determination to use profanity in contexts where it's not expected, or welcome; his use of two different vocabularies is perhaps 'unresolved'. But the research identifies two further connections that perhaps explain this after all. Firstly, 'There is a connection of swearing words with creativity as they are stored on the right side of the brain, the "creative brain".' Secondly, expletives are frequently thrown instead of punches, 'a remote form of aggression'.[65] And there it is on the cover of the book, Kennedy with his boxing gloves, presenting a book in which he takes his defiantly creative stance against all adversaries.

Kennedy of course complicates even this neat assessment. The point of the expletive as opposed to the physical punch is, according to the research, to avoid repercussions. Drummond may no longer be around to swing physical or verbal punches in return, but who knows what consequences of rejection have been set in motion by the book, reinforced by negative reviews. The thing is, Kennedy doesn't care, and I can't help admiring that spirit in an age where career and money dominate, and ultra-caution is the order of the day, dictated by the corporate sponsors of your every move.

I'll admit to some surprise that Kennedy went quite so far as he did. John-Erik Jordan suggests that we respond to swear words differently to other language. We don't decipher them in the same way, they're simply 'concentrated lumps of emotion'.[66] But if that's correct, it still leaves us with some difficulty in responding to a flow of them, especially when some are put in capitals. Swear words, as Jordan points out, are typically used for emphasis, as are capitals, so we're getting a double whammy of left hook and right jab, a lot to take. In *Uncensored!* Kennedy supplies us with an initial Glossary, so there is indeed meaning attached, as well as a barrage of raw emotion. You either buy into the glossary, or you might as well opt out of the whole book.

But just when we're left reeling from all this, further theories step in to help out. According to Jordan, swearing, particularly 'ritual insults among friends', is related to group solidarity. And Emma Byrne, author of 'The Absolute F-cking Best Swear Word For You', says that a choice swear word is 'a product of the values of the people who surrounded you growing up. In particular, it depends on the emotional responses of the people whose opinions mattered most to you when you first tried out those words.'[67] Kennedy's language, highly individual, is also the language of his tribe, the musicians and friends he has surrounded himself with, away from the traditional classical arena. And for all its combative tropes, it's inviting the reader to join the tribe. It is, bizarrely, a welcoming gesture, while also fending off the people he already thinks are irredeemable. As Byrne says, 'The most cathartic swear word is never going to be a universal.' No way will everyone like Kennedy's book.

Kennedy's use of 'vulgar' language in referring to Drummond is payback for the latter's criticism of Kennedy's vulgarity, but Kennedy does in fact use Sterne-like asterisks at one point, in describing Drummond as 'a BULL****frog'. That's rather more witty. Either way, the hatred of Drummond, though thoroughly understandable, is not really commendable. The rant in *Uncensored!* will hopefully have put the need for further abuse to bed.

Before he opted for the harder-core language of *Uncensored!*, Kennedy's vocabulary was peppered with other terms that seemed to hail from a different era. Interviewers sometimes felt that they needed a translator. Prominent amongst the oddities was 'monster', a term that could be variously applied to a concerto, a conductor, almost anything. The conductor Klaus Tennstedt was a monster, and returned the compliment, calling Kennedy 'little monster'. (One might call that a pseudo father/son relationship, perhaps not inappropriately, given how Kennedy, abandoned by his father, would turn his back on conductors.)

We don't necessarily choose words because of their multiple meanings, or derivation, and yet their richness, and sometimes their inherent ambiguity, is what appeals, however unconsciously. 'Monster' is certainly an interesting one. The latin *monstrum* is an 'omen', itself deriving from *monere*, 'to warn'. But a broader set of meanings for the noun includes whatever is out of the usual course of nature, a marvel, or prodigy; and for the verb, to reveal, show, advise or teach. If something is monstrous, it's mighty – or outrageously wrong or absurd. Here, then, is *furore* within a single word. If something is truly marvellous, it may almost be a guarantee that some will find it *in*credible, *un*believable, and dismiss it.

There are other monsters that we're presented with, versions of Frankenstein's monster, sewn together from different parts; so-called marvels that have more to do with manufacturing – and marketing of a much more cynical type than John Stanley ever dirtied his hands with. The band put together artificially, as part of a television process, is a prime example of how image can be made to matter more than musicianship – or the music itself. Kennedy hates that with a passion, and sees classical music going the same way:

> What's happened in classical music is the same as what happened with the teen bands ... with all the make-a-pop-star-on-telly shit. It seems that it's so much better if the band sounds like the last band, instead of a band making new shit. How Frank Zappa or Marvin Gaye would fare on these new shows I dread to think - they'd probably be dumped on the first possible occasion.[68]

From a different angle, András Schiff concurs, pointing the finger (again) at record companies:

> I think an image is your personality, your choice of repertoire and the way you approach music. The trouble starts when record companies want to make your image for you. If you are not very firm in your ideas, you let them make it and that's dangerous.[69]

If anything, Kennedy's image was an absolute statement that the record company had nothing to do with it; after all, would they really sanction such *vulgarity*? EMI had made a pretty firm statement on that front in dismissing The Sex Pistols. But they were nevertheless trying to manipulate him, and he resisted.

> It was OK being marketed as a pop star as long as it was true to what I was ... but you can't stand still. People expected me to carry on being this punk violinist who played Vivaldi, but I

didn't want to become the Val Doonican or Des O'Connor of classical music. That was when things got unreal.[70]

Here we have Kennedy decrying 'cheap', just like Schiff. But for Kennedy, 'cheap' is more associated with 'bland', and 'formulaic'; also television's endless supply of instant gratification:

> People should be given the chance to concentrate on something for more than five seconds. Look at MTV – the camera angle changes every shot. Everything is fantasy. Music isn't just about that. It's a grounding process which can liberate the mind.[71]

This description of MTV sits uncomfortably with Kennedy's own *Four Seasons* film, which uses some of the same techniques. As already discussed, his approach was indeed grounded, but it nevertheless came in for criticism, as did the later Brahms video. And this criticism was enough to prompt Kennedy's post-Brahms re-release of the Sibelius and Tchaikovsky concertos, with the strapline 'just listen' and an image-free cover. It seems to say, 'if you don't like images, then I'll bleep them out'. The album cover's black page here is really a *blank* page.

Kennedy's further point was argued at length in his sleeve notes:

> there has been a growing consternation amongst some traditionalists (who perhaps mistakenly think that they are also automatically 'purists') that the use of visual imagery in conjunction with classical music is detrimental to the potential understanding and enjoyment that the listener can get from the music alone.[72]

He continues with a complementary argument, railing against the traditionalists' preference for verbiage. He goes on the attack, categorising them as *writers*, 'implanting their own probably superficial ideas in the head of the listener by means of the printed word'. He ends with a barely concealed vulgarity about the worth of their efforts: 'it might seem wiser to use the printed page for a more basic purpose than reading!'

All this leads to a sort of 'anti-sleeve note':

> trying to get people interested ... by sharing my knowledge ... that you can get a great deal of pleasure from bars 66-69

leading to the introduction of the second subject of the
Tchaikovsky concerto, would appear to be highly unethical.

The rant reaches its conclusion with a democratic punch that
teeters on the brink of being anti-educational: 'What these guys
would prefer not to face is that the arts are a great leveller, and
that qualifications or background don't have anything to do with
art's deeper understanding or who it belongs to.' Having got all
that out of the system, it's time simply to say 'Anyway, whoever
you are, I hope you enjoy this album.'[73] Amusingly, the text is ©
Dr Nigel Kennedy.

He's adamant that he's right, but also embattled. You could
argue that saying nothing – using no words as well as no images
– would be a cleverer tactic, but that might have been too subtle.
He needs, somewhat ironically, to spell out his message, as he did
again at the Proms in 2008:

> Talking about the music is bad karma – it's almost like admit-
> ting that no-one will understand the music unless I talk a lot
> of rubbish about it, so I don't really like doing that. If a great
> actor performs Shakespeare then you don't need all those
> books about Shakespeare: it becomes abundantly clear.[74]

This feels like Kennedy *contra mundum*, but he's not alone. Nicola
Benedetti writes, 'innocence, that lack of technical understanding, enhances your visceral reaction',[75] and Clemency Burton-Hill
initiated the Open Ears podcast for similar reasons. As a television broadcaster, having spent many years 'telling people what to
listen to and how to listen', she decided to do something different:
getting people to present and listen to music from an emotional
perspective. The podcast features 'comedians, bartenders, fire-
fighters, taxi drivers [of course], teachers'.

> There must always be a place for rigorously intellectual appre-
> ciation of classical music for those who want it, but a working
> knowledge of the complex technicalities that underpin what
> we hear is a privilege enjoyed by a tiny percentage of listeners.
> Most people falling in love with, say, Dido's Lament by Henry
> Purcell – apparently the UK's favourite aria – are unlikely to be
> getting their kicks from spotting that passus duriusculus; it's
> probably not being able to identify the tierce de Picardie at the
> end of Dvořák's New World Symphony that makes it endure.[76]

This is well put, certainly in regard to 'most people'. Even those who would defend 'intellectual appreciation' (and in writing this book, I'm a hypocrite if I don't count myself amongst them) are unlikely to disagree with the notion of music's emotional core – and affect. And yet eyebrows were raised when Kennedy once spoke about 'emphasising feeling',[77] as if that were a crime worse than electric amplification. All sorts of other emphases are permitted in interpreting music. Why should the emotional heart of it be out of bounds? I suspect the same plaintiffs turn a blind eyebrow to the worst type of emoting that we witness on concert stages all the time, the florid 'I'm *so* moved by this' gestures. A recent Proms performance of Bach's Matthew Passion was one of the worst examples. 'Bleed, loving heart...' sang the choir while the keyboard player/conductor was grinning and waggling his head in that dreadful manner so beloved of some classical musicians. He appeared to have no grasp of the words whatsoever. Are people actually trained to have no feeling for the music they play? It got worse: 'Weep mankind for your sins' – Grin! Grin!

As a sham, that performance ranked with footballers rolling around in agony when they've received a tap on the ankle. And yet, when I shared my thoughts on social media, at least one friend disagreed with me, having witnessed nothing wrong. That's the degree to which people can be conned by fake emotion, as they are by fake injury, by fake news – by all the fakery that would whip up a storm at the expense of more searching enquiries.

A typical 'cheap' trick at Kennedy's expense – and ours – can be seen in a *Record Collector* article of 1996. The photo of Kennedy that appeared on his *Let Loose* album is accompanied by the caption, 'Nigel Kennedy takes a machine gun to the musical establishment in 1987'.[78] If you haven't seen the image, you might be thinking of some hell-raising publicity photo in which Kennedy, with a terrifying snarl (of which he is indeed capable) brandishes an actual gun, or mimics Paul Nicholas playing Frankenstein's monster-cum-Hitler at the end of *Lisztomania*, his electric guitar spraying machine gun bullets into anyone in his path. In fact, the photo shows Kennedy (despite fist) in a quiet, calm pose. The way he cradles his guitar across his lap has been monstrously distorted by the words. A violent metaphor is born

and members of the establishment 'under fire', who might well
have been comrades in a less savage revolution (or a 'small-scale
rebellion', to use the Warner Classics line), lose interest in his
cause, or turn actively against him.

It makes me think again of Paul Gascoigne, another sublimely
gifted but difficult character – and regular victim of the press.
They built him up – into an easy target, both for their further
column inches and his own inclination to self-destruct. Neither
Gazza nor Kennedy did much to tone things down. Kennedy for
instance commented, 'Someone called me The Gazza of the Violin;
that's a very flattering description 'cos Gazza's out of his head,
man!'[79] It was perhaps inevitable that the two outstanding talents
of their generation in their respective fields would get together, as
England once more dared to dream of football glory at Italia '90.

Kennedy's friendship with Gary Lineker, which arose through
their roles in The Magnificent Seven, was key to the connection.
Kennedy and his girlfriend Brix Smith both tell the story in their
books of their chaotic arrival in Sardinia, where the villa they
were due to share with Michelle Lineker, Gary's wife, wasn't
ready. (Wives were not allowed to stay with the team.) According
to Smith, 'Nigel went mental'[80], but things were resolved, thanks
to Michelle Lineker's connections with ITV, and with the bonus
of various TV set-ups for Kennedy, who was now given exceptional access to the England camp. From thereon, the 'chaos' was
more predictable: 'accidental' provision of vodka for Gazza, and
champagne for everyone on the yacht owned by a friend of Villa
chairman 'Deadly' Doug Ellis.

There is a YouTube video of Kennedy entertaining the players,
and it is fascinating how Gazza, who was the creative genius but
also the maverick in that England squad, is the one who is most
clearly entranced. Ian Hamilton, in his book Gazza Agonistes,
describes Gascoigne as 'a kid who has never really had time
to grow up',[81] a phrase that some would say applies equally to
Kennedy. There's a clear affinity between them.

Two years later, Gascoigne would settle in Italy playing for
Lazio, and his treatment by the press there was markedly different. The Italians were strangely tolerant of his behaviour. In
Gazza Italia, an expanded version of his original text, written in
the run up to the 1994 World Cup, Hamilton writes: 'In Italy …

they regarded his nuttiness as an important aspect of his gift—and the gift was what mattered most of all.'[82] In the same way that Gazza's indiscretions were simply 'part of the package' for the Lazio supporters, Kennedy fans are mostly willing to treat his more reckless tendencies with a similar shrug. Others of course react in horror, and the trashing of a hotel room in time-honoured rock star fashion is bound to come across as either juvenile, attention-seeking, or both. It may of course be the accidental result of over-ferocious partying, but it is perhaps more wilful than that, and not simply for publicity purposes.

Kennedy will apply the phrase 'do some damage' both to partying and to playing a classical concerto. What matters, it would seem, is that the experience is intense, even 'dangerous', with nothing treated as sacrosanct. And this points to another similarity, at least in Kennedy's view, between music and football (and indeed partying), the idea of the 'result' being unpredictable – that is, when music is truly alive. Hamilton points to the alternative scenario: 'With a pop star or an opera singer, when you turn up for a performance, you usually get more or less what you go to see, or hear',[83] and for Kennedy that whole idea of 'expectation' is anathema, as indeed is the 'sacrosanct'.

Edward T Cone observes that 'more knowledgeable audiences tend to regard a composition as a received text', and highlights

> the subtle and pervasive influence of a special kind of ritualism, one that inappropriately transforms many of our musical performances into liturgical services and that encourages our audiences to respond to them accordingly ... The performance is taken by the cognoscenti, not as a lived experience, but as the reverent reading of a sacred writing.[84]

The implications of this are pronounced by Kennedy in the direst terms: 'If you do the same thing every night, that's the death of music.'[85] There is of course no *furore* surrounding such a predictable performance.

In the England camp, Kennedy performed – guess what – 'Spring' from *The Four Seasons*, but with Brix Smith on guitar, the whole thing veering quickly into an improvisation. Never, even among the hundreds if not thousands of more 'formal' renditions, have two of his performances been the same, however closely related. As Eric Cantona said, rather mystically, of playing at Montpellier FC: 'Our mission was to interpret *The Magic Flute*, every Saturday.'[86]

England's Italia '90 experience ended quite literally in tears. Gazza played brilliantly in the semi-final against Germany, but when booked for a foul, knew he would be out of the final. When it then came to a penalty shoot-out, the tearful Gazza clearly wasn't going to be one of the takers as the manager Bobby Robson had originally planned. And so it was that he stood by while Chris Waddle blasted his shot over the bar. Watching Gascoigne's perfect penalty in the shoot-out against Germany six years later, at Euro '96, it's easy to convince yourself that he would have scored that night in Turin. But Robson and Lineker knew Gascoigne well, and how emotion – unfaked emotion that rocks you to the core, the type that leaves a grown man crying in the middle of a football match – was, in that instance, a debilitating factor.

According to Brix Smith, Kennedy wouldn't go to the third-place play-off match against Italy, saying 'What's the point?'[87] I understand the sentiment – Gazza's tears ran deep – but somehow find it immeasurably sad, especially from such a true football supporter. Rudyard Kipling, in his poem 'If', suggests that we need to be able to 'meet with triumph and disaster / And treat those two impostors just the same'.[88] On another day, Kennedy would surely agree. But on 7 July, 1990, The Three Tenors were preening their fake football credentials as a curtain raiser to the final in Rome, while in Bari, the Nigel Kennedy of football wasn't allowed to play. Hard indeed to see why the Gazza of the violin would want to be there.

'Incident' of one sort or another seems to have followed Kennedy and Smith Start on their travels. On a tour of Australia, invited to play to industry executives and local dignitaries in a smart Melbourne hotel, Kennedy spied an artwork that he considered 'too ugly to exist'.[89] The assembly was aghast when he deliberately let the sculpture – made by a famous Australian artist, and worth £13,000 – drop from his hand. So too was John Stanley, who had his work cut out to avoid a major outrage in the papers.

This story, shared by Smith, is shocking and yet curiously related to how Kennedy's *Four Seasons* was treated, treasured by some and abhorred by others. Had Nicholas Kenyon's review wiped Kennedy's recording off the map, he might well have said 'That's better', as Kennedy did to his astonished hotel audience, staring at the fragments. Such behaviour, real or imagined, is the act of someone who believes in the value of his own aesthetic judgement – and his right to assert it. We are used to critics asserting that right, not so much to artists – certainly not when they use actual vandalism as their critical weapon. That can hardly be condoned, but I'm almost as shocked when András Schiff says that 'Nigel Kennedy is very bad taste';[90] Kennedy, the awful figurine that Schiff is just itching to let drop.

There is of course something more primitively miscreant in Kennedy's behaviour, misbelieving in authority. The chapter in *Uncensored!*, 'My Police League Table', provides plentiful evidence, as well as interesting and certainly amusing 'defence'. And Smith's recollection of their time in Florida is full of colourful misbehaviour unrelated to any aesthetic considerations. 'Because there were so many rules at Disney World, it was natural for Nigel and me to want to break them.' They drove a Disney golf cart to the supermarket, leaving Orlando's traffic in near chaos. 'We bought so much food we couldn't fit it into the golf cart, so we tied sirloin steaks to the roof of the cart, Fred Flintstone-style.'[91] You can picture Paul Gascoigne doing the same thing. Gazza's actual visit to Disneyland Paris in 1992 is the stuff of legend: a three-day bender while he should have been training with Lazio; still 'smashed' at the following day's match in Seville, he scored a goal that had even Maradona looking to the skies in disbelief.

Performing while wrecked is (or was) more commonplace amongst footballers than classical soloists, but Kennedy has managed it, with apparent pride. 'I hit the f***ing pilseners last night, man' he said to an interviewer in a Prague concert interval in 2008[92]. That's the sort of thing to appeal to one crowd but most definitely not another, even if the performance doesn't suffer, which in Kennedy's case, almost miraculously, it doesn't seem to. He's not Keith Moon passing out on his drum kit, or the Alex Harvey I saw dragged from the stage in 1978, whisky in hand, by his own fellow musicians. Within the musical arena, at least, he's always master of his own demons.

Clowning, on or off stage, is one thing. Further along the eccentric spectrum, petulance, crankiness, and at the far end, violence, are less charming. Gazza fighting with Mickey Mouse in Paris probably wasn't as pretty as his later goal. In Florida, Kennedy lost it with Brix Smith, kicking and stamping on a cuddly Mickey Mouse that she'd been given. He also barely contained his rage when a waiter took away her plate while he was still eating. (I hate that American custom too, but custom it is.) Smith describes Kennedy's own eating habit as rather strange.

> He had a particular quirk when he ate. He revolved his plate in a circle with his hands, turning it round and round, inch by inch, to line up particular food on the dish in front of him. He always did this.[93]

Weirdly, I've found myself doing that too. It must be somewhere on the different 'spectrum' of impulsive to obsessive compulsive disorder. Those who go so far as to separate all their food, having brumotactillophobia, are said to 'have issues with flexibility'. They're 'methodical, giving great attention to detail in everything they do'.[94] That might well apply to someone who practises Bach four hours a day, but such people also tend to keep neat and tidy houses, which most definitely doesn't match the 'absolute chaos' that Smith was first faced with in Kennedy's Hampstead house.[95] Perhaps there is only so much discipline and ordering that a life can accommodate, before everything else spills out in all directions. Or maybe the Kennedy contradictions are simply 'something else'.

Smith's therapist, Eva Loewe, referred to Kennedy as a 'High Chair Tyrant', someone having 'unresolved issues from his formative years'.[96] That seems pretty undeniable. But Smith also witnessed Kennedy suffering a very physical manifestation of the toll taken by those same formative years.

Pain in the neck

The neck scar that would cause disruption to Kennedy's career was already evident in footage of him busking in New York. It's not uncommon for violinists to suffer from this problem; in some cases they are forced to abandon playing altogether. It has a variety of names: fiddler's neck, violin hickey; 'acne mechanica' is how dermatologists ruthlessly refer to it. In its less vicious

guise, it's almost a badge of honour, showing how much you practise. Benjamin Herbert, working for Christie's on the sale of a
Stradivarius, required a hickey to be in evidence before allowing
just 'anyone' to try out the instrument. Personally, I would have
reached for my Dracula make-up.

The mark is basically caused by the material of the violin, or
chin rest, reacting with sensitive skin. The particular way you
'hug' the violin can exacerbate the problem.

The chin rest was only introduced to the upper side of the
violin in the 1820s by composer Louis Spohr. It's common to see
images of old instruments without them. A shoulder rest *under*
the violin only came into use mid twentieth century, and many
top soloists have not made use of them, including Heifetz, Grumiaux, Kreisler, Stern and Menuhin, one of the reasons being that
the clamp limits the resonance of the instrument. Kennedy has
followed suit. Ill-fitting chin-rests or shoulder-rests can contrib-
ute to a hickey, as chin-rest manufacturer Lynne Denig explains:

> The hickey comes from crushing layers of skin at one point
> along the jaw ... Bacteria enter the wound, and a hickey is
> born. It's like buying an ill-fitting pair of shoes—where the
> shoes don't fit properly, they'll rub your skin, and you'll get
> skin irritation.[97]

A raised shoulder, compensating for the poor fit – or as a natural
form of 'hug', can make things worse.

Brix Smith describes how the operation on Kennedy's neck
proved particularly complicated, and became a rather different
badge of honour:

> We were surprised Nigel had any neck left at all. Nigel insisted
> the doctors save the massive cyst of keloid scarring they
> removed that day. He brought it home in a jar and kept it on
> a shelf in the music room. I kept thinking 'Eleanor Rigby'.[98]

The operation actually went 'horribly wrong', and Kennedy
couldn't perform for several months; even when the neck finally
healed, it was going to take as long again to get back into practice.
Meanwhile, 'everyone was threatening me with million-pound
lawsuits because I wasn't playing in Germany ... I had to ask, do
these people care about me or are they trying to get blood out of a

stone?'[99] But an anxious time was also party time. He 'let his inner child go wild, unchecked'.[100] There were three-day-long parties, with 'hash brownies and chocolate-chip pot cookies'.

This was a phase that would continue long after the neck was healed. If it was party time it was also time for serious reflection. The demands of the classical touring circuit were proving a pain in their own right. As Kennedy said to Peter Culshaw, 'If music is a journey, how the hell do you know what you want to play in four years' time?'[101] He had been touring Europe, Japan, Australia, New Zealand, America and Canada, and in 1992 he decided on a break.

It wasn't just the touring, it was the '"mental midgets" and "ignorant" jobsworths with little understanding of what it takes to play an instrument' that forced his hand. As Dalya Alberge relates, Kennedy 'found himself unable to work with EMI executives who were more interested in repeating previous successes than allowing artists the freedom to create'. Some weren't really fit for the job at all. 'There literally was some geezer who'd managed to sell a certain number of fish-fingers and then he was head of classics. It was a strange mix of a lack of credibility and qualifications.'

> It's a shame that people don't trust the instinct of artists who have the experience of playing in front of audiences. We know what might turn somebody on or off because we've tried it out in public and that's the best barometer you can use. To have to go by some preconceived theory made by people who've probably hardly picked up an instrument in their life is a bit like me saying 'well, I think an aircraft that shape might be really nice and I don't know anything about aerodynamics'.[102]

He bemoans that fact that so many 'wonderful musicians' have become 'burnt out, fettered and held back'. All he ever wanted for himself, really, was the chance to do a bit of this and that.

> I'd be able to do an album with Ornette Coleman one minute, then play Beethoven the next. But that confuses people. So for the moment I'm going to keep playing my stuff. And if that doesn't work, I'll move out of England to somewhere they'll accept it. The main fear I have is that music here is too polarised. Like the 'NME' have been telling us we have to like Blur and Oasis, and in five years' time they'll be telling us we're idiots for still listening to them. That's just as bad as the

elitism of the classical world. So I may have to go and look for a healthier environment. But I won't go crawling back to the classical world with my tail between my legs.[103]

I find it interesting how an 'entrenched' position can also be an expression of true freedom – with all its hazards. It's a typical Kennedy enigma. Through dogged resistance to cultural conformity, he preserves his personal, creative horizons, within which he's subservient to nothing but his own self-styled outlaw status.

Journalist Mark Lawson caught up with Kennedy around this time and witnessed his free-form approach to life – and driving:

> The interview over, Nigel freewheels his psychedelic BMW down the Malvern Hills, released (so he says) from the straitjacket of the classical concert circuit; but constrained still by the bonds of fame, a vast, strange talent, and the chemical and mental temptations they bring.[104]

Kennedy's BMW (and later a Jaguar XJ6) was crudely spray-painted in Villa colours, with added graffiti. Brix Smith recalls his pastime of freewheeling the vehicle in greater detail:

> At the top of a long, steep road, he would take the car out of gear and pull his feet away from the pedals. Not only would he take his foot away from the brake, he'd take his hands from the steering wheel too. He'd reach to the sky, as if on a roll-ercoaster. The car would then pick up speed and 'free-wheel' down the hill, gathering huge momentum. It was forbidden to put your foot on the brake ... One night, while driving home in the darkness through the Malvern Hills, Nigel decided to take the game one step further.... He wanted to 'off-road' and attempt to 'roll' the car down the hill sideways.[105]

Here's an artist's sketch, made a few centuries earlier, by Laurence Sterne, describing – with an inter-textual flourish of the pen – how his character flourishes his stick in the air, saying 'Whilst a man is free—'.[106]

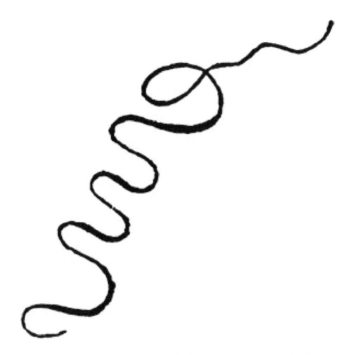

Freedom ... but it's Kennedy's 'one step further' that causes trouble, and risks alienating the biggest fan or friend, not to mention life or limb.

'Free' is an adjective that gets applied to many things: free verse; free jazz ... Free verse hardly gets that 'dangerous', but free jazz remains controversial, gripping or unintelligible, depending on how willing you are to 'hold on'. A free spirit might seem a universal 'positive', but as these pages have, I hope, shown, that's far from the case. Ian Hamilton's comment about Gascoigne is revealing in this context: 'Gazza would remain unspoiled, or remain spoiled, as some might think.'[107]

John Stanley's policy of 'containment' was never going to be foolproof, not where such a gifted fool was centre stage. And so the furore continued. Here's Schiff, again:

> People say that Nigel Kennedy misbehaves but that he plays like a god; but I think he misbehaves and doesn't play like a god. I don't think his violin playing is anything extraordinary; you can find violinists like that in every music school. It is all marketing.[108]

I believe that Schiff is wrong. Kennedy plays, if not like a god (after all, who can define that?), in a way that is utterly exceptional. But even if you disagree, then what he has done is surely important. More people enjoy classical music as a result of his crusade. When Schiff says, 'the public for good music today is a hundred times bigger than it was in the time of the composers',[109] he's not meaning to thank Kennedy, but he does so nevertheless. Kennedy, ironically, is less optimistic, and statistics are grim: the vast majority of children are unable to name one classical composer. Is it not worth creating a bit of a storm to put that right, even if Vivaldi is the only composer to crawl onto the radar for a while? What did Vanessa Mae with electric violin and wet white dress do to *harm* classical music? The only danger, as Kennedy rather brilliantly quipped, was to herself: electricity and water don't really mix.

Since originality and risk are so controversial, maybe furore is exactly what we want. The alternative is manufactured bands and careers, and a classical world that doesn't look to the horizons, preferring to hide behind conservative ideals. 'I don't think Schubert wanted to be particularly original', says Schiff. 'Today it's one of the main criteria for an artist. You cannot be deliberately original. You have to be true and honest to yourself.'[110] On the last point, I agree. So much of what Schiff says seems reasonable, and yet he has a serious Kennedy blindspot. 'I'm not against selling millions of records but won't reach out for the people who buy Nigel Kennedy.' Why? 'I despise that kind of thing.' Why? 'Because it's very bad music.' How he must hate to appear on Decca and Deutsche Grammophon compilations along with Kennedy. He doesn't appreciate Kennedy's particular way of being absolutely true and honest to himself. But let's hear him out:

> There is integrity, musical and personal, in past performers –
> Schnabel, Edwin Fischer, Cortot, Adolf Busch, Casals. There
> is an integrity and a huge culture behind their music. It is not
> just entertainment, it is a crystallisation of European culture.
> There is a great problem today with taste - what is good taste,
> what is bad taste? To me the Three Tenors are very bad taste;
> Nigel Kennedy is very bad taste. Maybe people will say that
> I'm a snob. It is not the popular factor that bothers me; it is
> when people sing badly or play badly that bothers me.[111]

I'm guessing Schiff wasn't anywhere near Italia '90. But Pavarotti a *bad singer*? Nigel Kennedy a *bad player*? For Schiff, cultural engagement is even more important than technique. Too right, but there's the rub. What, exactly, is cultural engagement? It means one thing to Schiff, another to Nigel Kennedy. Schiff talks of 'integrity', but what on earth does such a phrase mean? He wouldn't begin to understand how 'culture' might relate to affiliations beyond his own horizons, to free jazz, or to the Aston Villa or England football tribe.

Alfred Hickling writes that Kennedy 'takes culture very seriously indeed. It's those who approach the arts in a falsely reverential fashion who are the real philistines.'[112] Kennedy comments:

> The problem in this country is that we don't see classical music as part of our root culture. So we approach it in this ridiculously gentrified manner, and play the music in an uptight fashion completely alien to the blokes who wrote it. I mean, Beethoven and Mozart were two of the greatest geniuses who ever lived – but they also knew how to have a good time.[113]

This tallies with what Langston Hughes said of Louis Armstrong and Co, also with what Kennedy has said about 'fiddlers': 'I would not set one classical violinist above a great Irish fiddler in a pub', he said to Helen Wallace.[114] High artistic achievement can emerge from environments utterly unlike those prized by Schiff.

> The best audience I played for was in a pub in Dublin, elbow to elbow with people and mugs of Guinness. I was playing with a local violinist and the audience was so quiet that you really could've heard a pin drop. That's what I'm after. As long as I get that, the career doesn't matter.[115]

There's nothing like a good debate. But there's also nothing as awful as a bad argument. I wish András Schiff could recognize how Kennedy, like Schiff himself, has rejected the idea of being moulded by the industry. Cultural engagement, or identity, is not necessarily a straightforward matter. Sometimes, though, there's a simple issue at the heart of it. As Paul Gascoigne said, 'I want to be mesel'.[116]

Free Verse

it starts with a mischievous smile
a sideways
glance at the passenger
who doesn't at first realize
the car's out of gear
and that the driver's taken his feet
off the pedals
though something feels
different
strangely at ease
gradually picking up effortless speed
down the empty road
but just as she's beginning to enjoy it
he takes his hands off the wheel
thrusting them in the air
before rummaging
in the dashboard clutter for an Ornette
Coleman cassette
and ramming it into the deck
so that now as it plays
she can't hear herself think
above her own scream blending
with the saxophone's wail
and the claret and blue jaguar
with its already indecipherable scrawl
is becoming a blur
that she sees from afar
careening down the hill
with herself inside
cowering from the broken white
lines like silent gunfire
streaming into the bonnet

Chapter 6: Interval
Alone at the Frontier

As Gregor Samsa awoke one morning from uneasy dreams he found himself transformed in his bed into a gigantic insect. ...

O God, he thought, what an exhausting job I've picked on! Travelling about, day in, day out.—Franz Kafka

I don't have to be what you want me to be. I'm free to be who I want.
—Cassius Clay/Muhammad Ali

Who, or what, was Nigel Kennedy, circa 1992? David Bailey's photograph of him used for the Brahms album cover is strange enough, but Lord Snowdon's portrait photo the following year is downright weird – Frankenstein's monster with a Villa scarf. Why he's wearing a fur coat, I have no idea. Add the John Lennon pink shades, a velvet doctoral cap, a carpet bag slung over the shoulder, and an unstrung violin held on the wrong shoulder, and perhaps you get the picture. The fact that such famous photographers were giving it a go is significant; that they floundered is even more so. The most curious thing is how neither gives any inkling of musical joy, and even the oddity is unnatural, contrived.

Perhaps the absence of so much as a smile does fit one side of the story. Kennedy had had enough of the classical circuit and the effect of its drudgery. He had split, amicably enough, from John Stanley, and while looking for another manager, was doing all the admin himself: 'If you're doing seven hours' phone work a day it's not very good for your central musical identity.' He'd also had enough of negative critique.

> When, like, every musician I'm playing with says I'm playing better than ever before, and then you get totally opposite opinions coming out in print, I think that has to be some mistake from the media profile or something ... I've got to look for a situation where it just works naturally.[1]

The problem with his neck was in some ways a useful catalyst for his self-imposed 'exile' from the classical world. And while he couldn't play the violin, he could still develop as a musician: 'It wasn't all negative – I got to try the cello and sax and got better on the keys.'² He was also trying out the guitar, even the mandolin. Asked by Charles Searson if he really had time to *study* such a range, he replied, 'Well, it's self-taught, but by listening to other people and seeing what they do, which is quite a valid tradition of tuition, I think, in other forms of music.'³

He also got to see all four seasons in his own garden, something he would repeat in 2020-2. It was a time for reflection. If the public portraiture was confused, this was a phase in which Kennedy could redefine himself on entirely his own terms. The scenario is in stark contrast to Menuhin's eventual predicament: 'The curiosity of my life ... is that I can pursue only what I am committed to.'⁴ Menuhin was hugely fulfilled, in many ways, but didn't have time to learn any music if he wasn't scheduled to conduct it. He was no doubt frustrated by Kennedy's 'withdrawal', but he would also have understood it.

Kennedy and Brix Smith were now living in the Malverns. Relocation to Elgar country came about through a chance meeting between Smith and Stephen Duffy, in New York, both being artists on the Fontana label. Duffy was a founding member of Duran Duran, later a co-writer of Robbie Williams's songs. He also formed the band The Lilac Time, the name of which was taken from the Nick Drake song, 'River Man', a song that Kennedy would include on his *SHHH!* album of 2010, the lyrics sung by Boy George.

> Going to see the river man
> Going to tell him all I can
> About the ban
> On feeling free.

The alternative 'plan' in the song is for 'lilac time', which perhaps matches Kennedy's Malvern time. When Smith and Kennedy visited Duffy's home in Malvern, they immediately loved the place, and decided to move to the area themselves, into 'Moon Sun House'. It was an escape from the pressure of London, and reasonably close of course to Villa Park. Smith bought a pug that they called Satchmo, after Louis Armstrong. Kennedy bought her a white pony, called Lucky. Ken Russell's depiction of Elgar on white pony, riding across the Malvern hills, comes to mind.

Had Kennedy 'given up' classical music? No, though he's threatened to on many occasions since. He was however giving prime consideration to his own personal projects, while also working with a range of contemporary artists.

His role as what might be called a 'session musician' started back in 1986. The term 'session musician' more properly applies to those who make such work their prime focus, but many star names have turned their hand to the jobbing role. Rick Wakeman worked on albums by Cat Stevens, John Williams and David Bowie. His keyboard contributions to Stevens's 'Morning Has Broken' (for which he was apparently paid a whole £10) and Bowie's 'Life on Mars' are fundamental to the character of those works. When Bowie died, and Nicholas Freestone, organist at St Alban's Cathedral, was moved to pay tribute, he was essentially playing Wakeman's keyboard part. Chris Nickol, organist at Kelvingrove Museum in Glasgow, followed suit; it became quite a thing.

Jimmy Page played guitar for Shirley Bassey, Petula Clark, Donovan, The Kinks, The Who, Jeff Beck, and more. Both Page and Wakeman – like Kennedy – might more properly be described as 'guest' or 'featured' artists, even if they were sometimes uncredited.

Kennedy seems to have been given full acknowledgement from the start. He had made sufficient headlines, and demonstrated both his musical excellence and maverick tendencies sufficiently to appeal to rock musicians looking to break the mould of their own, different world. They didn't just want 'some violin'; they were interested in the particular quality that Kennedy could bring to their creations. For his part, Kennedy was keen to work with those who, in his opinion, were bigger, more influential, indeed better *musicians* than many jobbing 'classicos'. These collaborations enabled him to take a 'supporting role', the very opposite of what was required of him on the concert stage in the 80s.

His first appearance as guest to 'rock royalty', as he describes them, was on the Kate Bush track 'Experiment IV'. The track was released as a single, and was the one 'new' track on *The Whole Story* album of 1986. He also appeared on the video, with actors such as Hugh Laurie, Dawn French, and Peter Vaughan of Peckinpah's *Straw Dogs* fame, but the video was considered by the BBC too violent to be broadcast on *Top of the Tops*; when Kennedy appeared on a related edition of the *Wogan* show, it was within a 'recreation'.

Kennedy and Bush would work together again on *The Sensual World* album of 1989. He plays violin on 'The Fog' and viola on 'Heads We're Dancing'. Dave Gilmour of Pink Floyd is another significant guest. The following year, Bush was one of the surprise guests when Michael Aspel captured Kennedy with his big red book on *This Is Your Life*. A further collaboration was on *The Red Shoes* (2011). Kennedy plays violin on 'Big Stripey Lie' and both violin and viola on 'Top of the City'. Once again, the further guest list was impressive, including Eric Clapton, Prince and Jeff Beck. It underlines how, in this rarefied sphere of popular/rock music, high level collaboration is if anything the norm.

Not everyone 'gets' Kate Bush, just as not everyone 'gets' Nigel Kennedy, but her reputation as a serious artist, working against the grain of many of her contemporaries, remains high. Kennedy would have admired her resolve to release 'Wuthering Heights' as her debut single, in defiance of EMI executives. Brendan Matthews, who teaches creative writing at a college in New England, makes a big deal of Kate Bush in his class on Emily Brontë because, he believes, 'Bush has spent decades defining a space for women artists as visionary creators'. This strikes me as fertile ground on many fronts, not only the matter of empowerment, but how artists and new artworks respond to the past; it opens up 'conversations about art, where it comes from, who it ignores, and who gets to make it'.[5]

Bush, like Kennedy, is often wonderfully 'over the top' – and unrepentant. For that quality alone, she's found favour in otherwise unlikely quarters. John Lydon, aka Johnny Rotten of The Sex Pistols, is an admirer. 'It's not about rolling in the money, it's about the joy of knowing what you have done has touched people's hearts. You just can't beat that.' 'She might be a bit wild for some, but those on the edges clearly gravitate to her like Pooh Bear to a pot of honey.'[6] As Matthews says, 'Kate Bush is authentically herself',[7] and is that not a prime requisite for any great artist? It's certainly something to appeal to Kennedy. Whether there should be a Kate Bush Masters Programme, as has been suggested, is another matter altogether.

Kate Bush was the first female singer to have a number one hit with a song of her own writing; as with Kennedy's solo classical recordings, his guest work was starting at the top. Next up was Paul McCartney, who asked Kennedy to play on 'Once Upon a Long Ago', with George Martin producing. McCartney equates the lyrics of the song with the 'cut-up' technique of William S Burroughs. It's a sequence of seemingly random, semi-meaningless lines that actually do make sense if you go with the flow. The individual lines also hold personal memories.

> 'Picking up scales and broken chords' refers again to why I never wanted to learn music, because it was 'da-da-da-da-da, da-da-da-da-da' – one five-finger exercise after another. I couldn't stand that. Bored the hell out of me. It put me off learning notation.[8]

The words also refer to anxiety dreams: 'playing guitars on an empty stage'. McCartney simply asked Kennedy for something 'romantic'. Kennedy's interpretation of that word was initially off the mark, unsurprisingly, perhaps, given that he was also working in the world of big romantic concertos. A much simpler, more Beatlish sense of romance was required.

Kennedy's contributions to such songs were often small, and low-key, but he always aimed to make a real connection with the material. Judie Tzuke was particularly grateful for the heartfelt quality of his input, as Dave Ling recounts:

> Judie has to stifle a tear as she recalls Kennedy's contribution to the 'Turning Stones' track 'Sound of My Sister's Tear'. 'I hadn't told him the song was about losing my sister because it was extremely emotional, but Nigel picked up on it and said, "I don't know what this is about but I believe it's extremely important to you". His string part makes me cry when I hear it. And he got really emotional about it too.'[9]

Their introduction was by a curious route. Tzuke writes, 'I was asked by *The Times* if I would review some CD players with him, and we got on really well.' She underlines her collaborative instincts – and frustrations:

I don't see Nigel's music as being alien to mine. In fact, I'd like to do more of that type of thing in the future. Working with classical artists or in film soundtracks is something that really appeals to me, but it's difficult to make people aware of the fact.[10]

On *Wonderland*, Kennedy was once again her guest, along with Brian May (on separate tracks). Kennedy's short violin solo rises birdlike above the dreamy synthesizer seascape of 'On a Ship'.

In between these delicate poetic cameos, Kennedy played a role in one of the most infamous albums of the 80s. Talk Talk may now bring to mind a cut-price phone and internet provider, but in the 1980s the name signified a highly regarded band that had enjoyed considerable success with their album *Colour of Spring*. Their next venture, however, was no commercial follow-up. *Spirit of Eden* proved to be a deeply controversial album: a work of genius or insanity; the jury is still out, though NME has ranked it in the top 100 albums of all time. Kennedy agrees, calling it 'one of the greatest albums of all time, in any genre', though he takes no significant credit for its status.

As led by Mark Hollis, the recording was more of a classic 'happening' straight out of the 60s. The studio was kept in near darkness for months; as engineer Phill Brown recalls, it was lit only by 'a 1960s oil projector, a strobe, and four sound-activated flashing disco lights'.[11] Everything was shaped from a basis of improvisation. What emerged were 'six improvised pieces full of space and unhurried rhythm, stitching pastoral jazz, contemporary classical, folk, prog rock and loose blues into a single, doggedly uncommercial musical tapestry'.[12] Fyfe Dangerfield comments: 'this was obviously what was inside Mark Hollis's heart, and it feels like it. There's no notion of the outside world at all.'[13]

Hollis cites influences that bear a marked similarity to Kennedy's favourites: Miles Davis, Bartók, Debussy. The *Spirit of Eden* album is considered to have paved the way for 'post-rock' bands such as Radiohead, though 'post-rock' is a pretty loose term; it was first applied to The Beatles.

Phill Brown explains the 'process' of the recording: 'There was very little communication with musicians who came in to play. They were led to a studio in darkness and a track would be played down the headphones.'[14] Each musician would improvise over eight, differently drum-tracked versions. Brown would then 'mix down the best bits to a master track ... Sometimes ... all we ended up with was a few seconds of music.'[15] Kennedy's input was one of the more substantial 'survivors'.

Brown had first worked at Olympic Studios in the days when Jimmy Page recorded advertising jingles there, John Barry film scores, and Hendrix created his famous cover of 'All Along the Watchtower'. On *Spirit of Eden*, Brown himself ended up playing guitar with a bow (a la Jimmy Page) – encouraged to do so by Hollis, despite having never played guitar in his life. 'It's easy ... and you've had 20 years of watching musicians. Just move your hands around like everyone else. It's all chance.'[16] Chance did indeed play a huge part in the work. As Brown recalls, Tim Friese-Greene at one stage tripped on the lead of his guitar, which crashed to the floor. 'After the playback we erased the guitar part but kept the accidental explosion at the end, moving it to a more desired location in the song.'[17]

The idea was to use the recording studio as an instrument in itself; synthesizers, however, were not favoured by Hollis: 'Unless things are played with that feeling and that heart, they're not worth anything.' If feeling was paramount, so too was freedom:

> Freedom is to me when you have no need to compromise anything you do. In a fully free society, everyone would have the choice to choose his own way, not driven by arrogance and selfishness, but with respect and compassion for the people around him.[18]

The appeal to Kennedy's own ethos is clear. Alan Wilder comments: 'The meticulous and sheer bloody-minded, anti-establishment approach speaks to musicians who care passionately about their craft but find themselves diverted from their vision by outside influences.'[19]

Kennedy spent his first two days of 'studio time' just drinking with the band in the pub, and his final contribution was laid down in 20 minutes. His initial improvisations, however, didn't meet with the band's approval. 'After trying to dissuade him from performing in his traditional classical style, they finally bound the fingers of his right hand together with gaffer tape.'[20] Keith

Aspen, the band's manager recalls their quibble – 'He played too fast and too many notes' – but says that 'Nigel was a really good sport and happily went along with it.'[21] He ended up adopting a lightly bowed, whispering sound, something that he's used on many occasions since. His contribution was at least used; many other artists, including a whole choir, were dropped from the final mix. According to an apocryphal Mojo anecdote, 'an entire orchestra's work had but one aspect kept – the sound of the trombonist clearing the saliva out of his instrument'. That's unlikely to be 'true', but on a metaphorical level at least, it seems too good to throw away.

If the album is 'heartfelt', even 'raw', and as Hollis says 'feels like seven guys playing live in a room',[22] its effect was constructed in laborious fashion: 'every note is placed where it is. The album is an illusion.'[23] Comparing that to the 'real live recording' (of Beethoven) in which Kennedy took such pride, the contrast could not be more stark. But Kennedy the perfectionist clearly respected the different, meticulous approach to crafting a soundscape, an approach that had the additional merit of breaking with any number of conventions. The album was, shall we say, guaranteed to divide opinion. As Wyndham Wallace relates, 'even Q – who praised its "damn the consequences" attitude – conceded it was "the kind of LP that encourages marketing men to commit suicide"'.[24]

Kennedy would no doubt also have applauded Talk Talk's consequent battle with EMI, who loathed the album and claimed in court that it wasn't 'technically acceptable';[25] this was a 'get-out clause' that resulted in termination of contract. After this debacle, however, the standard clause was modified, 'commercially satisfactory' becoming the typical requirement; a case of 'battle won' leading swiftly to 'war lost'.

*

When Kennedy first recovered from his neck operation, and had touring dates still to fulfil, Stephen Duffy accompanied him to Australia and New Zealand, 'playing a couple of songs to cut the amount of time he had to play the violin. You can imagine how that went down.'

> Whilst on tour we decided to make an album of songs joined
> together by improvised transitional pieces that would link
> them all together. It was to be called Music in Color, a phrase
> attributed to Syd Barrett that I read in an American magazine
> – hence the spelling – along the lines of: he left art school and
> gave up painting to make music in color.[26]

The phrase has many associations. Messiaen, who was also a
poet, famously saw and heard music in colours, and gave musical
instructions accordingly.[27] He described his chords as having
a 'rainbow' or 'stained-glass window' effect.[28] Van Gogh took
piano lessons specifically to learn more about tonal colour. The
singer Lisa Gerrard, who has composed and sung on various film
soundtracks, including *Gladiator*, says, 'When I do my scores, I
don't do them so that you read them: I do colours.'

> I spend a lot of time with that person's piece of music and I
> find the colours that happen and shapes. Then I know when it
> comes to me having to go to a studio, and I'm asked to impro-
> vise over the music, I have an understanding of what they do.
> I don't read it: I respond to the colours on the page ...[29]

Asked if she ever doubts her process, she responds: 'Sometimes
there's a certain amount of anxiety about singing but all it is is
waiting for the gate to open.' As Amanda Helen Roff points out,
Gerrard's phrase about gates 'calls to mind many others used in
the task of attempting to explain the creative process or a process
of enlightenment',[30] notably William Blake's famous phrase, 'the
doors of perception', taken up by Aldous Huxley – and Jim Morrison in naming his band, The Doors, more of which later.

Music in Colors (as it became, opting for the less interesting
plural), took a while to see the light of day, not least because of
Kennedy's delay in adding the string parts. 'I think we waited
a year' says Duffy.[31] Given that it was recorded in such isolated
instalments, it's more coherent than might be expected. There are
times when the joins seem to show – the first florid violin inter-
jection comes out of nowhere, but perhaps that was the point, and
it's clear that Kennedy gave real thought to how electric violin,
in particular, could be used in a variety of ways. It feels as if we're
back in a pseudo-Vivaldian laboratory. Kennedy's search for an
electric violin that was capable of realizing his ambitions took him

to David Bruce Johnson, who developed the violectra. Johnson's violectras are all hand-crafted, but Kennedy's (multiple) instruments are also customized – in Aston Villa colours, claret and blue. A more recent addition even featured Villa's gold lion crest, and the motto 'Prepared'.

I'm no synaesthete, I admit, but I don't find the songs themselves particularly redolent of colour, and the colour concept is somewhat trivialized by the artwork, which depicts a snack dispenser stocked with variously coloured bags of who knows what. It's a nice touch, though, to have 'featuring Dr Nigel Kennedy' as almost invisible text along the bottom of the machine. More vivid imagery is found in the lyrics: 'It Sparkles' opens well with 'The advent calendar of her eyes'; in 'Galaxy', 'The passing years leave vapour trails / or silver patterns like those of snails'. The album gets stronger as it goes on, and Kennedy's contribution is crucial. Perhaps the best track is 'Holte End Hotel', which refers to Villa's fabled Holte End stand where Kennedy, Duffy and Brix Smith were regular fans. (The stand was demolished in 1994 and rebuilt, following new safety principles in the wake of the Hillsborough disaster.) The simple lyrics are hauntingly effective:

> Holte End Hotel
> Where I live
> All year around
> In my dream
> Where I live
> By the ground
>
> I'll meet you where the lane from Witton stalls
> They hurry when the voice of football calls.
>
> Holte End Hotel
> Falling down
> Down down down
> Ballroom days
> Lochead plays
> Balding crown.
>
> I'll meet you where the lane from Witton stalls
> They hurry when the voice of football calls.

Listening to this, and other tracks on the second half of the album, I find myself thinking of The Lightning Seeds,[32] and the pop of that period that had *charm*. It's not just the footie ('Three Lions') connection, though it does make me think that Kennedy/Duffy could have really nailed a football anthem if they'd wanted to.

The planned transitoires on *Music in Colors* proved to be a useful solution to incorporating Kennedy's 'late' additions to the album. The solution worked well, and the transitoire would become an important component of Kennedy's later recordings, *A Very Nice Album*, and *The New Four Seasons*.

Stephen Duffy was also involved in what would become a long association between Kennedy and Donovan. Brix Smith was working on her second Adult Net album and needed extra material, beyond the songs she'd written herself. Encouraged by Duffy, she settled on a personal favourite, Donovan's 'Hurdy Gurdy Man'. Duffy played guitars on the track, Kennedy the violin. Their meeting with Donovan set a long friendship in motion, but the track itself caused problems. Kennedy demanded approval of the final mix, and Phonogram wouldn't run with it. In the end, the track appeared on the compilation album, *Island of Circles*, with Donovan covers by a variety of artists. Kennedy would later duet with Donovan on guitar for 'Eldorado', a song from the 1996 album, *Sutras*. A dozen years later, 'Donovan' would be the opening track on the Nigel Kennedy Quintet's first album, and in 2022 the musical partnership would flourish yet again.

Of all the rock royalty's rave reviews of Kennedy's contribution, Robert Plant's stands out. For his *Fate of Nations* solo album, he'd recruited some Indian musicians but was unhappy with their performance, so he got hold of Kennedy and says, 'this guy saved our lives'.[33] This is pretty high praise, considering that Kennedy is credited as playing on a single track. But it's the opener, 'Calling to You', and it sets the tone for the whole work. It's a hard rock number and Kennedy fits right in, his solo work towards the end of the track taking it full circle to its mystical beginning but with driving power.

The CD insert[34] has four central pages referring to the problematic state of the planet, notably the polluted air so many of us breathe; motor vehicles are portrayed as the main cause. The pages also highlight the human culpability for the amount of radioactive waste (from war) and acid rain (from burning fossil fuels) and the contamination of the seas (from oil spillages). In four accompanying images, two children and a teddy bear look on. Plant's song, 'Calling to You', questions where this is all going to end. It calls to all of us, with an insistent refrain.

It's the final two tracks, 'Great Spirit' and 'Network news', that are most explicitly anthems raging against 'environmental terrorism'. They stop short, though, of mentioning man-made global warming explicitly, so nothing for Kennedy to argue about. Also playing on *Fate of Nations* was Doug Boyle, who would become a regular guitarist for Kennedy's own projects. It was a rich period of musical connections that were set to last.

In August 1992, Kennedy was amongst musicians who gathered at Peter Gabriel's studio near Bath, to improvise together and record. The studio was conceived by Gabriel not just as a place to record, but to meet other artists, songwriters and poets, to exchange ideas and see what happened during 'recording weeks'. In the early 90s, dozens of artists from all over the world came to play. Present in that summer of '92 were Bill Cobham (drummer with Miles Davis and the Mahavishnu Orchestra), Massive Attack, Jane Siberry, and Alex Gifford (formerly saxophonist with the Stranglers). Kennedy played some quartets with Electra Strings (a trio including Caroline Lavelle): 'it was someone's birthday, and it was two in the morning, and the string quartets seemed just right for dancing to ... you can imagine the sort of thing', writes Clive Bell.[35]

Kennedy's own composition, 'Ginger', co-written with Sagat Guirey, is nearly thirteen minutes long, and comes across primarily as an improvisatory duet with saxophonist Andy Sheppard, plus Guirey on guitar, underpinned by Gifford on bass and percussion from Nana Vasconcelos. Kennedy writes:

> when you've got musicians like that all in the same room it's better not to go in with too many preconceived ideas. And when you're recording it's a shame if you're isolated in Perspex boxes. On this tune the dynamics were shaped by us as we played: it's just the sound of the encounter of those particular individuals in that particular room.[36]

Andy Sheppard was similarly happy with the process. 'Nigel played me the tune, I played it back, and two hours later we'd recorded it. No headphones or fancy separation, it was like a living-room situation. Nigel's improvising ability amazed me.' He also makes a telling comment about dealing with Kennedy generally: 'he's the only guy in the world who can be eight hours late and, just when you're thinking I've had enough of this, he arrives, and he just has to play three or four bars and you forgive him everything.'[37]

True to form, Kennedy did test people's patience on a number of occasions. There were improvised 'studios' throughout the property, including one on the lawn, and that didn't work too well when Kennedy decided to blare out 'Purple Haze' on electric violin from his open window. On another occasion he revved his battered BMW, splattering various people in mud. Small wonder that they took revenge and re-customized his Villa vehicle with white emulsion.

The 1992 recording week included Simon Jeffes, founder of the highly regarded Penguin Café Orchestra, a loose musical collective with a truly remarkable origin. Jeffes, best known in other circles as producer of the string arrangements in the Sid Vicious version of 'My Way', had an epiphany of sorts while in the South of France in 1972. It began when he was 'in bed delirious, sort of hallucinating for about 24 hours'. He had a vision in which all soul seemed to have leaked from the world. But this was then countered by a wholly different train of thought:

> A couple of days later I was on the beach sunbathing and suddenly a poem popped into my head. It started out 'I am the proprietor of the Penguin Cafe, I will tell you things at random' and it went on about how the quality of randomness, spontaneity, surprise, unexpectedness and irrationality in our lives is a very precious thing. And if you suppress that to have a nice orderly life, you kill off what's most important. Whereas in the Penguin Cafe your unconscious can just be. It's acceptable there, and that's how everybody is. There is an acceptance there that has to do with living the present with no fear in ourselves.[38]

This is also Kennedyland. When Kennedy talks about going *the other way* – away from the security of an Arts Council-funded life – he is essentially heading into the Penguin Café.

In the Real World café, serendipity loomed large. John Cage had just died, prompting Jeffes to come up with an homage, 'Cage Dead', on which Kennedy plays. The work riffs on the letters/notes within the two words of the title. Jeffes comments, 'I recognised his name as a strong melodic harmonic cell and quickly wrote this piece which simply spells his name in canon over four octaves, three durations and two transpositions a fourth up and a fourth down.'[39] Robert Sandall adds: 'Alongside this riffing on the CAGE theme, was a piano part playing the notes DEAD in free time.'[40] The beat poet Michael Horovitz just happened to be there, having 'arrived with a random busload of poets',[41] and his voice was recorded using a walkie-talkie. In length, the piece is an exact match for Cage's famous work, 4'33". Horovitz had been part of the 'International Poetry Incarnation' that hit the Royal Albert Hall in June 1965, with Allen Ginsberg, William S Burroughs and others, kick-starting a British counterculture movement. For Horovitz (whose hero was William Blake), poetry was 'a vital and democratic force that needed liberating from the academic world and the printed page'.[42] His mission was to bring poetry to the masses, but when he appeared in the Albert Hall again the following year, the event turned so rowdy that poetry events were banned there for eighteen years. Keith Emerson might have smiled. Horovitz had published the work of John Cage in his *New Departures* magazine, and would later edit McCartney's poetry collection, *Blackbird Singing*. He believed passionately in the close association of poetry and music, and campaigned for the Oxford Professor of Poetry position to be inclusive of both music and visual art. Ginsberg also made an effort on the same front, nominating Donovan for the role in 1967.

In 'Cage Dead', the composer's demise becomes the occasion for further creativity. Death plays a similarly pivotal role in a Horovitz poem, 'For Felix Mendelssohn'. The poet begins by saying 'how I'd love / to have been him', before realizing 'if I had been him, / I'd be dead.' It feels like a throwaway joke, but then it takes another turn, as Horovitz wonders 'perhaps I *was* / Felix Mendelssohn / in another incarnation / closed to me // — till now.' And as if that doesn't give us enough to think about, in terms of an artist's power to take hold of our lives, Horovitz moves on to further musings, seemingly simplistic, but profound:

Listening again
to his Songs Without Words on the radio,

it strikes me
that if I am indeed

anything like

a composer
I have to

stop talking   — and get on

with the music.[43]

In the Real World café, the 'busload of poets' were there as fellow musicians, their words aspiring to song.

'Cage Dead' may have been conceived in cerebral fashion worthy of Alban Berg, but it similarly transforms into something soulful. As a memorial piece, it gained new life when the *Union Café* album (2017), featuring the instrumental version of the song, was reissued to mark the twentieth anniversary of Simon Jeffes's death, from a brain tumour, a mere five years after his Real World appearance.

The Penguin Café Orchestra's musical offerings don't conform to any easy categorization. It's music that thinks outside of the box. The band and its various reincarnations are hardly household names, and yet retain a cult following. Certain tracks have been extensively used on film, television and radio, so it's possible that a very significant number of people have appreciated their music without having heard of them.

Brian Eno welcomed the Penguin Café Orchestra to his own label, Obscure Records, in 1975. He says of Jeffes:

> Given his individuality, his non-allegiance to any particular musical category, and the unfailing eclecticism of his vision, Simon Jeffes could easily be marginalised as an English eccentric – and thus sort of overlooked.
>
> The truth is he discovered a huge musical territory – stretching along the border regions of the whole United Nations of music – and he wandered through it fascinated and, apparently always smiling. These pieces are reports back from those borderlands.[44]

Those 'border regions' might equally apply to the Real World territory Gabriel established, and in which Kennedy took part.

A Real World album, *Arcane*, featuring work by Jeffes, Kennedy et al, was released in 1994. Kennedy also contributed to a further Real World album that emerged from the same gathering. *Dream* (1995), originally intended as a 'traditional' album of Indian music by the mandolin virtuoso Uppalapu Srivinas, became a collaborative work of improvisation, steered by Michael Brock. Kennedy plays on two of the four pieces, 'Dance' and 'Run'. Srivinas was heralded as a worthy successor to Ravi Shankar, and his work with Kennedy raises inevitable comparison to the Shankar/Menuhin partnership, and its meeting of Eastern and Western idioms. Once again, Kennedy seems to have been drawn, albeit almost by chance, to tread in his teacher's footsteps. But the nature of the collaboration certainly had no precedent. The various improvisations – by Kennedy, Caroline Lavelle, Nana Vasconcelos, Jane Siberry and others, sometimes in front of an audience – were recorded and later pieced together almost in Talk Talk fashion. Even recordings of Indian bicycle bells were added to the mix. As with many of the Real World solo albums, there is not so much as a title on the cover, going one step beyond Kennedy's 'just listen' idea.

Lavelle, primarily a cellist and singer, had worked as session musician with Massive Attack, The Fall, and with Radiohead on *The Bends*. At Real World, she made an interesting point about the limited role usually assigned to string players in such situations: 'We usually come in right at the end but this time there are some production ideas coming from us. String players don't get a chance to have ideas like most musicians.'[45] This greater creative scope came partly from Gabriel's generous concept, but Kennedy's presence made the very idea of 'relegating' string players a nonsense. The status of the session violinist had been transformed.

In his commentary on the week, Neville Farmer writes, 'Lavelle remembers Kennedy from her schooldays and wouldn't play with him earlier in the week. Now they are like sparring partners.'[46] She joined him on stage for the public concert given on the penultimate day (where various other artists, including Boy George, joined the throng), and on his wittily titled Heroes and Villans tour the next year. Kennedy subsequently contributed to her *Spirit* album of 1995, adding an eastern-tinged violin part to 'Forget the Few'.

A third Real World compilation album from the various recording weeks was finally released in 2008. Its title, *Big Blue Ball*, is a reference to an astronaut's description of planet earth. This is Gabriel's personal take on the phrase 'world music', namely, that 'All other divisions seemed ridiculous and arbitrary, because there's the planet, the whole thing.'[47]

Arcane is described as a 'WOMAD Production'. Gabriel was a major supporter of WOMAD (World Music, Arts and Dance) having created it in 1982, losing a small fortune into the bargain. He was also appreciative of Kennedy, and picked a Kennedy/ Kroke track as one of five new world music releases recommended and featured on a CD issued free with *Songlines: Top of the World* magazine No. 54. Kennedy later performed at WOMAD with Kroke in 2004. He would eventually refer to the festival as 'all corporate and painfully politically correct'.[48] He also criticizes the festival (and/or the BBC) for copyright infringement: 'they used one of my songs for their BBC transmissions without asking or crediting me. (If that had been done to a World musician there would have been an outcry.)'

The Real World connection is evident in several of Kennedy's other collaborative works produced during the 1990s: Jane Siberry, Nana Vasconcelos and Caroline Lavelle feature on *Kafka* (recorded with Peter Gabriel's producer Dave Bottrill). Kennedy also contributed to The Stranglers' album, *About Time*. Some might have viewed this as confirmation of Kennedy's punk tendencies, but from the start The Stranglers were an unusually 'musical' so-called punk band, with innovative bass playing by Jean-Jacques Burnel soon matched by captivating keyboard input from Dave Greenfield. Those two distinctive, creative forces remained, but vocalist Hugh Cornwell had been replaced by John Ellis and Paul Roberts by the time Kennedy (and Caroline Dale) joined them to record 'Face' in 1995. In truth, the band were past their best, though *About Time* is perhaps an underrated album, and 'Face' is one of the catchier tracks, nicely structured, with Kennedy's violin giving it a lift. The Stranglers both heralded punk and outlasted it, by a mile. They were still going strong in 2020, when Greenfield died of Covid-19.

Kennedy would continue with occasional guest appearances. The final one of the 90s was with Lukan, whose frontman Jamie Evans also had a Stranglers connection, having appeared as solo support act for Hugh Cornwell. But Kennedy's main focus was now on major projects of his own – bringing together many Real World musicians and others in support of his personal musical vision, first on *Kafka*, then *The Kennedy Experience*, his reworkings of Hendrix. First, however, there was a concerto to be played.

Frontiersman

> The way we are living,
> timorous or bold,
> will have been our life.[49]

These words from Seamus Heaney's 'Elegy' for his friend, the great American poet Robert Lowell, resonated deeply for me the first time I read them. They were instantly lodged in my repertoire of 'poetry by heart'. And they came to mind the moment I read the following words by Dave Heath, in relation to his violin concerto written for Kennedy in 1993.

> Alone at the frontier,
> alone where all is clear,
> no matter what they say,
> live your life your own way,
> don't be ruled by fear,
> follow me to the frontier

Heath's lines are less concise, and his message less nuanced: it's a clarion call 'to boldly go' (using as many split infinitives as you like), and makes clear that it's a lonely path. Heaney allows for the 'timorous' but in a way that still urges us to be true to ourselves. I say 'us', because Heaney's use of 'we' is a general address; he's not just talking about himself and his friend. Heath's words suggest something similar: should you venture, 'alone', to the frontier, you'll be joining a kindred spirit; you won't be alone at all. There'll be other penguins in the frontier café.

Heath and Kennedy first came together in 1979. Following Kennedy's admiration for his early work, *Out of the Cool*, Heath wrote *Rumania*, which Kennedy performed with John Lenehan at the Wigmore Hall in 1982. (Another of Heath's works from 1982, *Fight the Lion*, is dedicated to none other than Muhammad Ali.) Then there was *Let Loose*. There's considerable, mutual admiration: Heath considers Kennedy to be 'without doubt one of the most individual and emotionally expressive players who has ever lived';[50] Kennedy says of Heath's flute solo on *Kennedy Meets Gershwin*, that 'it's worth getting the album for that alone'.[51] In 1989 Kennedy performed *Out of the Cool*, rewritten for violin, with the Kansas City Symphony Orchestra. At Kennedy's request, the piece contained a two bar phrase that was repeated, to allow for Kennedy to improvise. Heath remarks that the improvisation was 'highly unusual, in that the sounds [Kennedy] produced from the [acoustic] violin, by the use of ponticelli and bowing effects, were almost electronic sounding'.[52]

Heath's comments about composition seem close to Kennedy's opinions and experience:

> There is intellect involved, but that's not my starting-point. Perhaps it's because I started as a flute-player. You begin by playing other people's music. As you progress you get a clearer idea of how you want to play, you want to control more things. It seems perfectly logical that you should end up wanting to write music. For me, a composer has to go out there and play to get a feel of what's going on.[53]

For his next concerto, Heath went further than *Out of the Cool*: the violin part would be wholly improvised throughout. 'Nigel's only request was that the piece should be "right to the edge of my musical imagination".'[54] As if this wasn't sufficiently experimental, Heath incorporated a beat box choir and raga sections, and staged the piece against an extraordinary visual backdrop, 'a 40ft high piece of graffiti street art'. Described by Heath as a 'street concerto', *Alone at the Frontier* was played (in its various incarnations) over three consecutive nights in 1993 by Kennedy and the Minnesota Orchestra, conducted by Edo de Waart. Improvisation was itself taken into new realms. 'Nigel at one point walked into the audience, gave his violin to a young fan and sat next to her listening to her play!----------outrageous and totally off the wall, but that's Kennedy for you.' According to Heath, Kennedy 'blew the roof off the place' and there was 'a 20 minute standing ovation at the end', though this is qualified by Ted Quanrud:

some of the audience was applauding, many others were
lustily booing or heading for the exit. Some of us were collapsed in our seats, convulsed with laughter over the silliness
and stupidity of the whole thing. [Heath] also fails to mention
that in addition to the (all-white) rap choir and graffiti daubed
backdrop by some 16-year-old, the performance also featured
the Minnesota Orchestra's percussion section armed with car-
penter's tools attacking a length of steel I-beam like a bunch of
maddened Gibichungs out of Wagner's Ring.[55]

The American critics were similarly savage in their opinions, and
the planned tour of the US was abandoned. Heath suggests that
the label of 'disaster' was one of the reasons Kennedy then stayed
away both from orchestral concerts and the US for some time.
But he stands by the work, his 'gift to Nigel'. 'The USA critics and
musical establishment are entitled to their views but for myself, I
am proud of what we did. This recording is hardcore, not for the
fainthearted, and represents Nigel at his most extreme.'

The film from the Minnesota event is sadly no longer available
on YouTube, nor are Heath's accompanying comments quoted
above, but remixed audio is available on Heath's own YouTube
channel. The score (of 136 pages)[56] details the instrumentation,
which includes a 'crasher' – 'two springy plates of sheet metal
which when hit sound like a cross between an electronic snare
and a whip', and 'a large industrial metal object (iron girder or
iron vat)'. There's a smoke box specified, and indication that the
lighting effects are operated by the conductor. Precise directions
are given with regard to amplification and electronic effects,
positioning of loudspeakers, and the soloist's path from podium
into the arena. There are instructions such as 'whole orchestra
stamp feet'; 'soloist jumps in the air – and as his feet hit the floor
everyone stamps (except perc)'; 'percussion ignores the rhythm
of the orchestra & vice versa'. As the piece draws to its end, the
choir sings the 'frontier' words as above; the 'soloist slowly walks
out of hall playing F blues scale (Hendrix style)'. It finishes with
the 'choir sounding like the sea'. Heath's final encouragement is
for people to 'Make the piece your own.'

Is that an incitement to musical chaos? Have the accepted
rules of composition been thrown out? I find myself thinking of
an episode of the comedy series *Black Books* in which Bernard

and Manny, despairing of the 'drivel' in children's books, decide to write one of their own. They limber up at their blackboard in the middle of the shop as if to splatter the rectangular space with ideas like Jackson Pollock filling a canvas. 'No rules' says Bernard. 'I get it – anything goes!' replies Manny, getting in the mood, but 'Nooooo!' screams back Bernard. It's a distinction perhaps too subtle for its own good: the difference between creative freedom and mindless abandon. It is easy to dismiss seemingly anarchic musical compositions, but one only has to look at Dave Heath's score to see how meticulously the 'anarchy' has been crafted. The amount of thought and preparation that goes into a 'disaster' can be immense.

The critical mauling of Heath's concerto is reminiscent of previous examples of outrage, such as the contempt for *Façade*, a collaboration between poet Edith Sitwell and composer William Walton in 1922. The staging, in particular, was highly provocative, Sitwell reading her poetry using a megaphone poking out through a screen. But the critical reaction provoked public intrigue – and therefore success through notoriety. *Façade* (primarily on account of the questionable poetry) has ultimately faded away, but the critics couldn't quash the public's fascination with something so *odd*. Today, critics seem to wield more power, and 'opening nights', certainly for expensive film or theatrical productions, dictate a work's fate.

When Paul Simon and the Nobel-prize-winning poet Derek Walcott collaborated on a musical, *The Capeman*, the critics were somehow determined to trash it, as 'one of the biggest flops in Broadway history'.[57] Simon was often cited as being disdainful of Broadway, having said in interviews that he hoped to reinvigorate what he saw as a stale musical form. Broadway music, he said, had 'ended up in a weird cul de sac – probably because it was never energized by rock and roll'. Theatre producer Rocco Landesman responded to Simon's statements: 'The idea that you can at a strike rewrite an art form is a little presumptuous. I can't say the people in the theater community were rooting for Paul Simon after all the things he said about Broadway.' Simon's 'disdain' is a pretty close match for Kennedy's 'contempt' for the classical music scene. But a staged concert – even one as outlandish as *Alone at the Frontier* – doesn't take the financial risk of a Broadway production. With sufficient will, it can probably limp on through its scheduled tour, though where would be the joy in that, if the sample audience had proved so resistant. Alternatively, it can vanish with a degree of grace, but perhaps no less disappointment for those whose artistic vision was invested.

Are we, today, more conservative, less open to the avant-garde than ever before? Stravinsky's *Rite of Spring* may have been ridiculed in *Le Figaro*, 1913, as 'laborious and puerile barbarity',[58] but it quickly came to be admired. To my mind, it would be a real privilege to witness the premiere of a ground-breaking work, be that *The Rite of Spring, Façade, Capeman, Alone at the Frontier*, or something as yet unimagined – even at the risk of angry bewilderment. But the critics don't want that. 'Drivel That They Paid to Hear'[59] wrote one critic of *Façade*, which is cynicism of the worst order, using a warped notion of financial prudence as the whip; it's calculated to deter us from imaginative curiosity, scaring us away from *odd* and steering us instead towards the bankable banal.

Tom Service makes the interesting observation that 'difficult' music, meaning dissonant music, is actually much closer to the sound world around us than is the artifice of classical harmony.[60] We should really find Dave Heath's sheet metal crashings easier to assimilate than a Mozart symphony. Dissonance is in any case a relative concept, which has evolved over time. As Grout states, 'chords that would have been unthinkable in the sixteenth century were accepted easily at the end of the nineteenth century'.[61] And yet, we seem to be fiercely divided in our tolerance, in ways that make little sense. Some have ears for thrash metal, but not Dave Heath; some have ears for Stravinsky, but not Nirvana. The Berg concerto has elements of dissonance to rank with anything in *Alone at the Frontier*.

But even if something seems 'laughable', isn't that something to relish anyway? Can't we enjoy sheer craziness, the *really wild* frontier? According to the joke – 'How many ears has Davy Crockett?' – the *wild front ear* is his third. Maybe members of the audience for the Heath/Kennedy concerto needed one of those. Or maybe The Third Ear Band should have been roped in, the rather brilliant improvisatory group that composed the soundtrack for Polanski's *Macbeth*, and opened the Rolling Stones' famous free concert in Hyde Park, 1969. Their second album, aka *Elements*, featured 'Air',

'Earth', 'Fire' and 'Water', the very same that comprise Kennedy's *Four Elements* album of 2011.

Kafka

The Real World, as it were, had confirmed Kennedy's belief in spontaneity, and not even the 'Frontier' experience diminished it:

> I believe absolutely in the spontaneity of the moment, however thoroughly an interpretation is planned. Whether a decision is made half-a-second before you play it or 10 weeks before, there's always room for manoeuvre. Improvisation doesn't really mean random, though someone like Thelonious Monk, or a classical equivalent like Alfred Cortot, can make it sound random and inevitable in the turn of two notes. That's because there's always an underlying purpose at work. A respect for structure. There has to be. I think you only really get to be free when you understand the importance of discipline.[62]

Kennedy's *Kafka* album of 1996 involved plenty of improvisation, but was also highly crafted. A couple of the tracks combine programming with live acoustic performance, something that Kennedy reckons was unusual at the time. The emerging 'theme' was that of change, and for Kennedy *Kafka* was a more engaging title than *Metamorphosis*. 'From Adam to Eve', co-written with Duffy and Brix Smith, is a song about gender transformation. 'Transfigured Night' is another song explicitly about change, set in the Malvern Hills. As with the Elgar t-shirt worn on the cover of *Let Loose*, the composer is still a presence:

> Hello Edward Elgar
> I feel your spirit here
> I'm here too
> Hills dark yet light
> Transfigured into something new

There's a dreamy quality to much of the album. It's a much more relaxed work than *Let Loose*, and a better one, more confident.

> For once I wasn't having to ask myself questions that the composer wasn't around to answer. That was strange – and liberating. I've always believed that presenting and nurturing

melody was one of the things I did best, so here was my chance
to get back to some basic melodic principles and be true to
them. That's something I've learned from musicians with
nothing to prove, musicians who knew how to be satisfied
with less, people like Miles Davis.[63]

The reference to dead composers doesn't entirely make sense,
because Kennedy was on a mission to arrange Jimi Hendrix
material. He wanted to include it on *Kafka*, but liaison with the
Hendrix estate proved too complex at that stage. The final *Kafka*
track, 'Breathing Stone', does use elements of Kennedy's later
Hendrix arrangement of '1983...(A Merman I Should Turn To Be)',
the title of which would have fitted the 'change' theme perfectly,
but it's a passing fragment, uncredited.

Kafka features not only the Real World mates (and some songs
are listed as 'copyright control/Real World Music') plus Stephen
Duffy and Brix Smith, but also Dave Heath, Doug Boyle, Donovan
– and Stéphane Grappelli, who is the only one given 'featured
artist' status, on 'Melody in the Wind'.

As indicated in Kennedy's comment above, melody was a
hugely important element of the project, and the crucial memo-
rability of a melody is something that he stresses: 'I start playing
these melodies on the piano then if I can remember it the next
morning I know it's a good song and if I've forgot it, it means that
it was shit.'[64] This seems like a pretty good test, and one that is
given further scrutiny by the poet Miroslav Holub. In his poem
'Brief Thoughts on the Theory of Relativity', Holub describes a
meeting of minds where poet Paul Valéry asks Albert Einstein
what he does with his thoughts: 'Write them down / immediately
they come to you? / Or wait / till evening? Or morning?' Einstein's
response is politely dismissive of the very question:

> Monsieur Valéry, in our craft
> thoughts are so rare
> that when you have one
> you certainly won't forget it
>
> Even a year after.[65]

Is the songwriter blessed with more frequent original thoughts?
McCartney, certainly, has produced a prolific stream of melodic
ideas that would seem to pass the 'sleep on it' memory test even

for the casual listener. But quite how 'Yesterday' or 'E=mc2' first came into being is much harder to grasp. For many of us, the beautiful simplicity of mathematical equations is bewildering, and I suspect that, for most people, musical composition is a similar mystery. In 2021, when we finally gained access to the extensive footage of the Beatles at work in Peter Jackson's documentary film *The Beatles: Get Back*, we were able to witness something of the 'mystery' playing out in real time. Mystery, in the best sense, remained, but to witness its manifestation was entrancing. It was particularly interesting how one person's initial idea (McCartney's) came to fruition as a result of the collaborative process, and the development of *Kafka* would seem to have been along the same lines.

Watching McCartney doodle his way into 'Get Back', you can see how the Hofner bass guitar was crucial to the thinking, but a particular instrument isn't always the focal point. Kennedy tends to avoid having the violin too much in mind when he writes, and Ruth Slenczynska makes a related point about Rachmaninov: 'One reason why [he] was so great as a teacher is that he did not think like a pianist, he thought like a creative artist ... He dared to do things that mere pianists don't do.'[66]

On *Kafka*, Kennedy plays not only acoustic and electric violins, but also viola, cello, piano, and mandolin. Some of the album's strongest melodies are also the simplest, and even if they are played on the violin, they don't originate in any violinistic virtuosity, quite the contrary. Melody, after all, is not driven by virtuosity; it needs space in which to breathe, and for the weight of every melodic movement – however light or brief – to be fully felt. Kennedy says: 'I'm looking at the gift of playing a simple melody, with the meaning it has. A lot of rock guitarists, or classical violinists, embarrass themselves when they have to play a simple melody and can't.'[67] And the simplicity principle applies to more than melody: 'even if I'm writing for an orchestra, I'll simplify it and make sure that it stands up as a song and isn't just technical. I like to speak from the heart.'[68] For *Kafka*, this principle affects the texture – and the way many of the individual songs emerge very quietly. And having emerged that way, they don't 'blow it' by going over the top. 'I like that essence of space. All music comes from silence in the first place and you need to be aware of that. Sometimes I've become tired of hearing myself play lots of notes, and when playing with others I'm often asking them to play less.'[69]

'Melody in the Wind' puts melody visibly in the title. The opening melody is extremely simple, with a phrase exchanged between two soloists. It's the simplest possible version of what Kennedy dealt with in his Menuhin School audition, responding to a melodic phrase with one of your own. The scrap of melody, passing from one instrument to another, is then taken – as if on the wind – to a higher realm, before the wind picks up, with the voices blown together, in unison, before that larger pattern repeats, then varies, and melody is pulled in any number of directions, and for however long Kennedy decides the wind should blow that day, before it subsides, and the melody comes back to rest. It works well with two violins, and the airy feel of it is perfectly suited to Grappelli, though the piece has been played by a number of co-soloists on different occasions: Mostafa Saad, for instance, took part when it was performed at the Proms in the Park, the same evening that the Palestine Strings joined Kennedy for *The Four Seasons* in the Albert Hall. But it's also been performed on the oboe (on the *My World* album of 2016), and as a violin/guitar duet with John Etheridge, on *Later with Jools Holland*, in the year of its release.

Perhaps the strongest of all the *Kafka* melodies is in 'Fallen Forest', a track that supposedly references Nottingham Forest's relegation from the Premier League. But that has to be a joke, unless Kennedy is a seer, since Forest weren't actually relegated until 1997, the year after *Kafka* was released. The more obvious connection to depleted woodland makes better sense, as the melody is haunting. It's once again simple, based around a triad in a pattern that repeats and falls, although the final movement is upward, so the sense of falling, and melancholy, resolves into a wistfulness. And as with many of Kennedy's melodies, it keeps moving – straight into a further development of the idea, a balancing melody in another fluctuating pattern. The accompanying harmonic shifts are as simple and subtle as the melody, the whole piece achieving a reflective beauty, with emotional power.

With various vocalists involved, some of the melodies on *Kafka* are indeed sung – and in a variety of styles. The whole

Holte End crowd contributes to 'I believe in God', a monotone chant built around the 'Ooh Aah' football chant that some will have heard rhymed with 'Cantona'; in Kennedy's song, 'God' is of course the Villa player Paul McGrath (though in a certain other ground at the time, God was Matt Le Tissier ;-). The accompanying electric 'violin jam' is more melodic; the two elements work well together and pack a real punch. On other tracks, Siberry and Lavelle's vocals are more narrative, and lyrical, without being particularly compelling melodically. It's the contribution by counter-tenor David Roscarrick-Wholey that is most remarkable, unexpected – and highly effective. It's also a statement of sorts by Kennedy about classical singing, which I'll say more about in Chapter 9. The counter-tenor voice is typically a 'pure' sound, less 'wobbly' than a mezzo-soprano or contralto. It bucks the trend of vocal expectations; and in that respect it's counter-*cultural*. A man singing in what is generally regarded to be a woman's vocal register can be disconcerting. The most disturbing example is the castrato. In the sixteenth century, when women were excluded from church choirs or the stage, gifted boy singers were castrated before puberty, extending the life of their high voice at the expense of their sexually mature life as an adult, a classic case of prioritizing – with barbaric pragmatism – a youthful gift over natural development, creating a monster. In those terms, the word falsetto (false voice) seems appropriate, but there are of course natural means of achieving falsetto, as demonstrated not only by the many classical counter-tenors such as the superb Andreas Scholl, but also soul and disco groups of the 70s, such as The Stylistics and The Bee Gees, and the many pop and rock singers who use it as part of their vocal technique, such as Freddie Mercury and Justin Hawkins. On *Kafka*, the counter-tenor seems to hail from an era far removed from the other musical influences; they come together in a way that is transformative, resulting in a work that resists any easy musical or historical classification.

With *Kafka*, there was also an 'EP' release, *Autumn Regrets*, with three of the main album tracks plus 'Mixamorphosis I'. The asterisked sleeve note reads: '* This music is from the album "KAFKA" available now for loads of money.' That seems to be a less than veiled comment about the general price of an EMI album. EMI seem to have run with it, or perhaps not noticed.

The Kennedy/Hendrix Experience

When Jimi Hendrix arrived in London in 1966, many fell under the spell of his hypnotic guitar playing. Freddie Mercury, having seen Hendrix perform 'Hey Joe' on the BBC, saw him live at least fourteen times within a few months. The attraction was three-fold: his extraordinary ability as an instrumentalist; the innovative nature of the music he played; and the charisma with which he presented it. That combination is rare indeed, especially when all three elements are perfectly bonded. You can see why an ambitious writer/performer would want to learn learn learn. At age eight, at the Menuhin School, Kennedy was obviously not following Hendrix around the country as Mercury and others did so obsessively. In fact, it wasn't until he was sixteen or so that he was even aware of Jimi Hendrix. For Kennedy, back in the sixties and early seventies, music 'had to have a violin in it', so his favourites were 'the Mahavishnu Orchestra, Flock, Family, groups like that'. It was the link with jazz that led to his interest in soul, rhythm and blues, and more psychedelic rock. He realized that Hendrix was an exceptional figure within that world, but was still 'more impressed by John McLaughlin ... because his chord sequences had more in common with classical music and jazz, while Jimi's were simpler'.[70]

Kennedy was intrigued when he first heard the Kronos Quartet playing 'Purple Haze'. 'I thought it was great that a string quartet was doing it, but immediately I could imagine loads of different ways of playing it.'[71] His affinity with what Hendrix created was not guitar fixated or even dependent, although he acknowledges the significant role of the electric guitar in the twentieth century: 'I think that sense of line has been developed on the guitar more than on any other instrument this century.'[72] There have inevitably been many guitarists covering or 'imitating' Hendrix, but Kennedy reckoned that a violin would offer a more interesting angle. At the same time, he felt the 'classical' approach of the Kronos Quartet lacked the necessary rhythmic drive. Just as Hendrix was pushing the guitar towards 'orchestral' sounds, the violin and other strings could be used in new ways.

As Kennedy tells it, The Hendrix Foundation contacted him after he went on a kids' TV show and played 'Purple Haze'. His version of 'Fire' then appeared on a Hendrix tribute album, *Stone*

Free (1993). As mentioned above, he had intended a number of Hendrix arrangements to feature on *Kafka*. Releasing them on an album was postponed, but the six tracks were ready for his comeback recital in 1997, played by The Kennedy Collective, and would emerge as *The Kennedy Experience* album in 1999. For the cognoscenti, it's obvious enough, but you have to look quite hard to find reference to Hendrix on the album insert. It's right down at the bottom of the page of small-print acknowledgements: 'Written by Jimi Hendrix (1942-1970) / Used by permission of Experience Hendrix'.

While Kennedy's *Four Seasons* had capitalized on pop's three-minute character, the tracks on *The Kennedy Experience* go totally the other way. The longest is over fifteen minutes. Unsurprisingly, none of the album got airtime on British radio.

Interviewed by Neville Marten for *Guitarist* magazine in 1999, Kennedy looks and sounds exceptionally focused, and lucid, offering more technical detail about his work than he tends to in relation to classical music:

> I use [the electric violin] either with a Boogie head and a Marshall 4x12 or the other way round, because I like to have the warmth of one and the brightness of the other. I like to use old pedals, and I've got a Crybaby wah-wah, set at different angles for different sounds.
>
> On the Hendrix album, I used the acoustic violin with a bit of 'imagination' afterwards. For the live versions it's an acoustic with an LR Baggs pickup at the bridge, so I can go through all my pedals. But I like it simple; I don't want to end up with a rack, where I've got to be a computer scientist to deal with it. But, the old stuff sounds better through a violin; it triggers all these things in a different way.[73]

Not every violinist would be remotely interested in this attention to the electronics; Kennedy however is enthusiastic about it as an integral part of music making. But although his Hendrix excursions began as 'a power trio-ish scenario', with Kennedy playing electric violin over the top, and he still goes electric when he chooses, his first recorded Hendrix pieces went the other way. As he says, 'when I'm playing electric violin, my style veers more towards the Santana type of sound than Jimi's. So a lot of [*The Kennedy Experience*] was done using the acoustic violin.'[74]

He inevitably mentions the famous Hendrix 'stacked fifths', which he compares elsewhere to Bartók's harmonies based on similarly stacked intervals. His approach is to play them 'four or eight times as slow', making 'harmonic relationships out of that over the root harmonies that he's got in his songs'.[75] It's a way of using Hendrix material to form something that sounds, at times, remarkably different. Another major reason for the difference is the fact that Kennedy's arrangements don't use drums; the rhythm is achieved by the ensemble playing, and the acoustic nature of the ensemble accentuates the effect. Asked how 'the Purple Haze chord and other Hendrixisms translate to the violin', he answers:

> It's quite good because that hacking thing, you can do that with the bow quite animatedly and with a fair amount of aggression. When you hear strings whacking away like that it's as exciting as an electric guitar. But Jimi was inventing that and there was an emergency to it. To recreate that same energy, I don't think you could do it on the electric guitar again. It's good transferring it to players who are doing it for the first time on instruments that don't usually do it. To give it that same sense of discovery and aggression.[76]

Hendrix's own brand of aggression was particularly sinuous, and Kennedy mentions the crucial variety of influences he brings to his interpretations, 'a mixture of jazz discipline and classical, with a slight rock sensibility from my own playing'.

> I love timing in music and I think that looseness is all about timing and the way the lead voice relates to the engine-room of the band, which in my case is the guitars and bass. It's the way that you play over that stuff; behind the beat, which is more my natural disposition as well. Then you get that great tension between what's making the thing work and what's pulling it around.[77]

His ensemble reflected that creative mix. The more classically trained members had their parts fairly extensively notated, while the bass and guitar parts were more improvised. But the 'whole' was still flexible. 'I've got certain figures which I can call up with hand signals, so it doesn't have to be the same every time. Sections can go round and round...'[78] Once again, the 'project' was both collaborative and personally driven – both in terms of interpretive vision and performance.

In the programme note for the 1997 recital, Kennedy refers to the 'Hendrix Concerto ... I am writing which is still in development'.[79] At other times he has talked of a 'Suite'. It would seem to be an ever-evolving concept that manifests itself in various ways at various times – notably in the six-song *Kennedy Experience* and *The Four Elements* (more of which later), but also in endlessly varied concert encores. *The Kennedy Experience* got no airtime on British radio because it didn't fit any of the categories. There's a sense, perhaps, that *The Kennedy Experience* falls between two potential directions: the concerto-style ambition (perhaps still a masterpiece waiting in the wings) and the individual songs that might be more popular were it not for their length.

I say 'songs', but Kennedy's Hendrix pieces do not generally include any lyrics. The exceptions are the Hendrix-influenced parts of *The Four Elements*, but their lyrics are newly written. Kennedy's renditions of Hendrix songs put both vocal melody and guitar parts into his violin mix, with the original lyrics becoming seemingly irrelevant. I, for one, am not at all bothered by that. If I look at the lyrics, I'm not hugely impressed. They are not the reason for Hendrix's fame. Monika Dannemann, Hendrix's close friend, feels differently. She also cites the fact that some of the lyrics were improvised, and those of us who have been involved with jazz and poetry events know how difficult that is to pull off.

The Kennedy Experience doesn't, in my opinion, focus on the 'line' that Kennedy mentions, and reveres. As mentioned above, there are other aspects of Hendrix's 'genius' that are worked. Kennedy would later show great skill in transferring a vocal line to the violin, his version of the George Harrison song, 'While My Guitar Gently Weeps' being a good example. 'Voice' can transfer, very effectively, between one 'instrument' and another. Gesualdo's madrigals, for instance, were sometimes performed by viols rather than voices. But *The Kennedy Experience* is at a slight remove from either vocal or guitar line. It's Hendrix's inner, 'poetic voice' that comes to the fore.

It's interesting, however, to encounter versions of Hendrix songs on which Kennedy plays that do preserve the lyrics. There are three on Jarek Śmietana's 2009 album, *Psychedelic*: 'Fire',

'Little Wing', and 'Crosstown Traffic' (which is otherwise unre-corded by Kennedy). All three offer a very different account of Hendrix, and of Kennedy's interpretation, since he is no longer responsible for the lyric line.

If Hendrix's lyrics generally are of little great worth, a couple of lines stand out for their relevance: 'I have only one burning desire, / Let me stand next to your fire.' That's what Kennedy and others who have fallen under the Hendrix spell desire most of all. Some outstanding musicians, guitarists in particular, have bowed down in awe of Hendrix. Both Brian May and Pete Townshend have said how he made them feel they either had to *shape* up or *give* up. Freddie Mercury didn't have that worry; he wasn't a guitarist. Nor is Kennedy, whose admiration seems altogether more free to follow its own direction, if still in close proximity to the fire.

When The Jimi Hendrix Experience played their 'electric church music' in Stockholm, January 1969, Hendrix gave what was prob-ably the most bizarre of all his eccentric introductions to a song. 'Spanish Castle Magic' was 'recorded in 1733 ... from the Benjamin Franklin studio'. Wtf? It began to make sense, possibly, when he dedicated another song ('Voodoo Child') 'to all those people who can actually feel and think for themselves and feel free for themselves'. The anti-authoritarian Franklin would certainly fit that description. But 1733 is an intriguing date, the year Handel, for the first time, reworked a biblical story, 'Deborah and Athalia'. That might seem a meaningless connection, but in 2016 'Handel and Hendrix in London' was established as a joint museum, the composer of 'electric church music' matched with an acknowl-edged musical 'great'. Handel had lived at 25 Brook Street, in Mayfair, and Hendrix lived next door at number 23, albeit two centuries later. The 'Hallelujah Project', as it was rather hilariously called, has restored the Brook Street properties and is presenting Hendrix memorabilia as significant archive material, an import-ant musical story. Amongst Hendrix's personal record collection, preserved in the apartment, there were, rather remarkably, two copies of Handel's *Messiah*, as well as those of Dylan and The Beatles. *Sergeant Pepper* is the most worn of the hundred odd albums. Hendrix played a version of the title track as the opening number of his gig at the Saville Theatre, just three days after the album had been released, a feat that, while not perhaps rivalling Mozart's memorizing of Allegri's 'Miserere', was nevertheless remarkable. McCartney, who was in the audience, considers it one of the greatest honours he has ever been paid.

Kennedy has often cited James Marshall Hendrix as one of the great 'classical' composers. With the establishment of the museum, his assessment would seem to have received official endorsement

Excess

Writing about Hendrix in 2000, Robert Wyatt, who toured with The Experience in 1968, said, 'He was very scared of being boring.'[80] Echoing that feeling, Freddie Mercury said, before he died: 'You can do what you want with my music, but don't make me boring.'[81] But perhaps the figure who personifies that attitude – with all its attendant trials and tribulations – is the famous hellraiser and drummer with The Who, Keith Moon.

It was in the Berlin Hilton, 1966, that Moon developed an inclination to destroy hotel rooms and throw furniture from the windows, on one occasion specifically a television into the hotel pool, an act that Kennedy would replicate at the Berlin Grand Esplanade in 1992. If you're looking for a further chain reaction, on-stage rather than off, there's Townshend abusing his guitar, followed by Hendrix setting fire to his (though this was in fact at his manager's urging), and Kennedy following suit in the abortive attempt to burn his violin.

There's a considerable urge to copy or tread in the footsteps of our heroes. Even the trailblazers have their influences. Keith Moon's idiosyncratic drumming bears an uncanny resemblance to that of jazz drummer Gene Krupa. And Moon's general behaviour (if anything so wild can be called 'general') seems to be modelled on the piratical persona of actor Robert Newton. On one level, it all *makes sense*. But Moon took 'bad' public behaviour to hitherto unknown exhibitionist heights. 'Everything you've heard about Keith Moon is 100 per cent true, and you've only heard 10 per cent of it',[82] says Alice Cooper, who took to hiding when he knew Moonie was in town. Townshend, interestingly, had no truck with Alice Cooper, as he fell for the stories about chickens being beheaded onstage. You shouldn't always believe what you read in the press.

Kennedy has deliberately followed in some of his rock heroes' footsteps. In 2005 he finally achieved his mission to play at the Cavern in Liverpool, as the Beatles had done. Unfortunately, the occasion was marred by the theft of his electric violins while his band were having a meal in Chinatown; they were only recovered seven years later when they came up for auction. But five years earlier, another, bigger dream was realized when Kennedy was one of the star guests joining The Who at the Royal Albert Hall. He played the violin part on 'Baba O'Riley', a version of what featured on the album *Who's Next*. Keith Moon was long gone by the year 2000, but Kennedy's involvement owed everything to Moon, as it was he who had initiated the violin solo (and produced it), having persuaded Dave Arbus, violinist with the band East of Eden, to be part of the recording.

In a trivial way, I know first hand the desire to connect with that rock star world. In 1983 I wrote to Pete Townshend, when he was associated with Faber poetry. Perhaps I was taking my cue from Heaney's lines already quoted: 'The way we are living / timorous or bold / will have been our life.' Bold it had to be. 'Good stuff' replied The Who's guitarist to my poems, on his Eel Pie letterhead. It means a lot to have a frontiersman take note of what you're doing, when you're otherwise in the wilderness. Townshend was of course the intellectual in the band; imagine Moonie's response. Moon, in California, living next to Steve McQueen, was himself courting favour with some of Hollywood's heavyweights. He hoped that Sam Peckinpah – the ultimate maverick in the movie world – would remake *Soldiers Three*, with Moon, Ringo Starr and Harry Nilsson. (The original had starred Moon's hero Robert Newton.) Sometimes, though, the eccentricity squared formula just doesn't work.

Moon's friend and minder Dougal Butler writes, 'Moonie is a lunatic but he's right in the tradition of great British eccentrics.'[83] That gives him Tristram Shandy credentials, but Moon somehow blew them, just as he did his own drum kit on repeated occasions. 'He was trying to make people laugh and be Mr Funny, he wanted people to love him and enjoy him, but he would go so far. Like a train ride you couldn't stop.'[84] Some would say that Kennedy's eccentricity and his determination to have a good laugh goes similarly way beyond a joke. It is perhaps the nature of comedy to tread a path close to tragedy. But tragedy in the original sense is no accident; it's inevitable. Moon's death may have resulted from a confluence of chance factors, but it was also the conclusion of a self-destructive arc. It was certainly a great loss to the band and the music world more widely. For a while, no one could adequately substitute for his drumming, including (by his own admission) Kenny Jones. It was eventually Ringo's son, Zac Starkey, who would get somewhere close. Almost a quarter-century later, Kennedy's *Kafka* bass player, Pino Palladino, faced a similar challenge in taking over from John 'The Ox' Entwhistle, whose heart attack was related to his consumption of cocaine.

Kennedy would make further forays into the world of 'classic' rock, notably with *The Doors Concerto* of 2000, exploring Jim Morrison's music, which I'll talk about further in the next chapter. But 'the doors' in a metaphorical sense, had been opened. In 1992 Kennedy commented, 'At some point, I'll have to think about whether it's my responsibility as a musician to get into heavier drugs simply to find out more about music.'[85] It was a somewhat provocative remark (and some were quick to rise to the bait in ways that Kennedy deplored), but it smacked of a serious link to the heroes who, in Kennedy's view, had achieved such great things: Hendrix, The Who, The Doors.

The Doors took their name from Aldous Huxley's book of 1954, *The Doors of Perception*, itself a reference to a work by the poet William Blake, *The Marriage of Heaven and Hell*: 'If the doors of perception were cleansed everything would appear to man as it is: infinite.'[86] Huxley is also the name of Kennedy's Weimaraner dog. Huxley (the author) writes about his experience of taking the drug mescalin, and listening to a variety of music under the influence. His comments about the works of the sixteenth-century composer Carlo Gesualdo are particularly interesting. Gesualdo, Prince of Venosa and Count of Conza, wrote music that was at once sublime and utterly unlike anything else of its era. The chromatic harmonies are almost Wagnerian. But Gesualdo also presents us with a problem that is now more pertinent than ever. He murdered both his wife and her lover but was, astonishingly, acquitted of any crime. Does that affect our judgement of his music? The current wave of 'cancel culture' would suggest yes. Historically, however, there's a case for suggesting the opposite, that notoriety of the worst type has provoked our interest. As Alex Ross comments,

> If Gesualdo had not committed such shocking acts, we might not pay such close attention to his music. But if he had not written such shocking music we would not care so much about his deeds. Many bloodier crimes have been forgotten; it's the nexus of high art and foul play that catches our fancy.[87]

The same might be said of Keith Moon. The outlandish behaviour seemed essential to the musical style, and effect. And yet it surely went too far. Isn't that the risk, that chaos comes to reign, to the detriment of art – and even human survival? That everything meaningful falls apart? Huxley's acknowledgement of this, with regard to Gesualdo's 'chaos', is revealing:

> 'And yet', I felt myself constrained to say, as I listened to these strange products of a Counter-reformation psychosis working upon a late medieval art form, 'and yet it does not matter that he's all in bits. The whole is disorganized. But each individual fragment is in order, is a representative of a Higher Order. The Highest Order prevails even in the disintegration. The totality is present even in the broken pieces. More clearly present, perhaps, than in a completely coherent work. At least you aren't lulled into a sense of false security by some merely human, merely fabricated order. You have to rely on your immediate perception of the ultimate order. So in a certain sense disintegration may have its advantages. But of course it's dangerous, horribly dangerous. Suppose you couldn't get back, out of the chaos...'[88]

Also focusing on Gesualdo, Mark Steinberg of the Brentano Quartet comments that 'although mescaline is perhaps inappropriate in a public concert setting, the music alone may inspire such reveries in those with the right combination of attention and sensitivity'.

> Startling juxtapositions and contrasts, discontinuities and disruptions had been a part of Gesualdo's expressive arsenal from the start. But, just as we all know of people of strong

character who come to be more completely themselves as they age (in fact, it seems to be a truism), so do the madrigals in the final book, Book VI (1611), exhibit an even greater density of these characteristic moments such that they do, indeed, threaten to whirl into chaos. The amount of emotional turmoil we can precariously contain within our lives is on occasion fantastically large. At times we feel we just barely manage to cheat the forces of collapse.[89]

Sometimes one's lifestyle choices get in the way of art. Sometimes art gets in the way of one's personal life. And sometimes, lifestyle and manic art are so inextricably entwined, that they thrive while destroying everything around them. Keith Moon is flailing away somewhere within that picture, though somehow still defying quite *where*. Anyone tapping into that eccentric *modus vivendi* is taking a big risk. Even Jim Morrison, who died aged twenty-seven – like Hendrix, Janis Joplin, Brian Jones, Kurt Cobain and Amy Winehouse, the list is extraordinary – had a more measured, philosophical view of things when he sang, in *An American Prayer* (1978): 'O great creator of being, grant us one more hour to perform our art and perfect our lives.'

1996, the year of *Kafka*'s release, was a big year for Kennedy. Aston Villa won the League Cup, and Kennedy became a father, his partner Eve Westmore giving birth to Sark Yves Amadeus. Yes, the son of the violinist famed for outrageous behaviour as well as phenomenal musicianship was given the same middle name of the 18th-century composer famed for the same two traits. Mozart's middle name was itself a playful adaptation of his christened name Theophilus, 'loved by God'. But he didn't seem so blessed when his own first child, left at home with a nurse while he and his wife took a trip to Vienna, died of an untreatable fever. Three more of their children failed to survive infancy; that was the nature of the times. Two sons who did survive both had a reverential attitude to their father. Young Karl would sit in Mozart's study, mesmerized, watching him compose. The sons were clearly tolerant of the flip side to his behaviour.

Mozart loved to party, and let most of his earnings slip away. The giggling, filthy-minded child, as Peter Shaffer portrays him in *Amadeus*, was like a prototype Moonie in that respect. But Keith

Moon took parenting to a new level of neglect. Strangely, his daughter, Mandy, doesn't rate him as either a good or bad father; he was simply not there, which on any normal scale counts as bad, but in Moon's case was probably for the best. When he once threw a wine bottle in the rough direction of his wife, a piece of the smashed glass cut his daughter's face. She nevertheless wishes she had got to know him better.

Am I comparing Mozart and Moon as musicians? Of course not. Moon himself identified as a drummer rather than a musician. And yet, as Kennedy likes to say, The Who 'changed the course of music',[90] and Moon was a vital element of the quartet. It's entirely possible that more people know of him than they do of Wolfgangus Amadeus Mozartus, as the composer self-identified.

Kennedy may have aped some of Moon's antics, but he has always had an utterly different, responsible attitude as a father. His split with Eve Westmore raised the possibility of Sark lacking a father figure, just as Kennedy himself had suffered. But 'my son comes first',[91] he said when Sark was four, and he was organizing his touring around his access time. He was also concerned about his son's education – from when Sark was only three. At the risk of being seen as 'a bit of a fucked-up old Tory underneath',[92] he insisted his son should go to a school that offered real *structure*. And he used that same word in regard to music education: 'I'd prefer him to study guitar or piano first, to get a feel for structure and harmony.'[93] That was balanced, however, with a sense of musical fun: 'he was given a trumpet for his birthday. We took him to the Villa-Chelsea cup final, and he was the only one of us that could make a noise with it!'[94]

By 2021, Sark was facing a jail sentence for alleged dealing in cocaine, which undoubtedly put a strain on the relationship with his father. It's not for me to comment on that here, except to note the darker places to which chaos may drag us.

'Suppose you couldn't get back', wrote Huxley, back to the future, as it were. It's a big risk. The more recklessly you adventure, say, within a cadenza, the more difficult it will be to return to the safety of the written score. And the path back from a wild-man reputation is similarly fraught. In Hendrix's case, the path was frequently blocked by his manager, Mike Jeffrey. Hendrix's first guitar breakage was an accident, which prompted him to smash the instrument in rage, and the audience reaction encouraged Jeffrey to demand more of the same. It was largely an exploitation, and those who gave Hendrix drugs he didn't want, and spiked his drinks, were also to blame in building an image from which it was hard to escape. But he desperately wanted to. Even Keith Moon, in his final year, was trying to stop drinking and regain some control. It proved too hard, too dangerous in its own right.

When Keith Moon died in 1978, from an overdose of a drug intended to address the effects of withdrawing from his alcohol addiction, I was back-packing through Montana. An open-topped jeep pulled up at the side of the road, and the bearded rocker in mirrored shades yelled out, 'I've just heard the news. I've chucked my job, and am heading for Alaska. Wanna ride?' His total luggage appeared to be a spade. On that occasion the timorous me was in charge.

Who Are You?

Behind Zak Starkey's blue eyes
there's Uncle Keith, headphones taped to his head
as if awaiting ECT, explosives
hidden in his drums.

Another legend wakes
in a Soho doorway. Policemen,

they're learning your name too –
in London, Warsaw, Frankfurt, Berlin,
Madrid, New York...

You flick your bow in the air, deft
as Moonie twirling a drumstick
like a magician before he
smacks it into place, perfect
-ly in time with his own wayward sense of the beat
; crash; cr-
ash, and burn...

At the Albert Hall it's for 'Baba O'Riley'
that you get in on the act you've always revered,
taking the (dreaded) harmonica solo
back to its roots
and beyond.

The rehearsal starts badly.
You're Daltrey's guest
so Townshend's in a mope

but the performance is a triumph –
your final thrash of the bow
an absolute match
for the guitarist's trademark jump.

The Ox, on bass, is simply breathing in and out.

Townshend: 'Nigel Kennedy!'

You've never been happier.

But still – 'Who *are* they, who *are* they'
sing the opposition.

Daltrey turns the mic
to the audience – us – and wants to know
'Who the fucking hell are *you* –
you, you, you, you, you, you, you, you-u-ou!'

Chapter 7: Bach to the Future

In the excitement of communication with his audience, Nigel went perhaps a little too far; but it is my hope and belief that thanks to his classical training he will find his balance again.—Yehudi Menuhin

People talk about our dumbed-down culture. But when 5,000 people pay to hear Bach played on a solo violin, there's hope for Western civilisation.—Richard Morrison

Menuhin's comment, above, was published in his revised auto-biography of 1996, the year before Kennedy's 'comeback' recital. Menuhin may well have felt vindicated by that comeback. He died two years later, in Berlin, the same year that *Classic Kennedy* was released. That year however also marked the release of *The Kennedy Experience*: Kennedy's return to classical discipline was matched by an equally disciplined reimagining of Hendrix. Menuhin would probably have applauded both, just as he surely marvelled at Kennedy's Bach/Bartók/Hendrix recital combination.

It's possible that some fans, having nodded at Kennedy's criticism of the classical establishment, and preferring his *Kafka* mode, saw the so-called comeback as selling out. But when I hear that phrase, I always remember film director Monte Hellman preferring to call it 'buying in'. Kennedy was 'back' – but on his own terms. His recital presented a radical new take on a type of classical concert that had sometimes proved tedious even for the most conservative of musicologists. In *The New Musical Companion*, Eric Blom comments that violin recitals, in particular, 'tend much more to become exhibitions of executive personality than of music as such'. He bemoans the narrow repertoire, and

a certain traditionalism that seems ingrained in most fiddlers, who would rather play Bach's Chaconne for the hundredth time than dig out an almost certainly less imposing but fresher work. And the Chaconne itself has often shown that violinists are too apt to expect their public to find fiddling interesting in itself, simply as a feat and a science, for they seem quite

oblivious of the fact that unless this masterpiece is performed
with the uttermost perfection it remains a lifeless abstraction
and, it must be confessed, a sore trial to the mind and ear
alike.[1]

All of this Kennedy turned on its head: the narrow repertoire;
the (absurd) notion of 'uttermost perfection'; and the idea that
personality is exhibited at the expense of the music. Bach was at
the heart of it, and Kennedy has become increasingly outspoken
about the composer's music and its legacy.

Fast-forward: In 2011, Roger Wright, director of the BBC
Proms, invited Kennedy to play solo Bach for a whole (late night)
concert. Kennedy responded, 'Well, that evening won't exactly be
a holiday – but it's a challenge I can't refuse.'[2] He added, onstage,
that he'd had to lay off the booze for at least a week, in order to
prepare. It was the first time a solo Bach concert had ever been
scheduled in the Royal Albert Hall. Some were quick to complain
that it wasn't a whole concert of solo Bach: Kennedy came on
stage saying what a lonely job it would be, so he had the 'ghosts'
of fellow musicians with him, and a drum, 'to create a placebo
effect'. The second part of the concert did indeed go beyond Bach,
and for Kennedy that was entirely logical, in ways that I'll explain
below. I find it interesting that the props were in place from the
start. They could so easily have been brought on in the break
before the 'ghosts', in the form of Rolf Bussald, Yaron Stavi ('from
Palestine/Israel') and 'social experiment' Krzysztof Dziedzic
joined Kennedy to play jazz adaptations of Bach – and more. But
Kennedy isn't interested in conning anyone.

In the first part of the evening, Kennedy presented first Bach's
Prelude from the E major Partita, then the full Partita No. 2 in
D minor, the colossal masterpiece that includes the aforementioned Chaconne. As if in reference to Blom's 'sore trial', Kennedy,
in his introduction, jokily mentioned the 'killer concentration'
involved, 'just as much for you as it is for me'. But what followed
reaped the highest rewards from that dual effort. Spotlit, surrounded by semicircles of candles, the man who notoriously
can't keep still in performance hardly moved, just occasionally
adjusting his poise as if to accompany a harmonic shift. It was a
performance of the highest intensity – both as an act of inward
reflection and a communicative force that reached the furthest

parts of the hall with that highly personal absorption intact. Not only was each individual movement superbly shaped; the larger structure was conjured and held with matching artistry. There were times when it was hard to believe the sound was coming from a single instrument, such was Kennedy's eloquent command of the harmonic and contrapuntal layers; the complex polyphonic texture. Looking at the score, one might be forgiven for thinking it was written for four parts. Four notes frequently appear as a chord that the violinist must somehow render as one within the ongoing rhythmic movement, with certain notes within a chord needing emphasis; Kennedy's performance gave marvellous weight to the bass in particular.

Could anyone seriously have taken more of that intensity? 'Man, I need a beer' was Kennedy's own reaction. When the 'ghosts' were made manifest, the relaxed swing of 'Das Pendel' (The Pendulum), based initially on Bach's 'Air on a G String', felt exactly what was needed, and led into a Grappelli-like take on the double violin concerto. The light touch was entrancing, as if the ghosts were subtly materializing. Kennedy would later make an interesting comment about the drums, in particular: 'I was inspired by busking groups which only use a snare. I was also inspired by the playing of Ed Thigpen with Oscar Peterson and the kind of drum style on Erroll Garner's albums. The drums are almost inaudible but vitally important.'

'Das Pendel' was effectively an encore that was included in the printed programme. The more justified quibble, from some quarters, related to what came next, a set of four Fats Waller numbers that lasted half an hour, pieces that would eventually appear in some form on Kennedy's *Recital* album of 2013. Did this overbalance the programme? Possibly, but something needed to follow the Partita, and Kennedy stressed Fats Waller's credentials as another 'harmonic master'. This was a typical case of Kennedy making a point, but it was done with panache (and the double-stopped harmonic progressions were indeed delightful). In Blom's terms, the Fats Waller contribution was the fresh, 'less imposing' work that complemented the complexity of the Bach; the audience left with a spring in their step – *and* the emotional power of the Bach still holding them in thrall. And let's face it, for every shake of the head and online whinge about what they had or

hadn't paid to hear, there would have been thousands more wondering where Kennedy's traditional jazz encores had vanished,
had he not gone down that route. Signing off the broadcast, Suzy
Klein summed it up well: 'A rather unexpected double bill, but
what would you expect of Kennedy but the unexpected.'

After the Proms concert, Kennedy hit the headlines not only
for his intense performance, but for what he said in the programme: 'Specialists are pushing Bach into a rarefied and effete
ghetto which leaves many people thinking that Bach's music is
merely mathematical and technical – I see it as my job to try and
keep Bach in the mainstream and present his music with, rather
than without, its emotional core.' He went on to be remarkably
specific – about the decade (the 1970s) when 'three horrible things
happened'. In the firing line were The New York School (lacking
'rhythmic ingenuity, dynamic sophistication and architectural
awareness'), The Russian School ('philosophical masterpieces end
up sounding like shallow showpieces'), and the 'Authentic Period
Specialists' (beyond the pale).[3]

When it comes to his own approach, Kennedy talks in almost
mystical terms about playing Bach. 'The music gives us the
wisdom of 300 years ago – as a performer, you can complete that
circle, of everyone experiencing the same thing at once.'[4] This is
a fascinating comment, which might easily be misinterpreted by
someone unfamiliar with Kennedy's personal approach. Does it
mean that performances over 300 years have been the *same*? No:
the circle is completed by engaging with what Kennedy views as
the real spirit of Bach, and there are many who would echo this,
in their own terms. Icelandic pianist Víkingur Ólafsson holds dear
a comment he once heard, that 'Bach is a free country'. He points
out how a Bach score includes

> hardly any indications as to *how* you should go about shaping
> them in performance. Every element is up for debate: tempi,
> dynamics, proportions, articulation – the list goes on. ... it is
> simply unavoidable for the aspiring performer not to become
> something of a co-creator.[5]

In recognizing how successive generations bring an 'inescapably contemporary sensibility' to bear on Bach's music, Ólafsson
reaches the conclusion: 'In that sense his music is contempo-

rary rather than classical. It has the potential to feel more or less as new today as it did 300 years ago.' Ólafsson's comment is uncannily close to what Kennedy says of Bach (and other great composers) and his remarkable Bach recording of 2018 offers a palpable demonstration.

Of course, the idea of a 'free country' will always be anathema to some. Of Jacques Loussier's 1960s jazz versions of Bach, a New York Times critic wrote:

> There is a certain sort of sensibility that is actively appalled by the very notion of popularizing Bach—or any classical composer, for that matter. This listener's sensibility is one of those, and so he found the Tuesday evening performance at a sparsely attended Carnegie Hall by the Jacques Loussier Trio tiresome and offensive.[6]

A large public, however, adored it. Impressively, Loussier sold even more copies of his Bach recordings than Kennedy did of *The Four Seasons*. And his version of 'Air on a G String' was the soundtrack to Hamlet cigar advertisements for some 30 years.

Loussier's re-imaginings of Bach coincided with more scholarly re-evaluations of how Bach might be performed. 'A bone of contention was in what is called "notes inégales"' (unequal notes), a seventeenth-century phrase that indicates how 'individual notes in classical music were often varied according to the whim of the performer – not unlike twentieth-century jazz'.[7] This idea – spanning centuries – adds further depth to Kennedy's concept of completing the circle; an ever-evolving re-evaluation of the past through contemporary practice. Just as Vivaldi needed 'discovering' in the early twentieth century, Bach, according to Kennedy, was put 'back on the radar' by George Enescu, who passed the baton to Menuhin (and by inference to Kennedy himself). 'Bach to the Future' was the title of a Kennedy tour, but it might well have applied to Loussier's interpretations, or, for that matter, the very different, techno-driven versions by Wendy Carlos.

Carlos's versions of Bach on Moog synthesizer date from around the same time as Loussier's jazz, though the *Switched-On Bach* album wasn't released until 1968. That sold over a million copies too. Her aim was to make 'appealing music you could really listen to', as opposed to the 'ugly' music being produced by the avant-garde. Purists of course disliked it, though none other than

Glenn Gould (whose renditions of Bach Kennedy admires) said, 'The whole record, in fact, is one of the most startling achieve-ments of the recording industry in this generation and certainly one of the great feats in the history of "keyboard" performance.'[8] Carlos used her Moog arrangements for Stanley Kubrick's *A Clockwork Orange*. She also contributed to the score for *The Shining*, re-working material by Berlioz.

The absolute precision of the playing, made when the Moog was monophonic, and each key had to be meticulously released ahead of the next note, is certainly at odds with the concept of 'notes inégales', closer perhaps to the 'cold-blooded', 'machine-pulsed' jazz derided by Blom. With his dislike of computers, it's not Kennedy's style either. But Bruce Eder comments on the 'finely wrought nuances, in timbre, tone, and expressiveness.'[9] That might come as a surprise, unless you've spent time with an analogue synthesizer's array of voltage-controlled oscillators and filters. But then, so too might Kennedy's mention, in his Bach Prom notes, of 'expressive intonation'. We so often encounter criticism of intonation that varies from a received idea of per-fection – Menuhin, Sammons and Kennedy, to name just a few have been in the firing line – but as Bach's *Well-Tempered Clavier* demonstrated, intonation is a matter of choice. Bach would have played on keyboards tuned in different ways. Tuning, like rhythm, can be fixed or free according to purpose. And however we react to Carlos's precision, to Loussier's bending rhythms, or to Kenne-dy's creative but highly controlled approach to everything on the (invisible) page, what all these interpretations show is that Bach can be treated in many different ways and find converts, fans, and fresh inspiration for all but the most die-hard conservatives.

Kennedy's criticism of those 'destroying Bach's legacy' was aimed not at the Loussiers and Carloses but at music academies instilling specified approaches in their students, with overt virtuosity the main focus. There were, unsurprisingly, quick ref-utations. Professor Jo Cole, Head of Strings at the Royal Academy of Music, wrote a letter to *The Guardian*, championing the 24 violin teachers at the Academy who shared 'a tireless dedication to nurturing young musicians and preserving at all costs their stu-dents' evolving artistic personalities as communicators through music. We encourage students to take risks in live performance and follow their muse.' She went on to say, 'I don't recognise the perfectionist clones described by Nigel Kennedy, because they don't survive as musicians.'[10] The final comment is intriguing, as it doesn't actually dispute the fact that such clones may exist; they just suffer. Who, then, is to blame?

Kennedy's near dismissal of the New York School points the finger at Ivan Galamian. As mentioned in Chapter 2, Dorothy DeLay fell out with Galamian, and some notable violinists, including Itzhak Perlman, transferred their lessons from Galamian to DeLay. As Perlman comments, 'His teaching method was Scare You to Death.'[11] But perhaps the most controversial aspect of his teaching was his idea that absolutely anyone could be taught to be a fine violinist, an idea that is at once appealing and appalling. It would seem to contradict everything that Menuhin and others believe. Another pupil, Peter Oundjian, puts it harshly, commenting how 'People always said Galamian could make a violinist out of a table',[12] and points to his surely mistaken view that merely playing something 2,000 times will make it better. Here, perhaps, lies the birth of the cloned violinist.

Of later 'New York' violinists, Kennedy is appreciative of Lara St John, specifically her understanding of Bach. Echoing Kennedy's thoughts about clones, St John comments: 'As for all those young musicians that sound like each other, I weep for them. I had a teacher who came straight out of Galamian's workshop, and the best thing I ever did was leave her little factory.'[13] Like Kennedy, she pushes the boundaries of where Bach might go. Alongside her more conventional recordings, her album *re: Bach* makes use of world music, jazz and pop idioms, in arrangements by Magnus Fiennes. A notable difference is that St John doesn't rework or reimagine the material herself in the way Kennedy does, but her principle is the same: 'I think what Bach wrote is so strong that it welcomes many kinds of treatments.'[14]

I find some of the *re: Bach* tracks are made slightly tedious by the monotonous nature of the percussion. Kennedy has always shunned that effect. He rejected the drum machine Brix Smith used on their Donovan recording, and Damon Reece's programmed percussion on *The New Four Seasons* is remarkably subtle. Percussion, especially when it's banal, is probably the number one irritant in the 'updating' of classical music. But *re:*

Bach is certainly fresh in its approach, and Lara St John's playing thoughtful and engaging. Other notably inventive recordings include her 'Bird's Eye Spring', in which she plays Vivaldi while filming with a GoPro camera on her head, and her versions of the Bach concerto in A minor accompanied by a highwire gymnast. Crowning all these achievements, however, is her YouTube video, 'Four Seasons Total Landscaping' – as she describes it, 'a musical, artistic version of the Trump Campaign's November 7th international press conference in a suburban Philadelphia parking lot between a crematorium and a dildo shop ... Lawn & Order! ... Make America Rake Again!' St John's presence as a 'social media violinist' puts her in stark contrast to Kennedy, whose nominal facebook page is, shall we say, 'under-used'. But that's another example of diversity, the anti-clone heart of how musicians go about their business and connect with us in different ways.

Other violinists whose renditions of Bach are admired by Kennedy include Arthur Grumiaux and Isaac Stern. The latter, who like Kennedy had a passion for football, even watching it while he practised, was passionate, too, about the importance of individual musicianship. He is cited as remarking that 'the real question that needs to be answered is not how to play well, but why one chooses to play at all'.[15] (The same point is made by Dave Grohl, in what he says about John Bonham's drumming: 'Though he was technically mind-boggling, I wasn't so concerned with *how* he played what he played; I was more interested in *why* he played what he played.'[16])

Kennedy's Bach-centred 'comeback' recital of 1997 came at a time when that question was urgent. He demonstrated that important ability to do what Stern described as 'filtering the music through his feelings'.[17] On stage, that was broadly welcomed by all who witnessed it. And Richard Morrison applauded not *despite* Kennedy's 'antics' but rather *because* of them: 'his frisky couture and even friskier repartee are badly missed in what can be a pretty staid corner of musical life.'[18] Three years later, Kennedy took the further step of recording a whole album of Bach: four concertos, with the Berlin Philharmonic.

A recording gives critics more leisure in which to listen in repeated detail – and potentially find fault. Almost against expectations, Kennedy's Bach CD was welcomed with a similar warmth as that which greeted his recital. And like the subsequent Bach Prom, it's an immensely dedicated work, passion, technique and creative vision equal drivers in the quest to 'complete the circle'. There are touches which may surprise, namely the moments of improvisation, but as Rob Cowan comments in the CD notes, they are brief and entirely true to period practice. (Bach himself went much further, and was reprimanded for his over-elaborative organ accompaniments in church.) And yet, when I tuned into a 2019 edition of BBC Radio 3's *Record Review*, which compared various interpretations of Bach's E major violin concerto, and chose favourites, Kennedy's version didn't even get a mention. I thought back to the time I heard Kennedy play the concerto at the Festival Hall in 2010, and he only played the first two movements. A member of the audience shouted out 'What about the third movement?!', to which Kennedy joked 'I don't like it!' Perhaps that was enough to write his version off Mark Lowther's list of recommendations. In a 2012 edition of the programme, however, Nicholas Anderson acknowledged Kennedy's lyrical version of the double violin concerto:

> Kennedy is not known best for his Bach playing. Perhaps he should be, for I remember hearing him play the Andante from Bach's A Minor Sonata for unaccompanied violin as a tribute to Menuhin shortly after his death in 1999. It was beautifully done, with warm, yet restrained expressive power, virtues which I have not always associated with this artist.[19]

Those measured words, and indeed muted humour, were all delivered in received pronunciation turned up to an ultra-posh eleven. Also mentioned was the fact that the artist had for some reason dropped his first name.

No More Nigel?

The name Nigel apparently peaked in 1964, the year Kennedy first appeared on the BBC. In 2016 *The Sun* newspaper ran with the headline: 'THE END IS NIGE! Nigels are nearing extinction after no British babies were given the name last year.'[20] Kennedy's own abandonment of his first name, timed to coincide with his reappearance on the classical stage, was yet another cause for controversy. For some it seemed pretentious; for others it smacked of a new marketing strategy by EMI, aiming to restore a clean classical image and be rid of the 'bad boy Nige' associations that had been building up. The name had been an issue from the start: 'It was suggested by one senior [EMI] executive that no one called Nigel would ever make it. At which another executive said, "What? Like Adrian?", after which the objection was not raised again.'[21] When Kennedy himself dropped it, his story was that he simply didn't like the name Nigel, and he objected to those who thought there was anything more to it than that:

> I have been accused of gross arrogance when dropping my first name by some who think only having one name is seemingly (to the petty and mean-minded) comparing myself with other one-namers like ... Bach, Beethoven, Pavarotti?, Prince, the Osmonds, Family Lost in Space etc. What hasn't been noticed is my unprecedented humility when dropping the prefix Dr![22]

In just a few years' time, he would reclaim his much-maligned first name, saying he missed it. For a while though, the leaner moniker stuck, and seemed fit for purpose. There was less hype around his new releases, while their quality was undeniable. As Kennedy would later point out, 'In my absence, some fairly cynical marketing exercises were going on within classical music, which by comparison made me seem like a golden boy.'[23] He had always believed that the music should speak for itself; now it seemed to have a better chance.

The first 'Kennedy' album was a second recording of the Elgar concerto, at the invitation of EMI, to mark the company's centenary. As was Kennedy's custom, the concerto was played in concert (to great applaud) ahead of the recording. It was paired with Vaughan Williams's *The Lark Ascending*, with Simon Rattle conducting the City of Birmingham Symphony Orchestra. Elgar and Vaughan Williams make an unsurprising pairing, but the particular pairing on the album is highly apt, given that, in the Elgar Concerto, the solo violin is described as 'soar[ing] to remain poised over the orchestra like a lark over a summer landscape'.[24]

In its overall length, the Rattle recording is not so different to the earlier Handley version, but the individual movements vary considerably. Rattle's first movement is a minute faster; his second movement a minute slower. The 'drive' is more forceful, the reflection more expansive. The third movement of course combines those two elements, and is therefore, appropriately, much the same length in each case. I use 'Rattle' and 'Handley' as convenient terms; both recordings were the result of close collaboration between Kennedy and the conductor.

In the 'Kennedy' phase, this was the only recording to be led by anyone other than Kennedy himself. Kennedy and Rattle had worked together before, recording the Sibelius concerto, and Rattle – despite his superstar conductor status – was clearly 'ok' as far as Kennedy was concerned. Not long afterwards, however, they had a major disagreement, when Kennedy had to pull out of a performance of Sofia Gubaidulina's new concerto, owing to a further complication with his neck that prevented him from practising on his Guarneri but not from playing jazz on the violectra. As Norman Lebrecht chronicles, it was a distinction that Rattle failed to understand:

> 'He's cross with me for playing in a club when I should have been playing the concerto,' shrugs Kennedy, 'but I don't think it's any of his business what I'm doing.' Doing jazz, Kennedy demonstrates, he holds the fiddle to the front of his chin, rather than at the troublesome side. 'If Simon believed in me, and what I was saying was the truth,' he grumbles, 'he wouldn't have any problem with me playing a totally different violin technique with a singer-songwriter friend. But I'm not going to defend myself to him. He can do whatever the f--- he likes.'[25]

In 1997, this fallout was unimaginable, as the two formed what the *Gramophone* review called 'an inspirational alliance'. Andrew Achenbach found 'their interpretation positively brimming over with re-creative flair, intensity and danger', and that, 'from almost every conceivable point of view – authority, panache, intelligence, intuitive poetry, tonal beauty and emotional maturity – Kennedy surpasses his [earlier] achievement.'[26] But the crowning praise for this astonishing recording comes from David Owen Norris. For the BBC 'Building a Library' series, in 2021, he reviewed multiple recordings of the Elgar concerto, in discussion with Andrew McGregor, and the Kennedy/Rattle recording was in the mix. Kennedy's performance of the cadenza, that almost 'out-of-body experience' that floats within the final movement, was, they agreed, 'beautiful and daring'. Listening to the programme again, I find myself caught up in their discussion as if witnessing a kind of race. Suddenly there's Tasmin Little 'sailing to the end of it with great elegance', perhaps the winner, but then, as if the concerto itself is being revised in dramatic, real time, Norris brings in Lady Elgar, encouraging her husband to create a more impressive ending. Cue Kennedy's triumphant conclusion:

> It's like watching somebody go around the corners faster than you could ever imagine, but they don't come off – it would all be quite different if they came off – on the race track. It's not a question of speed, but it is that wonderful recklessness that actually succeeds.[27]

That description – the edge of the seat thrill – reminds me of Uffenbach's experience watching Vivaldi in Venice. Or imagining oneself in Doc's DeLorean in *Back to the Future*.

Norris admits that everything may be a matter of taste, and he admires other performances, but he doesn't waver in his assessment of Kennedy's achievement. He is inescapably caught up in a performance of such intensity that his review becomes part of the drama. We can almost believe that we have witnessed the miracle for ourselves, as some in 1998 were privileged. And there's further justification for using the word miracle.

As described in the previous chapter, Kennedy had taken time out from classical performance and recording, spending time writing his own music and working in other musical spheres. There were some, perhaps many, who suspected that he was there to stay. With the neck operation a further factor in restricting progress along conventional classical lines, there seemed to be the real possibility that we had seen the very best of Nigel Kennedy's prodigious technique. The 'reckless' lifestyle would surely take its toll. Some doubted that he would perform again at the level of his debut Elgar recording. So to return to the stage *with that very same piece* was an act of astonishing bravery, a different kind of recklessness; and the stakes were high. To positively thrive on that, delivering, as Norris calls it, a reckless performance – and to triumph, was an artistic, indeed a *human* endeavour of the highest order. In a world where there are countless new performances and recordings of major works, relentlessly, year by year, there are few that not only announce themselves with fresh emphasis but also last the test of time as representative of greatness, and I believe both Kennedy's Elgar recordings are amongst them.

More lines of poetry connect for me here, from Thom Gunn's poem 'In Time of Plague'. Going further, even, than Seamus Heaney's lines quoted earlier, Gunn writes of those injecting themselves with heroin that they are 'testing themselves against risk, / as a human must'. Never mind the specifics of heroin and plague, the poetic statement strikes me as true, whether the chosen risk is small, as for most of us, or recklessly huge – sheer folly a mere hair's breadth away.

Vaughan Williams's *The Lark Ascending* derives from a poem by George Meredith, written in 1881. The music was composed in 1914, ahead of the outbreak of World War 1, but not performed till 1920. As a consequence, its simple, pastoral theme was destined to convey an element of nostalgia. A review of the first performance praised the work because 'It showed serene disregard of the fashions of today or yesterday. It dreamed itself along.'[28] Today an immensely popular work, its seeming simplicity belies its radical departures from British music of the time, with its impressionistic use of the pentatonic scale, and rhythmic freedom (the cadenza has no bar lines at all), the violin embodying the lark within the poem – 'both the bird's song and its flight', as Vaughan Williams's poet-wife Ursula put it so well.[29]

Vaughan Williams includes the opening and closing sections of the poem in his score, together with six central lines, evoking the poem as a whole, an act of partnership between music and poetry reminiscent of Vivaldi's *Four Seasons*.

> He rises and begins to round,
> He drops the silver chain of sound,
> Of many links without a break,
> In chirrup, whistle, slur and shake.
>
> For singing till his heaven fills,
> 'Tis love of earth that he instils,
> And ever winging up and up,
> Our valley is his golden cup
> And he the wine which overflows
> to lift us with him as he goes.

Till lost on his aerial rings
In light, and then the fancy sings.

A notable absence is one of the poem's most famous lines, 'seraphically free from the taint of personality', which I discussed in
Chapter 5. The phrase *is* used both by EM Forster in his short
story 'The Machine Stops' and by Hawkwind in their 2016 album
of the same name; its application to a machine world is irresistible.
But if we consider the line in the context of Vaughan Williams's
lark, it's immediately problematic. The lark of the poem is not
simply a seraphically free line of notes in the score; embodied
by the violin it is played by a human character, musical freedom
expressed through an individual personality. Intriguingly, the
display of personality, as reviled by Geoffrey Hill, is still held at
bay; the music is so intrinsically free that the personality of the
violinist is unlikely to distort it. Nevertheless, one only has to look
at the sheer time taken to perform the work in different recordings to register marked differences. It can take under fourteen
minutes, while Kennedy's version is 17.37.

'Can you hear the lark ascending?' sings Kate Bush in 'Pro-
logue' from her *Aerial* album of 2005 (which also features actual
birdsong). Her line echoes the dual depiction of song and flight
identified by Ursula Vaughan Williams. In 2018, a work by Chris
Pye did the same – in wood. His 'Lark Ascending' music stand
was one of the works commissioned from members of the Master
Carvers Association to mark the 300th anniversary of the birth of
Thomas Chippendale Senior, the great eighteenth-century wood-
carver. Pye's music stand features lines from the poem spiralling
up around the central pole, with a carved bird suspended from
the decorative top. Further to the commissions, I was asked to
write associated poems, including 'Air', part of an Earth/Water/
Fire/Air *Quartet*:

A clean ascent, inscribing the visible grain of the air
with its poetry, its spiralling grace; each wingbeat
beating new song into being, each bird's-eyed note
of the melody intent on a distant, dizzying frontier.

The Lark Ascending has remained a touchstone for Kennedy, who
performed it in its original arrangement for violin and piano with

Peter Skellern on *Private Lives* (BBC) in 1984, and the orchestral version of 1921 at the Last Night of the Proms in 2013. He evokes its style and mood in his adaptations of radically different material, such as Hendrix's 'Little Wing', while 'Air' from his own *Four Elements* makes for a direct comparison. At the Proms, Kennedy claimed to have difficulty memorizing the piece, on account of the 'elusive structure', he said to Richard Morrison ahead of the event. 'I play it over and over and hope. Just have to pray that it sticks on the night, man.'[30]

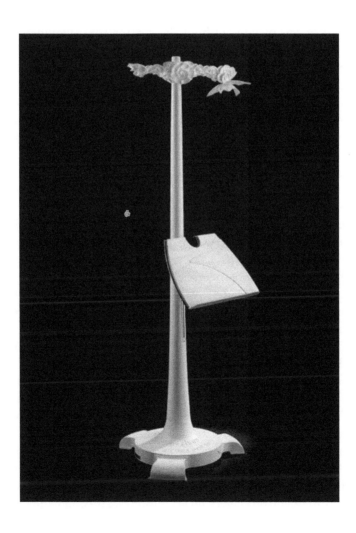

Chamber Music: a conversation

Kennedy's return to the concert stage in 1997 was a clear success, and yet, as Helen Wallace writes, 'The rapturous reception must have been both sweet and sour: the classical establishment were welcoming their local hero 'home' to a fold he still didn't wish to inhabit.'[31] His next recordings showed a preference for smaller-scale collaborations, chamber music rather than orchestral.

'Playing by heart', as discussed in Chapter 3, and which (of course) Kennedy did so effortlessly on that Last Night of the Proms, is of particular relevance to chamber music. The string quartet is a domain where one might imagine the scenario of all the musicians playing without the written score would be the norm; it has, after all, been called the musical equivalent of a conversation. Haydn's first quartets were published with the subtitle 'dialogued quartets'. And Goethe later referred to Beethoven's quartets as 'four intelligent people conversing among themselves'.[32] In the eighteenth century, conversation had itself 'been elevated to a bona fide art form worthy of meticulous cultivation, since displays of conversational wit carried great social cachet in Enlightenment salons'.[33] And since sport is a feature of my Kennedy musings, it's worth mentioning here how 'The repartee of a lively conversation was often compared to racquet sports – for a particularly adroit conversationalist would know just when to deliver a particularly witty riposte to "win" the volley.'[34] In considering the quartet, we clearly have to think of doubles, rather than singles, but there the analogy breaks down, as it's not a competition between two pairs, more a 'friendly' between four equal partners. The full equality of voices is key to the texture of a quartet.

The eighteenth-century French intellectual Madame de Staël highlights other key elements of conversation: 'speaking the moment one thinks ... displaying the understanding in all its shades by accent, gesture, look ... eliciting.'[35] She even compared the intoxicating effect of such conversation to that of liquor. These aspects of conversation relate well to the intimate musical development of a quartet, but are also clearly relevant to the mode of performance, where four musicians are in a close 'conversational' arrangement, typically a semi-circle, just as we might expect of a panel discussion on stage. And yet, despite all this, and unlike the panel discussion, where we would raise our eyebrows if panellists were to be reading their every word from a printed page, the quartet typically plays in 'orchestral' fashion, behind their music desks.

In 2016, however, the Chiara Quartet made headlines for performing Bartók's complete cycle of quartets from memory, building on previous, memorized performances of Haydn and Brahms. Their project was sparked by another form of musical 'conversation' – between the Takacs Quartet playing Bartók and a folk group, Muzsikas, playing Hungarian folk music. Key to this interplay was the fact that Bartók's own music derived in part from folk melodies passed down without written notation, evolving all the time. Performing such a melody was done from memory, allowing for improvisation, whether subtle or more substantial. Rebecca Fisher of the Chiara Quartet comments:

> In a sense, the goal *is* to improvise on the music, or to feel close to that improvisational process ... When we were first playing and memorizing the quartets, there's a stage where you feel like it's about the memory. We're always trying to get away from the score and the detail-oriented nature of memorization so we can be freer to feel spontaneous with it—to feel like we can improvise, even if we're really still just playing the notes.[36]

This tallies with what Kennedy has said about playing Bach: 'We know the music well enough now to let ourselves go. There's got to be ... an element of not trying to control everything but letting the vibe take control, letting the spirit of the music take control.'[37] Significantly, each player in the Chiara Quartet had to memorize not just their own part but the whole. The notion of spontaneous conversation may be an illusion, but the players are aware of every nuance of the debate – from all angles, which is precisely why the illusion is so effective. As Edward T Cone has said of dramatic dialogue, 'The actor who knows only his own part does not know his own part, for each role is defined in large measure by its connections with others.'[38] And the challenge for musicians is even greater. As Cone goes on to say,

> every ensemble player is continually confronted by a situation actors rarely if ever have to face: he and his colleagues are

performing simultaneously, not in turn. If he is to hear them,
he must do so while he is playing, as well as when he is silent.[39]

In this respect, the memorizing is different both from the concerto
soloist's process and the Aurora orchestra players' accomplishment. Conductor Nicholas Collon, who, as conductor, can hardly
escape the task he gives to his orchestra, also leads the proceedings without a score; he needs to know every part, though as
Kennedy might be quick to point out, he doesn't actually have to
play. Kennedy, speaking about his knowledge of *The Four Seasons*,
states, 'I have played it so much that I know every note that every
instrument of the orchestra is playing.'[40]

The particular skill of ensemble playing is a strong musical
virtue, and yet sometimes overlooked. Guitarist John Williams
has been outspoken about solo playing taking priority in education. In his opinion, students become proficient at performing
solo works from memory but struggle with ensemble playing.
He actually goes further, suggesting that they are 'preoccupied
with fingerings and not notes, much less sounds'.[41] Sight-reading
is another area of his concern, and his criticisms match those of
Menuhin when he visited the Central School of Music in Moscow,
the visit that clarified his own, different purpose in setting up
a music school. The Russian school seemed exclusively set on
producing soloists, to the extent that 'the orchestras of Moscow
and Leningrad consisted largely of disillusioned soloists'.[42] They
were also 'untrained to sight-read'. Menuhin wanted to nurture
more rounded musicians.

As an ensemble player, Kennedy benefited from Menuhin's
approach – and his own dedication to jazz, a form of music where
the idea of conversation is crucial (another reason to believe Kennedy's claim that playing jazz is good for your classical technique).
As Ingrid Monson writes, jazz is all about 'musical personalities
interacting, not merely instruments or pitches or rhythms ... At
any given moment ... the improvising artist is always making
musical choices in relationship to what everyone else is doing.'[43]
In the fully scored string quartet, those choices are of course more
subtle, almost a matter of performative illusion, as with actors
within a scripted play.

It is surely strange that this fundamental musical skill should
be so ignored. Perhaps it stems from what Peter J Martin identifies

as 'the widely held view of improvisational ability as a gift possessed by a few exceptional individuals'. Martin also calls that 'a
myth, the prevalence of which is related to the marginalisation
of improvisation in the western art-music tradition'.[44] Such mar-
ginalization is ideological, and surely goes against the grain of
our natural, quotidian inclinations. As Ingrid Monson says, 'all
social interactions, such as conversations, are improvised in the
sense that we do not – other than on ritual occasions – speak from
scripts. The routine encounters that constitute social life must be
enacted.'[45] In a number of non-Western communities and cultural
environments, improvisation – whether linguistic or musical – is
more the norm.

We don't immediately picture Kennedy playing quartets; we
don't tend to picture him sitting down at all. He doesn't care much
for Haydn, and surely cares even less about the idea of *refined*
conversation – that epithet alone might have persuaded him to
avoid the genre. But he has recorded one quartet, the Kreisler
String Quartet in A minor, featured on his *Kreisler* album of 1998
(another of those that he doesn't even mention in his summary of
albums in *Uncensored!*). The Kennedy Kreisler connection is significant. His grandfather, Lauri Kennedy, was cellist in Kreisler's
quartet that recorded his work at Abbey Road studios in 1935.
Intriguingly, a photo from that recording session shows them
playing with no sheet music.

In Eric Wen's notes to Kennedy's album, Kreisler is described
as 'one of the first "cross-over" classical musicians':

> Renowned for his interpretations of the great masterworks,
> he was also a brilliant exponent of the popular music of his
> day, and recorded such hit tunes as Irving Berlin's 'Blue Skies'
> and Rudolf Frimi's 'Indian Love Call'. Furthermore, a recital
> by Kreisler was an event.[46]

Like the film stars of his day, 'Fritz Kreisler was larger than life:
the conductor Bruno Walter once remarked, "He did not play the
violin, he became the violin."'[47]

Anne-Sophie Mutter recorded some Kreisler pieces in 2003,
with André Previn. Like Kennedy, she felt a personal connection,
having learnt the pieces when she was six, her teacher having
played in Berlin coffee houses like Kreisler himself, before fleeing

the city during World War II on account of her Jewish heritage. Commenting on Kreisler's own (recorded) performances, she refers to the many wrong notes: 'Only in my late teens – when I had become less fixated on accuracy – was I able to appreciate the quality of his playing. His sound was like a human voice, pure expressivity.' She goes on to make more general observations: 'Music making [in the past] was much more personal and eccentric, much more emotional. And those are the qualities I require of a musician.'[48] To which Michael Church adds: 'Players then had to survive by convincing a live audience, rather than by relying on records.'[49] Kennedy would undoubtedly agree on all fronts.

Kennedy's name may loom large on his Kreisler album, but there are distinguished partners in the venture. Bill Hawkes has perhaps the most extensive viola credits ever amassed. Like Kennedy he has worked with Robert Plant, and Kate Bush – before recklessly calling her 'massively overrated'. Violinist Rosemary Furniss was contemporary with Kennedy at the Menuhin School, one of the very first admissions. And cellist Caroline Dale had previously worked with Kennedy on his Hendrix project. 'He encouraged me to be a total musician who enjoys playing everything.'[50] Like Kennedy, she went on to perform with Robert Plant and Jane Siberry, also collaborating with Peter Gabriel, David Gilmour and many others from the rock world. It's telling that Kennedy, Dale and Furniss – all formidable soloists – should wish to work as equal chamber musicians.

At one stage, the photographer and designer of rock album covers, Storm Thorgerson, was engaged to design the Kreisler album. Thorgerson, famous for his Pink Floyd album covers, and many others, shot a photo for Kennedy at Camber Sands, Sussex. He comments:

> I designed the cover around the twin muses in Kreisler's life – playing and composing – and pictured them as female shapes, or silhouettes (in deference to the two major women in his life). They were connected to the one source, Kreisler himself, by means of strings – strings of the violin of course but also strings of attachment.[51]

The concept of 'twin muses' would seem to relate to Kennedy too, except the concept isn't quite right, which is perhaps a reason the image was rejected. Neither 'playing' nor 'composing' can really be said to be a 'muse'. They are passions, skills. Any connective strings might more appropriately be drawn between fellow musicians, reflecting a collaborative endeavour.

*

Kennedy's classical comeback was underlined by the release of *Classic Kennedy*, a collection of 20 tracks, of which only Vivaldi's 'Summer' Presto was familiar from Kennedy's previous classical recordings. The others pieces follow suit, in that they match that pop song brevity. In other respects they are remarkably varied, both in period and style, ranging from the meditative to the frenetic. The irony is that none of them are from the 'classical' era, generally defined as 1750-1830. Beethoven is simply too big. We skip from the Baroque to the Romantic, venturing on through Debussy's impressionism to Gershwin's jazz, in a way that makes connections while also offering contrasts of dynamics and mood. Some of the pieces might be found in any classic/classical compilation; others, such as William Kroll's 'Banjo and Fiddle' are much less well known. And the selection ends with Joni Mitchell followed by Kennedy's own 'Melody in the Wind'. Here Kennedy is making the point that contemporary, popular music is also worthy of classic status. Given that he champions Hendrix on that front, it's perhaps surprising that Hendrix doesn't feature here. But *The Kennedy Experience* album was released in the same year, with its longer, exploratory tracks; the two albums are very different, each benefiting from a single-minded purpose. The overlap is Kennedy as composer, confidently working within and across different musical realms. It was a rich and varied phase of work, which also produced the Bach album already discussed.

Kennedy's next collaboration was even more intimate than his Kreisler conversations: *Duos for Violin and Cello*, with Lynn Harrell. During the period in which Kennedy had withdrawn from the concert stage, he received a letter from Harrell, regretting his absence. Kennedy was immensely touched by that, and suggested that they work together. It was the type of top-level classical partnership that had proved elusive after the *Four Seasons* furore, but here was Kennedy now teaming up with a player whom he calls 'the greatest cellist of his generation and maybe for the last century'.[52]

It's another of Kennedy's resolutely uncommercial offerings, but also a predictably thoughtful programme of works. The album includes Bach – a single two-part invention written originally for keyboard. Arrangements of such pieces would soon feature in Kennedy's orchestral concerts as encores, Kennedy duetting with the lead cellist. But the two main works, by Ravel and Kodály, are probably less familiar. Between them, they span the same pre/post-war period as Vaughan Williams's *Lark Ascending* (and Ravel had briefly been Vaughan Williams's teacher), Ravel's being the later work, though first on the album. They offer yet more exploration of the pentatonic scale in their melodic weave. Both works owe much to Debussy: Kodály had fallen under the French composer's spell when in Paris, recognizing an affinity with the modal language of Hungarian folksong; Ravel gives Debussy a specific dedication. In other respects, the works are very different. In Ravel's sonata, and the composer's own words, 'The music is stripped down to the bone. Harmonic charm is renounced';[53] and for Paula Kennedy the music 'has an edge akin to the dry crackle of static electricity'.[54] To contrast that with Kodály's sense of colour, and space, seems central to Kennedy and Harrell's purpose – exploring the variety of soundscape that a particular instrumental combination can produce. The shorter baroque works extend that range, and the Handel Passacaglia is itself layered with interpretative metamorphosis: firstly, the development into a set of variations by Johan Halvorsen, for violin and viola; secondly into an arrangement by Michael Press for violin and cello.

They may both have been to Juilliard, but Kennedy and the 6'4" American Harrell cut very different figures. What they brought to their *Duos* was a matching ability to converse in music at the very highest level – and with such wide-ranging focus. Listening to their Kodály conversation, I have in mind László Eósze's suggestion that the 'serene' first movement 'may have been inspired by the majesty of the Alps'[55] where the composer used to walk. And I think, then, of Harrell in the mountains of Colorado, where he would fish. And of Kennedy, soon to find inspiration from walking in the Polish/Slovakian High Tatras.

When Harrell died in 2020, Kennedy searched in vain for coverage of his passing on the BBC website: 'They've got American TV reality stars and all kinds of stuff. For the world's greatest cellist, they've got no space. A shocking omission.'⁵⁶ Harrell's son Eben, however, wrote a wonderful tribute, remembering, in particular, those Colorado days, saying of his father: 'He fished because he enjoyed the poetics of dry-fly fishing ... the magic of summoning wild trout from the depths simply by dancing shadows across a river's surface.'⁵⁷ That's not only a beautifully musical description; it's a metaphor for any creative act.

*

With such a run of strong albums, Kennedy was thoroughly deserving of his BRIT Award in 2000, for 'Outstanding Contribution to British Music'. Controversy had seemingly gone away. 'Many critics have forgiven me and think I'm a good boy now because I'm middle of the road compared to people like Vanessa Mae and Bond – at least I didn't put drum'n'bass behind Vivaldi.'⁵⁸ The award, however, was in the inaugural year of the Classical Brits, and Kennedy wasn't happy about that, considering it a 'ghetto'. He would prefer there to be a classical section of the main BRITs. 'Why do they have to be separate?' he asks. 'Good music should be kept together. In America the Grammy awards cover all types. Put classical music away by itself and it's no longer fairly represented.'⁵⁹ Violinist Rachel Barton Pine, who has also played in a Chicago metal band, Earthen Grave, makes the same point: 'As much as I love all kinds of world music, folk music, rock music and pop music, we would be so much poorer if classical music wasn't a part of it.'⁶⁰ The irony, of course, was that the Classical BRITs were established in response to the growth of interest in classical music in which Kennedy had played a key role.

He received a second award in 2001, for 'Male Artist of the Year', but his relationship with the BRITs deteriorated in 2008, when – again somewhat ironically – the Classical BRITs didn't want him to perform anything from his Beethoven/Mozart album, but something of pop song length. A jazz number (most likely the Horace Silver track from that same album) was also rejected, so Kennedy chose Monti's 'Csárdás', which he planned to play with Bond, the glamorous all-girl string quartet. This was unacceptable, apparently, as Bond had not been approved by the BRITs selection process. The committee's further reasons included insufficient dressing room space. Quite how that equated to 'artistic differences' is hard to say.

Kennedy refused to play with the BRITs orchestra, and commented: 'Seeing that the words "music business" still place the word "music" first, I am not going to let some old farts dictate my musical decisions.' His manager, Terri Robson backed him up: 'I can't think of any other musician who would accept being told who to play with. He has been prevented from playing.' The BBC reported that the organizers claimed to be unfazed, and 'highlighted an appearance by heart-throb virtuoso David Garrett, who is said to be an heir to Kennedy's throne'.[61] It strikes me that Kennedy would never have been too happy performing on the same bill as Garrett. He would certainly have been outraged by that BBC comment. 'I am the prototype and the rest are clones!'[62] he said in a later interview with the German press. 'Violinen-Legende verreisst David Garrett' ran the headline; Kennedy, not the German Garrett, was the legend.

Garrett (born Bongartz) has lived a life that in some ways parallels Kennedy's while being everything that Kennedy is not. He has performed at the Champions League Final and at the Formula One Eifel Grand Prix. His albums straddle genres – and he writes much of the work himself. But at Juilliard, he earned extra cash not by busking but by working as a model. He has promoted Montblanc pens. He starred in a film about Paganini, whom Kennedy deplores. And one has only to watch him performing Monti's 'Csárdás' to grasp the difference between the two violinists. Heir to Kennedy's throne? The 'Bad Boy of German music', as Norman Lebrecht describes him, had missed a few of his classes at the Royal College of Music and covered Nirvana; that hardly made him Keith Moon. In 2016, however, he was in real trouble, accused by porn star Kendall Karson (real name Ashley Youdan) of causing her injury.

The details of the case were pretty lurid. The case notes from the trial included Youdan's claim that 'the violinist's "behaviour began to take a dark turn for the worse" on their first Christmas together, when [Garrett] responded to a Craiglist ad for a "sex slave," hoping he could keep this person in a cage.'[63] Lebrecht is scathing about the 'defence': 'Violinists are there to behave badly.

Paganini showed the way. The violinist is an "erotic phenomenon".'

In 2017, when asked about Garrett, Kennedy paid him the ultimate back-handed compliment: 'David can play the violin. He finds the right notes.' Then he became more critical, saying, 'I like to play new pieces. David plays last night's stuff', before getting on a roll. The interview by *Die Welt* rendered his comments in German: 'Käme David Garrett zu mir auf die Bühne, würde ich sagen: Runter hier!' Norman Lebrecht translated: 'If David came up to me on stage I'd tell him to fuck off.'[64]

Symphonic Rock

In 1999, sports agent and music producer David Fishof staged an event that presented 'classic' rock in classical orchestral style. Well, not quite, because the British Rock Symphony, as it was called, still made prominent use of the 'original' instrumentation: electric guitars, bass and keyboards, and standard rock drums. Fishof's concept was to 'add another dimension' to the music of a select few bands, and 'elevate it to another level'.[65] I suspect this irritated the classical community and most rock musicians in one fell swoop, representing a type of fusion that bore no relation to the original concept of the music, placing both worlds in an uneasy alliance. The featured 'composers', despite having every instrument available to them when the works were written, chose the precise combination used on their recordings. Why would it 'improve' them to be 'classicalized'? Kennedy, in *Uncensored!,* puts it even more strongly, claiming 'Symphony orchestras have bad rhythm' and have typically done rock no favours 'in their unkool attempts to be kool'.[66]

Fishof meant well. Another of his projects, still ongoing, is the Rock 'n' Roll Fantasy Camp, which enables members of the public to join well-known musicians in organized jam sessions; not so much bringing rock music to the masses (there being no need for that, compared with Kennedy's classical mission) but enabling active musical engagement between amateurs and professionals. On one level, the British Rock Symphony did something similar: it brought together types of musicians inexperienced at performing with each other. Fishof believed that the British Rock Symphony would deliver something that not even The Beatles, The Rolling Stones, Pink Floyd, Led Zeppelin or The Who could ever have imagined. As I have said, there's reason to doubt that they would have wanted to, and yet they all gave their permission, indeed Roger Daltrey was instrumental in the venture.

Fishof talks of combining 'the tender and beautiful elements of the symphony with the ferociousness and power of rock 'n' roll and, on some occasions, vice versa'.[67] I'm glad he added that final phrase, otherwise I would find his view of the symphony deeply problematic, but it also begs a crucial question: If both can be 'tender' and 'ferocious', why the need to combine?

The project was really about synthesis as a principle, a means of breaking down barriers. It was hardly a balanced partnership however; only the rock musicians were credited, though perhaps that's no different to a concerto recording.

The British Rock Symphony launched at the Royal Albert Hall before touring. Kennedy was not part of the tour, but contributed to the album that was released around the same time (1999). He recorded his parts in Peppermint Park Studios, in Hanover, while on a German tour, but bewilderingly claims in *Uncensored!* that it was in 2013. Despite misgivings about the project as a whole, he accepted because the chosen song was 'While My Guitar Gently Weeps' by George Harrison, and Zac Starkey would be drumming. He saw scope to do something genuinely creative that would develop the melodic power of the original, while making use of entirely new orchestration. He has otherwise steered clear of covering Beatles material, feeling that George Martin had already used strings to best effect. It's the only work on the album where the words are not preserved. The original vocal line is performed exquisitely on acoustic violin, and the 'guitar' solos on the violectra. While the solos may not be as extraordinary as the one performed by Prince at the 2004 Rock and Roll Hall of Fame induction event (for both George Harrison and himself, amongst others), the overall arrangement and performance is outstanding, revealing the full subtlety and power of the song, without being overtly 'guitarist'. It's a common misconception that Kennedy imitates electric guitar on the violin. Even with his Hendrix pieces he uses the violin to do something equivalent, indeed different, rather than imitative, deriving inspiration from guitarists in taking the violin into distinctive new territory.

Apart from Kennedy's track, the album somewhat disappoints. Was this the future of classical music – to be at the beck and call of rock? It really doesn't add much to the works, some of which had featured elements of classical instrumentation in their original versions, or previous performances. Led Zeppelin had performed 'Kashmir' with an Egyptian orchestra in place of synthesizers, and that wasn't just a 'backing'; it made prominent use of the Egyptian musicians' particular flair. The British Rock Symphony feels as if it's riding the coattails of bands for which orchestral textures were fundamental to their concept. The Eagles, for instance, worked closely with orchestral arranger Jim Ed Norman on their 1970s albums. Norman was still involved when the new line-up toured again in 2022; the performance of the entire *Hotel California* album was prefaced by Erik Satie's 'Gnossiennes No. 1'. And ELO (The Electric Light Orchestra) was by definition an 'orchestral' band. These and many other bands incorporated orchestral instruments for a very specific purpose. By contrast, 'adding some strings' doesn't automatically make something 'symphonic'. It's fundamentally the wrong word. George Martin's work with the Beatles was occasionally 'orchestral', but the arrangement of 'Yesterday', for instance, is for string quartet, a very different instrumental combination.

Daltrey makes a distinction: 'This record is a rock symphony album, not a symphonic rock record; it's rock 'n' roll to its core.'[68] I'm not sure the distinction makes full sense, but part of his meaning is to suggest the album is a *whole*, just as *Tommy* is a rock opera, not a collection of individual songs. I think it fails though, on that front. There is a certain consistency achieved through Keith Levenson's orchestration and arrangements, but it's precisely where it aims for broader structure that it falls apart. The medleys are poor; there's little coherence to the songs that are threaded together, not least in the final 'Celebration Suite' in which they originate from different bands (although that concept in itself seems commendable). Quite what The Rolling Stones are doing in the mix at all, I really don't know. Daltrey himself has recently called them 'a mediocre pub band'.[69]

The year after The British Rock Symphony album was released, Kennedy was involved in a more adventurous orchestral rock project: Jaz Coleman's *Riders on the Storm: The Doors Concerto* (2000). A former cathedral chorister, Coleman is best known as a member of Killing Joke (a highly influential band admired by Jimmy Page, Dave Grohl and many more), but he decided over-night – in Iceland, 1982 – to take on a parallel life as classical composer, subsequently bringing his two worlds together. Dal-trey's reference to 'symphonic rock' may well be to Coleman's work, *Us and Them: Symphonic Pink Floyd* (1995) and *Kashmir: Symphonic Led Zeppelin* (1997). Following on from those, Cole-man's concerto, inspired by the music of The Doors, and approved by the surviving members of the band, is dedicated to the memory of all those who died in the Vietnam war. As Coleman describes it, those two elements are closely connected:

> In the public's imagination, the music of the Doors has always captured the atmosphere of the Vietnam war. To rearrange the music for orchestra, as a tribute to all those who fought in Vietnam, was an idea I simply could not dismiss.[70]

I suspect that the most prominent link in the public mind between The Doors and Vietnam is the use made of The Doors' music in Francis Ford Coppola's film, *Apocalypse Now*. It was actually a matter of serendipity that led Coppola to use 'The End' as music over the opening scene: he spotted film footage of burning trees that was about to be discarded, next to a pile of records that included *The Doors*. He and Jim Morrison had been film school contemporaries at UCLA. At first it was just a joke – to begin the film with a song called 'The End'; then the real power of the idea took hold. Intriguingly, The Doors provided Coppola with the original tape, so that the version of the song in the film is different to that mixed for the album. Less than four minutes long, the trance-like sequence sets the tone for the whole three-hour film. The soundtrack also uses other 60s music, including songs by Jimi Hendrix, as well as Wagner's 'Ride of the Valkyries'. There's no musical blender quite like cinema, and it's where many people are most exposed to classical music, the associated imagery often forming a lasting association. Just as Coleman links The Doors and Vietnam, many will link Wagner's 'Ride' with helicopters heralding napalm death.

In Coleman's concerto the Vietnam connection is manifested musically. The work uses the Vietnamese pentatonic scale of Hoi Xuam, Vietnamese ornamentation in the solo violin part, and Vietnamese instruments are added to the Prague Symphony Orchestra. It would however be entirely possible to listen to the work without Coleman's album notes and not make the connection at all. Even the notes complicate the connection by referencing the composer's broader humanitarian and environmental thinking. He mentions the execution of Che Guevara, the 'farcical' detention of Pinochet, the Soviet invasion of Czechoslovakia, the plight of Romany people in Europe, and how global pollution may just overturn our obsession with sovereignty. Again, none of that is explicitly evident in the music, but it does make clear the heart and soul behind the writing, the real reason – beyond an interest in symphonic rock – for its existence: the *why*, as articulated by Isaac Stern earlier in this chapter.

The *why* of *The Doors Concerto* is what gives it an undeniable depth beyond its easy, melodious appeal, a depth enhanced by Kennedy's playing, which soars, but with a haunted, vocal quality similar to his treatment of George Harrison's song. In Kennedy's opinion, the work is a 'masterpiece', aka 'fukkin' fukkin' good'.[71] It's certainly enjoyable, and treats the original music both with respect and interesting liberty. I imagine some Doors fans find it lacks the band's raw edge, but it's delving into the other, more poetic side to Jim Morrison's writing; there's little that speaks of Morrison's self-destructive personality. If, in Blakean terms, the work is a marriage of heaven and hell, then the harmony and texture leans towards the former. There's a touch of Maurice Jarre's *Dr Zhivago* score in 'Spanish Caravan', and in 'Hello I love you', the melody is drawn out to sound something like the Cadbury's Flake advert circa 1985. That might sound unfair; I don't mean to be dismissive of the concerto's sensuous beauty. But I'm intrigued by the fact that symphonic rock should be so softcore in comparison both to its rock relations and contemporary classical music. *The Doors Concerto*, for instance, is probably 'easier listening' for many people than the Kennedy/Harrell Ravel sonata. It's all the more strange since Coleman himself is so hardcore, even abrasive by some accounts. He's as outspoken as Kennedy, indeed the two share a number of quirks. Like Kennedy, he's no big fan of computer technology. 'I don't use modern forms of communication unless it's a land line. I don't use computers ... I think that a lot of the great thinkers couldn't achieve what they did through a computer.'[72]

Coleman's 1982 decision to pursue a classical career as composer and conductor is markedly different to Kennedy's 'long childhood' of classical training. It fits with his radical concept of 'supersynthesis':

> I've documented a series of perfectly timed coincidences; it's a 30 year study of magical principals. For instance if you visualise you're a producer and you assume it from day 1 then you are a producer. It's a manifestation of dreams into reality.[73]

From day one? It's a question of belief. Coleman's classical transformation, training, whatever you want to call it, took ten years – the very same period identified by Andrew Robinson as the prelude to all breakthroughs, but ten years counts for nothing without the belief, the determination, the *why*. Coleman had it. Klaus Tennstedt, no less, hailed him as a 'new Mahler'. His 'theory' may sound fanciful, but he's utterly serious about it. He outlined his ideas in a book, *Letters from Cythera*, and said:

> This book will raise money for my next violin concerto. Classical music does[n't] really sell very many copies so I have to raise it somehow. I should spend it getting water on my Island in NZ but I put music first.[74]

Eccentric theorizing is probably excusable if music's the beneficiary. There was at one time talk of Kennedy recording a Coleman 'War Concerto', but maybe not enough books were sold.

Coleman was heavily involved with Sarah Brightman's eighth studio album, *Harem*, so it's perhaps no surprise that Kennedy is a contributor – to three tracks, one of which, 'Free', was also released as a single. He was also guest at a promotional concert broadcast on Canadian television. His input was hugely appreciated by Brightman, 'for bringing tears to our eyes with your beautiful playing'.[75] It certainly fits subtly into the unusual musical soundscape – Arabic with opera and disco in the mix, Allegri's

'Miserere' thrown in for good measure. Kennedy's solos show his instinctive grasp of unusual musical blends, and how the violin can complement a distinctive voice. Lebanese violinist Aboud Abdel Aal also plays a solo. He would later be involved with the Kennedy/Kroke album, *East Meets East*, produced by Coleman and John Stanley.

Nigel Revisited

Kennedy was continuing to help others with their major projects, but the time had come, it seemed, for him to issue an album that had 'commercial success' written all over it. When Kennedy's *Greatest Hits* album was first suggested by EMI, he wasn't keen, saying, 'Oh shit, am I already over the hill?'[76] But he came round to the idea, 'after all, how many classical violinists can truthfully claim to have a hit at all?' He also managed to subvert the concept by playing on the word 'hit'. The back cover of the album shows him wielding his violin like a cricket bat or tennis racquet. And a photo inside the booklet shows him in boxing pose, the same image that would be used for *Uncensored!*. David Garrett has since posed with his violin in the same way, possibly in response to Kennedy's swipe about the German's Stradivarius being difficult to keep in perfect condition, unlike his own more modern instrument made by Martin Bouette: 'you can even play tennis or cricket with it.'[77] Garrett wields his violin bat with the strings side forward, which would seem a little silly.[78]

Kennedy's *Greatest Hits* album is, perhaps unsurprisingly, not a 'hits' album in the traditional sense. Yes, it includes parts of *The Four Seasons* and other concertos ('ALL THE BEST BITS' as the tour programme put it), and a range of shorter works from *Classic Kennedy*, but it also includes two pieces not previously released: a movement from Bach's Sonata for Solo Violin in C; and the Bach Chorale 'Es ist genug'. These are treasures for which the whole album is worth buying. One might react against that, as a marketing ploy; personally I treat it as a welcome departure from the standard 'nothing new' approach of such an album.

I attended the Sheffield concert within Kennedy's Greatest Hits tour with my children, then aged thirteen and fifteen. At the venue, Sheffield City Hall, they were not allowed into the bar area, so they had to be left outside while I bought their soft drinks. We'd already experienced problems getting a meal beforehand. It seemed that children were not supposed to be out and about in the evening at all, let alone at a classical concert. I have to say I've never encountered anything like it before or since, but it shows what barriers, and preconceptions about concert-going, were in existence even at the turn of the millennium. And there are still pubs in this country that won't admit children, even for a meal. Thankfully, on that night in 2002, Kennedy helped my anger dissolve – in the most perfect way possible. Spotting a baby in the audience, he wandered offstage and delivered a lullaby.

As if by accident, *Nigel Kennedy's Greatest Hits*, to give the album its full title, reconnected him with his first name. It had in fact already crept back into use on the *British Rock Symphony*, and on Lukan's *Face Down*, to which he contributed; it makes life easier. (On 2012 tours, the word Nigel was hugely more prominent than Kennedy.) The first new recording in the new Nigel phase was another reconnection – with Vivaldi. He had already suggested that he might revisit *The Four Seasons*, saying in 2001, 'I'd love to have another go at it, with the hindsight of 12 years. That recording was in some ways a reaction against the immature way I thought authentic music was being marketed, and the concern with "correct" techniques.'[79]

It's a natural inclination for a musician to revisit works with which they have a strong affinity. Anne-Sophie Mutter has such a relationship with Mozart, always finding something new. Kennedy's new Vivaldi recording was announced not only as 'another go' at *The Four Seasons*, but 'a major new initiative ... a dedicated Vivaldi Project to understand and explore Vivaldi's genius. More than three-quarters of the composer's works have yet to be heard.'[80] Surely Kennedy was not going to embark on recording *everything*? Indeed not (and nor was a similar Bach project pursued). *Vivaldi* was followed by *Vivaldi II*, but that was it. The selection process was pretty rigorous. John Stanley comments that, in choosing a sonata to complement the concertos, 'all 12 were explored before deciding on No. 2'.[81] A similar selectivity is evident in the 'Progetto Vivaldi' undertaken by the Argentinian cellist Sol Gabetta, recording with Sony, 2007-13. There are 'only' 27 Vivaldi cello concertos, and even so, Gabetta recorded under half of them, adding violin concerto transcriptions, and pieces by other contemporaries. The fact is, some of Vivaldi's works are simply much stronger than others, and 'collected' works, even of a master such as Vivaldi, are unwieldy, and potentially repetitive. A 2023 Vivaldi project by Giuliano Carmignola acknowledges as much. Originally conceived as an extensive overview of the violin concertos, it had 50 in its sights, but after much deliberation eighteen were selected, spread over three discs. It's intriguingly titled *The Three Seasons of Antonio Vivaldi*, identifying three periods of Vivaldi's development, each represented by one of the discs. The attention-grabbing title may prompt some to wonder which of the four ubiquitous concertos has been dropped. It is in fact all of them, none making the cut; a bold move, with its marketing ploy also taking a risk.

Revisiting *The Four Seasons*, Kennedy included the Vivaldi sonnets in the album notes, for the first time. Both the original Italian and a modern translation are printed. Interestingly, the English version is different from that printed in the later *New Four Seasons*, though the difference is relatively trivial compared to the musical interpretation. The later version is just slightly more colloquial. Neither are attributed. Another departure is that Kennedy provides comments on every movement of every concerto. And as with the Bach album, there are co-soloists. Kennedy writes:

> I enjoy playing concerti with another soloist – actually I think a little bit more than doing a solo concerto, because there is someone to bounce off, there's someone else who can be a catalyst. It's an extra kind of 'Call and Response' collaboration of ideas, as opposed to me coming up with too many preconceived formulae. Having another soloist who might do anything at any time stops me being too rigid about my approach to the music and injects an extra freedom and energy.[82]

The *Vivaldi (I)* album includes a DVD – part chat, part performance, with Kennedy surrounded by candles, just as in his solo Bach Prom. The chat mirrors that which featured in the original *Four Seasons* film, but the comments are more measured. Nicholas Kenyon might just have approved.

Vivaldi II won the prestigious German Echo Award for Best Performance of Eighteenth-Century Music and the supreme Austrian classical award, The Amadeus Prize, for Best Instrumental Recording. Revisiting Vivaldi was a huge success for Kennedy, but he was about to take a major step into new territory – both musical and geographical.

Practice, Imperfect

Your morning routine:
Bach – the discipline,
a rinsing of the brain,
restoring the harmony
of mind and body;
how the night again
fails to destroy the day.

It seems mere routine
can sharpen a horizon.
I think of Einstein
taking the tram in Bern,
a theory of relativity
forming with each daily
passage and refrain.

And even the routine
of your technical study
is no mere practice
but a piece of poetry
taken freshly to heart;
both heart and memory
stronger with each beat.

Your evening routine
– chasing pleasures
in a Malvern bar –
is the breakthrough.
It's there you find her,
a country in her eyes;
their treasurable blue.

Chapter 8: England vs Poland

Nigel is an Englishman, but his heart is very Slavic.—Jacek Kaspszyk

Kennedy was jamming in his local Malvern pub when he met the Polish student Agnieszka Chowniec. He was still living with Eve Westmore and their son Sark at the time. Agnieszka 'had been sent to Malvern because her parents considered it a safe, staid town, little dreaming that the most iconoclastic fiddler in Britain lived up the road.'[1] They married in 1999, and so began Kennedy's love affair with Poland. Agnieszka took him to Krakow, where he started frequenting the many jazz clubs, naturally joining the musicians on stage, and being thoroughly welcomed. As Adam Sweeting has observed, 'Part of what attracts him to life in Poland is that people are more apt to accept all the things that make up his personality, rather than expecting him to play Vivaldi's *Four Seasons* all the time.'[2]

Alan Yentob interviewed Kennedy in Poland for the BBC's *Imagine* programme in 2010. The encounter involved 'an interesting selection of local vodkas, each of them powerful enough to stop a charging rhino at 40 paces'.[3] Among the Polish musicians who contributed to the programme was jazz saxophonist and club owner Janusz Muniak, who said of Kennedy, 'I was simply stunned by his unusual behaviour for someone who plays classical music, ... I was struck firstly by the perfection of what he played, and secondly by the untypical way he dressed. He broke all conventions.'[4]

Among the many other musicians Kennedy got to know were Jerzy Bawoł, Tomasz Kukurba and Tomasz Lato, members of the klezmer band Kroke (which is Yiddish for Krakow). It was actually when Kroke were performing in Cornwall in 2001 that Kennedy proposed a collaboration. Kukurba usually plays violin in the Kroke trio, but switched to viola and flute to accommodate Kennedy. The resulting album, *East Meets East*, contains an equal balance of material newly written by Kroke and Kennedy, and arrangements of traditional tunes, the strength of which has kept them alive in the collective memory. As Kennedy says, 'if it's not written down, it's got to be good if people are going to remember it'.[5] The title of the album is a play on the *West Meets East* albums recorded by Yehudi Menuhin and Ravi Shankar and released when Kennedy was still at the Menuhin School. Once again, Kennedy was following somewhat in the footsteps of his mentor, but giving things his own twist. Part of the Kennedy/Kroke album was recorded at Abbey Road studios, where *West Meets East* had also been recorded. Another 'meeting' was involved, in that the Palestinian violinist Aboud Abdel Aal also joined the band for the song 'One Voice'.

Kennedy's comments about Kroke underline the strength of their partnership, and the musical qualities they all valued:

> What drags me into Kroke's music so successfully is this spiritual reality they have. It's honesty and sincerity in their music ... Something we were all looking for was not to clutter the music up, and to just go for the honesty of the melody and let things speak for themselves.[6]

His further comments also echo the comments he made about co-soloists on his Vivaldi albums:

> With Kroke, they're a unit, and they're a very strong band – it's not like you're having to lead all the time ... We're swapping ideas, either verbally, but most of the time just musically ... It's a very fine, healthy, equal relationship.

As with Muniak's reaction to Kennedy, the Kroke band members were astonished by Kennedy's convention-free approach, in particular his ability to cross musical boundaries *while playing*. 'None of us imagined you could change the convention so suddenly', says Tomasz Kukurba about Kennedy's electric violin development of the klezmer song 'Kukush'.[7] The Kennedy/Kroke performance at London's Polish Weekend of 2011 was one of the most exhilarating concerts I have ever witnessed, and another of their performances can be seen on the *Spirits of Music* DVD (2002).

Kennedy's attachment to Poland deepened, and his musical relationships there diversified and flourished. In 2002 he became Artistic Director of the Polish Chamber Orchestra, once again following in the footsteps of his mentor; Yehudi Menuhin had been the orchestra's Principal Guest Conductor in the 1980s. In

a film of a Vivaldi concert in the French medieval citadel of Carcassonne, one can see the great rapport between Kennedy and
his new orchestra, which he leads around the stage in a stomping
encore of 'Purple Haze'.[8]

Kennedy's first recording with the orchestra came about by
chance. He'd been playing Elgar, and after the concert someone in
the street presented him with an album of a Mlynarski concerto,
thinking that it had the same late Romantic appeal. It took several
years for Kennedy to get around to listening to the album (and
even then he subsequently lost it), but the appeal was confirmed.
Curiously, the concerto was not even well known in Poland;
Emil Mlynarski was more famous as a conductor, and founder
of the Warsaw Philharmonic; his great-grandson, Wojciech,
an even more renowned poet. Kennedy was therefore working
somewhat from scratch with the orchestra and conductor, Jacek
Kaspszyk, in a way that worked well for both parties, learning
together. Kennedy compares the process – finding the rhythmic
pacing of the work, the colours and dynamic balances – to that
of a sculptor finding the desired shape within stone. Watching
excerpts from the rehearsals, on the *Polish Spirit* DVD, you can
see the delight – the sense of revelation – on the faces of orchestra
members (though there are also amusing moments when you can
see they're thinking 'Help!').

On the album (and DVD) the Mlynarski work is partnered
by the concerto by Mieczyslaw Karlowicz. As part of his own
preparations for this work, Kennedy went off to the High Tatras
that inspired it, 'to make sure I was in the right mindset', just as he
had visited Elgar country for similar reasons, some twenty years
earlier. He speaks of his experience in the Polish mountains as
having general benefits too: 'it's so important to go and ... refresh
yourself ... start from a new canvas ... that's what walking up a
mountain can really do for you; it can open up your life.'[9]

It's a fine album, also featuring two Chopin Nocturnes,
arranged by Kzesimir Dębski. But it's the filmed concert that I
find most astonishing, the sculpture finally revealed, with all the
contributing artists the very image of focused warmth, indeed
happiness. There is clearly a very close relationship between
Kennedy and conductor Kaspszyk, so close, in fact, that Kennedy
is able to turn away from him at certain points and communicate

solely with the leader of the first violins, Jakub Haufa. The rewards of proper rehearsal time have never been clearer. There are smiles galore, but also clear emotion in Kennedy's eyes, deriving not only from the emotional spirit of the music, but also, it seems to me, from the joyous completion of a significant musical journey several years in the making. John Stanley, director of the film, deserves much credit.

David Groves, the recording producer, comments how the project extends from Kennedy's recording of Elgar, and in a sense that's right. But it's also something entirely new: there's a lack of baggage. These are classical works, but unencumbered by anyone's expectation of how they should be performed. And Kennedy is working with an orchestra of which he is artistic director. At the end of the performance, he gives credit to Kaspszyk, but refers to him not as 'conductor' but 'accompanist'. It's a revealing remark. There's no doubt that, in bringing these little-known concertos to life, Kaspszyk's extensive knowledge of Polish music was invaluable. But Kennedy would soon be on a further mission in his work with the same orchestra: to lead without a conductor at all.

Menuhin's fondest memories of working with the Polish Chamber Orchestra were of recording Beethoven and Mozart symphonies, and it was those two composers that Kennedy now turned to. A couple of years earlier he had said, 'I'd like to have another go at the Beethoven because I did it right fucking slow last time.'[10] His new recording certainly addressed that issue. To put numbers in place of expletives, the first Kennedy recording (with Klaus Tennstedt) came in at 50.11; the second at 47.59. As with the second Elgar recording, it's the outer movements that are radically faster; the middle movement is considerably slower.

The urge to revisit works in this way has already been discussed, but the particular new take on Beethoven owes much to the more surprising decision to record Mozart too – and for the very first time. Kennedy transfers Mozart's bright, light touch to the Beethoven concerto, and transforms it. Its inner gravitas is still there, but not the ponderous romantic leanings. And it's the 'chamber music' approach, with Kennedy leading not so much from the *front* as from the *heart* of the ensemble, which enables such a collective deftness of touch. As David Groves remarks,

'Chamber musicians respond to the slightest inflection in the music making',[11] while James Jolly, editor of *Gramophone* magazine, comments: 'It redefines the nature of concerto work ... So often it's the soloist versus the orchestra; I think if the soloist is also the conductor it brings the two sides of the equation much closer together.' Jolly also highlights the 'interesting dynamic [with] a music director who is a performing musician ... the band knows that this person can play as well as they can, if not considerably better'.[12] Kennedy himself says: 'The positive reason for doing music without a conductor is the communication that the orchestra have with each other, as well as me ... we have a direct relationship with each other, which means that the musicians have to use their ears, their reactions, and their skill.'[13]

Anne-Sophie Mutter made a similar decision when recording her Mozart concertos three years earlier.

> I suddenly felt an urgent desire to do it right this time ... I'm not a conductor. But I am a leader – partly because it's my nature, and partly because I know exactly what I want from the score, and how to explain it to an orchestra and inspire the musicians. Mozart himself was also more instrumentalist than conductor, and in a humbler way I am trying to emulate him, using an enlarged chamber group, unifying and inspiring it with a single idea.[14]

She echoes Kennedy's thoughts not only regarding communication within the ensemble, but the greater interpretative possibilities that are achieved as a result: 'Because inspiration is the key – making people want to follow your idea, and be part of that recreative process which is so exciting when it results in dialogue that feels totally spontaneous.'[15]

Members of the Polish Chamber Orchestra seem to side with Kennedy wholeheartedly. They also acknowledge the huge challenge – not for them, but for Kennedy – in dealing with such a complex piece as the Beethoven concerto in this way. As Peter Alward (former President of EMI Classics) says: 'There's no doubt Beethoven is a very, very difficult piece for the violinist; to then cope with the orchestra at the same time requires a considerable amount of skill, and I think a lot of violinists fight shy of that.'[16]

The Beethoven concerto was on the right side of 'challenging', and the result was a performance of almost implausible rhythmic

cohesion and precision. (Compare the closing bars of the concerto in films of Kennedy's 1992 and 2007 performances, and
marvel at the latter's perfection.) Geoff Brown in *The Times* noted
'the crisp articulation of the orchestra's four repeated notes',[17]
which drive the entire movement, as do so many of Beethoven's
rhythmic opening motifs. He was also so impressed with the 'sensational pianissimos' in the slow movement that he wrote, 'Be
careful when listening to this: you may forget to breathe.' Others,
wouldn't you just know it, found such spell-binding playing too
slow: 'too slow to sustain a flowing line',[18] wrote Rob Cowan. You
really can't please all of the people all of the time. But 'very bold,
I'll certainly give Kennedy that', he went on, a sentiment echoed
by Norman Lebrecht: 'Kennedy is still prepared to rush in where
other violinists hide like mice behind the classical skirting.'[19]
And the boldness was particularly evident in the accompanying
Mozart concerto.

Mozart wrote his concertos before he was twenty, and they
are perhaps 'immature' works compared to the later piano concertos. The simplistic equation for a record company is that they
are perfect material for a young violinist. For some, it's a good
match: Anne-Sophie Mutter was performing them aged nine,
and with Karajan when she reached thirteen. The lightness of
the music may suggest that young violinists can knock it off, but
that's highly deceptive.

Earlier in his career, Kennedy had either shunned Mozart, or
experienced negative associations. His agent lost him that first
deal; and in one early concert performance, Kennedy returned
from his cadenza in the wrong key. It was therefore surprising
that he should opt to tackle Mozart now, though even in his
previous 'anti' comments there are indications of an attraction.
Back in 2000 he stated: 'I don't really get Haydn, Mozart and
Stravinsky; I can't deal with technique being evident, I have to
have it well buried in the music ... OK, with Mozart, the content
is pretty fine ... I might try the Sinfonia Concertante one day.'[20]
When Kennedy was guest editor for Classic FM, he actually chose
Mozart as Composer of the Month. And he had after all given his
son a Mozart name, Amadeus, 'in the hope that one day I'd love
Mozart, and it's finally happened'.[21] When he took the plunge, it
was not the Sinfonia Concertante after all, but the Concerto No.

4, with Beethoven the driver: 'I never before had a reason to do it, and it's my love of Beethoven and finding a way I could play that, that related to how I could play Mozart, which led to me making this album.'²² But there was also another informing factor, from the opposite historical direction:

> My hook was to think about all the Baroque music I'd been playing and apply that energy and momentum to Mozart. There are always two vantage points from one simple melody – a joyful tune that reflects sadness. You get two emotions off the same thing.²³

There's a chain of influence: the Baroque to Mozart, Mozart to Beethoven – all of which has taken time for the violinist to develop in practice. Add that concept of ambiguous emotion, and the long childhood of what is in effect Kennedy's first classical period album begins to make sense.

Kennedy's Mozart is supremely light. Anne-Sophie Mutter's version, by comparison, feels heavier. She loads it with a touch of romanticism that Kennedy intriguingly strips *away* in his new Beethoven. Her opening triads are vibrato heavy, which is curious, considering her comment that Mozart would probably 'occasionally prefer non-vibrato to a thoroughly saturated sound'.²⁴ Rob Cowan agrees that Kennedy's Mozart is 'very light and lively, sensitive too', commenting that it's 'actually "straighter" than his Beethoven',²⁵ but there's something in store that challenges any comparisons or conventional critique: Kennedy's cadenzas.

The principle of performing (or indeed improvising) one's own cadenzas has already been discussed. The authority to do so is summed up well by Jeremy Denk, who comments, on making up his own cadenzas for Mozart piano concertos, 'I feel I'd be cheating if I didn't.'²⁶ One might think that cadenza controversy might be over, but that wouldn't take Kennedy's ability to surprise into account. Here, his cadenzas not only roam beyond traditional Mozart territory, indeed the classical genre; they are played on a different instrument – the electric violin. It's the orchestra that riffs on the Mozart theme, while Kennedy soars lark-like, using pentatonic scale and bluesy tropes. It's dreamy, and that is an aspect of Mozart that is sometimes overlooked, though it's detectable even in Mutter's cadenza.

I smile, not only at Kennedy's daring, but at the almost childlike charm of it all. I smile, too, when I think of Eric Blom's comment back in 1957: 'One has heard performances of Mozart concertos sound as though their composer were indeed the "Austrian Gershwin".'[27] This comment is doubly amusing in the light of pianist Chick Corea's ingenious melding of Mozart sonata and Gershwin song, shown in a rehearsal video the year before his death in 2021. This was something that he developed from concerts where he would talk to the audience in between pieces. The programme *pause* was really a *link* to what was to follow.

> I found out if I just let my associative mind go from one thing to another, I would be playing Mozart and I would see the similarity in the lyricism of Mozart and the melodic quality of Gershwin, and I'd say, 'That goes together,' so I'd start putting two composers together to make one kind of two-movement suite.[28]

Echoing Kennedy, Corea states that he was not originally much interested in Mozart. It was only when he heard Friedrich Gulda play Mozart 'out of context', sharing the stage at the Munich Piano Summer, 1982, that he was suddenly excited. He went on to record Mozart concertos – with his own jazz-inflected musical cadenzas. His *Mozart Sessions* album of 1996 (with Bobby McFerrin) features two concertos performed this way, predating Kennedy's by a whole decade, so one might well wonder what the fuss was about come 2006. Rob Cowan, accepting Gulda's rendition of a Mozart slow movement as being 'jazzily off the beat', wrote of Kennedy's cadenza: 'the principle would be fine if the outcome really worked but the level of artistic incongruity is unacceptably high.'[29] Kennedy, true to form, pushes things a little far. I suspect it's the electric violin that does it, and there is indeed a jolt – the opposite of Corea's Mozart/Gershwin effect – when Kennedy changes instrument; one is almost forced to picture it, and/or wonder how it would look on stage. And the electric amplification, err, amplifies the effect. We're not supposed to miss it.

In the 2007 EMI film preceding the album's release, David Groves says, of 'the fact that jazz is a twentieth century artform', 'there is no reason why performers shouldn't bring another artform of [their] day into a performance of a classical cadenza'.

Alain Lanceron adds: 'If Mozart was living today he would bring jazz into his own cadenza.'[30] This is EMI working pretty hard to defend Kennedy's approach in the album they've invested in. Groves's comment is contentious, though I personally agree with him. Lanceron's statement, however, is slightly ridiculous. There's no point speculating on Mozart's 21st-century resurrection: it ain't going to happen. Such comments belong in the 'Vivaldi would approve' bin, and are not remotely interesting to Kennedy. His idea is simpler, to 'open the hearts, open the minds of the people who are listening – to another possibility in Mozart'.[31] This 'alternative' thinking matches the ambiguous emotion already identified.

Perhaps Lanceron's statement deserves a little credit. I'm thinking of how Baz Luhrmann adapted *The Great Gatsby*, Scott Fitzgerald's jazz age portrayed through a 21st-century musical lens that matches the modern cinematography. The film is presented to us in the *now*, not as a period piece. That is essentially Kennedy's approach too. But both he and Luhrmann only work with material for which they have a deep respect, indeed a passion.

Jeremy Denk describes his cadenzas for Mozart piano concertos as 'taking Mozart for a bit of time travel',[32] which is nicely put, and applies well to Kennedy's cadenzas. In a sense, *any* performance today of Mozart, or indeed any composer from 'the past', is taking the music on a journey across time, and a performance that does so explicitly is simply underlining that fact, with honesty. As Tom Service comments, 'The only real limit is the imagination of the performer, and their ability to take the listener into orbit, and return to earth', and he makes a comparison too with jazz, where in the hands of a master such as John Coltrane, the initial 'melody becomes a distant memory, a planet glimpsed from outer space'.[33] In Kennedy's cadenzas, orbit achieves an appropriate weightlessness. Time itself seems suspended, much as it does for Vivaldi's sleeping peasants in Kennedy's later version of 'Autumn'. The orchestra is still there, like mission control back on earth.

Is the orchestral thrumming in the Elgar concerto, and other examples of the 'cadenza accompagnata' perhaps acting in a similar way? Michael Steinberg, describing the conclusion of Elgar's cadenza, writes: 'And so we wake from the dream ... as violin and orchestra carry the Concerto to a swift, brilliant conclusion.'[34] The apogee of Kennedy's Mozart dream, in the first movement, is an extended cadence that takes us into a swift descent. For Cowan, it's like 'an angelic slap in the face'[35], which is actually rather funny, given the story Kennedy tells of his earlier Mozart experience. Stephen Pettitt, by contrast, says, 'Frankly, I enjoy it so much that I almost regret it when he gets back, rather abruptly, to the printed score.'[36]

Kennedy might seem to stretch our expectation of a cadenza to its limit, but there are other examples that make Kennedy look positively restrained. A few years earlier, the French violinist Gilles Apap, whom Menuhin championed as a musician of the future, performed Mozart's third violin concerto with a final cadenza of eight minutes – longer than the rest of the movement. It is a virtuosic display, for sure, and some critics have written at length about its serious purpose. Maiko Kawabata considers it a musical example of Bakhtin's 'heteroglossia',[37] in its amalgamation of musical languages: Scottish reel, Gypsy dance, classical Indian improvisation, bluegrass; Apap whistles the Mozart theme while slapping the violin; towards the end he changes it to the minor key, and throws in a reference to Mendelssohn. The question with all of this is: *why?* On one level it's fun; Apap is clearly enjoying himself, and when he breaks into a blues rock pastiche, singing 'I woke up this morning / Could not play my fiddle no more' most of us will at least raise a smile. But how long can a 'joke' go on? Apap's cadenza puts this to the test, and ultimately risks alienating the audience. Kawabata, in comparing Apap's 'heteroglossia' to Mozart's 'style of styles' fails to acknowledge a fundamental difference: Mozart's amalgamation of eighteenth-century musical styles is supremely blended; Apap's cadenza is characterized more than anything by its fragmentedness – he can't weave one thing into another. It's this, which, in the end, proves irritating for the listener. The cadenza is a mere agglomeration lacking the necessary musical shape or overall rhythmic direction to act as any kind of cadence. There's no synthesis. It's an endless, awkward sequence of 'ok, what next?'

Revisiting Kennedy's cadenzas to Concerto No. 4, I am immediately struck by the way he sustains each of the three interjections as a single, extended moment, in contrast to Apap's atomisation. The bluesy rhapsody of the first movement cadenza is echoed with sublime subtlety in the second, and the third focuses on directing the whole concerto to its unusually quiet conclusion, to bring the music home. Not only is the trajectory of each extemporization masterfully shaped; they work together to present a fresh but thoroughly coherent account of the work as a whole.

As Tom Service points out, in French, German and Italian there is no linguistic differentiation between cadenza and cadence. Service goes so far as to suggest that Freddie Mercury's bravura call-and-response episode within Queen's Live Aid performance was a cadence/cadenza – one involving 70,000 participants; 'the note heard round the world' an extended, improvised bridge between songs, 'Hammer to Fall' fittingly up next.[38] And as I go into an orbit of my own here, I think of Ted Hughes's poem, 'Cadenza', which ends:

> Blue with sweat, the violinist
> Crashes into the orchestra, which explodes.[39]

In another fascinating 'Cadenza' poem, Michael Donaghy steps into the soloist's shoes. 'I've played it so often it's hardly me who plays', the poem begins, as if in reference to having learnt by rote, rather than by heart. But then life takes over: the poem delves into past and future, and the way in which the moment makes everything new. The printed cadenza/poem is suddenly 'a tide of musics, cities, voices', and I think of the plural musics in Kennedy's Mozart. As the poem draws to a close, Donaghy writes, 'How did I get here?' The radio static featured in the poem's opening lines is 'Suddenly articulate with Mozart. / Consider the soloist playing that cadenza / Borne to the coda by his own hands.'[40]

Donaghy, now sadly departed, always performed his poems from memory, but they were nevertheless always different in their delivery. When Kennedy plays his cadenzas in live performances, not only the delivery but the content is different every time. What we're given on the album is an example, not a definitive version. And Kennedy's inclusion of Horace Silver's 'Creepin' In' on the Beethoven/Mozart album is similarly indicative of what he might choose in performance as an encore. It's typical of Kennedy to wind up a programme with a taste of something completely different, and it's likely to be differently different on each occasion.

The Silver is well chosen though, its classical bluesy line ensuring that we remember the previous orbit. Cowan wonders, 'why didn't Kennedy reverse the process and smuggle in the odd Kreisler reference', Kennedy having used Kreisler's cadenza in the Beethoven first movement. 'Missed a trick there mate!'[41] It's fondly said, as barbed comments go, but it also misses the point. For Kennedy, these are not constructed relationships; they are instinctive manoeuvres.

The Beethoven and Mozart album was the last that Kennedy recorded with the Polish Chamber Orchestra. By the time of the Polish Weekend he had formed an orchestra all of his own: The Orchestra of Life, 'made up of talented young orchestral musicians hand-picked by Kennedy, who were equally at home performing classical repertoire, jazz and contemporary music'.[42] There would, naturally, be no conductor. Lizzie Ball, leader of the Orchestra of Life comments: 'A conductor's just totally unnecessary with him, he's so much more than just a solo violinist ... we don't need one.'[43] Kennedy would stick with his new orchestra for some years, but it was never a plan for life, or a matter of ownership. He said, at the time it was formed, 'I'll be a nominal director ... Hopefully they'll get some ideas, make some splinter groups, develop as musicians and develop their own relationships with each other musically speaking, make some initiatives of their own.' The orchestra's jazz credentials were crucial for Kennedy, who said, 'I do try to get the orchestra to behave a little more like a jazz ensemble, to respond, call and response, that proactivity from each section ... something that not every director of an orchestra would ask for.'[44] A programme of Bach and Duke Ellington would present no problem. But Kennedy was also moving further into the jazz world, with smaller bands, first with a Blue Note recording, then with two albums featuring the newly formed Nigel Kennedy Quintet.

Kennedy's liking for 'call and response' reflects that early ability shown at his Menuhin school audition, but his attention to jazz while at school (having picked up a taste for it from his stepfather's recordings of Louis Armstrong, Fats Waller and others) was initially a hidden occupation, listening in secret on a portable radio in bed. That seems rather appropriate, given the long history of jazz, and the blues before it, as defiant, oppositional to the dominant regime. As jazz became popular in America, during the early part of the twentieth century, it was widely viewed by the establishment as dangerous. *The New York Times* of 12 February 1922 carried a front page report from Kansas City, where Ira Cammack, Superintendent of Schools had asserted that 'Jazz music has much the same effect on young people as liquor, and should be legislated against'. His speech to a thousand teachers concluded: 'I think the time has come when teachers should assume a militant attitude toward all forms of this debasing and degrading music.'

In Poland, under communism in the 1950s, there was a similar conflict, though a different scenario. Jazz was the musical expression of opposition to the system, but it was also an underground movement – often quite literally, in cellars. Jarek Śmietana says, 'there was a time when jazz was forbidden by government'. In Alan Yentob's words, 'listeners needed music that kept its secrets to itself. They found solidarity within the intricate cross-currents of jazz.' Solidarity, and also danger. Janusz Muniak puts it starkly: 'people risked their lives just to listen to jazz music.'[45]

Kennedy describes Polish instrumental jazz, in particular, as 'freedom music ... resistance music, because no one understood what the music was about. It couldn't be censored because there weren't words',[46] and it is generally instrumental jazz that Kennedy has pursued. 'Freedom music' – almost of any kind – inevitably appeals to Kennedy, and he has summed up his own jazz practice by saying, 'I just play what I feel like playing at the time. In fact, that's my definition of jazz - just play what it is you want to play.'[47] That is of course easier said than done. It's the remark of someone who happens to have an instinctive grasp of what, for others is an almost impenetrable set of rules.

Much is made of Kennedy introducing people to classical music, but the world of jazz is surely an equally closed book to many listeners, its principles arguably harder to grasp for non-musicians and classical technicians alike. Jamming to twelve-bar blues is one thing, but where jazz goes to – and how it gets back – can seem a mystery. And because it's so intuitive to those who 'can', there's rarely explanation. Or, if there is, it's in terms that are themselves mystifying. Even the so-called classifications can be baffling: Bebop, Hard Bop... 'Classical' and 'Romantic' seem positively obvious by comparison. And as with classical music, the more avant-garde end of the spectrum can seem frankly unintelligible.

As stated earlier, Menuhin lacked a true jazz intuition, but he articulates the crux of the matter pretty well:

> a rigorous structure must be mastered if creation is to flower at the moment of performance. Otherwise to improvise would be to invent a language on the spur of the moment. Grammar, syntax, vocabulary must all be known before the everyday miracle of speech occurs. So it is with improvisation. It presupposes a path between the mind's dictation and the fingers' obedience so short that it can't be measured, but the laying of the path is the work of technique and discipline developed in years of training.[48]

Menuhin never did the learning as a young musician, and as previously mentioned, needed to prepare his musical script when playing with Ravi Shankar, or with Grappelli. But even from this 'subordinate distance from genuine improvisation', he felt some of the precious vibe, being in the thick of a musical outpouring that would never be repeated, his senses attuned to everything that was happening in a heightened way.

If, like Kennedy, you get an early intimation of that vibe, as a child, it's likely to take hold; you follow it up with fanatical listening and self-instructed practice. That's the tried and tested path of most musicians outside the classical arena. In the late 1990s, however, the Associated Board of the Royal Schools of Music (ABRSM) introduced exams in Jazz (Grades 1–5) for piano. The set pieces included improvisational sections, with the performer required to fill in the empty bars with their own melody to fit the repeating chord progression. Nowadays, with Trinity College also offering such exams, proficiency in 'call and response' (or 'quick study' as ABRSM calls it) is also required, with ensemble playing an option. Charles Beale was the lead consultant in a programme that eventually offered the exams for wind and brass instruments too. All this seems on one hand positive, but on the other an anathema. Is it really a valid route to the heart of jazz? Kennedy would surely not give it the time of day. But stringed instruments are in any case not catered for, which raises the further question: why, when the single most famous classical musician of the era

– a violinist – was also enticing people into the world of jazz, was the violin excluded from jazz exams? ABRSM's own statistics show the number of children playing the violin gaining parity, from 1999 to 2014, with those learning the electric guitar. Brass and woodwind instruments are not even in the top ten.

Perhaps the argument was that teachers of the right sort didn't exist. After all, Menuhin himself would have lacked the credentials. And despite the example of Stéphane Grapelli and others, the violin was – and possibly still is – still seen as a jazz band outsider. As Kennedy has commented, 'It's compromising to adapt jazz music to the violin. Jean-Luc Ponty showed me that you have to adapt the violin to the music.'[49] Kennedy, like Ponty (who worked with Frank Zappa in the 60s and 70s), has made extensive and innovative use of the electric violin – customized for purpose.

There may be some logic, then, in the violin's exclusion. I can't help but suspect, though, that Kennedy's anti-establishment image may have had something to do with it. Other examples of jazz violinists were not only few, they were also mostly in the rebel mould. As Alfred Hickling comments:

> it's worth noting that some of the greatest hell-raisers in jazz history have been fiddlers – figures such as the first amplified player, Stuff Smith, who was said to have taken the apron strings off the violin; or the notorious joker Joe Venuti, who once astonished a New York hostess by arranging a platter of salad vegetables around his penis.[50]

Shortly before his death in 1978, Venuti, on meeting Kennedy, 'pulled out this Stradivarius and said, "I bet my fiddle's fucking louder than yours." It was, because he'd drilled a hole in it for a volume knob.'[51] This was possibly not the type of example that the ABRSM wished to encourage.

I can't find it in my heart to dismiss the whole concept of the jazz exam, though I do question the centrality of exams in music education generally. There are no doubt countless pupils who have gained real enjoyment – and useful understanding – in their introduction to various jazz skills. It would be interesting to know the subsequent paths they have taken. Within my own main field, I recognize how many good writers have emerged from creative writing courses, even though such courses have received plenty of criticism. And though I still find it hard to match a formal jazz education with the essential street credibility of the genre, there's no doubt that jazz courses at university, especially in the US, have been a success. They turn out 'employable musicians capable of "making it" in the outside world'.⁵² That's their mission, after all, but it also means that they play safe, tending to avoid, for instance, the type of 'free jazz' that is, apart from anything else, difficult to grade; it's a typical example of how academia's pursuit of excellence is fundamentally compromised. There is also an emphasis on solo virtuosity, mirroring the problem Menuhin identified in Moscow, where ensemble skills were of secondary importance. With jazz, that's surely a major problem.

Kennedy's self-instruction in jazz, born of single-minded hours of dedicated attention, is comparable to how a 'genius' such as Gascoigne or Messi hones their range of skills, spending every solitary hour available with a football. Then you need some like-minded friends, to extend that range, make it a team thing. Kennedy was fortunate enough to have a couple of friends at the Menuhin school who joined him in that process. Then he had the bigger luck of being introduced to Grappelli, and hence the circuit of small UK clubs, the New York scene, and finally the Polish musicians with whom he teamed up for a significant new phase of his working life. Jazz internationally may have 'cleaned up', no longer 'chasing the bird' (in reference to Charlie Parker's alcohol intake), and be performed in shiny new performing arts venues, but Kennedy still gravitates to the 'dirtier' side of jazz. That is where and how his new band, The Nigel Kennedy Quintet, was formed.

The headline story, however, was rather different, in that Kennedy's first jazz recording in this new phase was his *Blue Note Sessions* album of 2006. The Blue Note label was famed throughout the world, 'the most fabled jazz label of all ... the label behind the golden age of bebop in the 1950s and 60s'.⁵³ While the earlier *Nigel Kennedy Plays Jazz* was a charmingly lightweight offering, the *Blue Note Sessions* was an altogether more serious undertaking. Recording the album in New York, he worked with an impressive group of highly regarded jazz musicians. Amongst the eight joining Kennedy were Ron Carter and Jack DeJohnette, who, like Chick Corea, had performed with Miles Davis. Kenny Werner and Jo Lovano had worked together and recorded extensively for

Blue Note. Kennedy's 'decision' to record with such musicians on the prestigious label was equally a mark of acceptance. He was joining the jazz establishment.

Having respect for any *establishment* seems at odds with what we might expect of Kennedy, but it was clearly an important step for him, putting his self-styled jazz credentials to the test, while also asserting the nobility of the jazz tradition itself. His respect seems almost like reverence. Even conventions are suddenly ok, and in performance he wants an audience to observe them too – clapping at the end of solos, for instance, sometimes while he introduces the soloist in time-honoured fashion.

I suspect I'm not alone in finding the whole business of band members taking turns as soloist a rather predictable, sometimes even a tiresome routine, but it's a core part of the bebop style, which Kennedy's *Blue Note* album mainly adheres to. The different ideas and inflections that individuals bring to their solos are an important part of what the jazz fan relishes, and as Travis Jackson comments, a jazz ensemble is characterized by 'the individual sounds of *musicians* rather than the sounds of *instruments*'.[54]

The ways in which an opening melody dissolves into the improvised solos demands close listening if you actually want to 'understand' what's happening. The alternative is to let it wash over you – or switch off. For the players, the plot is (hopefully) not lost, but it may be beyond the listener's musical literacy. The various evolving solo drifts can seem to obscure the underlying pattern of chord changes – which are in any case, for the uninitiated, harder to recognize than the more obvious patterns of blues and rock; at a basic level, jazz chords are likely to add a complicating extra note – a sixth, seventh, ninth, etc (and sometimes several of those together) to the more recognized triad. And while we may recognize these harmonic leanings within jazz, there is then the danger that things that are *familiar* also feel too *similar*. The same can be true of the scales and other melodic manoeuvres soloists deploy; even the most inventive can become formulaic – 'licks' that others copy, akin, in a small way, to written cadenzas.

Kennedy is aware of other potential pitfalls: 'the last thing I want is someone taking a solo and just playing blistering notes for half an hour. That's all been done, and it's how you throw spins and what space you leave which actually gives some perspective.'[55]

With his Blue Note ensemble, that 'space' is well managed by all the musicians, and their interaction is excellent. The duetting (and sometimes doubling) of violin and saxophone is particularly impressive, with Kennedy's vibrato-free playing a perfect tonal match for the sax. There are nevertheless times when I would probably be heading for the bar, typically in the established numbers. I find Kennedy's own compositions are more distinctive in their mood. 'Stranger in a Stranger Land' makes a nod to Robert Heinlein's sci-fi novel, and foreshadows 'The Hills of Saturn' a couple of years down the line, but 'Maybe in Your Dreams' is the most atmospheric of all.

Kennedy subsequently toured his *Blue Note* numbers not with the New York musicians, but with his Polish 'Nigel Kennedy Quintet' (NKQ). There's a DVD of a Paris performance (and yes, of *course* he wanted to perform this music in Paris, where Grappelli's Quintette du Hot Club de France became legendary). The two recorded sets offer a slightly different choice of numbers to the album, and the added sense of how the music works live. The DVD includes another Kennedy composition, '15 Stones' (about 15 stones he saw in the Ryōan-ji garden in Kyoto, Japan), which would later appear on the NKQ's first release, *A Very Nice Album* (2008), the two discs of which are titled 'Melody' and 'Invention', in close reference to 'Harmony and Invention' in the title of the larger set of concertos to which Vivaldi's *Four Seasons* belongs.

A Very Nice Album is also a double: one disc is claret; the other blue. 'Hills of Saturn', on disc 1, is one of Kennedy's finest compositions, as beautifully crafted as the title is baffling. 'Everyone talks about the rings of Saturn, but what about the hills' Kennedy asks, by way of 'explanation'. In the CD booklet there's a little drawing of the hills, in Aston Villa colours, surrounded by the more familiar rings.[56] The track begins (and ends) pianissimo, with gorgeous, slowly shifting harmonies. Then comes the surprise, a shift of a different sort as the harmonies continue – at high volume, with aggressive percussion. The contrast is intense, but familiarity with the recording doesn't begin to prepare you for how the contrast is delivered live. At the Festival Hall performance, within Kennedy's Polish Weekend, I was sitting behind an elderly lady who quite literally jumped in her seat as the volume changed. It was an instant effect, Kennedy hitting a foot-pedal, and Krzysztof Dziedzic letting loose on drums.

In the *Imagine* film, Yentob asks pianist Piotr Wylezol, 'Why do you find it easy to play with Nigel?', at which Wylezol cracks up into the most spontaneous heartfelt laughter I have ever heard. 'Easy' is clearly the wrong word. Nevertheless, Wylezol says of Kennedy, 'He understands the rules of jazz.'[57] 'Rules' is an interesting term here, in that jazz has been changing its own rules throughout its history. The rules observed at Preservation Hall in New Orleans have elsewhere evolved in various radical ways. And despite Kennedy's Blue Note mission, his subsequent jazz compositions have roamed with freedom into other musical territories.

A Very Nice Album was not in fact labelled as jazz, simply as 'songs composed and arranged by Nigel Kennedy'. 'Boo Boooz Blooooze', for instance, is as its title suggests a raucous, drawling blues number, with Kennedy himself singing – not the sort of thing to appeal to a certain type of jazz purist. But the album featured plentiful *elements* of jazz, sufficient for the NKQ to be booked for jazz festivals – and suffer the consequences. Writing about the NKQ at the Cheltenham Jazz Festival in 2009, Alyn Shipton praised Kennedy's 'remarkable sensitivity in caressing a melody to life', but had quibbles. Not only did he dislike the 'empty bombast' of the 'backing band' (an odd description), he also took issue with Kennedy's sound. He found the 'gorgeous middle register tone' of Kennedy's violectra compelling until the volume was cranked up 'in his effects-laden Hendrix style, his sound screaming and distorted'.[58] But the variety of tone and effect produced by the violectra and pedals, as played by Kennedy, is of course its strength. As John Bungey states, it can move 'from sweetly melodic to Hendrix freak-out, often in the same song'.[59] Shipton's bigger criticism took aim at Kennedy's improvising skills: 'too often his lines abandon jazz timing and resort to dazzling ornaments culled from the classical violin repertoire without the melodic or harmonic reinvention that had been so richly on offer elsewhere throughout the weekend.'[60] Yet again, we see Kennedy criticized because of context. It's not surprising that Kennedy, in *Uncensored!*, mentions his disillusionment with 'the typical jazz scene'[61] as well as the classical world.

Bungey said of Kennedy's Blue Note phase that, 'for a man perceived as a maverick, his jazz tastes are pretty conservative',[62] but with the greater range of style – and style fusions – on the NKQ albums, Kennedy still received stick. His 'sweetly modal tunefulness' was deemed 'oddly dated ... The one thing the music doesn't do is swing.'[63] But swing was never an absolute require-ment of jazz (nor indeed was improvisation). Some tracks were dismissed as pop, and worst of all, it seemed, was the drift towards 'unironic prog rock'.[64] Jazz, however 'dirty', is considered sophis-ticated, prog rock not; there aren't any ABRSM prog rock exams. The Sex Pistols et al were supposed to have consigned 'progres-sive' rock to the musical dustbin, as if 'progression' can only go so far. Emerson Lake and Palmer's touring convoy of trucks laden with 40 tons of equipment encapsulated prog's relation-ship with absurdity, and its reputation as musical dinosaur, but ELP's arch-critic Johnny Rotten (John Lydon) would actually become neighbour and friend to Keith Emerson in California. It's with matching irony that the so-called 'punk violinist', Kennedy, should be finding further mileage for prog – through his adven-turing with jazz.

Truth is, prog rock always had a relationship of sorts with jazz. Certain Yes albums veer towards jazz, and one has only to listen to ELP's extended version of Aaron Copland's *Fanfare for the Common Man* to hear the two genres working together. The outer, driving rock sections embrace a wild and lengthy improvised middle section that asks very different questions of the music – and the listener; the composer too. Copland, who approved the version generally, wasn't sure what the middle part was doing there. I'll admit to feeling the same about some of Kennedy's jazz – or rather, I know very well why the middle ramblings are there, I just don't *like* them as much as the crafted opening and closing sections. 'Hills of Saturn' is one example; another is 'Father and Son', which is based on the 15th-century French setting of *O Come, O Come Emmanuel*. The beautifully phrased opening is exquisite, but then the saxophone takes over and I want to walk away. At the Cheltenham Jazz Festival, Alyn Shipton clearly heard a very different version, with only violin and piano, and I can imagine that working much better. Shipton admired how Kennedy's 'soaring solo ... retained the contour of the melody. The touch of genius that makes his classical playing so compelling shone through.'[65]

Not only was *A Very Nice Album* written and arranged by Kennedy; he also produced it, and this again seemed to be a problem: 'you wonder what would happen if a disciplined producer took him in hand', wrote Clive Davis.[66] One thinks of course about George Martin and The Beatles, a transformative partnership. But Phil Spector, revered at the time, would later have his work on The Beatles' *Let It Be* stripped right back to reveal a much better album at the core, the album that McCartney had envisaged in the first place. Why not trust the artist to engineer their own vision?

A Very Nice Album was followed by *SHHH!* (2010), with Krzysztof Dziedzic replacing Pawel Dobrowolski on drums, and Boy George covering Nick Drake's 'River Man'. In with the more recognizable jazz, there's the deep tranquility of the title track and the hard-hitting rock of the concluding 'Oy'. Once again, the diversity is almost guaranteed to infuriate, though for me it works. It resists the label of fusion, being more a musical pick 'n' mix – with attitude. In the press release Kennedy wrote, 'I love moving from one style to another' – it's what makes life interesting for me as a musician. It's a kind of trip we're all making together.' He won't have been bothered by Clive Davis commenting that 'Jazzers won't find much to detain them';[67] Kennedy by this stage had ceased to be interested in pleasing the connoisseurs. In *Uncensored!* he writes that he's now only doing what he loves: 'I'm keeping the amateur spirit. People use amateur in a disparaging way, but in fact, it's the real business about what art or musical sports could really be.'[68]

Davis finished his review of *A Very Nice Album* by saying, 'Heaven knows what next month's late-night Prom will sound like.'[69] Isn't that as it should be – a concert an unpredictable musical encounter? Kennedy's Prom of 19 July 2008 did indeed surprise, with an extraordinary guest performance by the legendary rock and blues guitarist, Jeff Beck, who would himself serve up an equivalent surprise by welcoming Johnny Depp to his stage in 2022.

Three years after the Prom would come a concert, or rather a chain of thirteen of them, taking surprise to a new level.

Nigel Kennedy's Polish Weekend

All this, I am aware, sounds fanciful and is perhaps misremembered, written up. But if it is: well, that is the spectator's fate—we watch but in the end we have to guess.—Ian Hamilton

In 2011, The NKQ was at the heart of the most outrageously ambitious event of Kennedy's career to date: a three-day 'Polish Weekend' that he curated at London's Southbank Centre, celebrating Polish music and culture. It coincided with the 200th anniversary of Chopin's birth in what was being dubbed 'Polska!' year. At the heart of the weekend was Kennedy's 'World Cup Project', a screening of the England vs Poland football match of 1973, in which England – for the first time ever – failed to qualify for the tournament. Kennedy's band engaged with a group of Polish musicians in providing a semi-improvised soundtrack to the otherwise silent footage. It exemplified Kennedy's profound association between music and sport, football in particular.

Curiously, the match in question is not featured in *Uncensored!*, where Kennedy concentrates almost exclusively on Aston Villa matches, but it's one that has a genuine claim to legendary status. It took place at Wembley on 17 October, and was broadcast live on ITV with Hugh Johns and Billy Wright commentating. In the studio before kick-off, TV pundit Brian Clough – always a controversial character – was calling Polish goalkeeper Jan Tomaszewski a 'circus clown in gloves';[70] at half-time he still refused to retract his comment, but it was Tomaszewski who turned the whole match on its head, 'enter[ing] football folklore with a virtuoso, if unorthodox performance'.[71] The England team included sublimely gifted players such as Alan Clarke and Southampton's Mick Channon, but they just couldn't get past Tomaszewski, who dived at Clarke's feet to make a save in the early minutes and only found out later that he'd broken five bones in his left wrist. Tomaszewski comments: 'They were frozen during the game and the adrenaline meant I did not feel the pain.'[72] Years later, when Tomaszewski met up with Clough, the latter retracted his 'clown' comment. He said he was absolutely wrong, which must have been an all-time first.

It was an extraordinary match, totally one-sided, with England having 36 shots on goal, Poland only two. Two England goals were disallowed, the one by Mick Channon for no apparent reason. But football is cruel: the match ended in a draw. England failed to qualify for the first time ever, and Sir Alf Ramsey, hero of 1966 when England had won the tournament, was sacked. Clips from the match are available on YouTube (one with over a quarter of a million views) but it's unlikely that the match is much re-watched in its entirety. Kennedy however provided that opportunity during his Polish Weekend.

It was a 'long weekend' in more ways than one, extending into the May Bank Holiday Monday, with Kennedy scheduling thirteen concerts within the three days – and playing in eight of those concerts himself. 'I wanted to bring some Polish culture over to London and make the Southbank Centre into a miniature Poland for a while' says Kennedy.[73] He had been living in Krakow for nine years and felt that he had benefited enormously from the range of live music prevalent in Poland.

One of the concerts featured the Jarek Śmietana Band, with which Kennedy had collaborated the previous year on their Hendrix album, contributing to three tracks. For another, he assembled 'Nigel Kennedy's Chopin Super Group', which improvised on familiar Chopin pieces in ways that sometimes rendered them unrecognizable once the initial exposition was over. It wasn't just jazz that Kennedy would listen to in semi-secrecy at the Menuhin School; he used to listen to Chopin on 'propaganda radio from Poland', and here the two were mixed.

Bearing in mind what Donald Grout writes about Chopin, we shouldn't be too surprised by Kennedy's concept. Grout claims the composer's works 'have an introspective character and, within clearly defined formal outlines, contrive to suggest the quality of improvisation'.[74] Kennedy's greater liberty was perhaps to substitute 'introspection' with a more extrovert musical jam. And yet, as Lawrence Kramer comments, Chopin incorporates 'multiple dialectical patterns within a single continuous texture ... different patterns, superimposing ... on one another in a kind of loose conceptual polyphony'.[75] The Chopin Super Group put all that to a highly dramatic test, and as Yentob observed, 'Throwing Chopin into a musical blender was always going to be fraught with risks.'[76] It put a whole new slant on Kramer's further comment: 'the question that needs to be asked of this music is not what deep structure holds it together, but rather what motivates it to keep breaking apart.'[77]

There had been disagreements, it seems, between the various musicians. The singer Anna Maria Jopek had not been happy with how pianist Janusz Olejniczak (who played in Polanski's film *The Pianist*) was interpreting things. Disagreements may have been put aside, but it was clear that this particular event was under-prepared. Kennedy 'organizing' the stage at the beginning had the look of a worried schoolteacher ahead of a shambolic school play. He couldn't decide where to put his violin, and in the end decided to place it inside the open grand piano.

It was decidedly weird, but nonetheless engaging, and two things were particularly memorable. First was the performance of Chopin's Prelude No. 6 in B minor, arranged as a duet for piano and violin. Kennedy played what is usually the bass line of the piece, allowing the melody to soar above rather than underlie the chordal accompaniment. This was in some respects an obvious division of labour, though perhaps as a result more conventional than Chopin's original. (Yo-Yo Ma and Bobby McFerrin did something similar but more unexpected still with Gounod's 'Ave Maria', Ma playing the melody on cello and McFerrin *singing* the original Bach prelude accompaniment; intriguingly strange.) What makes it linger in the mind is the fact that Kennedy read this shortest of pieces from the music, startling for reasons that I discussed in Chapter 3. There was also no improvisation, and so it came across as a small oasis of calm within a rather manic event.

Equally memorable was something entirely different, Kennedy's decision for the Super Group to play, as an encore, a repeat of the Polonaise they had played earlier, to see if they could get it right. Who else does that kind of thing? It was an honest admission that the first rendition had not gone too well. There is another story of such behaviour, told by Helen Wallace, who remembers Kennedy playing *The Four Seasons* in Farnham, circa 1980.

> When it was over, Kennedy stepped forward... and apologised. A gasp swept through the blue-rinses. 'Hello, folks. I played that slow movement from "Winter" out of tune – let's

see if I can do better this time.' And off he went, beside a
noticeably tight-lipped leader ... [People] were reeling from
the shock of hearing a professional musician confess to having
played less than perfectly.[78]

That shock was echoed ahead of the Proms *Four Seasons* in 2013,
when Clemency Burton-Hill asked Kennedy if his fresh take
would be like hearing it for the first time. Kennedy replied: 'If I hit
all of the notes, that will certainly be for the first time!'[79] Perhaps
this refreshingly honest attitude owes something to Menuhin.
Tasmin Little, also a student at the Menuhin School, remembers
playing with her mentor in a string quartet:

> During an initial rehearsal he skipped a bar and was out of
> time with the rest of the group. He stopped, turned to me
> and asked, 'Tasmin, am I ahead of you all?' Stumbling for the
> appropriate way to reply in the affirmative, I said hesitantly,
> 'Well, only one bar...' His face broke into an enormous smile
> and he gave the lovely gentle chuckle that I knew so well. It
> did not worry him at all that he had made a mistake ... From
> that moment I learned that one should not be ashamed or
> frightened of making mistakes, as long as one learns from
> them, and that it is important to remember that we can never
> be 'perfect' musicians but can only strive to make the best
> music that we can.[80]

It was a rousing Polonaise that the Chopin Super Group delivered
second time around that afternoon. One got the impression that
Kennedy was now fully warmed up, just as the event was finishing. Luckily, he'd be onstage again within a few hours.

The daytime and evening Polish Weekend events were followed by 'Nigel's Front Room Late', jazz sessions that went on as
long as the Southbank Centre could possibly allow, with selected
audience members involved on stage. There was also a lot of
Kennedy kissing the hands of his female fans; my daughter was so
honoured, also with an ink-drawn heart, NK, and quintet graphic.
What I carried away was the sight of Kennedy playing while
holding a champagne bottle and a pint of Guinness. To requote
Ian Hamilton, 'All this, I am aware, sounds fanciful and is perhaps
misremembered'. After all, I had had a few myself by then.

As Adam Sweeting wrote for theartsdesk, 'the timetable had been ripped to shreds by the end of the opening Saturday'.[81] It was exhausting just to watch it, but exhilarating too.

The centrepiece event took place on the Sunday evening in the Royal Festival Hall. On the previous evening Kennedy had given it a plug: 'We have no idea how it's going to work, so if you want to see a total fucking mess, do come along.' It was originally a ticketed event scheduled to take place in the main concert auditorium, but Kennedy made a late decision to stage it in the foyer as a free event (with tickets refunded) in order to create the atmosphere he was after. The foyer backs onto the bar, and the whole place was draped with football flags and banners, with tables set up cabaret style.

It was very late getting started. Marshall Marcus, the Southbank Centre's head of music at the time, came on to thank us for our patience and assure us that things would be underway soon. 'There's just one problem', he said. 'He's called Nigel Kennedy.' One got the impression that the violinist was seriously trying the patience of his hosts, though I'm not sure the audience was too worried. Drinks were to hand, and delay only added to the sense of occasion and anticipation. Meanwhile the stage was filling with an almost implausible array of kit. Not only was Kennedy to be joined by members of his own Orchestra of Life, this time with electrified instruments; many other musicians featuring in other concerts were also involved. It was, essentially, Kennedy's 'English' team pitched against Polish rivals in a collaborative musical act of improvised commemoration.

On the big screen behind (and on additional monitors to the side) the fateful match was then replayed – without the commentary, although at one stage Barry Davies, the original commentator for the BBC's highlights had been rumoured to be taking part. Kennedy was keen on having the original Polish commentator, plus John Motson, and I can imagine Motty's humour having worked a treat. The soundtrack was instead that of the musicians onstage engaging in semi-improvised contest for the full 90 minutes. It was an event beyond any ready comparison – except, perhaps, to the bewildering nature of the original match. There was, of course, one crucial difference: in Kennedy's re-play the final score was a foregone conclusion; it was the music that provided the unpredictable drama.

Was it the chaos Kennedy himself had predicted? There were chaotic elements, certainly, but there were clearly structural principles involved. Each group of musicians deployed various themes, some of them familiar from other concerts or recordings. Kennedy, for instance, used melodies and riffs from his recently recorded album *SHHH!*; he was countered by a particularly high energy performance by the Polish violinist Sebastian Karpiel-Bulecka, whose band Zakopower had played the previous day, and made use of material some of us had already heard. That made sense, in that footballers too bring highly practised moves to their game. There were managerial hand signals involved in letting the other musicians know where to head next.

Kennedy was wearing his Aston Villa football shirt, as he so often does, and there were Villa banners as well as the national banners dressing the arena. To Kennedy followers this came as no surprise, and my earlier chapters have already mentioned his passion for football, Villa in particular. It does though need some further explanation, not least because Kennedy's own football reflections in *Uncensored!* are so personal and obsessively detailed that I suspect anyone other than Villa fans may find them bewildering.

The Beautiful Game

Until recent times, Aston Villa Football Club had a pretty dignified history; in Kennedy's words it was 'the greatest team in the world before American and now Chinese ownership'.[82] Founded in 1874, it was a founder member of league football in 1888. It's the Aston Villa stadium that gets mentioned by Philip Larkin in his poem 'MCMXIV':

> Those long uneven lines
> Standing as patiently
> As if they were stretched outside
> The Oval or Villa Park[83]

Kennedy's connection stems from 1964, the same year that he gained a scholarship to the Yehudi Menuhin School, and his mother remarried and moved to Solihull, near Birmingham. It was Villa Park where he found a new sense of home and belonging, as so many do in joining a tribe. 'He even wrote a poem about Villa's promotion prospects, 'We'll be Back!', for the school magazine.'

It was the vibe of the place that swung it, as his first match experience had actually been at the Birmingham City ground. Loyalty to the tribe then becomes paramount. Playing at the BBC Proms in 2015, he drew the line at joining in the performance of 'You'll Never Walk Alone', pointing out that it was a 'Liverpool song'. Partisan thinking, and behaviour, can be ruthless. It can also be grotesquely distorted, as evidenced by the disgraceful 'Hillsborough' taunting of Liverpool fans by some rivals. But as Kennedy states (albeit not in his own words) in *Always Playing*, 'tragedies such as Hillsborough leave a deep scar on every supporter – in fact everybody'.[84]

Many find such a sense of belonging; it is the extent to which football impinges on Kennedy's musical performances that is altogether more startling. Take this famous example:

When [Villa] won the European Cup in Rotterdam in 1982, Kennedy was playing a concert in Germany. He halted the concert and erected a giant screen so that he and the audience could watch the match before continuing his concert. 'It was the right result that night', he said. 'And the crowd enjoyed both the music and the football'.[85]

His Gershwin recording (2018) features 'Rhapsody in Claret and Blue' (the Villa strip); his business card sports those very colours and his electric violin is similarly customized. Even his BMW and house in the Malvern Hills were decorated to match. That might be considered an affectation, but Kennedy is open about the depth of the obsession: 'One time I took two years off the violin to watch the Villa, and I used to watch the Villa, the Villa reserves and the Villa youth team, every week ... some people would call that wasting your life.'[86]

When Kennedy made Poland his second home, he adopted Cracovia as a second allegiance. Like Villa it's one of its country's oldest clubs. When the Polish Weekend 'match' was staged it was, in a sense, Kennedy against Kennedy.

All of this is clear indication that, for Kennedy, football is a personal passion equivalent to music, and that he sees no reason to keep them apart. The title of the book, *Always Playing*, might refer to either. (The French edition, titled *La confession d'un violoniste virtuose hors du commun*, loses the meaning entirely.) When talking about rival Polish composers Karlowicz and Mlynarski he immediately reaches (jokily) for a football metaphor: 'Like Kraków's two football stadiums ... very close together, but very far apart.'[87] But he goes further, with statements about the relationship between music and football, and extending this to sport generally. 'I sometimes liken music to competitive sport. You see the great sportsmen and they are continually trying to improve. Even when they get to number one, they are never satisfied, they want to do more. Well, so do I.'[88] In the Polish Weekend programme he wrote: 'There's a similarity between music and football in that football brings a lot of people together and music is obviously designed expressly for that purpose. They are also both shared pursuits across all nations.'[89] He has also commented, 'For me there's an important correspondence between 40,000 people in a football stadium all wanting the same thing, that mass consciousness, and the performance of music.'[90]

More significant still are comments about managing and conducting, as in the 'Long-Gone Fathers' football chapter of *Always Playing*. Harbouring a scathing attitude towards most conductors, Kennedy states: 'Up until the 1960s there was the same lasting allegiance between a conductor and his orchestra ... just like a good manager and his team.'[91] And as he said to Peter Culshaw, in the run-up to the Polish Weekend, 'I'm a player-manager, I get on the field and direct the action.'[92] In *Uncensored!* he states: 'I see sport and music both as being forms of self-expression with collaboration, two beautiful things that people can benefit from.'[93]

It was the Brazilian footballer Pelé who, in 1977, made 'the beautiful game' a popular, recognized reference to football, though HE Bates would appear to have been the first to use it, in a *Sunday Times* article titled 'Brains in the feet.'[94] As that newspaper article indicates, the brainwork of football is not of a cerebral or academic nature; it is instinctive, and Kennedy – despite his substantial musical erudition – clearly favours an equivalent brainwork (and beauty) in music. A further, frequent reference, in describing football of the highest quality, is to poetry, and not just as an off-the-peg metaphor. In his contribution to the Poetry Foundation website, 'All Great Soccer Players Are Poets', Duy Doan comments:

> How often does Messi, for instance, with the game in the balance and his team depending on him to make the difference, summon the most imaginative, most beautiful solution possible? It's almost as if he doesn't know how to play any other way. When given the opportunity, Messi always opts for the memorable.[95]

Perhaps the most astonishing comment of all comes from Eric Cantona, who famously said: 'I will never find any difference between Pelé's pass to Carlos Alberto in the final of the 1970 World Cup and the poetry of the young Rimbaud.'[96]

I've already mentioned my debt, in writing about Kennedy, to the poet Ian Hamilton. Writing about Paul Gascoigne, he approaches his task as fan – both of football generally and of Gascoigne as an individual, and that's not the same thing as writing a hagiography. He says: 'Most soccer fans need to get hooked on the fortunes of a single player';[97] and 'you have to be part yob, part connoisseur'.[98] There's a fascinating exchange when Hamilton and Gascoigne actually meet:

> 'Have you ever played football?' asked Gascoigne.
> 'Well, no, not really, not ...'
> 'Well, fucking shut up then.'[99]

I feel at risk of a similar put-down. I play the violin (and football), but I'm a poor amateur, in awe of the artistry of Nigel Kennedy and Paul Gascoigne. Why am I so presumptuous in thinking I have anything to add to what such artists accomplish? I don't want to be a commentator (though there's an artistry to that, in the case of a Barry Davies or John Motson). I am more interested in being an interpretive narrator – like Kennedy in his recreation of England vs Poland.

On 30 May 2011, in the foyer of the Royal Festival Hall, even among those familiar with Nigel Kennedy's work – and the level of unpredictability that goes with it – few had any real idea what we were going to see or hear. Nor can we easily revisit it: almost no record exists of the entire, extraordinary weekend, apart from a few illegal recordings by members of the audience (despite the vigilance of Jude Kelly and others), and nothing at all of the World Cup Project itself. I seem to remember official cameras, but presumably the 'result' was not deemed acceptable for distribution. I doubt that Kennedy would have been worried about that. He believes, as do many other artists and performers, that a privilege belongs to those who attend – those who have paid money, travelled – and in the importance of the moment.

There were moments of brilliance. Towards the end, a snippet of the British National Anthem emerged, just as it might from the crowd. And when the assembly moved into the adjacent 'late room', it was as if to a pub near Wembley after the match, to celebrate or commiserate, but also to enjoy more music, fuelled by the sense of an event that had proved momentous – both historically and in its recreation.

Reviews were not altogether enthusiastic. John Walters, writing in *The Guardian* commented:

Kennedy's riffs were redolent of Hot Rats-era Zappa, electric Miles and white funk. There's nothing like Wembley and endless feedback solos to bring out one's inner bloke. The match was better structured than the music, though, as heroic goalkeeper Jan Tomaszewski made save after save against the vivid green pitch and K-tel ads of 1970s TV football. When Poland scored, the audience erupted, but the 'soundtrack' just riffed on until coming to an arbitrary halt. Combining football and music is a great idea, but it may need a more responsive lineup.[100]

Nevertheless, the same reviewer said, of Kennedy's earlier performance that same day with Kroke: 'He plays like an angel, pushing the terrific band's quasi-classical tone poems, rapturous rhythms and heart-tugging folk melodies to another level.' That 'angelic' performance included the most extraordinary cadenza of all, which I try to portray in the poem at the end of this chapter.

Kennedy is a performer who never gives less than total commitment – to his vision, his audience, or the moment – whatever the communal relevance or the aesthetic of that moment might be. Nor is he content for music to deliver what an audience is accustomed to. Even if the audience consists of 'fans', his instinct is to confound their expectations. Six years after the Polish Weekend, he provided the opening entertainment at the 2017 Australian Open men's final between Roger Federer and Rafael Nadal, highly appropriately, I thought, with a piece called 'Face-off', a hard-hitting electrified number deriving from Vivaldi's 'Summer'. Some of the online reaction, however, was appalled. As Kennedy himself puts it, 'My performance flushed out and riled a couple of fogies, mission accomplished.'[101] Just when his shock value might perhaps have worn off, there was Kennedy offending not the classical music establishment, as he did of old, but a differently conservative audience whose taste is middle-of-the-road bland pop. But bland, surely, never won a match, or nobly failed, while Federer, Nadal, Channon, Tomaszewski, Gascoigne and Kennedy have all thrown heart, soul, body and mind into the fray to make the world a richer place.

In 2014, a new football star made his debut for Aston Villa: Jack Grealish. Contrary to what the pundits might suggest, football is not all about trophies; it's not even about gaining the three points. Far more important than grinding out a result is the possibility of seeing something extraordinary – the genius of a Gascoigne or Le Tissier in action. Fans can suffer defeat with considerable consolation if they witness such football, and Grealish offered it match after match. Eventually he would get the chance to provide it for the England team too, though he has to date been woefully underused.

Grealish and Kennedy inevitably became friends, with mutual respect not only for each other's ability but also their application – and team mentality. Attending one of Kennedy's Birmingham concerts, in 2016, Grealish commented, 'It's unbelievable how talented Nigel is and how he has so much faith in the people around him. The show is not just all about him and he doesn't want to hog all of the limelight.' He also echoed Kennedy's comments about music and sport: 'I think all sportsmen could relate to the passion for what he does and it's great to see. You have got to try to become the best that you can be and Nigel shows how thousands of hours of practice always pays off.'[102]

As Grealish's comments make clear, the marvels offered by a talented individual are closely related to their performance within a team. And the player's allegiance is as important as the fans'. Sometimes this means the star of the team and darling of the fans becomes a pariah when leaving the club for fortune elsewhere, so it's interesting that Kennedy should have been gracious about Grealish leaving Villa for Manchester City; a case of empathy for an exceptional individual fulfilling his potential mattering even more than the tribe.

Grinding out a result, 'getting the job done'... the clichéd football phrases sound remarkably like the Brexit process; 'Brexshit' as Kennedy refers to it. For the Polish Weekend, he'd been able to bring his orchestra of Polish musicians, and other Polish bands with no questions asked. Brexshit changed all that, with freedom of movement between mainland Europe and the UK put under check.

The call for regaining 'sovereignty' was a mantra that few using it really understood. It led to a reduction in numerous freedoms and opportunities, while giving greater scope for a right-wing government to opt out of international laws protecting human rights and the environment. There was an immediate effect on touring musicians. Roger Daltrey might claim to have no issue with the new layers of bureaucracy, but for smaller bands or solo artists the burden may be insuperable. Elton John and others have been vociferous in their criticism of the barriers now imposed on touring musicians.

Kennedy didn't perform again in the UK until 2023, though the pandemic was also a significant factor. In the immediate wake of Brexit he vowed to leave the UK, as he didn't want to live in a country that was 'racist'; in his view the Brexit vote had hinged on the issue of immigration. But as *The Sydney Morning Herald* put it, he was 'stuck between a rock and a hard place'.[103] Poland, his other home, was also disappointing him; the move to ban abortion led him to call it a 'fascist' regime. And the qualities of life that had first attracted him were under threat. 'I chose Poland because it wasn't totally globalized, and it hadn't got Tescos and KFC and that.'[104] But by 2008, he was already bemoaning how 'the capitalist dream started taking over'.[105] At one stage he aimed to write a piece of music, *The Price of Freedom*, that would explore that change, 'the gains and losses of life in 21st century Poland', and use the speech patterns of those interviewed as melodic material.[106]

Kennedy's original, idealistic view of Poland was closely related to his views about jazz as 'a step away from the present world of ultra capitalism and globalization' where 'the musicians respect each other and their audience as equals – belonging to and contributing to the community, showing that another type of world is still possible'. Under his curation, in the Polish Weekend, those ideals were shared by Polish and English people together, in a border-free three-day event, the like of which is unlikely to be repeated – at least until the political landscape is reshaped.

It wasn't only jazz that was featured during the Polish Weekend. The programme included Bach; there was freedom of movement between musical domains, as well as countries. Kennedy wanted to showcase his new orchestra's renditions of Bach, as well as Duke Ellington, but it's particularly fitting that a German composer should have been highlighted. When English and Polish politics both proved problematic, Kennedy speculated on a move to Berlin. His dog Bully might well have seen it coming:

'Been all over Europe with me ... he's a real cosmopolitan character: a British bulldog, bought in Poland, who spends most of his life bombing along the German autobahns.'[107]

Kennedy sounds serious about Berlin, but if Germany were to reject his application for residency, then Alan Yentob's description of him as a 'musical vagabond'[108] would be both a shrewd assessment and a troubling reality. Meanwhile, Kennedy continues to occupy a patch of ground within Poland, far from the madding crowd, towards the Slovakian (and Ukrainian) border, with wolves and bears as neighbours. A bigger threat than the wild animals, however, is one particular human neighbour he decries in *Uncensored!*. It's not only politicians who can make one's life hell, though they do affect more people.

Perhaps Yehudi Menuhin deserves the final word at this point. In 1996 he commented, 'the "sovereign" state is a very bad custodian of peoples and their cultures'.[109] What we need, perhaps, is a more positive side to globalization.

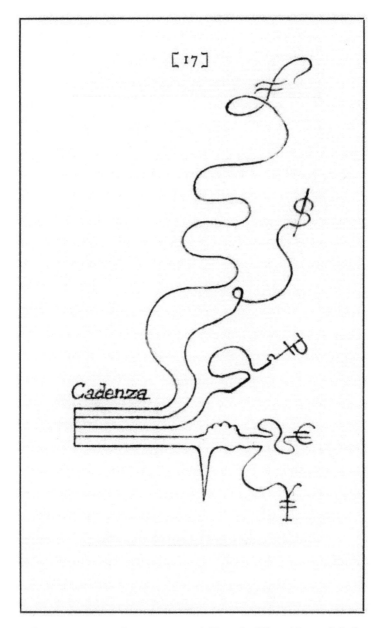

Cadenza: My version of Laurence Sterne's 'flourish of liberty' featured the lines of a musical stave going their different ways, morphing into Sterne's wandering 'lines of plot' and finally into monetary symbols.

Cadenza

30 May 2010

*an invisible line which is long
enough to let him wander to the ends
of the world and still to bring him
back with a twitch upon the thread.*
   —GK Chesterton

The improvised breaks
already out of hand,
the bow begins to thrash
against the strings,
its flayed filaments
drifting in a rosinous haze –
a savagery fuelled
by Polish spirit, stretching
the music to the point
where it must surely snap...

The spot-lit figure
writhes on the floor,
his violin somehow still
miraculously gripped
between shoulder and chin,
the bow finding space
to do more damage before
scraping to a halt
that could almost be
mistaken for defeat...

We hold our breath
in the dark – the music
hanging by a shred –
as the crumpled figure
uncurls, the music
cradled after all, brought
back from the brink,
small gasps of melody
feeling their way before
hurtling towards relief.

Chapter 9: Recycling
(It's Plucking Elemental)

It's a ceaseless process of enrichment that continues not only in their music but how we all listen to it and interpret it. And there's no blue bin anywhere that's marked transcendence or transfiguration, so that's why composers are different from municipal recycling plants: they disprove the entirety of Newtonian physics and find more, not less energy in the material they're recycling.—Tom Service

In Volume VI of *Tristram Shandy*, Sterne draws his famous lines of plot, to indicate how his narrative is going in a 'tolerable straight line'.[1] The idea that he has 'scarce stepped a yard out of my way' is of course deliberately laughable, as the meandering lines confirm. And here I am having followed in his footsteps. I wrote at some length of Kennedy's *New Four Seasons* in Chapter 3, but it's at this point in my story that he starts performing the new work, in evolving stages. His co-revisionists in the venture were from the Orchestra of Life.

As mentioned, the orchestra members were chosen for their musical versatility, and in Kennedy's view, their jazz credentials made them better equipped for tackling classical music – especially Kennedy's new interpretations. As he says of his own playing:

> I've learnt new scales through playing different types of music, like Indian raga scales, gipsy scales and harmonically-based jazz scales. It means I can think and play stuff in classical music that possibly violinists who didn't have access to other types of music could never do. It means I'm more flexible within classical music, to be a servant to the composer.[2]

He does however make one crucial distinction between the typical jazz and classical worlds: 'The basic difference between classical musicians and jazzmen is that, for the orchestral players, it's a job. For jazz players, it's an extension of their social lives.'[3] But with the Orchestra of Life, that division was blurred: for all the rigour of their application, it also appeared to be one long party. As the orchestra's name suggests, it was a joyous enterprise by design. One critic did take a swipe on account of the predominance of beautiful women, suggesting it should be called The Orchestra of Mid-life Crisis.[4]

The Orchestra of Life, itself an evolving ensemble, worked with Kennedy from 2010 to his most recent album of 2018. Their first recording (other than their contribution to *SHHH!*) coincided with Kennedy's move away from EMI to Sony, with a three-album deal. Kennedy's issues with EMI were well documented, and long-standing. He recalls how, in the 1990s, when Louise Mensch (then Bagshawe) was a press officer at the company, there was a fundamental lack of trust:

> They tried to get her to be a mole and tell them everything I was doing. But in the end she was telling me what was going on in EMI's head, which was far more difficult to get into because it was like a brontosaurus. It had a tiny head with a small brain and it was miles from the body.[5]

(It's tempting to take a Shandean detour into the world of Louise Mensch, who was a Young Poet of the Year in 1989, when Kennedy's original *Four Seasons* was released, and went on to be a Kennedy party-girl, as well as a Tory MP and generally controversial figure on many fronts, but that way madness lies.)

Kennedy's contracted albums were for the Sony Classical label, and yet none of the planned recordings were classical by any normal definition. *The New Four Seasons* (which would actually be the third of the Sony albums) were from the start on a mission to 'unclassify' themselves. *Recital*, the second album, featured primarily Fats Waller arrangements, plus jazz renditions of Bach as featured in Kennedy's Bach Prom, and other pieces whose origins range from Ireland to Brazil. Kennedy comments, 'I hope, mainly through my interpretations, but also because of the context in which I have placed all these works, to be able to shed new light on them. This is, after all, the function of an interpreting artist.'[6] He was reinventing the classical recital into the bargain.

The first album appeared to be a completely new work – by Kennedy himself: *The Four Elements.* 'Nigel Kennedy's New Masterpiece', the CD back cover proclaims; 'a suite of pieces which he conceived as his own 21st-century response to Vivaldi's *Four*

Seasons'. Not all the material was entirely 'new'; nor was the musical concept. Kennedy's friend Dave Heath beat him to it with a piece called *The Four Elements* recorded in 1995. Heath writes: 'The original idea behind this work was to create a companion piece for Vivaldi's *The Four Seasons* which would place it in a twentieth century context and complement the original work.'[7] Heath's order is Earth, Air, Water, Fire. 'Earth' begins with 'a huge storm out of which comes a chord representing life'. 'Water' begins with sound of actual running water.

Swiss composer Frank Martin had also written a set of short instrumental pieces bearing the same name (albeit in French) in 1964, 'a series of movements that evoked different landscapes, different phenomena' and 'sought to affect the emotions of the listener as concretely as possible'.[8] Wind instruments, particularly flutes, come to the fore in 'Air' but in some ways the four movements are strangely undifferentiated in their musical character. It would be interesting to challenge the listener with identifying the pieces 'blind'.

An even earlier precedent is Jean-Féry Rebel's *Les Elemens* (1737-8), composed a mere twenty years after Vivaldi's *Four Seasons*. The piece has ten movements, seven of which represent 'Chaos', during which phase of the biblical Creation story the four elements were ordered into 'nature'. Haydn's later *Creation* (1797-8) begins with a similar scenario, but Rebel's music is far more representational, its dissonance quite extraordinary, utterly outside its musical era. This makes perfect conceptual sense, but as eighteenth-century 'thinking' it seems brilliantly unexpected, as far ahead of its time as *Tristram Shandy*.

Disappointingly, perhaps, after such a provocative start, Rebel's composition settles down into a series of dance movements. A collaborative interpretation by the Akademie für Alte Musik Berlin and the company Sacha Waltz and Guests, in 2009, staged the work as contemporary dance, in a way that's pretty excruciating to watch on the available DVD. It demonstrates how music can become irrelevant when one is forced to focus exclusively on the 'dancer', in this case a grotesquely writhing man in his vest and underpants. The work was followed by a choreographed version of *The Four Seasons*. This was marginally more interesting, since the musicians came to the fore, but it was also fundamentally silly. In 'Spring', the musicians had leaves attached to their bows; in 'Summer', they played while semi-stupefied on the ground; in 'Autumn', they had apples placed on their heads, and one began to hope that William Tell, on an off-day, might appear and put them out of their misery. The willingness of the musicians to go along with it all was, in its way, astonishing, and Midori Seiler, as soloist, delivered a virtuoso physical performance atop ladders and under wintry sheets, her violin covered in fake snow. As pantomime, it had its inventive moments, and sell-out performances in Berlin were followed by an extensive tour, but I found it a travesty. The choreographer/dancer was the problem, self-centring the entire proceedings, failing to understand that the music itself portrays the pictures. As with the slogan of a certain theatre company, 'bringing drama to life', its artistic mission was simply gaga.

I mention all this in order to contrast it with Kennedy's so-called 'liberties', and to quash any suggestion that his treatments of Vivaldi have paved the way for inane extravaganzas. Kennedy's are always characterized by expressive, musical purpose.

Intriguingly, Darryl Way of Curved Air also wrote a violin concerto titled *The Elements*. He comments:

> This is a violin concerto I wrote and performed over 20 years ago now. Inspired by the programmatic music of Vivaldi's *Four Seasons*, I set out to find subject matter that I felt could be equally as evocative. I eventually chose to write a piece about extraordinary weather phenomen[a], such as Tornados and Floods, as they also have a seasonal element to them, along with plenty of dramatic potential.[9]

Weather distinguishes the three movements: 1. Tornado (Allegro); 2. Drought (Adagio); 3. Flood (Moderato). On YouTube the music is closely matched to mesmerizing film – the outer movements in black and white, the central drought in colour to capture the parched landscape most effectively and concluding with a slow zoom to a solitary yellow flower in the middle of a desert. Unlike the above-mentioned choreographed *Four Seasons*, Way's film demonstrates how a visual accompaniment can work in partnership with programmatic music, each artwork enhanced by the other.

Kennedy's *Four Elements*, then, had several precedents, but was of course unlike any other. On his recording the order is Overture—Air—Earth—Fire—Water—Finale. On tour, the Overture, Fire and Finale were omitted, replaced with an Underture, to bring things to a close. This track title change references The Who's rock opera *Tommy*, which features a wittily titled Underture mid way. Kennedy's tour featured *The Four Elements* and *The Four Seasons* back to back, and as Kennedy made clear, the new composition, written with extemporization at its heart, has the potential to go on for hours, so needed to be restricted.

What becomes apparent is that the 'new' work borrows from previous pieces, notably Kennedy's Hendrix arrangements. It's recycling – in a good way – material that's elemental to his musical thinking, which is, after all, a time-honoured musical practice. As Ólafsson comments, 'Bach frequently borrowed from himself'.[10] In Kennedy's *Elements*, 'Overture' reworks 'Third Stone from the Sun' (otherwise known as planet Earth); 'Air' owes much to 'Little Wing' with not a little *Lark Ascending* in the mix; 'Fire' has a similarly single-minded rhythmic drive to (wouldn't you guess it) 'Fire'; and 'Finale' uses themes and riffs from '1983...(A Merman I Should Turn To Be)'. But whereas *The Kennedy Experience* eschewed both lyrics and vocals, *Elements* brought them to the fore. The vocalists (Xantoné Blacq, Zee Gachette, aka Z-Star, and the Sahreal duo of Sarah and Rachel Wood) were given a significant creative role. Once Kennedy's programmatic concept was developed, with each element characterized sonically, he sketched a few words, 'thinking of a few snap associations with the particular element and giving those associations to the vocalist who I had chosen for the element'. The vocalists then had freedom to craft the lyrics however they chose, and as Kennedy says, 'This was a very rewarding way to work because it enabled the musicians to express themselves, as opposed to merely being instructed what to do.'[11]

This is classic Kennedy – a collaborative process, with co-musicians expressing themselves a priority. In performance, and recorded, the lyrics work well enough, but as printed in the CD booklet[12] (all in capital letters), they come across as rather banal: 'UNRESTRICTING ENERGY / LIGHTER THAN THE FLOW / TAKE A BREATH AND JUST RELEASE / AS YOU LET

YOURSELF GO' (from 'Air'). 'Earth' informs us that 'HER CREA-
TURES GREAT AND SMALL ARE / ALL OF EQUAL WORTH',
but rather more mysteriously mentions 'JEWELS BURIED
UNDER THE DIRT'. 'Water' is much better, the female vocal-
ists interpreting Kennedy's cryptic 'twilight depth' as a scene
of farewell, 'CALM AND THEN THE FLOOD' as they are left
'DROWNING, DROWNING, WHEN YOU LEAVE IN THE
DARK'.

It seems a shame that these lyrics were not further developed,
perhaps with a lyricist or poet. It was a lot to ask of the vocalists,
albeit a generous gesture. Kennedy wishes that a contemporary
poet had taken hold of Vivaldi's words, to accompany *The New
Four Seasons*, and there the words were not even incorporated
in the music. There again, a poet might have brought climate
change to the equation, which might have run counter to Kennedy's views.

As for 'Fire', it's a call to arms not against climate change but
for freedom, 'A PEOPLE'S REVOLUTION / BREAKING DOWN
OLD INSTITUTIONS'. It's fire as metaphor. Kennedy's snap association was 'the incendiary and reconciliatory spirit of mankind',
but although Gachette comes up with 'MILLIONS', then 'BIL-
LIONS' and finally 'TRLLIONS OF LIGHT YEARS OF LOVE',
the emphasis is on 'GIMME GIMME' clamour. The words were
admittedly written before the latest wave of disastrous forest fires
that caused such chaos around the globe, but I doubt if even those
cataclysmic climate events would have changed the upbeat vibe. A
single riff dominates, and it becomes rather tedious, saved by the
sumptuous electric violin overlays and interludes. But a relentless
'C'MON BABY' refrain, provided by Kennedy himself, punctuates
the entire track; it out-BABYs even Hendrix's repetitive 'Fire'
lyric. Towards the end, there are various bleeped out expletives,
and raucous chuckles from Kennedy, a taste of 'plucking elemental' things to come.

Kennedy plays various instruments on the recording, including guitar and Hammond organ. On tour, he took to the piano for
'Earth', as if he wanted to be at the heart of the 'grounding', unlike
his soaring role in 'Air'. He's a remarkably good pianist, as his
piano playing on his more recent Gershwin pieces has confirmed.

At the end of the album there's an 'Encore' subtitled 'It's Plucking Elemental'. Some might say the song, like the title, is a plain bad joke. Kennedy however was so enamoured with this piece of silliness that he wanted to release it as a single, but his 'Sony friends' deemed it 'unfit', and even the lyrics are excised from the CD booklet. Coming at the end of a substantial work, it's an amusing piece of fluff, with truly daft lyrics and rhymes ('if you're vegetarian you eat lentil') tonelessly delivered by Kennedy himself, though with his female singers adding rather sweet backing vocals. Kennedy sounds remarkably like Ian Dury, and when one remembers that an Ian Dury and the Blockheads song was Kennedy's top choice on *Desert Island Discs*, something – though I'm still not quite sure what – begins to make sense. (Ian Dury comments on the back cover of *Uncensored!*, 'Nige is an honorary blockhead.') For those who enjoy the main work, it's time to smile and shake one's head in fond despair, but although the accompanying video, now gone from the web, was also amusing, it's hard to imagine it acting as a calling card for the album, so the Sony friends were possibly right, though you can almost imagine the song having become cult listening. That's what happens to things that simply can't be judged by any normal means.

Remember that this was Sony *Classical*. And yet there, within the CD booklet, is Kennedy's note of thanks to Agnieszka and Sark for supporting his 'non-classical music'. Is this deliberately provocative? I imagine that, for some, the whole thing confirmed their worst suspicions, about Kennedy and/or the direction 'classical' labels were taking. Kennedy would either not have cared, or relished the controversy. I'm reminded of how the poet John Birtwhistle responded to such a critique by using the phrase as title for his next book: *Our Worst Suspicions*. One thing is for sure: the ground was prepared both for the unorthodox *Recital*, and the contemporary overhaul of Vivaldi.

The vocal style within *The Four Elements*, like *Kafka* before it, is most decidedly un-classical, at least in relation to the general perception of classical singing, with its intense vibrato. That's the focus of the majority of complaints from listeners to BBC Radio 3, some of whom, myself sometimes included, will switch off as soon as the warbling – sorry, singing – begins. For Kennedy it's a major bugbear. 'Clarse singing', he calls it.

It's a strange state of affairs, since singing is the one musical thing that almost everyone has had a go at. Maybe that's why we're fussy, even if we're poor singers ourselves. Kennedy has joked about his own singing voice. At the solo Bach prom, when introducing Fats Waller's 'How Can You Face Me Now' (and if that doesn't make sense, please backtrack to Chapter 7) he sang the words, saying 'and that's why I'm not going to do the melody like singing it, alright?' But he's still not shy of including his singing on the albums mentioned above, alongside the professional vocalists. It is, however rough and ready, the human voice, unadulterated by excess artifice. Many of us can relate to such a voice much more than we can to the voice of a trained opera singer. It's probably the case that more people would choose to hear Annie Lennox singing Dido's Lament than Janet Baker or Jesse Norman. I can already hear the cries of 'heresy', but the Lennox rendition on YouTube is remarkable, the simple purity of her voice recasting the Purcell aria as 'a lament for our dying planet', accompanied by a devastating stream of images. Another video of the same work, with the backing of London City Voices, shows a massive collage of their faces: human faces, human voices; our shared desire to communicate, to speak – or sing – to each other from the heart.

Where did it all go wrong, with classical singing? What started as occasional vocal ornament became the norm, a *tremolo* that varied the frequency and amplitude of the sound in subtle – or not-so-subtle ways; there's an interesting contradiction at work, which can affect the desirability of the sound produced. As Max Schoen comments, 'what is natural in the vocal vibrato would be considered pathological in other musculatures'.[13] Generally speaking, our muscles tremble as a result of fatigue, but with the voice, a controlled oscillation, tremolo, or vibrato, can in fact *prevent* fatigue. Its use therefore serves a particular purpose that *may* be beneficial to the sound. Francesco Lamperti distinguishes between the 'good effect' of 'a strong, vibrating sonorous voice' and 'bad vibrato, tremulous with vocal strain'.[14] Most of us can tell the difference, but even good vibrato can be tainted by association, especially if it's overblown. And if pitch fluctuates by more than one and a half tones, and/or the rate of fluctuation is lower than four per second, the vibrato is likely to be deemed a 'wobble'. Even when the vibrato is tighter, it is sometimes impossible to distinguish the note that is supposedly being sung, which surely oversteps the mark. Some rock, pop and jazz singers can of course be as excruciating as any 'clarse' exponents, but I'll resist naming shockers and personal hates.

Schoen makes the further point that a vocal tremor, good or bad, relates to human emotion: 'The psychological effect of the vibrato is probably due to the fact that the human ear has, because of the behaviour of muscle under emotional stress, come to associate a trembling with emotional expression.'[15] As listeners we may therefore either feel convinced and moved – or indeed conned, given that vibrato is a constructed effect.

The high-octane emotional arena of opera is where we find opinion most divided: we're either Inspector Morse (the fan) or Sergeant Lewis (the sceptic). Opera singers tend to use a substantial vibrato, for the simple reason they need to compete with an orchestra; the vocal projection required to hold one's own in a Wagnerian opera is far beyond the scope of a more natural delivery. Of opera singers, Pavarotti may well be particularly popular for the reason that he modifies the traditional tenor vibrato technique to suit his particular voice. He did so in order to sound recognizable, unique. Intriguingly, some say they hear him *talking* rather than *singing*.

The Wagner syndrome lingers on. As Arthur Benade writes, 'Vibrato ... give(s) the voice greater audibility, due to the independence of vibrato from rhythmic pattern of the music',[16] and this is true of other instruments, too. When violin soloists are at pains to stand out from an orchestra, they typically resort to too much vibrato. It became the norm in the early twentieth century to use it constantly, and many recordings reveal just how unwelcome it can be when used to excess. The trend has somewhat reversed, and Kennedy has tended to use less and less.

The trend is also evidenced in the popularity of classical singers such as Emma Kirkby and Grace Davidson, singing works from the Renaissance and Baroque. Zachary Woolfe writes, in reaction to hearing Kirkby, who was not formally trained, 'her pristine voice, perfect diction, and graceful phrasing ... reminded us that the primary role of vocal music is to communicate'.[17] Her singing may be aligned to musical periods several centuries past, but it accords with our current popular taste, and musical assimilation. The demise, if that's the right word, of popular vibrato was in no small part driven by the advent of the microphone, which enabled singers to maintain a natural, unforced delivery, and for every nuance to be heard (not that every singer or recording does this capability justice). And today, even when singing at full throttle, vocalists, to use the popular term, still resist what Kennedy calls 'warbling'. Any use of vibrato is more an expressive colouring.

Having mentioned Kirkby's 'pristine voice', and as an ex-chorister, I inevitably think of how the particular clarity of boys' voices has been favoured in English cathedral choirs. This has of course changed for good reasons, and since girls' voices are much more akin to boys' than to trained sopranos, there's really no 'argument'. But the clarity and communicative power of both boys' and girls' voices is particularly effective on account of that other 'microphone', cathedral architecture. I was bewildered when I first heard the treble voice of Aled Jones – with vibrato. Was that ultra-sophistication, or just *wrong*? The jury is probably still out.

An opposite challenge was posed when Sting decided to record songs by John Dowland, vibrato free. He came in for some stick, but also praise, for his 2006 recording, *Songs from the Labyrinth*. Here was a pop artist daring to appear on the Deutsche Grammophon label with an untrained voice. The outrage was a little strange, in that Elvis Costello had already made several Deutsche Grammophon appearances, starting in 2001 in collaboration with Anne Sofie von Otter; curiously, it's Costello whose distinctive style is closer to what people might call warbling. Anne Sofie – I can't bring myself to call her von Otter – meanwhile delivers an exquisitely calm version of McCartney's 'For No One'. Revealingly, she has described herself not as a singer of Lieder or of opera: 'I see myself as a musician, first of all, and secondly a singer, singing is my instrument.'[18]

Sting's Dowland project seems to me not only serious but, dare I say it, important – much like Kennedy's treatment of Vivaldi. It asks, of himself: how might I connect this music with a further audience? And it asks of us: how might we hear this music afresh, recycled by an unexpected yet relevant and sympathetic voice?

Vocalists of a strictly non-classical variety were a feature of Kennedy's *New Four Seasons* in its touring incarnations from 2012 onwards, though as previously mentioned, the vocals were gradually scaled back. It wasn't until late 2015 that the album, recorded apparently in 2014, was finally released, and there was a sense that it might have missed its moment, that Kennedy himself would have taken the work to other places by this stage. And was anyone really in the market for a third Kennedy *Seasons* recording? Kennedy had accused record companies of ripping off the public with the price of CDs. Why should people be expected to pay yet again for the 'same' work'?

It wasn't, of course, anything like the same work, and people had been paying good money to see Kennedy's novel recycling of the *Seasons* for many years. If he's played it 500 times, which he may well have done, then none of those 500 audiences have been treated to the same experience. I saw *The New Four Seasons* performed in both York and Sydney, with different ensembles, and though many of the musical tactics were the same, the results were not. Both, for instance, had Vivaldi's 'Spring' emerge from a sonic mist, but each occurrence was freshly contoured and coloured. For the 'repeat listener', the variance was an essential part of the joy.

At the Proms in 2013, the Orchestra of Life was joined by members of Palestine Strings. Clemency Burton-Hill pointed to the 'Arabic infused improvisations in a vivid and vivacious reimagining of a work that, as Kennedy points out, so often gets hijacked as background music, or a call waiting theme.'[19] Here's the rub: *The Four Seasons* as 'call waiting theme' is literally music on hold. It's a repetitive (ab)use, whereas Kennedy's multiple performances represent musical recycling at its most regenerative and rewarding. And when Kennedy's recorded version was released, even a tough critic such as Richard Morrison was, metaphorically at least, on the edge of his seat: 'I found some of it exhilarating, some infantile, the rest never less than startling.'[20]

My World

With Kennedy's next album, vocals were dropped but recycling was to the fore. Of the *Dedications* suite, three of the tracks, 'Melody on the Wind', 'Fallen Forest' and 'Solitude' were not 'new' at all, but they were given new treatments – and dedications, namely to those musicians who had inspired Kennedy over the years, 'opened doors in my mind, and in the heart'.[21] 'Melody', from *Kafka,* is dedicated to Grappelli, who played on the original version, where the melody is leisurely, and takes some time to emerge from the musical mist into which it finally disappears again after eight minutes. The new version (at 5.09) is much brisker, the melody quicker to appear and altogether more sprightly when it does, with Grappelli's echoing part played on the oboe. The new 'Fallen Forest' is more similarly paced to the original, though stretching to a further minute, and as with 'Melody', the central improvised section is very different. Its dedication to Isaac Stern is less obvious, given its previous association with Nottingham Forest's relegation, but since Stern used to practise while watching football on TV, maybe the joke just about holds good. 'Solitude' is dedicated to Menuhin. The newly dedicated version is less sombre, more lyrical. Its melodic theme is the most meandering, and yet in some ways the simplest. It's shorter than the original, and yet the theme feels even more repetitive; the nature, perhaps, of solitude.

The other two dedications are to Jarek Śmietana and Mark O'Connor. The first, 'Dla Jarka', is a sprightly piece that ventures into a highly dissonant improvisation. Śmietana, another Hendrix fan with whom Kennedy had so enjoyed working in Poland, died in 2013, and 'Dla Jarka' completes a quartet of dedications that are also in effect memorials. The fifth and final piece in the overall work, 'Gibb it', for Mark O'Connor, is the exception, a piece of pure *joie de vivre*. Like Kennedy, O'Connor has toured with Grappelli, and played a vast range of music in different styles, from bluegrass fiddle music to folk, jazz and classical. His own compositions are much admired, including his 'Fiddle Concerto', and 'American Seasons', which alludes to Vivaldi. 'The Improvised Violin Concerto' inevitably brings to mind the Kennedy/Heath 'Frontier' project. His 'country' credentials represent the one thing Kennedy tends to avoid at all cost, but O'Connor's award-winning Nashville appearances were no tales a trucker's love life, as Kennedy has caricatured the genre. Kennedy has not as yet worked with O'Connor, but his dedication comes with an explicit wish to do so.[22]

My World is very much an album of two halves, but both are in a sense *people* oriented. The second half is a suite of incidental music written for Agnieszka Kennedy's adaptation of Chekhov's *The Three Sisters*, which was staged at the Cockpit theatre, London, in January 2015, with Agnieszka playing the part of Masha; she was also responsible for costume design. Kennedy meets Chekhov – who, honestly, would have predicted that match? But despite his initial disinterest in 'the lives of some random bourgeois family',[23] he became fascinated with the play as a psychological study. For once, with music an adjunct to the drama, he can leave structure aside, and focus on atmosphere, character, human dilemma. The pieces are akin to his *transitoires* on other albums, though a couple of them adopt a greater presence: the Hendrix-laden link between Acts 2 and 3 (subtitled 'Fire'), and 'Masha', an accelerating and exhilarating full-blooded Russian dance, picking up on the earlier, muted Russian theme in 'Olga'. Even at a remove from original context, the suite of eight pieces is an engaging musical drama of its own, a sort of radio play without words. Who knows, it may even have led some listeners towards Chekhov for the first time.

In 2016 I had an unexpected chance to watch *Dedications* live, albeit at a remove. I was working in Canberra, Australia, following with interest Kennedy's imminent re-partnering with conductor Leonard Slatkin in Detroit. They were scheduled to play the Elgar concerto, a work they had previously performed together in New York, 1998, and again in London, ten years later. Despite Kennedy's much publicized views on conductors, Slatkin was one of the good guys. He had also conducted Dave Heath's flute concerto, *Free the Spirit*.

By good fortune, the full Detroit Symphony Orchestra (DSO) programme was being live-streamed, and I'd be able to watch, but it wouldn't be Elgar. A change of programme was announced; Kennedy would play Ellington instead, but it was Slatkin himself who clarified this rumour, saying, 'He had an injury to his left hand and the Elgar was simply not comfortable physically at this

time.' Kennedy would in fact be playing pieces from the newly
released album, *My World*. This, of course, was a red rag to certain
bulls – 'Ivan', for instance, who wrote, 'I would rather have my
prostate removed instead of listening to him play his own piece
of music.' But Slatkin slapped back, saying, 'All of us are thrilled
to have him back, no matter what he is playing.'[24] You can see
Slatkin back this up in his interview with Kennedy ahead of the
concert. 'We've missed you!' he begins, before asking 'Where
have you been?'[25]

I find Slatkin's comment – and question – intriguing. Who's
'we'? Slatkin only joined the DSO in 2008, the year he last worked
with Kennedy in London. He seems to be speaking for the American audience at large, if not for the whole classical concert circuit.
He was clearly aware of Kennedy's Polish adventure, so one could
take the question as somewhat staged, and yet it seems heartfelt.
It's also heartening, contradicting the vociferous Ivans of this
world who would prefer to think that Kennedy's eighteen-year
absence from the US marked him as *persona non grata*. It's true
that Kennedy's penchant for encores had previously been an issue
in the US, but that too was waved aside by Slatkin. On the night,
after the 'formal' programme, and 'Purple Haze', Kennedy was
joined in his encore improvisations by Slatkin at the piano, 'Rhapsody in Blue' and 'Chopsticks' in the mix (with a bit of Bonanza
thrown in). Finally, the conductor sat onstage engrossed in Kennedy's solo Bach.

With equal generosity, Kennedy put aside his general feelings about conductors. Significantly, Slatkin – like Previn – is a
composer as well as a conductor. He has also spent 'proper' time
with most of his orchestras; ten+ years in the case of the DSO.
As Kennedy commented in 2008, 'A conductor can galvanise the
troops and evolve an artistic programme and identity of style.
If they only give five or ten weeks a year [to an orchestra], how
can they do that?'[26] Slatkin was quick to agree: 'You wind up
with a kind of one-size-fits-all performance. It may be a faithful
performance, but it doesn't take it to the next level.'[27] Even if
performing the Elgar (again), they would no doubt have worked
in detail on a fresh rendition. As it was, the chosen work was new
to the orchestra, so a considerable commitment was required.
And Slatkin really enjoyed himself – not least in the rehearsals:

> I think when people watch this, they'll probably not think
> about all the work we put in this week. We've spent a lot of
> time, honing this, getting the style, getting everybody on the
> same page, as it didn't click right away, but every day we've
> been fine tuning this.[28]

Comparing the process to that of rehearsing Brahms, Bruch, or
Berg, he comments, 'Sometimes I think that people don't realize
that when you're dealing with a jazz or popular idiom, to make
it really work ... it's exactly the same thing, maybe even harder.'

For a conductor, working with a soloist's own material is an
unusual scenario, and one that rules out the ego-driven conductor's approach which is yet another of Kennedy's bugbears, and
he's not alone. In *The New Musical Companion*, Eric Blom comments, 'It is true that the [conductor] is often himself the star
performer, which can on occasion be extremely annoying.'[29] And
that was 1957, before the further rise of the celebrity conductor. In the same publication, Julius Harrison writes of 'individual
readings' that are a 'treasonable betrayal of the composer'. Such
a conductor, with 'an eye to personal advancement and avid for
any effect that will keep him prominently before "his" public,
upholds with consummate plausibility and with many an extrav-
agant mannerism his own spurious versions of the masterpieces
of music.'[30]

Blom also mentions instances of the conductor whose gestures
tell us, the audience, how to interpret the music, rather than let
us listen for ourselves.[31] That's the equivalent of the worst sort of
programme notes; excess signage. (The signage can also be pretty
basic – indicating that a part should come in, or be quieter, as if
no rehearsal had taken place.) And it raises questions about why,
in the case of filmed concerts, the camera should so often dwell
on the conductor, as if showing us how we are supposed to listen,
or how our emotions are to be governed. It's worth taking a step
back and considering just how absurd that is. I remember my
children howling with laughter when first faced with the sight
of a conductor at the Proms on TV; there's nothing like a child's
naïve inquisition to rumble pomposity.

Blom points to Furtwängler (who worked with Menuhin) as a
model of restraint, one who 'obtains with a minimum of outward
show a variety of sensational effects that have been carefully

drilled into the players beforehand'.[32] This is mainly well put, though Kennedy would have issue with the concept of being 'drilled'. For Kennedy, Barenboim and Tennstedt, and presumably Handley and Slatkin too, are the models.[33] You can see an example in the Tennstedt/Kennedy Beethoven performance of 1992: full of passion yet free of histrionics; the result of preparation, not drill.

In 2016, Kennedy's three-album contract with Sony was up, and he decided to do things differently; a case of *My World*, 'my way'.

> Rather than having monkeys behind desks chipping in and saying 'we think it should be like this' and having all those arguments, I just went and recorded it first. So there wasn't going to be any corruption of the musical process.[34]

He nevertheless took it to a record company, the Berlin label Neue Meister, part of the larger but still independent Edel company in Hamburg. Neue Meister has a highly specific remit: it 'brings together newly composed music by artists and composers who recognize no boundaries between the classical orchestra world, experimental art, electronica and pop music'.[35] It seemed a perfect fit, though the label fibbed rather in calling *My World* Kennedy's 'first album of his own compositions'. It is however still a *label*. Are such things today even *necessary*?

When Kennedy recorded his first albums, record companies were enjoying a revolution with the arrival of the compact disc. Claudio Arrau's recording of Chopin Waltzes was the first CD released, in 1979, but it wasn't until the mid 80s that CDs became more plentifully available. In 1984, vinyl records and cassette tapes were still the norm, and *The Four Seasons* was released in all three formats. The next revolution though, wasn't far away. In 1993, the Internet Underground Music Archive was set up in Santa Cruz, California, with music available to download, free of charge. Sony's online store of digital music files for sale, Bitmusic, was up and running by the turn of the century. All hell then broke loose with Napster's peer-to-peer file sharing service. 'Sharing' music was nothing new in itself; people had been making cassette tape copies of records for years, but MP3 music files were 'perfect' copies replicated at a single click. Apple computers, with a marketing slogan of 'Rip, Mix, Burn', were effectively encouraging the process – and the infringement of copyright.

The record companies tried and failed with their own digital stores. It was Apple – poacher turned gamekeeper – that succeeded, with its iTunes store set up in 2003. Within just a few years the sale of CDs was eclipsed by the sale of online files. But the latest success story obscured a major problem.

MP3 files are by definition inferior to the audio files on a manufactured CD, as the coding of the file involves some reduction or approximation – indeed a discarding – of data deemed surplus to requirements for the human ear. Making matters worse, in the early days the coded files were typically played through computer speakers or relatively primitive mobile devices. So throughout a decade of great technical advance, the sound quality of much of the music we heard was really pretty poor. Kennedy was outspoken in deriding the internet listening experience, and with good reason. It was further reason to prize the live concert or gig, though in reality some live venue sound systems can also be poor. As previously mentioned, I have heard Nick Cave perform on a grand piano so badly and unnecessarily amplified that it was excruciating.

Things improved somewhat with Advanced Audio Coding (AAC) files, and a new generation of compact speakers, and by 1998 Kennedy was changing his tune:

> I think downloading music at home via the internet is going to be a fantastic thing, because people will get music cheaper, and the choice won't be made by radio stations who are kind of bribed by record companies for their playlist and all of those inducements which are nothing to do with the public getting what they want, it's just a narrowing down of the choice.[36]

By 2020, with music streaming the new order, he would be saying, 'Luckily, record companies are like dead dodos now. They don't play such a big part in the music industry.'[37] And yet, in 2016 (and again with his next album two years later) he was still making use of them. Even today, the fact remains that artists are still reliant on all the middle men. Small initiatives that truly break the mould may work for unknown artists (e.g. Quadio bringing campus bands and artists to the attention of students) but otherwise the alliance of record labels and streaming services reigns supreme.

It's an uneasy alliance, since the labels still harbour ambition to stream for themselves, and there may be signs that the so called 'wall' between the two parties may be crumbling, but it's still a legal minefield,[38] and the average artist – let alone the maverick – is still a pawn in the money men's relentless marketing game.

The sort of bribery mentioned by Kennedy is well documented in Frederic Dannen's book, *Hit Men: Power Brokers and Fast Money Inside the Music Business* (1990). Such bribery doesn't go away, it just becomes more subtle – or not. Nor is it restricted to the music business. WH Smith employee Barry Pierce revealed that, '[w]hen the last Richard Osman [book] came out, Penguin bought the No. 1 spot on all WH Smith in-store bestseller charts, so it had to be displayed as the bestseller in every single store, whether it actually was or not'.[39] Who knows what financial persuasions are behind the algorithms creating playlists on iTunes or Spotify. Our old cassette tape playlists, even if shared 'illegally' with friends, are memories of a more innocent era.

At least Kennedy became free of his earlier contractual arrangements, which bordered on ownership. The smallest contribution to someone else's project, on a different label, came with the credit, 'Nigel Kennedy appears by kind permission of EMI Classics'. EMI still accounts for the majority of Kennedy's recording career, and it was a mixed experience:

> I wouldn't say that they were any worse than any other record company. They were very good in some ways. But that type of stifling of the creative impulse which is where all music comes from, it was impossible for me to carry on. There's a lot of random egos from behind the desks making it difficult for the artists.[40]

EMI was acquired by the Universal Music Group, and their spokesman reacted to Kennedy's comments: 'We will not comment on EMI under previous management, but can say that following our purchase of the company in 2011, Universal Music brought in new management, shifted strategy and invested in EMI and its artists globally.'[41] Whether their investment or new strategy would have benefited Kennedy, we'll never know. In the past, in Kennedy's own words, they were 'trying to deter me from doing creative work and just wanted me to do reinterpretations of popular repertoire from the classics'.[42] For every act of support, they had also been exploitative, though John Stanley would seem to have been compliant in the repackaging of old material into new compilations: playlists on CD.

In 2005 we got *Inner Thoughts*, the slow middle movements taken from various concerto recordings, with a mini-essay by Stanley championing it as a groundbreaking album, distinguished from 'faceless compilations ... collections of music with lifestyle titles and absolutely no central creative voice'.[43] On that last distinction, he is of course correct. And the album title was a clever one, suggesting access to Kennedy's imagination as well as ripping the concertos. It's also understandable that EMI (and Stanley as Kennedy's manager) would want to keep Kennedy's classical repertoire in the public gaze, even as the violinist's personal projects diversified. But even a sympathetic marketing concept can quickly degrade.

In 2009 EMI released a Kennedy compilation under their 'insp!ration' series. The album, titled *Nigel Kennedy, A Portrait*, claimed to be inspiration for 'unconventional music lovers' and 'a small-scale rebellion'. Each inspiration was ticked, as if part of a checklist. So far, so inoffensive, but in 2015, with EMI now owned by Warners, we were offered *Drive and Relax: Classics to go* (or *Klassik für Unterwegs* as Warner's original German Holding had it), with 'Der Frühling' Allegro from Kennedy's *Four Seasons*. The album cover explained:

> Rush hour in the city and endless traffic jams on the freeway? Just relax! On your way to work, after hours or on holiday travel? Unwind to tunes that reduce stress, put you in a happy mood, get you humming along ... and arrive in a good mood!

Ok, the happy mood and the humming along are passable, but it's stretching it to see Vivaldi's high-energy movement reducing stress. Other albums in the series took things a stage further, including *Heavenly Classics*, *Dinner Classics*, and – for when you want to take relaxation to an extreme – *Music of Silence*, the German 'Ruhe' (peace, quiet, calm) simplistically if not downright idiotically translated. Mozart had a pretty banal handling too: 'insp!ration for lovers of wonderful melodies [√] and the search for true genius [√]'. With the *Summer* compilation, you got all three movements of Anne-Sophie Mutter's version of Vivaldi's concerto, 'for people with the sun in their heart [√]' and 'relaxing summer evenings [√]' – the total opposite of what Vivaldi was portraying.

These banal, even misconceived playlists have been effortlessly superseded by online streaming. As physical artefacts they look like fossils chronicling the decline of a species. The Neue Meister output, by contrast, looks like a survivor, fit for its specialized purpose, and yet the unabated rise of streaming raises the question: is it time to take all CDs to the Oxfam shop or even the dump?

Of the two options (before I return to the heart of the matter), the first is preferable, a positive act of recycling that enables another listener to benefit from our personal purchase in a way that is entirely legal and proper. It is literally in our gift to pass music on in this way. And there is, bizarre as it may seem, no other easy recycling possible, since CDs in their entirety are classed as 'electronics', so can't be disposed of with your general plastic and metal. Disposal was of course not on anyone's minds when CDs were introduced. Their longevity, compared to scratchable LPs and stretchable tape, was touted as a major selling point. The same couldn't be said of their plastic cases – laughably called 'jewel' cases – which cracked and found any number of ways to fall apart.

The second option, where CDs end up in landfill, results in toxins leaking into the environment, a case of music as contaminant, but with charity shoppers very probably abandoning CDs too, it begins to look like an unavoidable reality.

There's little doubt that CDs will eventually no longer be produced. Whether the backtrack to vinyl will last is also questionable, given the supremacy of streaming, but who knows. The predicted death of the printed book seems to have stalled, as people are genuinely attached to the physical objects, which also offer a different physical experience for the reader. I can't imagine 'turning the page' being reduced to mere metaphor. But as I myself contemplate a cull of the music on my shelves, I realize what would be lost: the trappings of musical story – story such as I have explored in this book, and which I now feel the need to capture in its pictorial – and tactile – detail, before landfill claims the lot.

Kennedy's CD archive reflects the history of classical album design generally – and how his personal musical odyssey and aesthetic then deviated from that path. His later albums have stood out for their design, often being carefully and sometimes humorously matched to the man. Anyone streaming the music misses out.

The first Elgar recording in 1984 had its looks firmly in the past, with its archetypal 'classical music' cover: a painting, matched to the period of the music. The Tchaikovsky/Chausson release followed suit. The 'lighter' Elgar recording with Peter Pettinger, and its jazz partner, both released on the Chandos label, featured Kennedy himself, which set the pattern for a while, with or without conductor, Kennedy's image changing quite radically year by year. I've already mentioned the Sibelius/Tchaikovsky reissue on account of its sleeve-note polemics, and the cover underlined the argument, eschewing all imagery in favour of stark text on black. Thankfully, it was a one-off.

The Tennstedt Beethoven recording in 1992 was the first to break the mould in a more positive way. It features 'Man with a Violin Case', a sculpture photographed by Govert de Roos. The statue can be found in Amsterdam, between Marnixstraat and Tweede Hugo de Grootstraat. It's one of a number of works by an unknown artist that appeared around the city in 1982. The artist's identity remains a mystery, just as the sculpted 'figure' within the sculpted clothing is elusive. The figure is also known as 'the Man Running for Tram Ten, as the number ten tram line runs right in front of the statue'.[44] The sculpture is blue; the photo (or rather the cover, designed by P. Linard & Co. Ltd) is a slightly sepia black and white, with background removed. The effect is to make it even more surreal. It seems to herald a bold new approach to classical music. By Kennedy's later standards, the recording was of course somewhat old-fashioned, and the slight sepia tone sits well with that. For Kennedy's second recording of Beethoven, sixteen years later, the cover shows the violinist in silhouette, against woods in the High Tatras. He's carrying a violin case, just like the mystery man, the whole effect being to echo the earlier image. But this time it's Kennedy himself, pictured in his true surroundings.

For the albums recorded during Kennedy's 'sabbatical', the covers were varied. *Kafka*'s cover was dominated by Kennedy with violin, but also features a crowd, as if listening to him in a purple-skied arena. It is also the first album to introduce the Aston Villa claret and blue, which would be prominently used on four further albums. *East Meets East* comes complete with delightfully folksy sketches by Annabel Wright, and *The Kennedy Experience*, referencing Hendrix, features a violin on fire. Inside, it features the first photos of Kennedy to which an 'electrified' look has been applied, something that would reappear on *My World*.

For the rebooted classical Kennedy phase, things were de-Nigeled, a Deadly-style British bulldog for the Elgar/Vaughan Williams, and for the Kreisler (replacing the Storm Thorgerson image) Kennedy's portrait is a moody shot in black and white by Katarina Jebb, the eyes themselves in deep shadow. The effect is painterly, the face from another era. There are just two words on the cover: *KENNEDY* and *Kreisler*, two violinists. If you weren't totally familiar with Kennedy's image, you wouldn't necessarily know which musician the image related to. The Bach CD is more abstract, featuring a pastel painting by Rumen Rachev, with lines of overlaid and interweaving colour, the effect at once densely rich but bright. The CD liner opens out to a five-panel stretch, with different colour threads on the reverse. An online thumbnail image wouldn't begin to capture its effect. It's perhaps the classiest of all the album designs, muted yet bold. It's a minor but significant joy to open it, with the CD in matching design. It adds to the pleasure one feels in anticipation of the music. The cliché goes, 'don't judge a book by its cover', and while I'd concur with that in terms of judgement, book covers (as with the one you are holding) play a part in setting the tone of a production, and of course creating a useful sense of allure.

It's not only a CD's imagery that's valuable; there are the album notes, which may be available if buying the full album of digital files, but in a streamed listening world they are lost. Kennedy has often dismissed talking about music too much, but some of the mini-essays included with his albums are both insightful and informative (John Fordham's contribution to *The Early Years* collection particularly good). And without Kennedy's own note in *Recital*, I doubt anyone would appreciate how, in his homage to Dave Brubeck, 'the Bartók pizzicato at the end of the intro is Morse code for the words "take five"'.[45]

Plastic CD cases being so poor, card cases are much preferable, both more robust and aesthetically pleasing. (And if you do wish to dispose of them, they are easily recyclable.) A card case is almost always accompanied by greater attention to design detail; they are like miniature versions of the old gatefold double albums released on vinyl. Six of Kennedy's albums are sleeved in this way: *The Doors Concerto, A Very Nice Album, SHHH!, Polish Spirit, My World*, and *Kennedy Meets Gershwin* – plus the twentieth anniversary reissue of the original *Four Seasons*; that's a list of some of his most personal projects, packaged with matching personal stamp. And there's *The Early Years*, a set of (seven) CDs in card cases all within a strong card box (plus Fordham's great essay). The cover gives Kennedy's original *Four Seasons* image the Sex Pistols treatment (and when Kennedy was guest editor of *Classic FM* magazine, Mozart was treated the same way).

The *My World* case is also notable for its maverick typography: the capital Es are the 'wrong' way round, there's a solid dot for the 'o' of World, and a dot above a dash for the 'i' of Nigel. That's a radical statement about a world in which things are most definitely done differently to the norm.

When it comes to *Uncensored!*, however, not everything about the 3-CD box set makes sense. Of the cover image, which matches the book, Kennedy says, 'The boxing gloves kind of represent fighting back against bogus authority',[46] but that doesn't seem so relevant here. Kennedy's own compositions are together on CD3, separate from the concertos, so in a sense it's rather *classified*. And 'uncensored' music? It's almost the opposite: most of the concertos are presented only in part. There are excerpts from the book in the CD notes, namely from the 'Classical Music' and 'Rock Royalty' chapters. But the latter doesn't connect to the musical content, or even the heart of the full chapter, where we encounter McCartney et al. It refers to 'the following ROCK ARISTOCRACY'[47] but the excerpt cuts off before we even know who they are. The colours on the CDs aren't even right. It all seems a bit half-baked, and I wonder what the point is. Who is the intended audience? It was of course a great idea to have a boxed set of CDs to accompany the book, but how much more interesting it would have been to have a new, highly personal recording

– of the new concerto 'Für Ludwig Van', coupled perhaps with a radical new version of the Beethoven itself.

If streaming the music misses out on these physical accompaniments (and still, for the time being, the best quality sound), in another sense streaming is the perfect delivery mechanism for Kennedy's 'unclassified' notion of music. The average person may well find 'classical' music's category system rather less intelligible than the equivalent classification system by which we identify biological species. It smacks of an arrangement almost calculated to exclude the uninitiated. And even Kennedy himself comes a cropper when putting forward his own looser groupings ('My Concerto Recordings' and 'My Albums') in *Uncensored!*. The rather illogical nature of the 'system' results in some albums being overlooked completely.

The metadata and algorithms by which music streaming services operate are rather different, treating everything as a 'song', or 'track'. As Tom Service comments, what seems at first like heresy actually makes more democratic sense:

> [it] isn't necessarily about putting things in a box, or pinning a butterfly in its case. Instead ... to define something is also to understand its connectedness to everything else ... at the same time every piece can be its own species, and every genre can be its own node on the network.[48]

In this scenario, musical hierarchies disappear, and we have instead a diversity of unique musical offerings, related in a multitude of subtle ways. The current technology may still be clunky, serving up a crude menu of 'like that, then try this', but the Kennedy factor already means that a serving of Bach, Bartók and Hendrix is possible. We may mistrust machines to dictate our listening, but if their programming is sufficiently sophisticated, they are more generous gatekeepers than, for instance, those erstwhile self-appointed guardians of the classical music secret society. As Max Richter comments, those guardians were protecting their cultural capital and, 'at a certain point a large part of the audience just went, "you know what, if you don't care if I listen, well I'm not going to listen"'.[49] By contrast, the machine will serve us any song without judging us as listeners. As Tom Service says, 'enjoy the uniqueness of whatever musical species you're loving right now and surf on to the next node of the network'.

Tom Service comments on the 'bigger biome ... in which everything is a song, because everything is music, everything is sound'. But what about the even bigger biome, that of the third rock from the sun, the ecological system within which all our music reverberates? Is music a part of that ecology, and therefore a player in the drama of its survival or collapse? Is there more to it than the green credentials of CDs and their packaging?

There does seem to be a new awareness of the role that music can play. The Proms in 2022 included 'Earth Prom', an audio-visual celebration of the BBC's natural history unit, with music by Hans Zimmer and George Fenton. In January 2023, a BBC Symphony Orchestra concert at the Barbican, 'Our Precious Planet', combined music with the 'Cinesthetics' of artist Grégoire Pont. Violinist Patricia Kopatchinskaja now conceives all her concerts as acts of awareness, enlightenment even, but insists that everything derives from the music itself: 'I'm not trying to give any music a new coat of paint. My aim is to penetrate to the real quintessence of a work – to what it means for us today, in the here and now.'[50] Her 'Dies Irae' concert at the Lucerne Festival 2017 concluded with the old Gregorian Dies Irae chant while metronomes ticked under the audience's seats, stopping one by one as the lights went out. She has presented Beethoven's 'Pastoral' Symphony with a carefully staged set, including a black veil hanging above the orchestra, invoking the first performance of Haydn's *Seven Last Words*, not to mention Sterne's black page, 'a veil of mourning that is at once a projection surface and a theatre prop', as the designer Lani Tran-Duc describes it.[51] She found within Beethoven's respect for nature a contemporary story about our destruction of the environment. The Mahler Chamber Orchestra, with which Kopatchinskaja has worked on the project, has its own environmental agenda:

> We are measuring our carbon footprint ... We try to be as efficient as possible in our travel planning, to stay at certified hotels near the venues, to use public transport as much as we can. Above all, in our planning we consider artistic, financial and environmental factors equally, and we work on raising awareness in our global network.[52]

Where does Kennedy stand on the issue? His comments about Greta Thunberg in *Uncensored!* seem harsh. In interview, he says, 'Relatively speaking she's just a child',[53] which is also a little strange, given his own childlike tendencies. But although he's sceptical about man-made global warming, he is nevertheless an ardent environmentalist. As a teenager studying in New York, commenting on there being 'lots of violence and unhappy people', he also remarked, 'I don't think people are meant to live in polluted air'.[54] More recently he has said, 'I hate to think of dolphins swallowing plastic. I went through a phase of leaving plastic packaging outside the supermarket. If they want to propagate it they should deal with it.'[55] In his Polish village, he's built a house of wood and straw: 'even the tiles are made of wood. The drains are made of wood. Everything's made of wood, and it's a beautiful feeling being surrounded by this warm substance.'[56] And most significantly, his music (numerous free concerts, for instance) is a contributory factor in the health of his local community. That's just as important, in its way, as a 'crusading' concert by a Kopatchinskaja. The diversity of contribution is part of what matters, as with the diversity of species themselves.

Menuhin makes an interesting connection:

> Just as Sir Julian Huxley is so deeply concerned with the preservation of wild life ... so do I feel that strong encouragement of string playing is required to preserve our species from extinction, as has already nearly overtaken our predecessors and inspiring violinistic colleagues, the gypsies of Eastern Europe.[57]

This is more than mere metaphor. Menuhin is talking not only about human skills but human beings themselves. And every violinist, saved from extinction, becomes a potential force for enriching the world. That's the nature of creativity, of art itself. Art (deserving of the name) is no vandal. At the Globe Energy Awards of 2007, held at the European Parliament in Brussels, Robin Gibb of the Bee Gees and – yes – Kennedy provided the music, while America in particular was called out as an environmental terrorist. 'Words' was the song they performed together: 'words are all I have' goes the lyric; words – and music.

As Tom Service suggests, in the quotation at the head of this chapter, the creative recyclings of musical material by a Bach or

Kennedy are cultural enrichments of our world. Even revisions of work are either efforts to *do things better*, or offer thoughtful alternatives (and revising poetry is much the same). Walton, having revised his viola concerto, was happy for both versions to exist in the world. He simply expressed his own preference for the latter. Multiple recordings of classical (and other) works are also gifts of multiplicity, of choice.

Even before he wrote the incidental music for Chekhov's *Three Sisters* Kennedy talked of branching out: 'I'd love to write music for films. That'd be wicked!'[58] I'm tempted to imagine an 'Earth Prom' with film accompanied by Kennedy rather than Hans Zimmer. *The New Four Elements*. But I guess there might have to be a (plucking) bad joke at the end.

Shuffle

He was meant to be playing the Elgar concerto with Leonard Slat-kin but changed his mind a few weeks ago...—Norman Lebrecht, 4 May 2016

He had an injury to his left hand and the Elgar was simply not comfortable physically at this time. All of us are thrilled to have him back, no matter what he is playing.—Leonard Slatkin, 4 May 2016

I would rather have my prostate removed instead of listening to him play his own piece of music.—'Ivan', 4 May 2016

I attended the concert, which was fabulous. One standing ovation after another.—Stephen Calkins, 8 May 2016

from slippedisc.com

For Elgar, read Ellington. A twinge in the arm. A new reality you have to accept. If the cartilage scrapes, so might the bow. You drink to ease the pain and remember the drink that made you fall. For Ellington, read Elgar. What might have been niggles like a flickering of bone.

For Ellington, read Elgar. A twinge in reality. A new drink you have to accept. If the arm scrapes, so might the bone. You drink to ease the Ellington and remember the Elgar that made you fall. For cartilage, read pain. What might have been niggles like a flickering of the bow.

For Elgar, read pain. A twinge in the bone. A new bow you have to accept. If the Ellington scrapes, so might the cartilage. You drink to ease the Elgar and remember the Ellington that made you fall. For drink, read reality. What might have been niggles like a flickering of the arm.

For Elgar, read drink. Ellington in the bow. A new cartilage you have to accept. If the bone scrapes, so might the Ellington. You drink to ease reality and remember the twinge that made you fall. For pain, read arm. What might have been niggles like a flickering of Elgar.

For Elgar, read arm. A flickering of pain. A new Ellington you have to accept. If reality scrapes, so might the twinge. You drink to ease the cartilage and remember the bow that made you fall. For Ellington, read Elgar. What might have been niggles like a drink of bone.

For Elgar, read cartilage. A twinge in the bow. A new arm you have to accept. If the flickering scrapes, so might the drink. You drink to ease the Ellington and remember the pain that made you fall. For Elgar, read bone. What might have been niggles like an Ellington of reality.

For Elgar, read Elgar. A twinge of pain. A new flickering you have to accept. If the cartilage scrapes, so might the reality. You drink to ease the drink and remember the arm that made you fall. For Ellington, read Ellington. What might have been niggles like a bow of bone.

For Elgar, read reality. A twinge of Ellington. A new Elgar you have to accept. If the bow scrapes, so might the pain. You drink to ease the bone and remember the cartilage that made you fall. For arm, read Ellington. What might have been niggles like a flickering of drink.

Chapter 10: Wundercodger

Nothing odd will do long. Tristram Shandy did not last.
—Samuel Johnson

'At 60, Nigel Kennedy is well on his way from wunderkind to we hope wundercodger.'[1] So wrote John Bungey in *The Times*, reviewing the 'Nigel Kennedy and Friends' concert at the Royal Albert Hall in 2017. 'What a waste of talent' wrote 'Robert' in the comments. No one else chipped in, so the argument was not developed, and it begs the question of how, exactly, such a disappointed listener (or more likely merely a judgemental reader of the review) might wish Kennedy's talent to have been 'saved', and for what. Maybe 'Robert' was talking about the contributing friends, such as Robert Plant, and Jean-Luc Ponty, Kennedy's electric violin guru; who knows. The review gave the gig four stars out of five, 'an epic, meandering journey from baroque to hard rock ... laced with moments of brilliance'.

Prior to singing 'Kashmir' for the first time since Led Zeppelin's 2007 reunion at London's O2 Arena, Plant harked back to Kennedy's role as saviour on his *Fate of Nations* album. He quipped, 'I don't know whether this is payback or what'.[2] Kennedy had often thrown the Kashmir riff into his improvisations, for example at the Proms 2015 performance of Monti's 'Csárdás'. Here was the chance to really go for it, with the song's original co-creator.

In some ways, the event was reminiscent of The Who's Albert Hall concert with friends, ten years earlier. But while that had been in aid of the Teenage Cancer Trust, and was a clear-cut rock gig, Kennedy's event was part of the Hall's 'Love Classical' festival. That, presumably, was one bone of contention for the non-Plant Robert. Kennedy's programme, true to his musical ethos, was a playlist that didn't play safe. Plant may have stolen the headlines, but the friends came from diverse musical fields; Georgi Andreev played Bulgarian gadulka in folk tune duets with Kennedy's violin.

Brix Smith Start was there in the audience, along with many others who had known Kennedy for years, either as friends or followers – grown up with him and/or his music, I'm tempted to say, but therein lies another issue. Kennedy had hit sixty. Co-codgers Ponty and Plant were even older, though thoroughbred rockers of that age are viewed as graceful miracles of survival. The 'waste of talent' remark was closely related to a view of Kennedy as someone who hadn't grown up at all.

As discussed in Chapter 2, the child is often revered, but while the importance of 'the long childhood' is (or should be) recognized, there comes a time when people begin to shake their heads with disappointment or outrage – that someone appears to be stuck in the groove, refusing to grow up in conventional terms. Kennedy is bullish about it. Writing about the choice of music for his *Recital* album, he states, 'All of this repertoire is music which I have either grown up with or feel as if I have grown up with, bearing in mind that growing up is something I haven't been overly interested in so far.'[3] On his 60th birthday, he was asked how he felt about growing older, if he 'had grown wise with the years', to which Kennedy replied, 'No idea. It hasn't happened to me yet.'[4]

Other comments, over the years, have presented a rather more complex assessment: 'I think you grow within yourself even if you never grow up', he said in 1996.[5] A decade later came the bewildering claim, 'I celebrated my 50th birthday when I was 37'. He expanded on this by saying, 'I don't know what's going to happen in the next five years ... my agenda is always to meet other musicians, who are inspirational.'[6] He's found many such inspirations, as the Albert Hall event made clear, and they typically testify to Kennedy's spontaneity. Al Ayoub, the guitarist playing with Kennedy in Detroit comments: 'he lives in the moment more than anyone I have ever met.'[7] James Jolly backs this up: 'Kennedy remains one of those violinists, rather like Gidon Kremer and Isaac Stern from the generation before him, for whom the inspiration of the moment is a major part of the musical persona.'[8]

If you live in the moment to such an extreme extent, then time as it governs so many people's thinking becomes almost irrelevant. You might be 37, you might be 50: what does it matter if you're ploughing a new musical furrow with all the intensity of *now*? If such constant spontaneity is still yours at 60, and beyond, it may give the illusion of eternal youth. For some, that's admirable. As the Stranglers' song 'Duchess' has it, 'Duch of the terrace never grew up / I hope she never will'. And Theodor Adorno's comment about Alban Berg, that 'he succeeded in never becoming an adult',[9] is revealing because of the use of that word *succeeded*. It's an achievement, as if opting out of the standard progress of maturity, a deliberate self-casting as a pseudo Peter Pan, merits applause. Adorno's comment, though, is heavily qualified: Berg held adulthood at bay 'without, however, remaining infantile'.

There's the rub. Kennedy's detractors are quick to see nothing but infantile behaviour: his eternal youth viewed as failure not accomplishment, cause for derision, not applause. Ironically, the early image – of a child with a gift beyond his years – is part of the problem. There's a wonderful photograph taken by David Farrell that shows the very young Kennedy facing the Queen Mother, with two other middle-aged ladies looking on, full of smiles – smiles of admiration, for sure, but I can't help thinking there's a degree of condescension too. 'How very grown up', they seem to suggest, welcoming the very sight of a little boy with violin instead of, say, a football, while the boy would no doubt have given anything to make the swop at the time. One can only imagine their contrasting disapproval, should they have seen the same 'boy' using his violin as a cricket bat in later years. The 'waste of talent' comments are grounded in that photo from the early 1960s.

The issues surrounding Kennedy's early years have already been discussed, but it's interesting to relate those discussions to what the poet and essayist Francis Thompson writes about Percy Bysshe Shelley's problematic childhood: 'So beset, the child fled into the tower of his own soul, and raised the drawbridge.'[10] This could be a description of Kennedy 'the dormouse' at the Menuhin School, longing to be a child unencumbered by adult expectations. And in Thompson's view, the self-preserved nature of Shelley's childhood, 'unaffected by the intercourses that modify the maturity of others into the thing we call a man', is precisely that which fostered his particular creativity.

Thompson mentions how 'Shelley's life frequently exhibits in him the magnified child. It is seen in his fondness for apparently futile amusements, such as the sailing of paper boats.'[11] Kennedy has shown equivalent fondness, taking futile amusement to a Moonie level with his invention of Kitchen Golf. As described in *Uncensored!*, complete with detailed, futile 'rules', the game was first played by Kennedy and his partner in idle fun, Gary Lineker, demolishing the Kennedy household's crockery. It perhaps marks the line between childlike and childish, though it possibly has its origin in accident – the time when, in the Lineker house, Brix Smith had asked Gary about cricket, and the resulting demonstration and practice took out a collection of Royal Dalton figurines.[12]

Kitchen Golf is also an example – almost an emblem – of how, if you live in the moment, consequences don't seem to matter. Destruction of some sort is inevitable, and in the most extreme scenario, the risk of *self*-destruction looms. 'It's better to burn out than to fade away' goes the line in Neil Young's song 'Hey Hey, My My (Out of the Blue)', a mantra that's been repeated in songs by Def Leppard ('Rock of Ages') and Queen ('Gimme the Prize', used in the film *Highlander*). Kurt Cobain's 'suicide note' also quoted it, leading to the perception that 'burn out' = death. John Lennon had already interpreted it this way, in his spat with Young. 'Making Sid Vicious a hero, Jim Morrison – it's garbage to me. I worship the people who survive', he stated in a 1980 *Playboy* interview, to which Young responded, 'Rock'n'roll doesn't look that far ahead. Rock'n'roll is right now. What's happening right this second. Is it bright? Or is it dim because it's waiting for tomorrow – that's what people want to know.'[13] As Young makes clear, the physical burn-out of the artist is not the point (though it may be a risk). He's championing the absolute commitment to the moment, and the passion that entails, over the relative futility, for the artist, of letting caution dictate, or sheer longevity steal the disappointing show.

When the pandemic of 2020-21 caused widespread lockdown, the concept of living in the moment was disrupted. Musicians everywhere were deprived of their live tours. Like Kennedy, Dave Grohl – drummer in Cobain's band Nirvana, and more recently the driving force of the Foo Fighters – also spent some of his unexpected downtime writing an autobiographical book. Towards the end, he writes:

> I still forget that I've aged. My head and heart still seem to
> play this cruel trick on me, deceiving me with the illusion of
> youth as I greet the world every day through the idealistic,
> mischievous eyes of a rebellious child who constantly seeks
> adventure and magic.[14]

This could be Kennedy, except for the linguistic style – and the
idea that it's all a 'cruel trick'. Intriguingly, he adds: 'I still find happiness and appreciation in the most basic, simple things', much
like Kennedy enjoying the changing seasons in rural Poland.

Grohl thrives on the deception, the illusion. For Kennedy, it's
no deceit; it's simply how he is, almost determinedly so. And his
wilful prolonging of youth has been matched by a rugged determination to control his own life in a way that far outstrips the
mundane steps towards adulthood taken by most of us. He was
only in his early teens when he emerged from his withdrawal at
school with the realization that it was all up to him: 'I was the
only one who could change my life quality, and I'd better get on
with it and start enjoying something instead of feeling miserable
about it.'[15] He's wonderfully matter-of-fact about the whole thing:
'Life's what you make it, full stop.' But you have to find huge
inner resources and confidence to go solo like that. The fact that
Kennedy, a mere five years down the line, was muscling on stage
in New York jazz clubs says it all.

Shelley clearly had a similar, inner strength. He emerged from
his childhood withdrawal with radical social and political views,
a defiant attitude – and an exceptional artistic sensibility and
mission, all of which was sustained (although he died tragically
young) by the inherent child. How ironic, that conventional
'grown-ups' should find it harder to nurture those challenging
qualities. The poet and essayist Mary Karr remarks how 'James
Joyce once said that everyone starts out as a poet, then realizes
it's too hard.'[16] That would accord with Ken Robinson's chart,
'The Decline of Genius' (referred to in Chapter 2), which shows
our decline in metaphorical thinking. If Joyce is right, the chart
not only depicts a failure of education, it also reflects a loss of
nerve by the child in fathering the man – a man with sufficient
childlike qualities to last the distance as a poetic spirit. Kennedy
is a brilliant example of the child mustering nerves of steel – and
holding them throughout his career. It's a much harder act – the

'discipline of deliberate indiscipline',[17] to use Philip Gross's words – than simply toeing the line.

It was bullying, such as drove Shelley to withdraw into himself at Eton, that led a certain Harpo Marx to drop out of his New York public school aged eight. Wouldn't you just know it, but Kennedy – in another decidedly odd birthday celebration – joined Harpo for his 100th. In an extraordinary black and white BBC film of 1988 the violinist and harpist perform a version of Liszt's Hungarian Rhapsody No. 2. The duet is of course a mash-up: Harpo's performance is from the Marx Brothers film *A Night in Casablanca* (1946) (mistakenly credited by the BBC as *Stage Door Canteen* (1943)). Kennedy faces him, edited into the frame, and softened to match the low resolution of the archive footage. Rather appropriately, they're in the 'treasure room', within the original film's narrative. Equally fitting is that the scene (just ahead of the clip used) features a crew member's shadow. It's almost as if Kennedy emerges from that historical glitch.

Kennedy's monologue introducing the film, with deadpan delivery to camera, is equally surreal:

> I was in the supermarket the other day ... buying a pack of pork sausages, which wasn't much good because I'm veg-etarian, and this bloke ... standing next to me said 'it's my hundredth birthday this year. Do you want to come to the party?' And I looked round and it was Harpo Marx – pretty cool cat. So I'm not sure if it was a figment of my imagination but like, if he was alive today he would be 100.[18]

The dates tally: Harpo was born in 1888. Here were two eccentrics from different generations playing music together and defying time into the bargain; a single moment spanning the decades. It's the fact that the Liszt veers into jazz that makes it so persuasive, as if the two musicians are improvising together in 'real time', whatever that is. At the beginning of the sequence, Harpo picks a feather from his sleeve; Kennedy echoes this, plucking one from his own shoulder. At the end, Harpo's wide-eyed expression of glee appears to be directed straight at Kennedy. They are remark-able eyes, which the poet Robert Lowell referred to as 'old eyes too young', in his poem 'Harpo Marx',[19] written when he met Harpo on set a few years before the actor's death.

Kennedy's film is cleverly contrived; bizarre it may be, but Harpo as Kennedy's accomplice somehow makes sense. Harpo was an accomplished musician, but he was largely self-taught. Not only was his technique unorthodox, he even tuned his harp the 'wrong' way. A maverick musician, then, but also a maverick actor, and individual. In the age of the talkies he chose a silent persona. That made him seem a naïf, a simpleton almost, but his comic prowess was sophisticated. He was the consummate trickster, and yet here he's tricked by the trickster Kennedy, who plays it straight, not quite yet the lookalike for Harpo's contemporary Stan Laurel, as he would be a few years down the line.

Drawing by Lara Munden

I can even see a resemblance in portraits of Shelley and photos of Harpo. In a parallel universe, I reckon Ken Russell might well have used Harpo in his madcap Shelley biopic.

Thompson's further comments about Shelley might apply directly to the Farrell photograph of Kennedy:

> An age that is ceasing to produce child-like children cannot produce a Shelley. For both as poet and a man he was essentially a child.
>
> We, of this self-conscious, incredulous generation, sentimentalize our children, analyse our children, think we are endowed with a special capacity to sympathize and identify ourselves with children; we play at being children. And the result is that we are not more child-like, but our children are less child-like. It is so tiring to stoop to the child, so much easier to lift the child up to you.[20]

This again is surely not unrelated to Ken Robinson's 'Decline of Genius' chart. We make such big efforts in the name of nurturing future generations, and they're so often misguided. Andrew Robinson has yet another angle on this. He acknowledges that in our current era, there is talent all around. 'More scientists, writers, composers and artists than ever earn a living from their creative output' but where, he asks, is the next Darwin, Einstein, or Mozart? 'Even in popular music, the genius of the quality of Louis Armstrong, The Beatles, or Jimi Hendrix, seems to be a thing of the past.' Time may come up with a positive answer, but Robinson has doubts, with good reasons:

> First and foremost is surely the ever-increasing profession-alization and specialization of domains ... The breadth that feeds genius is harder to achieve today than in [previous] centuries ... Had Darwin been required to do a PhD in the biology of barnacles, and then joined a university life sciences department, it is difficult to imagine his having the varied experiences and exposure to different disciplines that led to his breakthrough.[21]

Robinson imagines other similar, negative scenarios, and then goes on to say: 'A second reason appears to be the ever-increasing commercialization of the arts. True originality takes time—at least ten years—to come to fruition.' This, as discussed earlier, is the principle argument in Robinson's book, but he makes a further point about the time it takes for significant originality to be rec-ognized. 'It is much less challenging, and more remunerative, to make a career by producing imitative, sensational and repetitive work, like Andy Warhol.'

A third reason given is more curious, but equally compelling:

> our expectations of a modern genius have become more sophisticated and discriminating ... The 'long hair, great black hats, capes, and cloaks' of the bona fide Victorian hero, iron-ically mentioned by Virginia Woolf, are now period pieces, concealing complexes more than genius.[22]

This is a very different point. It seems to say 'we're no longer fooled', which is fair enough, but it also, surely, suggests that we may be too ready to dismiss the eccentric dress and behaviour of a Kennedy as nonsense, or worse, to use those things as evidence against his greatness.

As discussed in previous chapters, Kennedy's 'ten years' (to use Robinson's yardstick) were complex, fraught yet also richly rewarding. An utterly original man and musician emerged. He never succumbed to the musical equivalent of that PhD on the biology of barnacles. He never resorted to a life of producing imitative art. There have been risks of repetition, but those have been driven in part by the record companies saying 'Yeah, more Vivaldi! Where's Vivaldi's fifth season?'[23] That was one reason why he took time out – time in which to develop his art, rather than churn out more of the same; a five year booster to the next ten-year breakthrough.

But 'sensational', yes, that charge cannot be denied. There is a difference though, between art that is sensational and correspondingly superficial, and art that employs a level of sensationalism to achieve its real purpose. My view is that Kennedy's output is most definitely in the latter category. And after the early forays into outlandish dress (such as the ill-fated costume for the Berg concerto performance), Kennedy's attire has actually been rather unremarkable. It settled down, quite early on, into either the standard grunge, first acquired from the Camden market in an emergency, and which now seems almost quaint, or the equally standard Aston Villa shirt, the only surprise being the occasional change of player's name on the back. None of it is really enough to register on the chart of 'great black hats, capes, and cloaks'. Curiously, though, it still sets Kennedy apart from the rest of the bunch – of male performers, that is. Women's colourful attire has long been the norm. There's been an expectation of glamour, though 21st-century women have apparently taken things too far. Yuja Wang, for instance, has been criticized for wearing 'itsy bitsy dresses and five-inch heels'.[24] She insists her choice of clothing is not for sensationalist reasons, and that fashion bores her; she simply wears what she wants. That would seem a pretty basic principle, in this day and age, and yet prejudice of one sort or another is always there with a tut tut. Perhaps I'm guilty of that too, in finding the sight of a soloist wearing tails in 2023 rather absurd.

Kennedy Meets Gershwin

A commitment to the moment was evident in Kennedy's teenage scotch-fuelled decision to join Grappelli on stage at Carnegie Hall. Gershwin's 'Lady Be Good' was a regular feature of their many performances together, and in 2017 Kennedy was playing it again – and recording it as part of a whole *Kennedy Meets Gershwin* album. The original seized moment was still alive, but Kennedy was also transforming the material, in new arrangements.

Gershwin lived a mere 38 years, in which he established a colossal reputation that hasn't faded. He didn't burn out, in the rock'n'roll sense, but he did, curiously, start to imagine that he could smell burning rubber. That was a symptom, along with blinding headaches, of the brain herniation and subsequent haemorrhages from which he died. His breakthrough work, *Rhapsody in Blue,* came some ten years after he started his musical career in New York's Tin Pan Alley. After ten more years he wrote the groundbreaking *Porgy and Bess*, a work that was considered to defy all categorization. He found his final, natural musical home in Hollywood writing soundtracks for film.

You might think *Kennedy Meets Gershwin* sounds like an unusually commercial project, given Gershwin's popularity. It looks like a further retreat from 'contemporary' jazz. Gershwin was a contemporary of Fats Waller, whose songs Kennedy had arranged for the *Recital* album. Kennedy admits that there have been times when he 'could have been pressurised into making some kind of commercially viable music' but insists, 'I've never done that, I've always made the music and worried about the commerciality of it later.'[25] His Gershwin album is not the Gershwin many would expect. It's a world apart from *The Glory of Gershwin* album produced by George Martin in 1994, to celebrate the 80th birthday of Gershwin's lifelong friend Larry Adler, the harmonica player. The vocalists on that album included Peter Gabriel and Kate Bush, two Kennedy favourites, and they and many others do a very creditable job, but there's little that's surprising. All the contributions, apart from Adler's 'Rhapsody in Blue' on harmonica, and Courtney Pine's 'Summertime' on sax, are straightforward vocal renditions of songs. When Anne-Sophie Mutter tackled Gershwin on her *Tango and Dance* album with André Previn, she too aimed to inhabit the vocal line, albeit on violin, rich with vibrato. Previn makes an interesting point about the necessary *feel.*

> You can take a great American orchestra and give them a Strauss waltz – and it just sounds wrong. It's correct, but it isn't right. Then you can take a British or German orchestra and try to do Gershwin – same thing, because they didn't grow up with it. But any kid here in New York, by the time he's a teenager, knows how Gershwin goes.[26]

He was obviously convinced that Mutter had what it takes, and the result is certainly enjoyable – one might even say commercial. Her set-list is all from *Porgy and Bess*. Kennedy's is very different, as is his approach. He brings the whole range of his other jazz forays, and his classical experience, to bear on the material. He was also, it should be remembered, a 'kid in New York' during his time at Juilliard. His claims to be a perfect fit for the material go further:

> For me, Gershwin's work is epitomised by three main ingredients: the fusion of jazz and classical music, the beautiful melodic influences of Jewish culture and the unique energy of New York City. This music fits my skill set and experience so well that if playing this music was a job my interview would end with my securing immediate employment with the employer deciding not to interview any other applicants.[27]

If the arrogance here wasn't so funny, it would be pretty irritating. Mutter might well convince the hypothetical employer, albeit for very different reasons. Kerenza Peacock's album *Someone to Watch Over Me* was hailed by Gershwin's nephew as 'the best arrangements and playing of my Uncle's songs I have heard!'.[28] Kennedy's list of Gershwin 'ingredients' is handpicked to suit not just his skill set but his inclinations as interpreter. For a start, he has a phobia about the 'abrasive pseudo cultured singing and two dimensional acting'[29] that has tinged most of our Gershwin encounters (though he excuses versions by Louis Armstrong and Ella Fitzgerald). The comment about singing comes as no surprise. The interest lies in how Kennedy does it differently, using his violin not only as an alternative solo 'voice', but as part of an investigative ensemble working its way to the heart of the music. Significantly, he also puts the violin aside to play piano instead. In some places, the relation to 'song' has all but vanished.

It all begins with 'Rhapsody in Claret and Blue', the one piece devoid of song even in Gershwin's original. Kennedy adds Aston Villa 'Claret', but in other respects he strips things back. Given that Gershwin's piece is seventeen minutes long, and that Kennedy so often extends things way beyond the expected limit, taking a mere two and a half minutes to skip through this substantial masterpiece is a startling opening gambit. But there you go: expectations are out of the window. It's a million miles from the simple, glorious rhapsody that opens Woody Allen's film *Manhattan*.

'Summertime' is similarly overhauled. If there's one Gershwin track that almost everyone knows, even if they don't know who wrote it, it's this. Kennedy had already recorded a version as an 'extra' on his *Four Seasons* 'Summer' single. Here, though, the melody is almost deconstructed into breathy fragments, accentuated by Dave Heath's breathy flute. It's as if Vivaldi's tortuous Italian summer has crept in. It's contemplative, wordlessly exploring the full depth of the lyric. As with the opening rhapsody, it's almost austere, and it's interesting how Kennedy's image on the front of the CD (with violin) and on the booklet inside (with piano) is also sombre, monochrome, utterly unlike Mutter's beaming image on her CD. He's even formally dressed (relatively speaking), which works, bizarrely, as a form of dressing *down*. His expression is studied. He looks – shock horror – slightly elderly!

There's even a rather old-fashioned feel to some of the tracks, moments when you feel the former punk violinist is donning a cardigan and slippers. 'Our Love Is Here to Stay' would keep even Philip Larkin's tapping toes happy. They would no doubt curl though at the interpolated Kennedy composition, 'Time'. It's an appropriate title, given the time-*travelling* across musical styles. Kennedy includes another of his own compositions, a 'Fantasy' on 'They Can't Take That Away From Me'. The longest track on the album, it's positioned, rather amusingly, after Gershwin's 'How Long Has This Been Going On'.

It's in these final tracks, 'Fantasy' onwards, when the Gershwin catalogue has been scoured for every possible musical inflection, that Kennedy's youthful exuberance comes to the fore. 'Lady Be Good' is redolent of his teenage partnership with Grappelli, but digs into the rhythm with a hard-hitting rock-style intensity. It's full of the *joie de vivre* that so often characterizes the conclusion of a Kennedy concert. It even encores itself with (finally!) vocals in the form of Kennedy shouts, before the whole thing signs off with a distant, angelic chord.

The Gershwin tour also featured a new composition, *The Magician of Lublin*, inspired by the 1960 novel by Isaac Bashevis Singer. For Kennedy, the story offered another opportunity to reflect musically on the massive changes to Polish life over the past century. But while the unrealized *Price of Freedom* project had intended to focus on recent narratives, using contemporary voices, the focus this time was on fictional characters of the past. Kennedy wanted to 'capture the vibrancy and colours'[30] of a world that's now gone, and he couldn't have chosen better material. Ted Hughes was a big fan of Singer, describing his writing as 'blazing with life and actuality ... powerful, wise, deep'.[31] Kennedy uses a string ensemble to portray the characters of the story, a classical foundation into which he weaves Jewish melodies and jazz. The eponymous magician, Yasho, is quite literally a trickster. He also shows absolute dedication to his itinerant profession, and his level of artistry sets him apart from his peers. In an intriguing parallel to a British violinist of the early 1980s, the magician is paid much more poorly than his foreign counterparts. His personal life however is a mess, and he ends up in penitent confinement. Any similarity between Kennedy and the magician only goes so far.

Interviewing Kennedy about his prospective 'Freedom' project, Jessica Duchen had been quick, perhaps *too* quick, to compare it to work by Steve Reich.[32] In 'Different Trains' (1988), Reich had written directly about the holocaust, not only pitching the sound of his own mundane train travel visiting his parents against the forced passage of Jews to concentration camps, but also using the actual testimonies of holocaust survivors, both as audible words and as melodic material. Just as the spoken words seem to sing, the blended stringed instruments, fractionally displaced in time, seem to speak. The viola is a natural accomplice, its range being so similar to the human voice. The writer Jonathan Freedland stresses the importance of keeping strictly to archival fact in dealing with material of such gravity, and Reich refers to his piece as 'documentary' with some justification. Kennedy's 'Freedom' material was less sensitive, and I have no doubt he could have pulled it off as a creative as much as documentary project, though to be in any way imitative of Reich, as Duchen provocatively suggested – even in a less repetitive vein, as Kennedy was quick to counter – was perhaps best avoided.

Freedland, himself a fiction writer, objects to 'creative' historical narratives such as *The Boy in the Striped Pyjamas*, the 2006 novel by John Boyne. There's no need, or excuse, in his view, for inventing stories around traumatic events where documentary evidence abounds.[33] His point is of course valid, and many agree with him, especially about that particular book, but I find myself resisting a general prohibition. How often do we use that phrase 'it's hard to imagine', when referring to the past, or even the current traumas of others? Artists of all kinds, using their imaginative skills, help us to grasp what otherwise baffles or eludes us. Even Reich's work is imaginative, combining disparate actualities into a time-travelling, 'fictional' collage.

The Magician of Lublin is a work of fiction and yet Hughes refers to 'life and actuality'. Poland's cultural past is alive on the page, the writer's imaginative feat as marvellous as any conjuring trick. That's what drove Kennedy to create an artwork of his own, a further embodiment – in musical form – of life miraculously preserved in art. The incidental music for Chekhov's *Three Sisters* showed Kennedy's flair for writing music to accord with a dramatic narrative. *The Magician of Lublin* takes that to a new level, not least as a structural whole.

*

What of Kennedy's peers, and other long-toothed Wunderkinder? Does defiance of age go with the breed? Or is the typical path into dignified elder-statesman-hood? Menuhin was still recording aged 83, in defiance of a deteriorating technique, but he had long committed himself to educational work and humanitarian causes. That became a defining characteristic, as much as his musical ability. For some, a shift towards education is a direct result of physical incapacity. Julian Lloyd Webber, for instance, took on the role of Principal at the Birmingham Conservatoire after an injury to his bowing arm. Maxim Vengerov suffered a shoulder injury while weightlifting, in his early 30s, and moved more into conducting, also founding a music school in Israel. Later, he recovered. But he, like Menuhin, had already established an ambassadorial profile, working with UNICEF, also playing in a number of Holocaust memorial concerts.

Kennedy has had injuries – he even broke his fingers while playing football at the Menuhin School – but he claims that his technique has nevertheless always been improving. He is though only 64. He hasn't as yet been drawn into the educational arena, despite various overtures. The earliest was from Princess Diana, no less. After the Prince's Trust gala concert of 1989, DJ Annie Nightingale introduced Kennedy to Princess Diana and asked her if she'd like Kennedy to teach her sons the violin. 'I wouldn't let you within a million miles of them' was Diana's response. 'Shocking, your royal monstrette',[34] said Kennedy. But Brix Smith claims Princess Diana took a 'very personal interest in Nigel'. 'She flirted outrageously with Nigel in front of me. She invited him to the palace, to give private violin lessons to William and Harry.'[35] More recently, Julian Lloyd-Webber has invited Kennedy to run a masterclass at his Conservatoire. Kennedy is reluctant, saying, 'I don't think it's a place where I should be telling late teenagers or people in their early twenties what to do.'[36]

Kennedy the late teenager had been at Juilliard, reacting against the whole system. One of his contemporaries there was Yo-Yo Ma, the cellist, and the two characters make for an interesting comparison. Brix Smith remembers calling on Ma's New York apartment, 'in a modern tower block'. It had 'white decor and was scrupulously clean', the almost exact opposite of Nigel's own place, which was 'in an old building, and the hallways and common areas smelled like boiled cabbage and old ladies'.[37] For Ma, growing up, music was the family business; like Kennedy, he too dropped out of Julliard, and has engaged with a similarly eclectic repertoire, recording American bluegrass and Chinese music as well as traditional classics. He's worked with James Taylor and Carlos Santana, matching Kennedy's work with Donovan and Robert Plant. He's done his share of oddball stuff, duetting with Elmo on *Sesame Street*, for instance, when he also used his cello to imitate the sound of Hoots the Owl on sax. Like Kennedy he performed with Bobby McFerrin (and Mark O'Connor) but admitted to being terrified by McFerrin's improvisation.

He's won numerous prizes, and – here's the first difference – they are just that bit shinier than Kennedy's awards: not just Grammys rather than Brits; he's received the US National Medal of Arts, the Presidential Medal of Freedom, and dozens more. Like Kennedy, he has an honorary doctorate, his from Harvard. He too has been a vocal supporter of human rights, and Kofi Annan appointed him a Peace Ambassador for the United Nations in 2006. He's a member of the World Economic Forum board of trustees, and gave an extensive interview at the Forum in Davos 2020, commenting, 'One of the reasons I could be here and be useful ... is to talk about culture in general. Culture does not build walls; it builds bridges.'[38] He makes all the right noises – about the importance of inclusivity, access, 'the building of trust, the seeking of truth'. He's fully committed to action on climate change. When, in 2022, he was awarded the Birgit Nilsson Prize, presented by the King of Sweden, in recognition of an outstanding contribution to the world of music, Ma closed his acceptance speech with a promise – 'a commitment to practice the values Birgit Nilsson held so dear: joy and humor, closeness to the land and to nature, and a life in balance with others and with our planet.'[39]

All this might sound a little grandiose. Is it really within a musician's remit to act on such a global, political level? 'Trust, truth and service' sounds like an admirable mantra, but what does 'a global network of aspiration' actually mean? Spoken by a poseur, it might mean nothing, but Ma is both sincere and efficacious. His 'Bach to Work' initiative (in 36 cities on six continents) and his Silk Road Project have both nurtured significant cultural exchange and understanding. Of the latter project, Ma relates a revealing experience. Unlike his previous, numerous conservatoire classes, where students typically focus on technical questions, on the Silk Road in Amman people were asking him very different questions: 'why do you do this, why is this so important', poetic questions; 'they quoted poetry, they talked about philosophy.'[40] It was this line of questioning (which connects so clearly with comments I've quoted earlier by the disparate talents of Isaac Stern, Jeremy Denk and Dave Grohl) that defined the subsequent focus of the project on *passion-driven learning.*

Despite starting on the cello aged four, Ma claims he was 49 when he actively decided he *wanted* to be a musician – and 'to examine the preconditions of creativity ... the petri dish that's necessary for something to grow' (the alternative was a sleepwalking, touring career, where he might have morphed into 'the salesman that doesn't know where they are', yet another version of Kafka's beetle). He believes that 'finding places ... where these things can happen is our future'. I understand – indeed share – that aim, but is it necessary to be a musician, an artist, to make the quest? Part of me says no, and Ma admits that, if he was a teenager again, he might well have chosen a different path towards 'solving problems', 'bringing people together'.[41] But I also know first hand, as a practising writer running a writers association, the difference that makes. You're *invested* in the petri dish experiments: the listening and learning cuts both ways. The bureaucrat doesn't understand, or stand to benefit from the petri dish in the same way.

Despite his lofty missions and associations, Ma is down to earth – and humorous. 'I've never been able to keep a day job, so I work nights', he jokes. His greatest goal is simply 'to be useful in my waning years'.[42] Connecting with young people is for Ma a fundamental part of that. Of all his awards, he has cited the Fred Rogers Legacy Award he received in 2014 as the one he probably values most. Rogers was a hugely admired US children's television presenter – no ordinary TV host, as the multi-talented Rogers conceived, wrote, acted, produced, even composed music for his shows. Ma's reverence for Rogers is closely related to his comments about Birgit Nilsson, that she was 'one of our great musical role models, an artist whose attention was directed outward, toward young people'.[43] That, for Ma, is the most important thing, if (classical) music is to be relevant to successive generations, and play a positive role in shaping our future. He's good at it, and admired for it. There were of course many – including George Martin – who admired Kennedy for similar reasons, packing concert halls with young people. And yet there were those, as discussed in Chapter 5, who were dismissive of that, in a way they would never be with Ma. Some pioneering work is done within the frame of establishment rules; other from without. And our personal feeling (or prejudice) about individual character no doubt steers our reaction.

In his Davos interview, Ma says 'in culture, you never break things, you're always trying to construct',[44] but is that true? I'm thinking of Greg Lake's comment about breaking down barriers, 'doing some damage', and Kennedy's use of that same phrase. The petri dish isn't always an immaculate environment. Sometimes, perhaps, the dish itself has to be smashed. That's what punk rock in the 70s seemed to say. Youth was in revolt, and there weren't that many in the musical establishment applauding punk for connecting with young people. But for all the anger and rebellion on the surface, punk had considerable thoughtfulness, sincerity, even an element of childlike romance at its core. And for all its monotonous traits, it often had captivating melody combined with inventive rhythmic drive, almost Mozartian, the very opposite of what contemporary classical music was up to, and indeed 'progressive' rock.

It was John Peel who, in 1970, referred to ELP's Isle of Wight Festival performance as 'a tragic waste of talent and electricity'.[45] The 'electricity' bit was particularly insulting. But there it is again, the wasted talent accusation. Emerson was 26, Lake 23, Palmer 20; young ages indeed to be accused of wasting anything. They had only just formed their band, having left The Nice, King Crimson and Atomic Rooster respectively. The Isle of Wight Festival featured The Who, The Doors and Joni Mitchell amongst others; it was prestigious company, and ELP's decision was to be bold, to push the boundaries of what rock music might do. It's surprising that no one criticized them for wasting gunpowder too, as Emerson used a couple of antique cannons, fired from the stage, as part of their adaptation of Mussorgsky's *Pictures at an Exhibition*.

Peel obviously didn't *like* it, but part of his objection was probably bound up with an objection to overt virtuosity. Punk, with its 'anyone can do it' ethos, was soon to come to prominence and be preferred. 'Virtuosity itself is one of music's curses',[46] writes Blom in the *New Musical Companion*, and Philip Larkin's critique of modernism goes even further: Pound, Parker and Picasso (let's form the supergroup PPP while we're about it) were guilty of 'irresponsible exploitations of technique in contradiction of human life as we know it'.[47] For Blom, there's compensation: 'The one thing that redeems the out-and-out virtuoso is, to put it paradoxically, that he is doomed to perdition. He has his day, vanishes, and does not take long to fall into oblivion.'[48] But therein, surely, is the real waste of talent.

What should it be saved for? Peel perhaps approved of Emerson's solo work writing film scores, which he did very successfully from the 1980s, though for some reason he turned down *Chariots of Fire*. But Emerson's great love was live performance. He kept going as long as he could, but the nerve problems in his right hand that began when he was 50 recurred in chronic form, ultimately pushing him to take his own life, a tragic waste of talent to put all other talk of waste into sharp perspective.

For the talentless critic 'Robert' to accuse Kennedy of wasting his talent at the Albert Hall is wrong on many levels. There's another word for his welcoming the likes of Plant, Ponty and Andreev to the classical stage, and it's 'inclusivity', a principle that in most contexts is universally lauded. While some make noises about inclusivity in a self-righteous manner, Kennedy has always put the concept into practice. And just as he's built bridges (to use Ma's phrase) between musical categories, he's equally keen to desegregate people, their identities and views. He's working on an album on that theme with Cleveland Watkiss, himself a prominent, practical advocate of music in education and the community. 'Look, let's deal with things together', writes Kennedy. 'Rather than unfortunate minorities, let's be a fortunate majority with everyone in it.'[49]

Kennedy's most forceful stance on segregation came at the Proms in 2013, playing with members of Palestine Strings. He took the opportunity to make strong comments about 'apartheid', which were then censored by the BBC in its subsequent broadcast, 'because it does not fall within the editorial remit of the Proms as a classical music festival'.[50] The powers that be will endorse a humanitarian mission when it sits comfortably with their own, not when it's too maverick for their charter, a clear case of dual standards. 'Earnests' (as we might call them) can be exclusive as purists.

Kennedy has refused to play in Israel, just as many bands refused to play in apartheid South Africa's Sun City. Maxim Vengerov is amongst those who do, but then he sees himself as an Israeli citizen, and his visits as part of the ongoing struggle. 'Always when there's a conflict, I feel I'm a soldier with my rifle in my violin and bow. This tradition is from my predecessors – Isaac Stern used to do the same.'[51] It's a conscientious stance; but conscientious objection is sometimes as important as taking up arms. Kennedy objected strongly to the war in Iraq instigated by Bush and Blair, and joined thousands in Trafalgar Square on 20 March, 2004, playing Bach on his violectra as black balloons were released into the sky as part of a coordinated global protest.

You can say that music unites. You can say that football unites, as FIFA President Gianni Infantino did at the opening of the Qatar World Cup 2022, an event plagued by controversy. His simplistic message was built on a foundation of nonsense, lies and misdoings. Somewhat more honourable, naïve rather than morally duplicitous, was Queen's defence of their Sun City appearance. In 1985 they were the heroes of Live Aid, helping to raise money for drought-stricken Ethiopia, but only a year earlier they'd been the villains, chastised even by the United Nations. They were committed to playing to racially mixed crowds, believing that such a stance was a force for good, but drummer Roger Taylor now admits it was an error.

Queen's music itself was apolitical. Freddie Mercury in particular didn't want to be an activist: 'Look, I don't want to get involved in all that. I want to go round the world playing songs that people can enjoy.'[52] That's an honest enough attitude, even if apolitical art may be something of an illusion. Kennedy has many political leanings, but his primary drive as a musician is equally simple: he wants to enjoy himself. 'Being an autonomous musician avoiding conductors is all he's ever wanted to do' says Kathy Evans, 'other than being a London cab driver'[53] (and yes, I can actually picture it – the gregariousness, being in control, knowing the terrain but deciding on the niceties of the route according to what's happening on the day).

> I might be a really boring motherf---er but I'm really happy with the way life is going. I don't think I'm any wiser now than when I was a teenager. What I wanted to do then is exactly what I'm doing now, so in that respect everything justifies itself 100 per cent.[54]

Not every musician can follow in Menuhin's UNESCO footsteps. Sometimes, pure, unencumbered musical entertainment is one's best offering. But let it not be said that Kennedy has no interest in helping future generations. Despite his rejection of Lloyd-Webber's invitation, he does have educational leanings – and strong beliefs. He has 'dismissed the idea that London needs to spend £278m building a new concert hall, arguing that he would rather see money invested in schools, giving children access to instruments and teachers.'[55] Speaking further about

Lloyd-Webber's invitation, he says, 'I might go and work on Bach ... help the students by working with them, rather than telling them what to do.'[56] His distinction is both egalitarian and anti-establishment. 'I'd like to pass on a few things, but in a way which is not teaching, because teachers or professors, they do it in a way which is convenient for them.' There are of course such 'lazy' teachers, but I feel the need to defend the better breed, which includes not only the full-time professionals, but those like Ma, O'Connor (the O'Connor Method now an established teaching technique), Benedetti and Vengerov, who put their own lifelong learning to the test by sharing it with their younger counterparts. Vengerov, who works with pupils at the Royal College of Music, says it's always been in his genes to work in his way. 'I feel that I'm their age, and I'm also a student ... this is one of the miracles, when you're standing in front of the student. I'm sure I'm learning more.'[57] If it weren't for his anti-teacher rhetoric, Kennedy would probably admit the same. His work with the young Orchestra of Life would surely qualify.

More unexpectedly, Kennedy has even described plans for a school in Birmingham, 'next to Villa', with 'every racial denomination'. It's partly a social mission. 'I want to bring these young kids together, even if it's just playing hand drums at first ... music is a great collaboration, it's possibly even better than football.' His vision is to help kids from the Indian and Pakistani communities, 'lots of cultures and different financial backgrounds' with both music and football, in conjunction with Aston Villa.[58]

There's a similarity here to what Yehudi Menuhin did in the last few months of his life at Stoughton Grange School in Guildford, not so much in the particular focus, but the desire to do things differently, with an inclusive purpose. Menuhin worked with twelve eight-year-olds, attempting to prove that 'all reasonably musical children can learn the violin'. After his death, his ex pupil Rosemary Furniss continued his work there. The 'experiment' was seen in a BBC documentary, *Menuhin's Children*, witnessed by Humphrey Burton, who writes that 'few of them demonstrated any special aptitude but for Yehudi that was not the point ... the participants would benefit from such an experiment in learning to conquer a craft'. Menuhin's own words provide the final summary: 'It will be useful throughout their lives. I don't think they'll ever regret it.'[59] As with Kennedy's plan, the focus was not on practising the violin fours hours a day, but offering a range of young people a sense of what is possible, what they might achieve at their chosen endeavour. Sadly, a promotional clip of the film is currently all that is in the public domain.

I know, from personal experience, how taking professional writers into schools can have a transformative effect – not in producing professional novelists or poets but instilling a sense of creative possibilities and self-confidence in pursuing one's dreams. Such 'experiments' have been particularly effective when the visits have been sustained. As Andrew Motion, Poet Laureate at the time of my own project, remarked, pupils were offered 'the chance to make heartening discoveries of themselves, and to deepen and diversify their connection with the world. If they produce important works of art, we shall all be grateful. If they don't we'll still be grateful: they'll have learned what it is to be educated in the round.'[60] I was inevitably pleased to learn how, after Menuhin's visits to Stoughton Grange, the children had written poems about the experience.

The producer of the BBC programme, Colin Bell, has also written poems inspired by Menuhin, one of which – a 'Fibonacci poem' – is printed below. He also relates that, sadly, the BBC declined the idea of following the children's further progress. It's a familiar picture: no one willing to make the modest investment into longitudinal studies that would, at the very least be hugely interesting, and potentially provide evidence of the value of longer-term creative interventions.

Yehudi Menuhin
(22 April 1916 – 12 March 1999)

Birth
name
The Jew:
Yehudi.
Rabbinical son
born to shame anti-semitics.
A name honoured not silenced – violin's wunderkind.
Humanity sung in music,
the fiddle his voice.
Yehudi
the Jew,
still
sings.

Our
last
meeting.
Menuhin,
the maestro and me.
His violin laid to one side
serenely walking, quietly talking, looking for Spring,
melancholy February's
transfiguration.
Seasons end.
Karma's
death
smile.

＊

As Andrew Robinson's comments quoted earlier in this chapter
suggest, there may be a diminution of genius upon us. With
specialization so early in education, it's increasingly less likely
for a 'Renaissance prince' to emerge, or a guitar playing tennis
star, even a classical soloist who is also a composer. (Yes, we have
poet-musicians/performing composers in the field of popular

music, and that's partly because *training* plays a lesser part in what they do; no one is telling them to put away their pen because they're supposed to be practising the violin.) An additional issue is that specialization makes it less likely for any achievement to be widely appreciated. Ironically, our 'age of information' is a further, worrying complication. Robinson refers to a conversation he had with Arthur C Clarke, in which the famous science fiction writer spoke of a 'fractal future':

> Although everybody is ultimately connected to everybody else, the branches of the fractal universe are so many orders of magnitude away from each other, that really nobody knows anyone else. We will have no common universe of discourse. You and I can talk together because we know when I mention poets and so on who they are. But in another generation this sort of conversation may be impossible because everyone will have an enormously wide but shallow background of experience that overlaps only a few per cent. As time goes on, all the great classics—who will even know who they are?[61]

Robinson highlights an extreme example where two separate groups of US scientists were working in the same field independently of each other: 'one group was literally unable to understand what the other group was talking about, because their two approaches to the physical phenomenon they had discovered differed so radically.'[62] Are we approaching a time when experts – or even casual listeners – within a certain musical field won't even overlap in what they know? Where even fans of a Yo-Yo Ma and a Nigel Kennedy won't share common ground – won't even know of the other's existence, especially if the streaming services on which they increasingly rely don't make the connections? Even the type of furore discussed in Chapter 5 may prove elusive. I found it odd that Jessica Duchen, writing about Maxim Vengerov in 2020, called the violinist 'the nearest thing the world of the classical violin has to a household name',[63] as if Kennedy had never existed. But her statement proved prophetic, in that Vengerov cultivated an online presence during the pandemic, and has now reached 170 million followers. Vengerov may well deserve them, but we need to remember that there are also multi-million followings of the inane. As Robinson says, 'Without a community of experts, sharing "a common universe of discourse", there can be no meaning to terms like "exceptional creativity" or "genius".'[64]

For now at least, the term 'Wunderkind' is generally understood; it's a term of astonished admiration. 'Wundercodger' is more confusing, 'codger' being an elderly eccentric, a term of affection, perhaps, but also of mild derision. There's possibly a dash of 'curmudgeonly' in the mix. Sheer longevity is confusing enough, not least because those blessed with it flaunt it in such different ways. 'Mick Jagger shakes his bum and attempts to convince his audience that time has stood still since the mid-70s; Dylan confronts us with not just his own mortality, but ours, too.' So wrote Dylan fan John Harris in 2011.[65] Let's be honest, both those musicians are still delighting their fans. As for Kennedy, he's playing it both ways, with his 'Lady Be Good' Gershwin swagger, and studied *Lublin* solemnity. But there are still no real models, or understanding, of how the classical musician can make us think differently, as they age, about the music they play. Part of that I'll attribute to what I'll call the Schiff Syndrome (on account of his remarks about Bach):[66] a reluctance to let classical music be muddled up with life. If composition isn't recognized as being inextricably involved with human predicament, growth, experience and decay, how is the performer's interpretation, as that of a fellow human being, to be an imaginative match, bringing their own predicament – their own life's journey – to bear on the process in a meaningful, sensitive way?

The question is complicated by the whole Wunderkind phenomenon. As Kennedy says, 'Menuhin was playing Bach on a fantastic spiritual level when he was a teenager'. Where do you go from there? Conversely, 'If you hear someone play vacant when they're 18, they're going to play the same type of shit when they're 50. You can't learn pathos or profundity.'[67]

I have mentioned what I find to be the captivating, deeply moving nature of Kennedy's concerts. His performance of *The Magician of Lublin* in 2018 was every bit as enthralling and technically assured as his South Bank recital some twenty years earlier. Yet there are those who have seen him play (not just listened to CDs) who might agree with Alexander Larman, calling Kennedy 'an erratic, often brilliant figure hellbent on pursuing his own agenda',[68] the suggestion being that such a 'hellbent' trajectory is a waste, that the acquisition of wisdom, that we tend to expect with age, is being wilfully ignored. Kennedy however would see the whole of that comment as a compliment. 'As a musician you can be whatever you want. It just comes down to how stubborn you're willing to be.'[69]

Holding to youthful ideals (with all the associated follies, dangers) when conventional wisdom says that you should be ageing gracefully, is fraught with disapproval, and rejection. But conventional wisdom can be bogus wisdom. The wisdom we might expect of our seniors, and especially the establishment, is often lacking. 'Prudence', in particular, has been called out. In February 2023 one tabloid newspaper referred to the Governor of the Bank of England, surely a pillar of the establishment – and embodying one might hope a degree of financial wisdom – as 'The Plank of England'. 'There's absolutely nothing better than being lectured about fiscal prudence by a prat with a £575k-a-year job, is there?'[70] 'Prat': it's the term of abuse that's been flung at the youthful Kennedy. There's no monopoly on terms of abuse.

The values and credentials of the establishment may have been rumbled (a good thing), but so too the Wunderkind – or indeed Wundercodger – may have been superseded by the talent show 'star', the wannabe who impresses the jury of lowest common denominatory judges (a bad thing, surely). It's possibly the Schiff Syndrome working in reverse, and (old) age isn't fashionable. As Kennedy says, 'In the old days, they could get a 70-year-old into the studio because he had something new to say about Chopin. But even Rubinstein or Glenn Gould would find difficulty now in being allowed to record what they wanted.'[71]

For —kind or —codger, however, it seems the sheer fact that they play music at all holds them in good stead. A recent report suggests that 'playing an instrument is associated with small but detectable cognitive benefits over a lifetime'.

> The ageing rocker clinging on to their youth may be a figure of mockery, but research suggests they should be envied for their sharpness of mind.
>
> Researchers have found a link between learning a musical instrument in youth and improved thinking skills in old age. People with more experience of playing a musical instrument

showed greater lifetime improvement on a test of cognitive
ability than those with less or no experience, a paper from the
University of Edinburgh has said.[72]

It's not only the 'Wunder—s' that should find consolation here;
it's all of us who have dabbled, and persisted, for sheer pleasure.

One of the minor pleasures of *Uncensored!* is the James Bond
spoof with which Kennedy introduces the Aston Villa chapter
(M diverting Bond's Moscow mission to a certain town called
Birmingham, with a big swipe at the 'centres of political correct-
ness in Manchester and London').[73] It's deft comedy, posing as a
dream, a sequence that reviewers might have done well to highlight. There's not an expletive in sight. One Bond, Sean Connery,
makes other appearances in the book, and it's the lighter, comedic
aspect of Bond that Kennedy plugs into. It's not only entertaining,
it's revealing of the truly child*like* quality at the heart of all the
childishness. But by some strange coincidence, the latest of the
newer, darker Bond films, *No Time to Die*, was arriving in cinemas
at the very same time, with an altogether more serious message
at its close. M quotes from the writer Jack London, and the words
reverberate with much of what this chapter has been about:

> I would rather be ashes than dust! I would rather that my
> spark should burn out in a brilliant blaze than it should be
> stifled by dry-rot. I would rather be a superb meteor, every
> atom of me in magnificent glow, than a sleepy and permanent
> planet. The proper function of man is to live, not to exist. I
> shall not waste my days in trying to prolong them. I shall use
> my time.[74]

It was a fitting epitaph for Bond. And yet, it seems he may yet be
recycled, to give us still more. The franchise lives on.

But should Bond have the last word here? I might go back to
Shelley, who wrote, 'Poets are the unacknowledged legislators
of the world'.[75] I count Kennedy, Menuhin, Yo-Yo Ma and many
other musicians as such legislative forces, 'mirrors of the gigantic
shadows that futurity casts upon the present'.[76]

When You're Sixty-Four

Macca will be at Glastonbury
headlining on the Pyramid stage
while you're in the High Tatras
taking care of Huxley,
the old dog almost unable
to move. You carry him
everywhere, like a priceless
fiddle. I admire you for this
as much as I long to hear
you play again – and you yearn
for more city lights. Ludwig Van,
for whom you've written a concerto,
never made it this far, his deafness
worse than we're likely to know.

The ruptured tendon
in my left hand is of no real
consequence to the world,
but should your fingers fail
(never mind losing your hair)
however many years from now
we would all be significant losers.
Meanwhile, every milestone
is good for a laugh, a memorable
party – reason to believe we're
somehow ahead of the game,
still ready to take advantage
of whatever talent, huge or small,
remains as we grow old.

Chapter 11: Encore

One is fun, why not two?
And if you like two, you might as well have four
And if you like four, why not a few?
Why not a slew?
(More! More!)
  —Stephen Sondheim

Are we there yet? Not quite. There's more, as there always is at any Kennedy concert when the scheduled programme reaches its conclusion. It's a significant feature of his performances – and his party-animal attitude to life generally. The energy appears unabated: there's always a desire for more music, even after the audience has gone, and only the hardcore inner-circle of friends and musicians remain, with more glasses of this or that to keep the more wheel spinning.

Sondheim's song 'More' was written for the film *Dick Tracy*, and sung by Madonna. It was released in 1990, the very year of Kennedy's post-*Four Seasons* heyday. Its joyous mantra proclaims the belief that if something is good, then even more of it is better still. We know though – don't we? – that there's a limit, a danger of too much, a reckless excess, a problematic addiction. That's all too clear in the Keith Moon story. Perhaps, but at the critical moment, we're all susceptible to wanting more of a good thing. As Christopher Hope (Daniel's father) writes in a poem about Schubert, dedicated to Yehudi Menuhin, 'He went down as well as new wine / at *The Blue Hedgehog* among encores of empty glasses'.[1]

The joy in Kennedy's encores is there to see in the various filmed concerts. In the Carcassonne *Vivaldi* film, Kennedy delivers a riotous version of 'Purple Haze' that sees the whole collective trooping off stage and back again in an ever greater ascent into glorious mayhem. In the *Polish Spirit* film, where the concert is staged more conventionally, there's less wild adventuring, but an element of danger nevertheless. In the heavily improvised part of Monti's 'Csárdás', during which Kennedy walks through the orchestra, it would appear that some of his fellow musicians have little idea where he's going, musically, but when the tune comes back at the end, at an almost impossible pace (even the conductor's arm can hardly keep up), they are rapturous. If the main programme doesn't give scope for improvisation, the chosen encores surely will.

For Eric Blom, however, the whole encore scenario is a disaster waiting to happen:

> To end with a flashy group of show pieces seems to me the height of folly, for that is simply asking the most cultivated section of the public to depart early and only the indiscriminately omnivorous to remain to clear up the leavings of the feast, and rapaciously to demand more and more.[2]

He's talking about the conclusion of the scheduled programme; we haven't even got to the encores, for which Blom reserves his greatest scorn, calling them 'a ridiculous convention, and the artist who conforms to it too readily is to be regarded with suspicion'. Blom died in 1959, and could never even have imagined the type of encore that Kennedy would unleash, turning that idea of 'conforming to convention' on its head. Blom, under a pseudonym, wrote a crime novel, *Death on the Down Beat* (1941), in which a conductor is shot. Writing in a later era, the author might have chosen a violin soloist as his target.

Originally, the encore was more to do with the word's slightly different meaning of 'again'. If an audience had enjoyed a particular operatic aria, they would call for the soloist to repeat it; they didn't after all have any means of listening to it again back home. The practice fell into disrepute, and the Italian conductor Arturo Toscanini famously banned encores at La Scala, and at the Metropolitan Opera in New York, during his tenures in the early years of the twentieth century. Strangely, however, it still goes on, albeit less frequently. Its close relative is the curtain call, for which Pavarotti apparently holds the record for reappearances – '165, after a 1988 performance of *L'elisir d'amore* at the Deutsche Oper Berlin. Apparently the applause lasted 1hr, 7 minutes, less than his personal record of 1hr, 30 minutes.'[3] That, by any standard, is absurd. It's like putting a track on permanent repeat, or a child's endless demand for the same game over and over again.

Andrew Robinson highlights early controversies: 'During its first run in Vienna in 1786 Mozart's three-hour opera *Le Nozze di*

Figaro ... received so many encores that the length of each performance was almost doubled.'[4] The Irish tenor Michael Kelly wrote that 'those in the orchestra I thought would never have ceased applauding, by beating the bows of their violins against the music desks'.[5] The opera is considered a sublime combination of music and poetry, its libretto by Italian poet Lorenzo da Ponte adapted from a play by Beaumarchais. And yet, there were only nine performances of the original production, and a furore around its subsequent run in Prague was countered by relative disinterest in Italy.

The encore was revitalized with avengeance in the rock concerts of the 60s. Gone was the clamour to hear something *again*; now it was a case of wanting something *else*, something different. While this occasionally meant something entirely new, which the audience hadn't heard before, more often than not it was a popular hit reserved for a crowd-pleasing finale. A hit, or hits; 'and if you like two, you might as well have four'. Some bands started to overdo it, so that the scheduled concert was little more than an extended prelude. That was also a recipe for predictability: everyone knew what would be kept until last. And with increasingly sophisticated stage production and programmed lighting effects, it was all pre-planned, lacking spontaneity. 'More', in the true sense, was no longer on offer, with venue closing times compounding the problem.

Kennedy, unsurprisingly, has done things differently. His encores may be semi-prepared, but even old favourites are presented in a new guise. A sense of digression is fundamental to the plan. He is also a master of shifting the mood, following a rollicking 'Csárdás', for instance, with the ethereal calm of 'Danny Boy', concluding with a silence that the audience must force itself to break with applause. It's as if he's taking his lead after all from Blom, who writes, 'the artist may produce a sobering effect by the simple expedient of giving something short and quiet by way of an extra, instead of a gratuitous exhibition of brilliance that only excites a craving for still more'.[6]

As mentioned earlier, there have been times when Kennedy has met with opposition. In the US, certainly during Kennedy's early touring years, the whole practice of encores was frowned upon, the main issue the cost of overtime pay. The bottom line was a twisting of Sondheim's further lyric: nothing *is* better than more. For Kennedy that's an anathema, a 'nine-to-five' attitude that runs counter to any meaningful musical event. English orchestras (though not all of them) have fallen short in his opinion too, for their attitude to preparation.

> There is a kind of blasé, laissez-faire attitude, a jobsworth atti-tude, where they are satisfied with being second-rate. They have forgotten what a first-rate result is. If I were playing on Boxing Day in Germany, you can be guaranteed that those musicians would turn out at 10 o'clock on Christmas morning to get the standard right.[7]

In Germany, he and his fellow musicians not only benefit from adequate rehearsal time, there is also scope for extended encores, sometimes real marathons. That only works if everyone is genu-inely enjoying themselves to the max.

Sometimes concert programmes are extended for the simple reason they start late, and there have occasionally been skirmishes with Kennedy's own fans. At Birmingham Symphony Hall in 2017, Kennedy 'risked a riot' by not even appearing until 7.50pm, '20 minutes after the advertised start'. After the first few pieces, he tuned his violin, saying 'I could have done this before, but better late than never!'[8] It's a standard Kennedy joke but perhaps he should have given it a rest on this particular evening. The 20-minute interval started 45 minutes late, and then lasted 45. It is claimed that a fifth of the ground-floor seats were empty by the end of the performance. The Albert Hall 'friends' concert had similar problems. Eric Blom would definitely not have approved: 'Quite plainly, it is the duty of all who attend a musical function, a duty to art, to other people and not least to themselves, to be punctual.'[9]

In 2018 Kennedy was back in Birmingham with his 'Kennedy Meets Gershwin' tour. A noticeboard in the foyer announced:

NIGEL KENNEDY
7:30pm* – 11.00pm*
(Interval 20')*

* timings are approximate

Someone came in late, and Kennedy quipped, 'Don't you like Bach?' It was all good humoured; the little battle had to be played out.

That was the last Kennedy concert I attended before the widespread periods of lockdown during the Covid pandemic, when most concerts were cancelled. Not only were we not getting *more* music, we got *less*. We were deprived, in 2020, of Kennedy marking the Beethoven anniversary (250 years since his birth, or at least baptism) with performances not only of the Beethoven violin concerto, but a new concerto written by Kennedy himself, 'Für Ludwig Van'. The scheduled concerts were primarily in Germany and Switzerland, with the promise of English dates to follow, but nearly everything was scuppered, and the knock-on effect has been chaotic. The whole system of heavily advanced touring programmes has taken a big hit. A few 'When I'm 64' events have been taking place, with Kennedy already 65. This weirdness is rather fitting, given Kennedy's random birthday celebrations mentioned earlier.

A different kind of hitch prevented 'The Alpha Experience' from going ahead on the Rhine island Grafenwerth, Germany, in June 2022, a 'symphonic multi-media project' billed as 'Hendrix meets Vivaldi – Uli Jon Roth meets Kennedy'. By this time, live concerts were up and running again, but there was apparently insufficient rehearsal time for all soloists (including opera singers as well as Kennedy, a truly unexpected combination) and the Symphony Orchestra of Cologne to be sufficiently prepared. There was a further complication: the event (part of an open-air series of concerts) fell foul of pending legislation protecting the island's environment. The Alpha Experience went on hold for a year, while curiosity about it continued to grow.

Like Kennedy, Roth was hugely influenced by Hendrix – and Menuhin. He married Monika Dannemann, Hendrix's last girlfriend, who was with Hendrix when he died, and 'escaped' accusation of complicity, only to die herself soon afterwards. Her death was deemed to be suicide, though Roth claims otherwise. He dedicated a work to her memory, *Requiem for an Angel*, the title echoing the dedication of Berg's violin concerto. A Roth/ Kennedy collaboration seemed to make sense, and The Alpha Experience was to feature parts of Roth's *Requiem* and Kennedy's concerto, as well as Hendrix and Vivaldi. But how on earth was all that to fit within the larger, rather grandiose description of the event?

> The overarching theme of the evening is mankind's search for identity. It revolves around the age-old conflict between the forces of good and evil which is forever unfolding on the battleground of the human soul. Our deepest questions for what is right and wrong; our insatiable quest for superficial knowledge, while disregarding the distant voice of higher wisdom; our struggle for survival of the human race as a species in the face of an impending mass extinction.[10]

'This then veers into matters on which Kennedy is sceptical: 'Uli is deeply concerned about the increasingly ominous and accelerating progression of man-made changes to the ecosphere of our planet.' So for every VIP pass a number of trees will be planted in a dedicated 'Sky Forest' grove in the Scottish Highlands. The plan is Roth's, but while Kennedy might disagree with the logic, he'd hardly argue with the tree planting itself.

Vivaldi and Hendrix – it sounds like more of the same, rather than something different, but I was fully prepared to buy my ticket trusting the collaboration would find fresh ways to 'make it new'. And given Kennedy's recent comments ('Hendrix is like Beethoven, Vivaldi is more Des O'Connor'[11]), the direct combination was tantalising enough. Innovation for the sake of it can of course become self-defeating, and Kennedy himself has been at pains to avoid a Vivaldi rut, or musical typecasting of any sort, but more *anything*, where Kennedy is involved, has always meant more invention: 'more colour, more expression, more layers, more eccentricity, more spontaneity, quite simply MORE', wrote Helen White on her blog when *The New Four Seasons* was released, entranced by the 'bizarre genius' of its making.[12]

The event, however, was eventually cancelled. It's a mark of how major projects can come unstuck, but perhaps some further determination will make it happen. Meanwhile, Kennedy 'connections' have nevertheless been in evidence in live music taking off again. Alicja Śmietana, a founding member of Kennedy's Orchestra of Life, performed her late father's Jazz Suites at the Polish Cultural Institute in London; Kennedy played on the original 'Autumn' recording (there's also 'Spring', but no other seasons). The Kennedy/Kroke composition 'Lullaby for Kamila' was rearranged and played by cellist Sheku Kanneh-Mason and pianist Harry Baker on their 'Noisenight' tour, organized by Through the Noise as part of its mission to bring classical soloists to nightclubs. At Sadlers Wells, choreographer Stina Quagebeur staged 'Take Five Blues', a work deriving from Kennedy's 'Vivace' and 'Take Five' on the *Recital* album, and how, in those pieces, 'contemporary jazz and classical music are uniquely married together'.13 The work was originally created during the 2020 lock-down, and presented online, where it's currently still available.

All this is relatively low-key, yet significant. Kennedy made his impact firstly and foremost as a performer, but here we see recognition of his work as a composer. That, potentially, creates an even greater legacy – and a rare one, in that very few contemporary violin soloists write their own concertos as Kennedy and Mark O'Connor do.

With the world still reeling from the Covid-19 pandemic, Russia escalated its ongoing conflict with Ukraine with a military invasion. Amidst the devastating scenes of suffering, there were images of remarkable human resilience, including young violinists continuing to play while hiding out in basement shelters. Kerenza Peacock befriended some of them via Instagram, and co-ordinated a massed response in the form of videos from violinists around the world – '94 violinists in 29 countries' – all playing a Ukrainian folk song, 'Verbovaya Doschechka'.14 Later, at a fund-raising concert for the Disasters Emergency Committee Ukraine Humanitarian Appeal, Nicola Benedetti added a live solo to the online montage that Peacock had assembled.15

Kennedy, meanwhile, was doing his own thing, but in similar solidarity. He recorded a short film in support of refugees, playing an arrangement of 'Merry Christmas Mr Lawrence', originally written for the film of the same name by Japanese composer Ryūichi Sakamoto. Kennedy plays the piece accompanied by cellist Beata Urbanek-Kalinowska in the studio of his Polish home, little more than a hundred miles from the Ukrainian border. Kennedy makes the point that refugees from any war zone often flee with few of their belongings. Musicians may have to leave instruments behind. He, by contrast, is free to walk through the snow to the woods above his village, violin case in hand, and leave a handwritten sign: 'Violins Not Violence'. It's the name of a charitable organization founded by police officers in Los Angeles, which donates musical instruments to young people. His larger point is 'to highlight ... the inclusive healing qualities of music'.[16] It may seem a small gesture, given the refugees' greater plight, but it recognizes the important role of music in emotional resistance. It seems significant that a musician, David Bowie, plays the lead role as a prisoner of war in *Merry Christmas Mr Lawrence*. Kennedy's film begins with an English quotation from a poem by the exiled Bertolt Brecht, written at the outbreak of World War II: 'In the dark times, will there also be singing? There will also be singing. About the dark times.'

Music and poetry: they have always made their presence felt at times of human struggle, and where deep consolation is required. And much as I, as a poet, inevitably champion the power of poetry, and the poetry/music alliance, with each often aspiring to the other, I find myself putting ultimate faith in music above all else. In 2020 I co-edited a book of poetry titled *No News*. 90 years previously, the BBC announced that there was, apparently, no news to report, and piano music played on the airwaves instead. Poets from around the world responded magnificently to the task of commemorating the extraordinary happening, and yet nothing – in words – could possibly match the pure, contemplative offering of the musical broadcast. Even when music has been broadcast in place of more explicit news of momentous change, as when *Swan Lake* was broadcast as tanks rolled into Moscow with intent to overthrow Gorbachev in 1991, it has left listeners free, in one sense at least, to ponder the historical moment unencumbered by polemic or indeed *fake* news. When Russia invaded Ukraine in 2022, TV Rain, one of Russia's last remaining independent broadcasters, used the same music, before the channel was shut down by the authorities.

How often we use that phrase, 'there are no words'. But there is never 'no music' (nor is there *fake* music). Leonard Slatkin gave us Barber's *Adagio for Strings* at the Proms after New York's twin towers were attacked in 2001. On Christmas Day 2016, the plane carrying the Russian Alexandrov Ensemble, otherwise known as the Red Army Choir, crashed into the Black Sea, killing all 64 members on board. There was remarkably little news coverage. Kennedy, however, devised a musical tribute and memorial in the concerts he staged in Australia shortly afterwards. Music brought us not only the news but also a means for us to pay our respects. There may yet come a time of such cataclysmic order that the consolation of music will be irrelevant; no human musicians or listeners alive, and no news channels left to tell a story of any kind. But there on the Voyager Golden Record, sent into space in 1977, will be the music of Mozart, Beethoven and others, including Arthur Grumiaux's recording of Bach that's rated so highly by Kennedy, and Louis Armstrong's 'Melancholy Blues'.

Perhaps, when some non-human being encounters Grumiaux's Bach, alongside examples of the human voice, they will recognize the individual quality of the sound, compared with other violin music on the disc. That is what Kennedy admires – and what I admire in Kennedy – and it's more rare, and therefore precious than you would think. As Anne-Sophie Mutter says, 'since the violin is so close to the human voice, you'd think that would be the easiest instrument on which to create a singular voice. But we have lost the urge to search for it.'[17] And yet, perhaps when aliens with their stereotyped brains come to appreciate the immaculate craft of JS Bach, they will also be able to gauge how the mere notes are taken to another level of life by the artist of truly individual distinction; and how this instrument, the violin, the means to many a virtuosic display, can also speak of the human heart.

When Menuhin wrote how 'Classical music has suffered at the hands of the dogmatic and the mechanical', it was to highlight the 'spontaneous expressiveness and poetry' that a musician such as Kennedy promised as a much needed antidote.[18] What on earth would he have made of the new Steinway Spirio now available for a mere $200,000: 'a seamless melding of 21st-century technology and Old World craftsmanship' according to CEO Ron Losby.[19] It's a self-playing grand piano, using software that enables the keys and pedals to be used with the exact velocity of original performances. This, in a sense, is no worse than a traditional recording, in seeking to faithfully reproduce a worthy performance, but it's false in its claim to offer something 'utterly indistinguishable from a live performance'. If anyone disagrees, and finds the claim acceptable, try to imagine where the madness

might lead. The Spirio is an arguably brilliant refinement of the
pianola, the accomplishment of an irresistible 21st-century technical challenge, but with robotics and indeed artificial intelligence
still in their infancy, who is to say that a machine might not, in the
future, play a violin? (Or, for that matter, write a poem more convincingly than ChatGPT.[20]) It might even play it 'perfectly', (or) in
precise imitation of a particular violinist. Imagine watching that,
and calling it 'utterly indistinguishable from a live performance',
or even calling it 'legitimate' as a personal, authentic human act,
as publisher Simon & Shuster did this year in reference to Bob
Dylan's signature in copies of his book, *The Philosophy of Modern
Song*. The 'signing' was done by a machine, and the publisher had
the nerve to provide certificates of authenticity. The limited edition
copies retailed at £599. Dylan at least had the decency to apologize
when the stunt was rumbled. Live performers everywhere deserve
a similar retraction from Steinway.

There's something else that's troubling about the Spirio. Its
'spirit' seems to have a lockdown attitude, suggesting that we
should be happy to avoid the concert hall and have the live performance brought to us in our own living rooms. It's a sad scenario,
with added sad one-upmanship by virtue of the price-tag. The best
of lockdown music was driven by a very different mentality. Daniel
Hope's project, for instance, Hope@Home, set out to help people
through the difficult times, offering daily streamed concerts as an
interim means of musical communication. It was determinedly
social. The UK government's phrase 'social distancing' was always
wrong; it was physical distancing that was, for a while, required,
while alternative social proximity was the new need. Musicians,
amongst others, rose to the challenge of providing it.

One extraordinary aspect of global lockdown was the way in
which the passage of time seemed to change. Familiar parameters
seemed to dissolve. And even when things returned to 'normal',
it felt that perspectives had altered. That probably happens at
many periods of widespread disruption, a form of *fin de siècle* flux.
Was it coincidence that Max Richter's *New Four Seasons: Vivaldi
Recomposed* appeared as we blinked our way back into the world
as we thought we had known it? Richter comments of the work,
'you have different eras talking to each other', and that – on a large

or small scale – was the new norm. Richter goes further, saying, 'it's also recomposing the social structure of our classical music culture',[21] and we know – or at least I hope readers of this book will recognize – that the 'recomposing' reflects what Kennedy was up to in the 1980s.

For a while, after Kennedy's brave new connections of eras, genres, and musical audiences, the word 'crossover' loomed large, a term that Kennedy loathes. It's a marketing word that attempts to categorize a type of artist and music as a hip new hybrid. It doesn't say anything about what the artist is really doing, apart, perhaps, from appealing to those who can only appreciate a classical melody if backed by an electro beat, or, conversely, only recognize the merit of a Beatles song if warbled by an operatic tenor. Those 'crossovers' break no new musical ground in Richter's or Kennedy's terms. They're gimmicks of performance, rather than (re)compositional adventures. They also make for bland rather than genuinely innovative or thought-provoking concert programming. So let's be done with them, and instead enjoy exploring the musical terrain that Kennedy has led us towards, where more and more artists of genuine distinction give us exciting new programmes of work, their passion for many genres creating a rich musical exchange: the Kopatchinskajas, the Hemsings, the Peacocks, the Barton Pines – all those who, to use Richter's phrase, are 'rediscovering diamonds which were hiding in plain sight'.[22]

We no longer need to think of pairing Mendelssohn and Bruch for all the old reasons; or even Berg with Britten. We can now have Bruch and Shostakovich with Black Sabbath and Led Zeppelin in Barton Pine's 'Shredding with the Symphony' program (2015). It's no stunt; it derives from her deeply personal attachment to those diverse musical sources and styles. It's also worth remembering that part of the symphony orchestra's ambition was to be as loud as humanly possible, to reach a Led Zeppelin volume level before a stack of Marshalls was available. Kopatchinskaja's *What Next Vivaldi?* album of 2020 is similarly eclectic. And Daniel Hope says of his increasingly concept-driven output, 'I don't really do "conventional".'[23] Just when you thought that albums generally were in decline, there seems to be a drive to give them new purpose, with a touch of prog philosophy in the mix.

Patricia Kopatchinskaja can hardly envision a 'normal' concert any more. She believes not only in the *right* of contemporary musicians to reinterpret classic works with daring, but also in their *responsibility* to do so. The result may be unsettling, but also *right* in the other sense. Friedrich Nietzche imagines Beethoven, for instance, travelling across time, witnessing a contemporary performance and endorsing it:

> Well yes! That is neither I nor not-I, but some third thing – and if it is also not exactly *right*, it is nonetheless right in its own way ... and as our Schiller says, the living are always in the right.[24]

It is not only music that walks this tightrope of 'right'. Every stage production of classic drama negotiates the issue, and television adaptations of classic novels offer a particularly clear demonstration of the ever-changing currency of 'right'. They all begin with the same premise, that an anachronistic technology can be appropriate to the telling of the tale. But each time – as successive versions of the same material show – the technology has moved on. The very look of them changes radically, the change made more acute by changes in acting, dramaturgical and directorial style. Equally fundamental is the fact that the audience is a moving target. Communicating with contemporary viewers is a constantly changing challenge. As a result, re-viewing earlier adaptations possibly tells us more about the period of production than the age in which the story is set. To use 'All Along the Watchtower', the Dylan song famously covered by Hendrix, as theme music for the 2018 version of Thackeray's *Vanity Fair* would have been unthinkable in an earlier era, but that's the artistic jukebox we are now blessed with.

Nevertheless, not only do the so-called purists grumble on; there's also a rearguard conservatism forever waiting to reassert its own sense of 'right'. It was there as classical music took to the stage again in 2022. In Patricia Kopatchinskaja's view, concert promoters were running scared of her adventurous projects, saying 'please, play Mozart, Beethoven, we need to sell tickets because people are not coming anymore'. She believes they're getting it wrong, ignoring the need to speak to young people in particular, 'in the language of today'. When she asked her

14-year-old daughter why she didn't come to her concerts, her daughter replied:

> First of all it's extremely boring, it's very stiff. You don't talk to us, we don't know who you are ... you don't move on stage ... you are dressed like servants of the last century ... You don't play music of today, you always 'cover' ... what is covering? It's repeating all the time ... you need to find out new stories, things which are really relevant to everybody ... Be courageous.[25]

Every word of this connects with what Kennedy – right from the start of his career – has striven to put right. He's had the courage, something that others have inherited, but which so many more still need to embrace. It seems timely, given Kopatchinskaja's worry about promoters' caution, that Kennedy's achievement should recently have been highlighted in an episode of Magic Moments of Music, a series 'dedicated to stellar musical events that gripped the whole world and remained unforgettable until today'.[26] The supposedly 'unforgettable' may sometimes be forgotten. As evidenced by Rob Cowan's review of Kennedy's Beethoven/Mozart recording, we don't necessarily fully appreciate the bold, and how we need it in the nurturing of our own, crucial curiosity – something that Cowan downplayed, so disappointingly, when he deemed the recording merely for 'Kennedy fans, and the curious'.[27] Yes, it was certainly appreciated by Kennedy fans and yes, it was rewarding for those with musical curiosity, but curiosity is surely fundamental to human experience, and at the forefront of human achievement and evolution. 'Curious' and 'bold'. Those were the two words that prompted me to write this book.

Others echo my sentiment. Clemency Burton-Hill says about Max Richter, 'he is curious'.[28] Richter himself quotes John Cage: 'As artists, our business is curiosity.'[29] Nicola Benedetti comments: 'I guess we all need to jump at some point ... Dare to try, and if we are free and daring enough, our collective experience only deepens.'[30] This is as true of the listener as it is of the performer.

And yet, I find myself worrying that curiosity is being systematically withdrawn from people's lives. Earlier in this book, I questioned certain educational systems, but those reservations pale into insignificance alongside my rage on reading how the

British government plans to make maths compulsory until the age of eighteen, to 'leave them better placed for the data-intensive jobs of the future'.[31] Is that to be our role, as pseudo-machines? Imagine the uproar if music or poetry were to be made compulsory to a similar age. I myself would reject that, despite believing that the arts are ever more important in a machine-governed age. Compulsory anything, to such an age, is an absurdity for young people finding their own way in the world. But whether or not such absurdity is imposed, there's nevertheless a creeping sense that horizons are shrinking. Some barriers may have come down, but new ones emerge, like weeds recolonizing cleared ground. Despite the class-less environment of 'songs' on iTunes etc, there are new, artificial categorizations being introduced. On Netflix films are placed in multiple, almost meaningless boxes, in an algorithmically determined attempt to grab our attention. The result is both confusion and, paradoxically, a limiting sense of what is available. Meanwhile, specialist services aiming to thrive within a niche are no service at all to a catholic taste. Maxim Vengerov now releases all his new works exclusively through the IDAGIO classical streaming channel. For those (I imagine a huge majority) who don't use that, his works will go unheard. Similarly, those who make exclusive use of the service are shutting themselves off from broader musical discoveries. It's segregation, just as it was with the Classical Brits. Even on the egalitarian YouTube, things are not working in our favour. The last time I played a Miles Davis number it was interrupted by a self-promotional video from Nigel 'Brexit' Farage. The system cares nothing for the sincerity of our quest. Burton-Hill writes: 'Whatever your musical tastes or proclivities are, there is no question that music is a powerful means to transcend barriers across space and time, geography and culture, politics and society.'[32] That's an admirable assertion, but is it true, when our curiosity is sabotaged by the crass?

I find myself thinking once more of Bronowski's great book, *The Ascent of Man*. Towards the end he strikes a pessimistic note, utterly at odds with the main thrust, saying, 'I am infinitely saddened to find myself suddenly surrounded in the west by a terrible loss of nerve, a retreat from knowledge – into what?'[33] He dismisses the various whats and regains his own nerve, and I want to follow suit. Everything I have learned through listening to music, reading poetry and other literature, and encountering a broad range of other art, leads me to be positive. Certain key figures have encouraged me most, and Kennedy tops the list: a reclusive seven-year-old who made his own way through the system to astonish the musical world. 'We are all afraid', writes Bronowski, 'for our confidence, for the future, for the world. That is the nature of the human imagination.' It's through '[t]he personal commitment of a man to his skill' that the challenge is overcome.[34]

Bronowski, a scientist, writes that 'it is pointless to advise people to learn differential equations, or to do a course in electronics or in computer programming'.[35] His words were published 50 years ahead of the British government's current maths crusade. Somewhat extraordinarily, he continues by citing that very number: 'And yet, fifty years from now, if an understanding of man's origins, his evolution, his history, his progress is not the commonplace of the schoolbooks, we shall not exist.'[36] The worst has not come, but his warning remains apposite. Where in our curricula is the overview of humanity that he identifies as so crucial? It's far more important than mere maths. If the study of the latter must be forced on us, let's make sure that it includes Bach's fugues, and Fibonacci poetry. 'I often think in music', wrote Einstein. Isn't 'thinking' the one obligatory part of education?

In writing this book, I have unashamedly exposed the frequently eccentric nature of my own thinking. I had to ask myself, over and over again, *why* I was writing, and in almost every passage I also had to ask why I was taking it beyond the obvious field of reference. Then I decided to let go, to risk exceeding my welcome in order to find the unexpected, to push my own curiosity beyond the initial intent, to use Philip Gross's notion of 'free-search' to the full. A lot of what's in this book was nowhere on my radar when I first set out to write; it's not what I originally envisaged, which strikes me as a thoroughly good thing. Perhaps it's a modest blueprint for a new degree called Curiosity Studies. In exploring my admiration for Kennedy, admiration that no doubt marks me as a fan, I haven't hidden behind blinkers. On the contrary, I feel I've broadened my own horizons, as well as gaining a better grasp of the infuriating flip side to charm.

I've also come to appreciate many other violinists that enthral, but I hold to my opinion, which I share with so many others including the late George Martin and the artist Tom Phillips (himself a violinist and a co-contributor to the various projects at Shandy Hall), that Kennedy is the outstanding violinist of our times. I absolutely refute the idea that Kennedy has in any sense wasted his talent. But although I believe him to be a truly great musician, I've also resisted the temptation to call him a genius, primarily because we simply don't understand that word; there's no real definition. Yet it strikes me that while talent can be wasted, genius surely can't. It's simply *there* for us to recognize, marvel at, be transformed by – or to ignore, misunderstand, thereby missing an opportunity to enrich our lives or expand our horizons. As George Steiner suggests, in the quotation with which this book began, genius may come with associated dramas that some may find off-putting, but perhaps we should accept those as corollary, even as indications of exceptional human accomplishment that's been doggedly achieved. The only way genius goes to waste is if those who encounter it are dismissive, resisting its shining light, or worse – shielding others from its glow.

While musical events were being cancelled during the various 2020-21 lockdowns, there was another form of cancellation at work. The rapid rise of 'cancel culture' in 2019 began an increasing call for some prominent figures to be outcast on account of their views and/or conduct. In some cases, the call seemed justified, but cancel culture suddenly seemed to know no bounds, self-righteousness wielding extraordinary power. The phrase has its origins in a song by Nile Rodgers, 'Your Love Is Cancelled' – cancelled as if it were a TV show. But while cancelling a relationship is an individual's prerogative, attempting to block out another individual supposedly on behalf of the whole of society is another matter entirely. It's ironic that the phrase should have emerged from a work of art, as it is art that is often in the firing line. JK Rowling's views on gender sparked a call for the author to be cancelled, which is a short step from burning her books. For similar reasons, Graham Linehan is no longer credited as writer of *Black Books* and other comedies. In the case of poet Kate Clanchy, who had naïvely used terminology deemed to be offensive, the book in question was indeed withdrawn, though subsequently revised and reissued by a different publisher.

In 2021 I had a brush with cancel culture myself. I had collaborated with a highly acclaimed composer who was later found guilty of online crimes against women. Any further collaboration was clearly impossible, and even the completed work was relegated to obscurity. That was clearly for the best, but it raises questions about why and when we insist that art is too tarnished by its authorial associations to be valid. If Carlo Gesualdo had been writing music today, the rather bigger misconduct of murder would undoubtedly have seen him and his music cancelled for good. And yet we still listen to his madrigals and sacred works. Is it only the living who need cancelling? Is that why people want to cancel JK Rowling but not Michael Jackson?

In some cases of course the right to cancel is clear-cut; I doubt many people have Gary Glitter on their Christmas playlists these days. But dismissal is sometimes on the grounds of personal bias, and more often on account of an unwillingness to accept the flawed nature of most human behaviour, and the fact that art often derives from turmoil.

Three twentieth-century artists have inspired me more than any others – poet Ted Hughes, film director Sam Peckinpah, and musician Nigel Kennedy – and they each have a problematic reputation that causes some to dismiss their creative work. In the case of Hughes, his harshest critics view him as responsible for his wife Sylvia Plath's death. They are entitled to avoid his poetry, but I pray they never succeed in preventing others from enjoying it. With Peckinpah, the output is as controversial as the man, but it is nevertheless acknowledged as an exceptional, highly influential body of work. And Kennedy? Part of what I hope this book achieves is an explanation of why 'that awful man', as my fellow passenger on that train journey all those years ago was quick to call him, is nothing of the sort. But just as cancel culture was in full swing, Kennedy risked making things more difficult by writing *Uncensored!*, a book whose very title tells you it refuses to be silenced. It was packed with attitudes and language guaranteed to confirm some people's 'worst suspicions'. Even Richard Morrison, essentially a Kennedy fan, hated it. I haven't come across anything that could be called a positive review. I struggled with it at times myself, but it strikes me that *Uncensored!* is, in a strange way, an important book. It's important that such a book can be published – an honest account of grudges, follies, blindspots and obsessions, the unsanitized reality of a life and mind from which remarkable art has emerged. At the centre of the story is the attempt once made to silence Nigel Kennedy, one of the most significant musicians of our time, ruling out his appearance at the Proms for years, all on the basis of self-righteous opinion about what should and shouldn't be approved.

I'll be the first to admit that Kennedy's book is not as enthralling as the music he has made, but it's important, nevertheless, that we recognize the reality of lives where creativity flourishes. We cannot (or should not) disassociate art from life in the way András Schiff seems keen to do. It's part of its rich fascination, and reward. This applies to us as listeners too. As Max Richter says, 'When a listener encounters a piece of music, they're really bringing their whole biography, and all of themselves, into that experience. That meeting point is absolutely unique to them.'[37] The complication is there, whether we summon it or not. I'm brought back once more to Laurence Sterne, whose marbled page symbolizes that unique relationship between reader and text, the artwork and the individual who encounters it.

What 'more' might we expect from Nigel Kennedy? I feel it's unlikely that we'll see him playing Berg or even Mlynarski at the Proms. I suspect that Bach will be involved (and yes, that's now confirmed, with the Oxford Philharmonic in a 'Bach Now!' tour in November 2023), along with the utterly unexpected, though possibly with little furore. It's generally the case that when we clamour for *more* we're asking for the musician(s) to return to the stage, for more of their individual brilliance rather than more repertoire as such. That's surely the case at a Kennedy concert, where our very attendance is most likely in defiance of Blom, who advises, 'go and hear music, never … a performer, however eminent'.[38] Sorry, Eric, but it's not that simple. He knows it, really, and has to offer us the faux compensation of what he sees as inevitable, the 'satisfaction of seeing an idol tottering on its pedestal'.

The publication of *Uncensored!* presented the very real possibility of my idol tottering. For some, of course, he tottered long ago. But tottering is part of life – and the creative process. Watching an artist maintain their balance after all is a reward in itself. Kennedy as ever has plenty of new plans, amongst which are the 'inclusivity' album[39] and a double concerto for violin and didgeridoo, with William Barton.[40] There are no new Kennedy albums as yet, but he features on Donovan's new album, *Gaelia*, along with David Gilmour of Pink Floyd, and others, including Steve Cooney also playing didgeridoo. Donovan was Kennedy's surprise encore guest at his Festival Hall recital of 1997, the first Kennedy concert I ever attended. It feels as if a twenty-five-year-old collaboration is not so much on repeat as continuing to explore a musical friendship for our further musical delight.

If, for some musicians, encores seem merely to go through the motions, for others they provide a route into new musical territory. The tracks on the Kerenza Peacock/Pavão Quartet album, *Someone to Watch Over Me* (2006), are pieces they originally developed as encores, in live concerts. It's effectively a whole album of bonus tracks; 'more' has become the main attraction. But they don't pitch it that way, which strikes me as commendably honest. The context has changed. It's a new, full programme in its own right. The distinction is important because, it now occurs to me, there *is* fake music, or at least music that has less than honest designs on us. There's also music that doesn't come from the heart, that's all show, just as certain behaviour is a sham.

It's finally time to mention what I've ignored until this moment: Kennedy's so-called 'fake', 'mockney' accent. The perceived fakery has been enough for some people to dismiss him. On one level, I understand that, as yes – fakery should be rumbled. But for two other reasons I strongly believe those doubters are wrong. Firstly, a musician's accent, even if contrived, surely has precious little relevance to their music. Secondly, I don't believe it's a sham at all. Fakery is not in Kennedy's nature. He has that chameleon-like gift, as I've discussed, to adapt to different environments, and his accent has undoubtedly changed over the years, as the received pronunciation of his early years has been rejected in favour of something that feels more natural to him – and attuned to new environments. It roughens up according to context, and anyone who regularly finds themselves in football crowds will probably know how that happens.

Kennedy is passionate about truthfulness, the quality that he highlights in the playing of other violinists he admires, such as Isaac Stern.

> The thing that I love about his interpretations was that they were just completely truthful – a real truthful probing to the heart of the music he was interpreting. Truth is a fantastic commodity to have in music – if you're bullshitting it shows up pretty quick.[41]

Those who doubt Kennedy's truthfulness – in his playing or his attitudes – are I believe mistaken, and I hope this book will urge them to think again, to listen again, to re-encounter the man and his music without any former bias. The most open-minded of us may have blind-spots, and 'bad' reputations can live long, sometimes with little real justification. The very name Franz Liszt, for instance, is almost shorthand for excessive virtuosity, but Liszt, for all his virtuosic talent, was a crowd-pleaser without being a show-off. The very best can be dismissed or over-looked, and the apparent arrogance of their defiance in the face of critical rejection may compound the problem. Elgar's brilliance is now recognized, but no thanks to his bullish statement of 1900: 'it is curious to be treated by the old-fashioned people as a criminal because my thoughts and ways are beyond them.'[42]

Truthfulness – and serious, relevant purpose – underpinned Kennedy's Proms statement about Palestine (in contrast to his later Proms co-star's PR stunt, as Kennedy saw it). The humanitarian stands he has taken are characterized by compassion, humility, and a sense of how music and musicians have a meaningful role to play in the struggle. There are those who pay lip service to certain causes, just as some of the rich are happy to make charitable donations on a tax-saving basis. Kennedy is not one of them. Nor are his notable friends and peers, such as Lynn Harrell, who together with Helen Nightengale founded HEARTbeats, which 'strives to help children in need harness the power of music to better cope with, and recover from, the extreme challenges of poverty and conflict'.[43] I find it both fascinating and heartening that musicians of the highest order, Menuhin being a leading example, should also be prominent humanitarians. To think of these artists tottering on their pedestals is actually not possible. They are not there posing.

When I watch the film of Kennedy the sixty-five-year-old walking up the hillside from his village, stomping through the snow, violin case in hand, I can almost believe that the still diminutive figure in his woolly hat and coat is the child from all those years ago, full of trepidation and quiet resolve, not unlike the Ukrainian children he says he passes everyday, with their hopes, dreams and fears. Nothing about any of this conforms to what might have been predicted – of Kennedy the youthful virtuoso, the 'punk violinist', Blue Note clubber, or Hendrix obsessive. But that's *right*. None of those descriptions were ever sufficient.

Having questioned labels and the limiting nature of some classifications, it's perhaps not surprising that I searched for so long for an appropriate description of this book. Companion? Study? Critique? While writing, I have also been in residence as a Royal Literary Fund Fellow at the University of Leeds, helping students with 'critical thinking'. There may be some readers of this book who feel I am poorly qualified for such a job, on the evidence of these eccentric chapters, but I firmly believe that eccentricity was required, indeed that more of it is needed in academic circles where increasingly lifeless, jargon-based prose is becoming dominant, and conventions go unquestioned. As with the classical music establishment against which Kennedy reacted, academia seems happy to preserve its own rules at any cost – cost, that is, to the students each paying £28,000, or more if they come from overseas. Perhaps Rishi Sunak's wish that school pupils (with endless years of maths) are well prepared to 'manage their finances as adults' will encourage them to question such an investment. But the situation has actually just got worse. Sunak is now, in the summer of '23, attempting to purge the higher education system of what he deems to be 'low value' degrees: those that don't lead to highly paid jobs. He has the arts and humanities firmly in his sights, failing to understand how they foster creative and critical thinking, and the analytical skills so valuable to such a wide range of work; how, too, they may enrich people's lives – and benefit society – in ways that aren't necessarily measurable in financial terms. If you do wish to invest in a university course that will help you fulfil your particular potential, but without substantial financial prospects, forget it; it's a worthless pursuit, according to Sunak – Sunak *Educare*. We need a PM *Educere* before it's too late.

'Everything changes, and everything stays the same', writes Jonathan Coe in his brilliant post-Covid novel, *Bourneville* (2022). It's true, in so many fascinating ways. The old barriers are replaced by the new. Educational reform takes us back to the dark ages, but new and astonishing talent emerges nevertheless. The passage of life, exemplified by the recurring seasons, is a refreshing repeat. It's a picture of relentless change that is itself a constant. As we witness a musician play from memory, the music can seem to be conjured in the air for the very first time. New musicians then emerge with new interpretations, and so it continues. We as listeners hold memories of musical performances. Sometimes we can press *play* on our various devices and have those memories unfold in 'perfect' detail, or we may try to do something similar in our heads. But however hard we try, we cannot remember – sufficiently – the magic of a live performance. I have a very good memory of how thrilled I was at every Kennedy concert I have been to, but it doesn't amount to the thrill itself. That is why I want *more*.

I'm tempted to compare that to the football supporter who has seen it all, week in week out, but still wants to see the same formula in action yet again. The comparison works up to a point, though I need to be more specific, and make a distinction between *watching* a match, which can be done on TV, and *attending* a match, which is an entirely different experience. Sky Sports commentators make a big deal of saying, ahead of every game they cover, that 'it's LIVE', with an exaggerated emphasis bigger than my capitals can capture. That's a sham. It's a good substitute for being at the match, but it's not the same thing. Kennedy knows that, revelling in being part of the crowd at Villa Park, and it's informed his own concerts in a profound way. He has surely suffered matches where the players don't really 'show up', as the phrase goes, and concert-goers have suffered the same, when musicians have been going through the motions; never, though, at a Kennedy concert. I think of Patricia Kopatchinskaja commenting that '[a] really good interpretation has me sitting on the edge of my seat in rapt attention and full of astonishment'. That has been my Kennedy experience every time.

I have wanted to explain what it is about Kennedy's playing that strikes me as so special. I hope I have offered some insights, but I also realize that I set myself an impossible task, precisely because of what I have said above – that unless you are there in the moment, the moment lived by the artist to the ephemeral full, you can only have an approximate sense of its unique ability both to stir and still the soul.

I'll finish by borrowing yet again from Philip Larkin, who writes in his poem 'For Sidney Bechet',

> On me your voice falls as they say love should,
> Like an enormous yes. [44]

That 'voice' was a saxophone. For me, listening to Nigel Kennedy, it's been the voice of a violin.

One for the Road

– and maybe a double
for good measure.

The scheduled programme
is done, but not the buzz

that drives the applause
or the desire to linger

at the risk of a frantic dash
to the last train; our hope

for a frenetic Csárdás
too great a pleasure

to relinquish
on account of the inevitable,

tedious trouble,
and so we clap, and clap...

waiting for our bonus mix
of Monti and/or hardcore electric –

maybe Hendrix,
'Crosstown traffic'

('the reason I was late!') –
with something gentler,

wandering with 'Danny Boy'
into the audience, to pause

beside an exhausted baby,
when we feel the embrace

of slumber and dream
as you go up, up

another octave, though no,
no higher

('well not till later' ;-) ...
You dodge

your way offstage,
riding the invisible

punches – the crass attack
from gods, critics –

while meeting the joyous,
vigorous high-fives

from every best mate
waiting to discover

a further palace or skip
in which to recreate

a club in Greenwich Village
and *do more damage,*

which is just another way
of describing musical lives

lived to the full, the joy
that we – left with the hush

of *watch this space*
can only imagine. Irish

fiddler – 'O come ye back
in sunshine or in shadow.'

Appendix

The Four Seasons (original Italian sonnets compiled from the score)

La Primavera

Allegro
Giunt' è la Primavera e festosetti
La Salutan gl' Augei con lieto canto,
E i fonti allo Spirar de' Zeffiretti
Con dolce mormorio Scorrono intanto:
Vengon' coprendo l' aer di nero amanto
E Lampi, e tuoni ad annuntiarla eletti
Indi tacendo questi, gl' Augelletti;
Tornan' di nuovo al lor canoro incanto:

Largo
E quindi sul fiorito ameno prato
Al caro mormorio di fronde e piante
Dorme 'l Caprar col fido can' à lato.

Allegro
Di pastoral Zampogna al suon festante
Danzan Ninfe e Pastor nel tetto amato
Di primavera all' apparir brillante.

L'Estate

Allegro non molto
Sotto dura Staggion dal Sole accesa
Langue l' huom, langue 'l gregge, ed arde il Pino;
Scioglie il Cucco la Voce, e tosto intesa
Canta la Tortorella e 'l gardelino.
Zeffiro dolce Spira, mà contesa
Muove Borea improviso al Suo vicino;
E piange il Pastorel, perche sospesa
Teme fiera borasca, e 'l suo destino;

Adagio e piano - Presto e forte
Toglie alle membra lasse il Suo riposo

Il timore de' Lampi, e tuoni fieri
E de' mosche, e mossoni il Stuol furioso!

Presto
Ah che pur troppo i Suo timor Son veri
Tuona e fulmina il Ciel e grandioso
Tronca il capo alle Spiche e a' grani alteri.

L'Autunno

Allegro
Celebra il Vilanel con balli e Canti
Del felice raccolto il bel piacere
E del liquor de Bacco accesi tanti
Finiscono col Sonno il lor godere

Adagio molto
Fà ch' ogn' uno tralasci e balli e canti
L' aria che temperata dà piacere,
E la Staggion ch' invita tanti e tanti
D' un dolcissimo Sonno al bel godere.

Allegro
I cacciator alla nov' alba à caccia
Con corni, Schioppi, e canni escono fuore
Fugge la belua, e Seguono la traccia;
Già Sbigottita, e lassa al gran rumore
De' Schioppi e canni, ferita minaccia
Languida di fuggir, mà oppressa muore.

L'Inverno

Allegro non molto
Aggiacciato tremar trà neri algenti
Al Severo Spirar d' orrido Vento,
Correr battendo i piedi ogni momento;
E pel Soverchio gel batter i denti;

Largo
Passar al foco i di quieti e contenti
Mentre la pioggia fuor bagna ben cento

Allegro
Caminar Sopra 'l giaccio, e à passo lento
Per timor di cader gersene intenti;
Gir forte Sdruzziolar, cader à terra
Di nuove ir Sopra 'l giaccio e correr forte
Sin ch' il giaccio si rompe, e si disserra;
Sentir uscir dalle ferrate porte
Sirocco Borea, e tutti i Venti in guerra
Quest' é 'l verno, mà tal, che gioja apporte.

Notes

Chapter 1

1   Morrison 2021, n.p.
2   Sterne, 542
3   Smith Start, 276
4   Kennedy 2021, 18
5   Morrison 1997, 5
6   in Seckerson, n.p.
7   in Collins, n.p.
8   in J Pound, 32
9   in Bray, n.p.
10 in Chaffee, n.p.
11 in Nigel Kennedy's Greatest Hits tour programme 2002, 1
12 Christians, n.p.
13 in May, 122
14 in Byrnes, n.p.
15 Szwed, 12
16 ibid. 48
17 ibid. 307
18 Menuhin 1996, 391
19 Szwed, 196
20 ibid.
21 Kennedy 2021, 239
22 Morgan, 39-43
23 Foreman (video)
24 Kennedy 2021, 239
25 Morgan, 42
26 Smith Start, 313
27 in Yule, 51
28 Wakeman's later album release (*The Real Lisztomania*) showed his contribution in a much better light than the original soundtrack compilation.
29 Blake, xviii
30 Ebert, n.p.
31 in *TLS*, Lisztomania (audio)
32 Kennedy, n.p.
33 McDonald, n.p.
34 in Boswell, 449
35 Sterne, 542
36 Edwards appeared at the Olympics, finishing last in two events, in 1988, the year before Kennedy's *Four Seasons* release. Taron Egerton played Edwards in the *Eddie the Eagle* film of 2015.
37 Social and other barriers however persist. For a discussion of issues beyond the scope of this book, see Bull 2019.
38 Cowan, 62
39 Kennedy 1992(a), 32
40 Kennedy 2021, 30
41 Menuhin 1996, 412
42 in Savage 2023, n.p.
43 Gross, n.p.
44 Coe, n.p.
45 Sterne, 180
46 in Munden 1999, 15

Chapter 2

1   Kennedy 2007 (video)
2   in Burton, 403
3   Lawrence, 21
4   Lord, 4
5   Kennedy 1991, 1
6   Nigel Kennedy at the BBC (video)
7   in 'Nigel Kennedy's Polish Adventure' (video)
8   in Evans, n.p.
9   Kennedy 2007 (video)
10 Menuhin 1996, 25-6
11 in Grubb, n.p.
12 Bull, 27
13 https://www.bbc.co.uk/news/uk-64426333
14 Cauter, 8
15 Menuhin 1996, 57
16 ibid. 380
17 in Fenby, 33
18 Menuhin, in Burton, 405
19 Russell's film of 1969 was co-written by Fenby, on whose memoir it is based.
20 Fenby, 40
21 in Fenby, 12
22 Fenby, 23
23 ibid. 44
24 in Kennedy 1991, photo page following 28
25 One of Fenby's 'Interludes' (Interviews) however consists solely of photographs, and such an Interlude focusing on Kennedy might have been fascinating.

26 in Kennedy 1991, photo page following 28
27 Fenby, 133
28 Auditions can be strange. At my Winchester Cathedral voice trial there was also a written paper, and I remember one question: Which footballer was recently transferred for a record fee? It was the one question I knew I got right: Martin Chivers, from Southampton to Spurs, £125,000.
29 Kennedy at the BBC (video)
30 Fenby, 134
31 in Searson, 25
32 Menuhin 1996, 381
33 Kennedy 1996(a), 44
34 Menuhin 1996, 386
35 ibid. 273
36 ibid. 274
37 ibid.
38 ibid. 387
39 Anon. in Fenby, 73-4
40 Classic FM, n.p.
41 Goldblatt, n.p.
42 Kennedy 2021, 25
43 Menuhin 1996, 387
44 Fenby, 84
45 ibid. 91
46 Menuhin 1996, 427
47 Kennedy 2021, 22
48 in Smith, n.p.
49 Kennedy 2021, 22
50 in J Singer, n.p.
51 Fenby, 60
52 in J Singer, n.p.
53 ibid.
54 Kennedy 2021, 108
55 J Singer, n.p.
56 Fenby, 116
57 Kennedy 2021, 145
58 in Shave, 31
59 Kennedy 2007 (video)
60 in Cooke & Horn, 55
61 Hughes, L 2009(a), n.p.
62 in Iwazumi, n.p.
63 Menuhin 1959, n.p.
64 in Ainsley, 19
65 in 'Nigel Kennedy's Polish Adventure' (video)
66 in Nigel Kennedy's Greatest Hits tour programme, 4-5
67 in Royal Philharmonic Orchestra programme, 19
68 in Tango Song and Dance, 10
69 in 'Nigel Kennedy's Polish Adventure' (video)
70 ibid.
71 in Kennedy 2021, 30
72 Smith Start, 276
73 Bronowski, 423-4
74 Khomami, n.p.
75 Slenczynska, 38
76 ibid. 46
77 ibid. 31
78 Bronowski, 425
79 ibid. 426-7
80 Robinson, xxix
81 The School Run, n.p.
82 Fenby, 48
83 Menuhin 1996, 391
84 in Pentreath n.p.
85 in Coyle, 88
86 Robinson, 12
87 Research by Trinity College Dublin has confirmed that such small animals do indeed perceive more individual images per second. (see Anthony)
88 Robinson, 13
89 Robinson's book, Sudden Genius: The Gradual Path to Creative Breakthroughs, is presented, rather amusingly in this context, in Aston Villa claret and blue.
90 in TLS, What's the Point of Practice? (audio)
91 in Robinson, 11-12
92 in TLS, What's the Point of Practice? (audio)
93 ibid.
94 Burton, 402
95 in Robinson, 13
96 Coyle, 104
97 in TLS What's the Point of Practice? (audio)
98 in Wilde, n.p.
99 Robinson, xxiv
100 Larkin 1974, 30
101 in Bacharach, 123
102 The chart was presented within Ken Robinson's keynote talk at the 'Confident Creativity' conference in Glasgow, March 2005, and included in Class Writing (Owen & Munden 2006).

103 Corea, in Steffen, n.p.
104 Coyle, xxiv
105 in Cooke & Horn, 152
106 in Knights, 22
107 in Patterson, n.p.
108 Kennedy 2002, n.p.
109 Menuhin 1996, 391
110 Robinson, 11
111 Fenby, 44
112 Steptoe, 144

Chapter 3

1 Menuhin 1996, 274
2 in *Tango Song and Dance*, 11
3 *Nazareno*, Osvaldo Golijov's work of 2000, is itself a stylistic mis-match, portraying Christ's procession to the cross as a carnival romp.
4 Max Planck Institute, n.p.
5 in Cooke & Horn, 194
6 Max Planck Institute, n.p.
7 ibid. 195
8 O'Brien, n.p.
9 Francis Monkman's father, Kenneth, was the great champion of *Tristram Shandy*, setting up the Laurence Sterne Trust at Shandy Hall in 1967.
10 in Cooke & Horn, 16
11 Robinson, 295
12 in Robinson, 296
13 in Cooke & Horn, 99
14 in Bacharach, 708
15 in Cooke & Horn, 139
16 in Kennedy 1984(a), 2
17 Newman, 632
18 Tommasini, n.p.
19 in Sandved, 655
20 in M Kennedy 1999, 4
21 in Kennedy 1984(a), 2
22 in Grimley & Rushton, 2
23 Kennedy 2008, 9
24 Kennedy 2021, 248
25 Ferruccio Bonavia, in Bacharach, 666
26 Kennedy 1992, 3
27 Kennedy 1986, 4
28 ibid. 3
29 ibid. 6
30 in Burton, 231
31 In 2022 Randall Keith Horton

took the work in a very different direction, with Ellington family approval, in a symphonic arrangement as a concerto grosso.
32 Menuhin 1996, 345
33 Pierpoint, n.p.
34 ibid.
35 in Pierpoint, n.p.
36 Kennedy 2021, 261
37 Williams also made a memorable appearance playing 'We Won't Get Fooled Again' with Pete Townshend at an Amnesty International event, 'The Secret Policeman's Ball', in 1979.
38 in *TLS*, The Inbetweeners (audio)
39 One version of Bach's Fantasia in C minor (1787) includes a paraphrase of a Hamlet soliloquy by the poet Heinrich Wilhelm von Gerstenberg.
40 in Howes, 423
41 Berliner, 216-7
42 Kennedy 1991, 33
43 in *TLS*, The Inbetweeners (audio)
44 Larkin 1983, 297
45 Bhabha, 216
46 Muldoon 1983, 62
47 Menuhin 1996, 386
48 ibid. 353
49 Kennedy 2021, 44
50 Christopher Palmer, in Kennedy 1987, 3
51 Menuhin 1996, 353
52 More recently, James Ehnes has also recorded both works, though ten years apart.
53 Haylock, 30
54 in Kennedy 1987, 6
55 in M Kennedy 1989, 104
56 in Nigel Kennedy Quintet (video)
57 Tovey, 215
58 in Millington, n.p.
59 Kennedy 2021, 250
60 in Haste, 249
61 ibid. 306
62 ibid. 312
63 A commission for a concerto had in fact already been received, from the American violinist Louis Krasner. It was a case of 'repurposing'.

64   Grout, 706
65   At one stage, Kennedy hoped that Nyman would write him a concerto.
66   Johnson, n.p.
67   Dakss, n.p.
68   Derrick Puffett, in Walton, 76
69   Walton, 81
70   in Doggett, 132
71   Kennedy 1986, 4
72   in Nigel Kennedy's Greatest Hits tour programme 2002, 1
73   in Doggett, 132
74   My own black page for the Laurence Sterne Trust project incorporated strips of ciné film, seemingly black but containing a world of colour and light.
75   in Lawson, 18
76   in *TLS*, Playing at sight and playing from memory (audio)
77   ibid.
78   Poetry by Heart, 9
79   in *TLS*, Playing at sight and playing from memory (audio)
80   McCartney, 234
81   in Simpson, n.p.
82   in Niles 2021(a), n.p.
83   in *TLS*, Playing at sight and playing from memory (audio)
84   in Swafford, 452
85   in Royal Philharmonic Orchestra programme, 19
86   Menuhin 1996, 413
87   Kennedy 1991(a), 5
88   Morris, 72
89   ibid. 72-3
90   in Royal Philharmonic Orchestra programme, 19
91   Kopatchinskaja 2020, n.p.
92   Premieres are often an exception to the 'from memory' rule. Even if there's time to 'learn' the piece, it hasn't necessarily had long enough to be taken to heart.
93   Berry, n.p.
94   in Niles 2021, n.p.
95   Kennedy 2021, 255
96   Fenby, 77
97   in Niles 2021, n.p.
98   in Kennedy 2007 (video)
99   Kennedy 1992(a), 5
100 Sterne, 376

Chapter 4

1   Our modern term for a music academy, 'conservatoire' or 'conservatory', derives from the Italian for orphanage: *conservatorio*, from *conservare*, to conserve, or save (ie the children).
2   E Pound 1934, 251
3   Paul, 188
4   Bledsoe, n.p.
5   in Paul, 192
6   in Ticciati, n.p.
7   in *TLS*, The Real Red Priest (audio)
8   Ticciati n.p.
9   Kennedy 2002, 9
10 in Service, n.p.
11 in Ainsley, 19
12 in *TLS*, The Real Red Priest (audio)
13 in 'Nigel Kennedy's Polish Adventure' (video)
14 in *TLS*, The Real Red Priest (audio)
15 Spanoudis, n.p.
16 in Robbins Landon, 197
17 in Bacharach, 290
18 Schiff (video)
19 Spanoudis, n.p.
20 R Williams, 11-12
21 Snodgrass, 70
22 Menuhin 1996, 358
23 Kennedy 2021, 260
24 Edwards, 17
25 A useful account of improvisation in the baroque era is provided by Hyesoo Yoo, 91-96
26 Guilar, 30
27 ibid. 63
28 Muldoon 2006, 195
29 Leonid Desyatnikov developed Piazolla's work into further alignment with Vivaldi in 1996-1998.
30 Morrison 2013(a), n.p.
31 in Recomposed by Max Richter (video)
32 Kennedy 1989, 3
33 Benjamin, 69-82
34 de Campos, 315
35 Reynolds, 29

36 in Eco, 65
37 Nida, 159
38 Eco, 14
39 Raffel, 453
40 Jackendoff, 198
41 Susam-Sarajeva, 190
42 ibid. 191
43 Raffel, 456
44 Way 2018, 4
45 Carr has also written Requiem for an Angel, the title of which is strongly reminiscent of the Berg concerto's dedication.
46 Carr, n.p.
47 Kopatchinskaja 2020(a), 23
48 Nietzche, 242-3
49 in Kopatchinskaja, 32
50 Ticciati, n.p.
51 Richter 2022, 4-5
52 in Richter 2022, 4
53 Ginell, n.p.
54 Richter 2022(a), n.p.
55 Richter 2022, 7
56 Kopatchinskaja 2020(a), 13

Chapter 5

1   in Bacharach, 744
2   Gritten & Kelleher, n.p.
3   ibid.
4   in Black, 142
5   March, n.p.
6   Nickless, 27
7   Haylock, 32
8   Lebrecht 2001, n.p.
9   Kennedy 1991, 68
10 in Bacharach, 693
11 in Steffen 2020, n.p.
12 in Lawson, 18
13 in Black, 143
14 in 'Nigel Kennedy & The Four Seasons' (video)
15 ibid.
16 in Moss, n.p.
17 Kennedy 1991, 51
18 Venta, n.p.
19 in H Wallace 2000, 226
20 in Weingarten, n.p.
21 Lebrecht 1998, n.p.
22 Press Association, n.p.
23 L Hughes 2009, n.p.
24 in Cooke & Horn, 158
25 Billingham et al, 87-88
26 in Bacharach, 731
27 ibid. 711
28 Haylock, 30
29 in Black, 143
30 in Stedman, 374
31 in Haffenden, 86
32 Eliot 1932, 17
33 in Bacharach, 709
34 Kennedy 2021, 56
35 in Bacharach, 750
36 Calinescu, 14
37 in Fisher, n.p.
38 Bruns, 230
39 ibid. 260
40 Maguire, 42
41 ibid.
42 Hendrix, 74
43 in Schulte & Biguenet, 158
44 in Bacharach, 710
45 Burton-Hill, n.p.
46 Gager, n.p.
47 Kopatchinskaja 2022, n.p.
48 in Fisher, n.p.
49 Fenby, 1
50 in Fisher, n.p.
51 in Moss, n.p.
52 ibid.
53 Schiff (video)
54 in Black, 142
55 H Wallace 2006, 115
56 Kanter, n.p.
57 Baxter, 180
58 in Baxter, 211
59 Culshaw 2003, n.p.
60 in Black, 143
61 Kennedy 2021, 55
62 Stephens, n.p.
63 Jay & Janschewitz 2008, n.p.
64 Potter, n.p.
65 Jay & Janschewitz 2008, n.p.
66 Jordan, n.p.
67 Byrne, n.p.
68 in Byrnes, n.p.
69 in Fisher, n.p.
70 in Doggett, 133
71 in Ainsley, 19
72 Kennedy 1992, 3
73 ibid. 5
74 BBC Proms 2008, 6
75 in Burton-Hill, n.p.
76 Burton-Hill, n.p.
77 in H Wallace 2000, 25
78 Doggett, 132

79   in Hibbert, 5
80   Smith Start, 295
81   Hamilton 1993, 98–99
82   Hamilton 1994, 115
83   ibid. 14
84   Cone, 116
85   in Culshaw 2010, n.p.
86   in Hind, n.p.
87   in Smith Start, 302
88   Kipling, 496
89   Smith Start, 310
90   in Moss, n.p.
91   Smith Start, 314
92   in Preston, n.p.
93   Smith Start, 316
94   Tempesta, n.p.
95   Smith Start, 272
96   in Smith Start, 284
97   in Roberts, n.p.
98   Smith Start, 292
99   in H Wallace 2000, 25
100 Smith Start, 292
101 in Culshaw 2003, n.p.
102 in Alberge 2020, n.p.
103 in Doggett, 133
104 Lawson, 20
105 Smith Start, 293
106 Sterne, 490
107 in Hamilton 1993, 36
108 in Moss, n.p.
109 ibid.
110 in Fisher, n.p.
111 in Moss, n.p.
112 Hickling, n.p.
113 in Hicking, n.p.
114 in H Wallace 2000, 25
115 in Goldstein & Belfiore, n.p.
116 Hamilton 1993, 36

Chapter 6

1   in Searson, 27
2   in Culshaw 2003, n.p.
3   in Searson, 27
4   Menuhin 1996, 374
5   Matthews, n.p.
6   in Taylor, n.p.
7   Matthews, n.p.
8   McCartney, 559
9   Ling, in Tzuke, n.p.
10   Tzuke, n.p.
11   P Brown, 279
12   Thompson, n.p.
13   in Thompson, n.p.
14   ibid.
15   P Brown, 285
16   in P Brown, 287
17   P Brown, 286
18   in The Music Afficionado, n.p.
19   in Thompson, n.p.
20   W Wallace, n.p.
21   in W Wallace, n.p.
22   ibid.
23   P Brown, in Larson, n.p.
24   W Wallace, n.p.
25   P Brown, 288-9
26   Duffy, 1
27   Robinson, 51
28   in Grout, 690
29   in Roff, 85
30   Roff, 86
31   Duffy, 2
32   Founder of The Lightning
     Seeds, Ian Broudie, was also
     producer for The Fall, for which
     Brix Smith was guitarist and
     songwriter.
33   Plant's comment was made at
     the Nigel Kennedy and Friends
     Gala Concert, 2017.
34   Plant, 5-8
35   in Arcane, 4
36   ibid. 3
37   ibid.
38   in Sandall, n.p.
39   ibid.
40   ibid.
41   S Jeffes, in Arcane, 4
42   Field, n.p.
43   https://journals.jcu.edu.au/linq/
     article/download/2919/2873/5595
44   in Olivas, n.p.
45   in Farmer, n.p.
46   Farmer, n.p.
47   in Blair, n.p.
48   Kennedy 2021, 117
49   Heaney, 31
50   This, and several subsequent
     comments by Heath were taken
     from an online source no longer
     available.
51   Kennedy 2021, 276
52   Heath 1993, n.p.
53   in Kimberley, n.p.
54   in Heath 1993, n.p.
55   Quanrud, n.p.

56 Heath 2016
57 Time Magazine, n.p.
58 in TF Kelly, 307
59 in Greenfield, n.p.
60 in *TLS*, How to love new music (audio)
61 Grout, 709
62 in Seckerson, n.p.
63 ibid.
64 in Bray, n.p.
65 Holub, 6
66 in Romero, 40
67 in Reid, n.p.
68 in Bray, n.p.
69 in Reid, n.p.
70 in Doggett, 132
71 in BBC Proms 2008, 4
72 Kennedy 1999, 69
73 ibid.
74 ibid. 67
75 ibid.
76 ibid. 67-69
77 ibid. 69
78 ibid. 67
79 in Royal Festival Hall programme
80 in Powers, n.p.
81 in Sullivan, n.p.
82 Cooper, n.p.
83 Butler, 212-3
84 Butler, in Raisin, n.p.
85 in O'Hagan, n.p.
86 Blake, plate 14
87 Ross, n.p.
88 Huxley, 30
89 Mark Steinberg, n.p.
90 in Nigel Kennedy in Recital tour programme
91 in Ainsley, 19
92 in H Wallace 2000, 23
93 in Ainsley, 19
94 ibid.

Chapter 7

1 in Bacharach, 701
2 BBC Proms 2008, 3
3 ibid. 3-4
4 in Ainsley, 19
5 Ólafsson, 7-8
6 in Predota, n.p.
7 Robert Matthew-Walker, in Loussier, 1
8 in Pinch & Trocco, 131
9 Eder, n.p.
10 Cole, n.p.
11 in Strand, n.p.
12 ibid.
13 in Baer, n.p.
14 St John, n.p.
15 in Lunden, n.p.
16 Grohl, 68
17 Schwarz, n.p.
18 Morrison 2008, n.p.
19 Anderson (audio)
20 Lazarus, n.p.
21 Barry McCann, in Kennedy 2009, 4
22 Kennedy 1998, 9
23 BBC Proms 2008, 8
24 Kenneth Loveland, in Kennedy 1997, 1
25 Lebrecht 2001, n.p.
26 Achenbach, 52
27 Norris (audio)
28 Lee, 441
29 Vaughan Williams, 156
30 Morrison 2013, n.p.
31 in H Wallace 2000, 25
32 in Klorman, n.p.
33 Klorman, n.p.
34 ibid.
35 in Klorman, n.p.
36 in S Powell, n.p.
37 Kennedy 2005(a) (video)
38 Cone, 131
39 ibid. 132
40 in Evans, n.p.
41 J Williams, n.p.
42 Menuhin 1996, 379
43 Monson, 26-7
44 in Cooke & Horn, 140
45 ibid. 139
46 in Kennedy 1998, 3
47 ibid.
48 in *Tango Song and Dance*, 10
49 ibid.
50 in Williamson, 41
51 Thorgerson, n.p.
52 in Alberge 2020, n.p.
53 in Kennedy & Harrell, 3-4
54 ibid. 4
55 ibid. 3
56 in Alberge 2020, n.p.
57 Harrell, n.p.
58 in Culshaw 2003, n.p.

59   in Ainsley, 18-19
60   in Lanz, n.p.
61   in Media Wales, n.p.
62   in Nogge, n.p.
63   Lebrecht 2016(a) n.p.
64   in Lebrecht 2017, n.p.
65   in British Rock Symphony, 1
66   Kennedy 2021, 273
67   in British Rock Symphony, 1
68   ibid. 2
69   in Kreps, n.p.
70   Coleman, n.p.
71   Kennedy 2021, 267
72   in Gruar, n.p.
73   ibid.
74   ibid.
75   Brightman, 21
76   Kennedy 2002, 5
77   in Nogge, n.p.
78   https://www.classicfm.com/
     artists/david-garrett/guides/
     david-garrett-facts/world-re-
     cord-holder/
79   in Ainslie, p19
80   John Stanley, in Kennedy 2003,
     10
81   in Kennedy 2004, 3
82   Kennedy 2004, 2

Chapter 8

1   in Duchen 2009, n.p.
2   Sweeting 2010, n.p.
3   ibid.
4   in 'Nigel Kennedy's Polish
     Adventure' (video)
5   ibid.
6   in BBC News, n.p.
7   in 'Nigel Kennedy's Polish
     Adventure' (video)
8   Kennedy 2006(a) (video)
9   Kennedy 2007 (video)
10   in Hickling, n.p.
11   in *Nigel Kennedy plays Beethoven
     & Mozart Concertos* (video)
12   ibid.
13   ibid.
14   Mutter, 4
15   ibid. 5
16   in *Nigel Kennedy plays Beethoven
     & Mozart Concertos* (video)
17   G Brown, n.p.
18   Cowan, 62
19   Lebrecht 2008, n.p.
20   H Wallace 2000, 25
21   in *Nigel Kennedy plays Beethoven
     & Mozart Concertos* (video)
22   ibid.
23   in Clark, 27
24   Mutter, 6
25   Cowan, 62
26   in *TLS*, What's the point of
     cadenzas? (audio)
27   in Bacharach, 708
28   in Steffen, n.p.
29   Cowan, 62
30   in *Nigel Kennedy plays Beethoven
     & Mozart Concertos* (video)
31   ibid.
32   in *TLS*, What's the point of
     cadenzas? (audio)
33   ibid.
34   M Steinberg, n.p.
35   Cowan, 62
36   Pettitt, n.p.
37   Kawabata, n.p.
38   in *TLS*, What's the point of
     cadenzas? (audio)
39   T Hughes, 20
40   Donaghy, 12-3
41   Cowan, 62
42   in Nigel Kennedy's Polish
     Weekend programme, 5
43   in 'Nigel Kennedy's Polish
     Adventure' (video)
44   ibid.
45   ibid.
46   ibid.
47   in Hickling, n.p.
48   Menuhin 1996, 272
49   in Shave, 31
50   in Hickling, n.p.
51   in Hickling, n.p.
52   David Ake, in Cooke & Horn,
     268
53   Hickling, n.p.
54   in Cooke & Horn, 89
55   in Reid, n.p.
56   Kennedy 2008(a), 5
57   in 'Nigel Kennedy's Polish
     Adventure' (video)
58   Shipton, n.p.
59   Bungey 2008, n.p.
60   Shipton, n.p.
61   Kennedy 2021, 165
62   Bungey 2008, n.p.
63   Hewett, n.p.

64 Davis 2008, n.p.
65 Shipton, n.p.
66 Davis 2008, n.p.
67 Davis 2010, n.p.
68 Kennedy 2021, 165
69 Davis 2010, n.p.
70 in Bevan, n.p.
71 ibid.
72 ibid.
73 in M Brown, n.p.
74 Grout, 565
75 Kramer, 84
76 in 'Nigel Kennedy's Polish Adventure' (video)
77 Kramer, 72
78 H Wallace 2000, 3
79 in BBC Proms 2013 (video)
80 in Burton, 414
81 Sweeting 2010, n.p.
82 Kennedy 2018, 6
83 Larkin 1971, 28
84 ibid. 81
85 in Nigel Kennedy in Recital tour programme, 9
86 Kennedy 2017, n.p.
87 in Allison, 39
88 in Nigel Kennedy in Recital tour programme, 8
89 in Nigel Kennedy's Polish Weekend programme, 7
90 in H Wallace 2000, 26
91 Kennedy 1991, 87–88
92 in Culshaw 2010, n.p.
93 Kennedy 2021, 166
94 Bates 1952, 4
95 Doan, n.p.
96 in Hind, n.p.
97 Hamilton 1993, 13
98 ibid. 14
99 ibid. 102
100 Walters, n.p.
101 Kennedy 2021, 158
102 in G Young 2016(a), n.p.
103 Evans, n.p.
104 in 'Nigel Kennedy's Polish Adventure' (video)
105 in BBC Proms 2008, 4
106 in 'Nigel Kennedy's Polish Adventure' (video)
107 in Morrison 2013, n.p.
108 in 'Nigel Kennedy's Polish Adventure' (video)
109 Menuhin 1996, 394

Chapter 9

1 Sterne, 379
2 in Sweeting 2011, n.p.
3 in Hickling, n.p.
4 S Pritchard, n.p.
5 in Jury, n.p.
6 in Maddocks 2013, n.p.
7 in The Celtic, 6
8 Adams, n.p.
9 Way 2021 (video)
10 Ólafsson, 11
11 in Nigel Kennedy Tour Programme 2012, 6
12 Kennedy 2013
13 Schoen, 253
14 Lamperti, 18
15 Schoen, 253
16 Benade, 381
17 in Schwalbe & Partners website
18 von Otter (video)
19 in BBC Proms 2013 Prom 34 (video)
20 Morrison 2015, n.p.
21 in Detroit Symphony Orchestra (video)
22 Kennedy 2016, 8
23 ibid. 9
24 in Lebrecht 2016, n.p.
25 in Detroit Symphony Orchestra (video)
26 in R Powell, n.p.
27 ibid.
28 in Detroit Symphony Orchestra (video)
29 in Bacharach, 686
30 ibid. 181
31 ibid. 687
32 ibid.
33 Kennedy 2007 (video)
34 in Bray, n.p.
35 Original text from Neue Meister website: https://neue-meister-music.com/de/neuemeister/
36 in Sweeting 1998, 14
37 in Alberge 2020, n.p.
38 Mishra, n.p.
39 in Grant, n.p.
40 Alberge 2020, n.p.
41 ibid.
42 Sweeting 2011, n.p.
43 in Kennedy 2005, 3
44 Cityseeker, n.p.

45 Kennedy 2013(a), 4
46 in Lazarus 2021, n.p.
47 Kennedy 2021(a), 12
48 in *TLS*, What's in a Name? (audio)
49 ibid.
50 in Elbphilharmonie 2022, n.p.
51 ibid.
52 ibid.
53 in Hardy, n.p.
54 in Nigel Kennedy at the BBC (video)
55 in Hardy, n.p.
56 Kennedy 2021, 159
57 Menuhin 1996, 406
58 in H Kelly, 21

Chapter 10

1   Bungey 2017, n.p.
2   in Grow, n.p.
3   Kennedy 2013(a), 3
4   in Fulker, n.p.
5   in Seckerson, n.p.
6   in Nigel Kennedy Quintet (video)
7   in original Detroit Symphony Orchestra broadcast 2016
8   Jolly, 1
9   Adorno, 367
10 in FH Pritchard, 296
11 ibid. 297
12 Smith Start, 280
13 N Young, n.p.
14 Grohl, 370-1
15 in Hohenadel, n.p.
16 in Smiley, 122
17 Gross, n.p.
18 in 'Nigel Kennedy at the BBC' (video)
19 Lowell, 205
20 in FH Pritchard, 295
21 Robinson, 328
22 ibid. 329
23 in 'Nigel Kennedy's Polish Adventure' (video)
24 Maddocks 2017, n.p.
25 Kennedy 1996(a), 44
26 in *Tango Song and Dance*, 11
27 Kennedy 2018, 5
28 in Peacock, n.p.
29 Kennedy 2018, 5
30 in Nigel Kennedy in Recital tour programme, 3

31 in IB Singer, back cover
32 Duchen 2009, n.p.
33 in *TLS*, Steve Reich's *Different Trains*: Minimalism and Memory (audio)
34 in Kennedy, 2009(a), 5
35 Smith Start, 281
36 in G Young, n.p.
37 Smith Start, 285
38 Ma 2020 (video)
39 Ma 2022, n.p.
40 Ma 2020 (video)
41 ibid.
42 ibid.
43 Ma 2022(a) n.p.
44 Ma 2020 (video)
45 in Sweeting 2016, n.p.
46 in Bacharach, 709
47 Larkin 1983, 297
48 in Bacharach, 709
49 Kennedy 2021, 166
50 Huffington Post, n.p.
51 in Duchen 2020, n.p.
52 in Scarlett, n.p.
53 Evans, n.p.
54 in Evans, n.p.
55 Alberge 2016, n.p.
56 in G Young, n.p.
57 interviewed on *In Tune*, BBC Radio 3, 22 November 2022
58 Kennedy 2021, 166
59 in Burton, 508
60 in Owen & Munden, 67
61 in Robinson, 308
62 Robinson, 321
63 Duchen 2020, n.p.
64 Robinson, 308
65 Harris, n.p.
66 Schiff claims that JS Bach's music exists independently of his life. But he also considers it lucky that there isn't more biographical information available to us, which seems to express a fear that there is indeed a connection. See Schiff (video).
67 in Alberge 2011, n.p.
68 Larman, n.p.
69 in Shave, 32
70 in *The Daily Star*, 5 February 2022
71 in Byrnes, n.p.
72 *Guardian*, n.p.

73 Kennedy 2021, 192
74 London, vii
75 in CW Eliot, 377
76 ibid.

Chapter 11

1 Christopher Hope's wife, Elenor, was Yehudi Menuhin's assistant. Hope and Menuhin collaborated on a children's book, *The King, the Cat and the Fiddle*, published by Ernest Benn in 1983. Daniel Hope later commissioned a rendition by Bruce Adolphe for string quartet, piano and narrator.
2 in Bacharach, 705
3 Simeonov, n.p.
4 Robinson, 106
5 in Robinson, 122
6 in Bacharach, 706
7 in Lebrecht 2001, n.p.
8 in G Young 2017, n.p.
9 in Bacharach, 726
10 Roth, n.p.
11 in Simpson, n.p.
12 White, n.p.
13 English National Ballet, n.p.
14 Violinists Support Ukraine, n.p.
15 Benedetti 2022 (video)
16 in *Time News*, n.p.
17 in *Tango Song and Dance*, 10
18 Menuhin 1996, 428
19 in a facebook sponsored advertisement
20 Nick Cave provides a blisteringly powerful damnation of the AI 'writer', in one of his Red Hand Diaries posts: https://www.theredhandfiles.com/chat-gpt-what-do-you-think/
21 Richter 2022, 6
22 ibid. 10
23 in Smith 2014, n.p.
24 Nietzsche, 243
25 in Music Matters (audio)
26 'Nigel Kennedy & *The Four Seasons*' (video)
27 Cowan, 62
28 in Richter 2022, 5
29 ibid. 11
30 Benedetti 2021, 10
31 in *The Times*, 4 January 2023, 1
32 in Richter 2022, 10
33 Bronowski, 437
34 ibid. 438
35 ibid. 436
36 ibid. 436-7
37 Richter 2022, 10
38 in Bacharach, 695
39 Kennedy 2021, 166
40 ibid. 158
41 in McPherson, n.p.
42 Elgar, 244
43 in Tsioulcas, n.p.

Sources

Achenbach, Andrew 1998 Review of Elgar/Vaughan-Williams, *Gramophone* https://www.gramophone.co.uk/review/elgar-violin-concerto-vaughan-williams-lark-ascending

Adams, Byron n.d. 'Frank Martin: Les quatre éléments' (The Four Elements) American Symphony Orchestra https://americansymphony.org/concert-notes/frank-martin-les-quatre-elements-the-four-elements/

Adorno, Theodor 1986 *Berg: Der Meister des kleinen* Übergangs, in *Die Musikalishen Monographien*, Frankfurt am Main: Suhrkamp

Ainsley, Rob 2001 'You Looking at Me?' Interview with Nigel Kennedy, *Classic FM*, July

Alberge, Dalya 2011 'Nigel Kennedy accuses fellow violinists of destroying Bach's legacy', *Guardian*, 13 August https://www.theguardian.com/music/2011/aug/13/nigel-kennedy-violinists-bach

Alberge, Dalya 2016 'Classical "factory line"...', *Observer*, 20 November https://www.theguardian.com/music/2016/nov/20/nigel-kennedy-slams-colleges-for-stifling-musical-talent

Alberge, Dalya 2020 'Nigel Kennedy says record company 'jobsworths' drove him to withdraw from classical music', *Telegraph*, 3 May https://www.telegraph.co.uk/news/2020/05/03/nigel-kennedy-says-record-company-jobsworths-drove-withdraw/

Allison, John 2007 'Kennedy's in Pole Position', *Gramophone*, November

Anderson, Nicholas 2012 Bach Double Concerto, BBC Radio 3 Record Review, 13 October https://www.bbc.co.uk/programmes/p02tmmph

Anthony, Sebastian 2013 'Small animals see the world in slow motion...', *Extreme Tech*, 17 September https://www.extremetech.com/extreme/166694-small-animals-see-the-world-in-slow-motion-or-why-your-puppy-is-so-hyperactive

Arcane (Assorted Artists) 1994, CD, Real World

Associated Board of Royal Schools of Music https://gb.abrsm.org/en/making-music/4-the-statistics/42-shifts-in-instrumental-trends/

Bacharach, AL (ed.) 1957 *The New Musical Companion*, London: Victor Gollancz Ltd

Baer, Adam 2007 Bach to Bach with Lara St John, *Glass Shallot*, 26 September https://glassshallot.typepad.com/glassshallot/2007/09/bach-to-bach-wi.html

Bates, HE 1952 'Brains in the feet', *Sunday Times*, 16 November

Baxter, John 1973 *An Appalling Talent: Ken Russell*, London: Michael Joseph Ltd

BBC News 2003 'Eastern spice appeals to Kennedy', 13 June http://news.bbc.co.uk/1/hi/entertainment/2984574.stm

BBC Proms 2008, Prom 3 Programme

BBC Proms 2011, Prom 31 Programme

BBC Proms 2013 Prom 34: Nigel Kennedy, Vivaldi, *The Four Seasons*, 8 August https://www.youtube.com/watch?v=ngSHR3P-cCk

Benade, Arthur 1990 *Fundamentals of Musical Acoustics*, Mineola, NY: Dover Publications

Benedetti, Nicola 2021 *Baroque*, CD, Decca

Benedetti, Nicola 2022 'Violinist Nicola Benedetti accompanies real Ukrainian refugees' stories...', *Classic FM*, 29 March https://www.classicfm.com/artists/nicola-benedetti/violinist-concert-for-ukraine

Benjamin, W 1968 [1923] 'The Task of the Translator' in H Arendt (ed.) *Illumina-tions*, trans. H Zohn, New York, NY: Harcourt Brace Jovanovich,

Berliner, Paul F 1994 *Thinking in Jazz: The Infinite Art of Improvisation*, Chicago, IL: University of Chicago Press

Berry, Mark 2012 'Outstanding Brahms from Nigel Kennedy', 13 June https://seenandheard-international.com/2012/06/outstanding-brahms-from-ni-gel-kennedy/

Bevan, Chris 2013 'England v Poland 1973...', BBC Sport, 14 October https://www.bbc.com/sport/football/24445822

Bhabha, Homi 1990 *Identity, Community, Culture, Difference*, ed. J Rutherford, London: Lawrence & Wishart

Billingham, Mark et al 2014 *Great Lost Albums*, London: Sphere

Black, Johnny 1991 'Is this man a prat?', *Q Magazine*, October

Blair, Susie, 2014 'The Big Blue Ball project...', *The World*, 7 November https://theworld.org/stories/2014-11-07/big-blue-ball-project-defines-25-years-real-world-records

Blake, William 1975 [1790] *The Marriage of Heaven and Hell*, Paris: The Trianon Press/OUP

Bledsoe, EM 2016, 'Make It New', *Routledge Encyclopedia of Modernism*, 1 October https://www.rem.routledge.com/articles/make-it-new

Boswell, James 1887 *The Life of Samuel Johnson*, ed. GBN Hill, Oxford: Clarendon Press

Bray, Elisa 2016 Nigel Kennedy: 'I don't want to be in a country which is racist...', i online, 2 December https://inews.co.uk/culture/music/nigel-kennedy-benders-brexit-moving-berlin-i-dont-want-country-racist-an-ti-semitic-prejudiced-531883

Brightman, Sarah 2003 *Harem*, CD, EMI

British Rock Symphony 1999 CD, Point Music

Bronowski, Jacob 1973 *The Ascent of Man*, London: BBC

Brown, Geoff 2008 Nigel Kennedy: Beethoven/Mozart, *Times*, 11 April https://www.thetimes.co.uk/article/nigel-kennedy-beethovenmozart-8z7zv6vbkx5

Brown, Mark 2010 'Nigel Kennedy lines up soundtrack to 1973 England v Poland game', *Guardian*, 9 March https://www.theguardian.com/music/2010/mar/08/kennedy-improvisation-poland

Brown, Phill 2010 *Are We Still Rolling?* Tape Op Books

Bruns, Gerald L 1992 *Hermeneutics Ancient and Modern*, New Haven, CT: Yale University Press

Bull, Anna 2019 *Class, Control and Classical Music*, Oxford: Oxford University Press

Bungey, John 2008 Review: *A Very Nice Album*, *Times*, 19 July https://www.the-times.co.uk/article/nigel-kennedy-quintet-a-very-nice-album-hsqw2gwtfxn

Bungey, John 2017 Review: 'Nigel Kennedy and Friends at the Royal Albert Hall, SW7', *Times* 16 March https://www.thetimes.co.uk/article/concert-nigel-kennedy-and-friends-at-the-albert-hall-sw7-3sfkd6wx3

Burton, Humphrey 2000 *Yehudi Menuhin*, London: Faber and Faber

Burton-Hill, Clemency 2019 'We need to get emotional about classical music', *Guardian*, 8 October https://www.theguardian.com/music/2019/oct/08/clem-ency-burton-hill-classical-music-podcast-alec-baldwin-ian-mcewan

Butler, Dougal 2012 *Full Moon: The Amazing Rock and Roll Life of Keith Moon*, London: Faber and Faber

Butler, Dougal 2012 'Interview with Dougal Butler by Mark Raison', *Mod Culture*, 4 July https://www.modculture.co.uk/interview-mark-raison-meets-dougal-butler-keith-moons-right-hand-man/

Byrne, Emma 2018 'The Absolute F-cking Best Swear Word For You', *Time*, 23 January https://time.com/5115683/swearing-is-good-for-you-emma-byrne/

Byrnes, Sholto 2004 'Nigel Kennedy: "Antagonism vibes me up"', *Independent*, 16 June https://www.independent.co.uk/arts-entertainment/music/features/nigel-kennedy-antagonism-vibes-me-up-732420.html

Calinescu, Matei 1979 'Hermeneutics or Poetics', *The Journal of Religion* 57 (1)

Carr, Paul 2021 *Four New Seasons*, Goodmusic Publishing https://www.goodmusicpublishing.co.uk/products/GM313/four-new-seasons

Cauter, Gaynor (ed.) 2001 'Fishing in the gene pool', *Classic FM*, July

Chaffee, Keith 2019 'Music Memories: Clara Schumann', Los Angeles Public Library https://www.lapl.org/collections-resources/blogs/lapl/music-memories-clara-schumann

Christians, Ian 2016 *Discovering Classical Music: Vivaldi*, Barnsley: Pen & Sword Books

Cityseeker, 'Man with a Violin Case' https://cityseeker.com/amsterdam/721673-man-with-a-violin-case

Clark, Philip 2008 'True to Type', *Classic FM*, April

Classic FM n.d. 'An American in Paris', Gershwin Guide https://www.classicfm.com/composers/gershwin/guides/gershwin-facts/boulanger-7/

Coe, Jonathan n.d. https://jonathancoewriter.com/book/like-a-fiery-elephant-the-story-of-bs-johnson/

Coe, Jonathan 2022 *Bournville*, London: Viking/Penguin Books

Cole, Jo 2016 'Music students are allowed to follow their muse' (letter), *Guardian*, 27 November https://www.theguardian.com/theobserver/2016/nov/27/observer-letters-nigel-kennedy-royal-collage-of-music

Coleman, Jaz 2000 *Riders on the Storm: The Doors Concerto*, CD, Decca

Collins, Aengus 2003 'Music that goes with the gut', *Irish Times*, 8 July https://www.irishtimes.com/culture/music-that-goes-with-the-gut-1.365365

Coming Along Nicely 1978 Film documentary, dir. Patricia Foy, BBC2, 28 January

Cone, Edward T 1974 *The Composer's Voice*, Berkeley, CA: University of California Press

Cooke, Mervyn, and Horn, David (eds) 2002 *The Cambridge Companion to Jazz*, Cambridge: Cambridge University Press

Cooper, Alice n.d. https://www.sickthingsuk.co.uk/09-people/p-keithmoon.php

Cowan, Rob 2008 'A New Age Mozart and very quick-very slow Beethoven... Kennedy's creepin' in', *Gramophone*, July

Coyle, Daniel 2009 *The Talent Code*, London: Random House

Culshaw, Peter 2003 'They think I'm a good boy now', *Telegraph*, 14 July https://www.telegraph.co.uk/culture/music/rockandjazzmusic/3598616/They-think-Im-a-good-boy-now.html

Culshaw, Peter 2010 'Nigel Kennedy interview for Poland Weekend', *Telegraph*, 26 May http://www.telegraph.co.uk/culture/music/classicalmusic/7767278/Nigel-Kennedy-interview-for-Poland-Weekend.html

Dakss, Jonathan n.d. Summary of *Mahler*, dir. Ken Russell, IMDb https://www.imdb.com/title/tt0071797/plotsummary

Daltrey, Roger 2021 'The Who's Amazing Journey' https://codacollection.co/stories/the-whos-amazing-journey

Dannen, Frederic 1990 *Hit Men: Power Brokers and Fast Money Inside the Music Business*, New York, NY: Times Books

Davis, Clive 2007 'At Ronnie Scott's', *Times*, 22 April https://www.thetimes.co.uk/article/nigel-kennedy-mr2prmn3fhn

Davis, Clive 2008 Review: *A Very Nice Album*, *Sunday Times*, 22 June https://www.thetimes.co.uk/article/nigel-kennedy-quintet-a-very-nice-album-the-sunday-times-review-shr3lstcslh

Davis, Clive 2010 Review: *SHHH!*, *Sunday Times*, 9 May https://www.thetimes.co.uk/article/nigel-kennedy-quintet-shhh-htmnvxvkn8l

De Campos, Haroldo, and Gibson, Diana 2007 [1963] 'Translation as Creation and Criticism', in AS Bessa & O Cisneros (eds) *Novas: Selected Writings of Haroldo de Campos*, Evanston: Northwestern University Press

Detroit Symphony Orchestra 2017 Leonard Slatkin interviews Nigel Kennedy, facebook post, 1 September https://m.facebook.com/watch/?v=10154950633607616&_rdr

Doan, Duy 2017 'All great soccer players are poets', The Poetry Foundation, 24 October https://www.poetryfoundation.org/harriet/2017/10/all-great-soccer-players-are-poets

Doggett, Peter 1996 'Kennedy Meets Kafka', *Record Collector*, September

Donaghy, Michael 1988, *Shibboleth*, Oxford: Oxford University Press

Donovan: *Island of Circles*, CD, Nettwerk

Duchen, Jessica 2009 'Still playing the rebel...', *Independent*, 4 September http://www.independent.co.uk/arts-entertainment/classical/features/still-playing-the-rebel-nigel-kennedy-is-back-and-hes-showing-no-signs-of-mellowing-1781176.html

Duchen, Jessica 2020 'From prodigy to superstar', *Jewish Chronicle*, 14 May https://www.thejc.com/life-and-culture/all/from-prodigy-to-superstar-1.499747

Duffy, Stephen 2004 *Music in Colors*, CD, Harvest/EMI

Ebert, Roger 1975 Review: *Lisztomania*, 28 October https://www.rogerebert.com/reviews/lisztomania-1975

Eco, Umberto 2001 *Experiences in Translation*, University of Toronto Press, Toronto

Eder, Bruce n.d. Review: *Switched-On Bach*, AllMusic https://www.allmusic.com/album/switched-on-bach-mw0000976916

Edwards, Michael 2011 'Believing in Poetry', *Literature and Theology*, 25 (1), 10–19

Einstein, Albert 1987 *The Collected Papers of Albert Einstein, Vols 1–12*, Princeton, NJ: Princeton University Press

Elbphilharmonie 2022 Patricia Kopatchinskaja: *Les Adieux* https://www.elbphil-harmonie.de/en/mediatheque/patricia-kopatchinskaja-les-adieux/703

Elgar, Edward 1987 *Elgar and his Publishers: Letters of a Creative Life*, ed. JN Moore, Oxford: Clarendon Press

Eliot, Charles William (ed.) 1910 *English Essays: Sidney to Macaulay*, New York, NY: PF Collier & Son

Eliot, TS 1932 *Selected Essays*, London: Faber and Faber

English National Ballet 2020 'Take Five Blues', Ballet on Demand https://onde-mand.ballet.org.uk/production/take-five-blues/

Evans, Kathy 2016 'Nigel Kennedy on Brexit...', *Sydney Morning Herald*, 5 December https://www.smh.com.au/entertainment/nigel-kennedy-on-brex-it-useless-conductors-and-why-he-hates-mozart-20161202-gt2cno.html

Farmer, Neville 1992 'The World About Us', mu:zines http://www.muzines.co.uk/articles/the-world-about-us/2368

Fenby, Eric 1969 *Menuhin's House of Music*, London: Icon Books

Field, Douglas 2021 'Michael Horovitz obituary', *Guardian*, 11 July https://www.theguardian.com/books/2021/jul/11/michael-horovitz-obituary

Fisher, Paul 1997 'Catching Mercury', *Irish Times*, 30 January https://www.irishtimes.com/culture/catching-mercury-1.27144

Foreman, George 2016 'The best way to describe Muhammad Ali is beautiful', *Telegraph*, 5 June https://www.facebook.com/TELEGRAPH.CO.UK/videos/george-foreman-the-best-way-to-describe-muhammad-ali-is-beautiful/10154345127119749/

Fulker, Rick 2016 'Classical music star Nigel Kennedy at 60', *Deutsche Welle*, 28 December https://www.dw.com/en/the-classical-music-pop-star-nigel-kennedy-at-60/a-36923474

Gager, Trevor 2010 Review: 'Nigel Kennedy', Arts Hub, 16 February https://www.artshub.com.au/news/reviews/nigel-kennedy-180424-2296970/

Ginell, Richard S 2017 'Fire and ice: the best recordings of the Sibelius violin concerto', The Strad, 7 December https://www.thestrad.com/reviews/fire-and-ice-the-best-recordings-of-the-sibelius-violin-concerto/7351.article?adredir=1

Goldblatt, Cassidy 2016 'An American Lost in Paris: Gershwin Navigating the Classical Sphere', The Gershwin Initiative, University of Michigan, 21 September https://smtd.umich.edu/ami/gershwin/?p=987

Goldstein, Nina, and Belfiore, Michael n.d. Nigel Kennedy Biography, Musician Guide https://musicianguide.com/biographies/1608001157/Nigel-Kennedy.html

Grant, Katie 2022 'Publishers pay to get books on WH Smith 'bestseller' charts...', *Scotsman*, 22 January https://www.scotsman.com/business/consumer/publishers-pay-to-get-books-on-wh-smith-bestseller-charts-3537467

Greenfield, Edward 2002 'The Walton I knew', *Guardian*, 25 January https://www.theguardian.com/lifeandstyle/2002/jan/25/shopping.artsfeatures

Grimley, Daniel, and Rushton, Julian (eds) 2004 *The Cambridge Companion to Elgar*, Cambridge: Cambridge University Press

Gritten, David, and Kelleher, Kathleen 1991 'Not Just Fiddlin' Around', *Los Angeles Times*, 12 May http://articles.latimes.com/1991-05-12/entertainment/ca-2486_1_nigel-kennedy/3

Grohl, Dave 2021 *The Storyteller: Tales of Life and Music*, London: Simon & Schuster

Gross, Philip 2015 'A Walk in the Abstract Garden: How Creative Writing might speak for itself in universities', *Writing in Practice* 1

Grout, Donald J 1973 *A History of Western Music*, London: JM Dent & Sons

Grow, Kory 2017 'Hear Robert Plant's First 'Kashmir' Performance Since Led Zeppelin Reunion, *Rolling Stone*, 15 March http://www.rollingstone.com/music/news/hear-robert-plants-first-kashmir-since-led-zep-reunion-w472220

Gruar, Tim 2013 'Laughing Lines – Jaz Coleman Interview', Fresh Thinking, 24 May https://timgruar.com/2013/05/24/laughing-lines-jaz-coleman-interview/

Grubb, Jennifer 2016 'Violinist cheats death, fulfills destiny', CNN, 13 April https://edition.cnn.com/2016/04/13/health/turning-points-rachel-barton-pine/index.html

Guardian 2022 'Playing music in childhood linked to a sharper mind in old age, study suggests', 29 August https://www.theguardian.com/education/2022/aug/29/playing-music-in-childhood-linked-to-a-sharper-mind-in-old-age-study-suggests

Guilar, Liam 2017 *Anhaga: An exploration in poetry of narrative, memory and identity*, PhD thesis, Deakin University

Gunn, Thom 1992 *The Man with Night Sweats*, London: Faber and Faber

Haffenden, John 1981 *Viewpoints*, London: Faber and Faber

Hamilton, Ian 1993 *Gazza Agonistes*, London: Granta

Hamilton, Ian 1994 *Gazza Italia*, London: Granta

Hardy, Frances 2021 'Nigel Kennedy's symphony of rage...', *Mail Online*, 19 November https://www.dailymail.co.uk/news/article-10222743/Bad-boy-classical-music-Nigel-Kennedy-takes-aim-culture-wars-BBC-Proms.html

Harrell, Eben 2020, 'My father Never Stopped Reaching Out', Slipped Disc, 1 May https://slippedisc.com/2020/05/lynn-harrells-son-my-father-never-stopped-reaching-out/

Harris, John 2011 'The day I (nearly) met Bob Dylan', *Guardian*, 14 May https://www.theguardian.com/music/2011/may/14/bob-dylan-mysterious-rocker-turns-70

Haste, Cate 2019 *Passionate Spirit: The Life of Alma Mahler*, London: Bloomsbury

Haylock, Julian 1997 'Nige Fights Back', *Classic CD*, September

Heaney, Seamus 1979 *Field Work*, London: Faber and Faber

Heath, David n.d. *Alone at the Frontier*, YouTube https://www.youtube.com/watch?v=vpFhYSc5uWM

Heath, David 1993 *Alone at the Frontier*: Concerto for Improvised Instrument and Orchestra, Wise Music Classical https://www.wisemusicclassical.com/work/8313/Alone-at-the-Frontier--Concerto-for-Improvised-Instrument-and-Orchestra--Dave-Heath/

Heath, David 2016 *Alone at the Frontier* score, issuu 2 August https://issuu.com/scoresondemand/docs/alone_at_the_frontier_8313

Hendrix, Jimi 1969 'An Infinity of Jimis', *Life Magazine*, 3 October

Hewett, Ivan 2010 Review: Nigel Kennedy Quintet, *SHHH!*, *Telegraph*, 7 May http://www.telegraph.co.uk/culture/music/cdreviews/7692776/Nigel-Kennedy-Quintet-Shhh-CD-review.html

Hibbert, Tom 1990 'Who the hell does Nigel Kennedy think he is?', *Q Magazine*, September

Hickling, Alfred 2006 'If you need a pillock, call me', *Guardian*, 29 September https://www.theguardian.com/music/2006/sep/29/classicalmusicandopera2

Hind, John 2009 'Did I say that?', *Guardian*, 3 May https://www.theguardian.com/lifeandstyle/2009/may/03/eric-cantona-football

Hohenadel, Kristin 1998 'He May Not Look the Part, but ...' *Los Angeles Times*, 15 November https://www.latimes.com/archives/la-xpm-1998-nov-15-ca-42806-story.html

Holub, Miroslav, 1977 *Notes of a Clay Pigeon*, London: Martin Secker & Warburg Ltd

Hope, Christopher 1981 *In the Country of the Black Pig*, London: London Magazine Editions

Hope, Daniel 2004, *Berg and Britten Violin Concertos*, CD, Warner Classics

Howes, Alan B 1974 *Sterne: The Critical Heritage*, London: Routledge & Keegan Paul

Huffington Post 2013 'BBC to cut Israel 'Apartheid comment from Nigel Kennedy Proms broadcast', *Huffington Post*, 17 August, https://www.huffingtonpost.co.uk/2013/08/16/palestinian-proms_n_3766594.html

Hughes, Langston 2009 'Jazz as Communication', Poetry Foundation https://www.poetryfoundation.org/articles/69394/jazz-as-communication

Hughes, Langston 2009(a) 'The Negro Artist and the Racial Mountain', Poetry Foundation https://www.poetryfoundation.org/articles/69395/the-negro-artist-and-the-racial-mountain

Hughes, Ted 1967 *Wodwo*, London: Faber and Faber

Huxley, Aldous 2004 [1954] *The Doors of Perception*, London: Vintage

Hyland, Paul 1979 *Purbeck: the Ingrained Island*, London: Victor Gollancz Ltd

Hyland, Paul 1984 *Wight: Biography of an Island*, London: Victor Gollancz Ltd

Iwazumi, Ray 2015 'Dorothy DeLay and Her Legacy', *Julliard Journal*, May-August https://journal.juilliard.edu/journal/1505/dorothy-delay-and-her-legacy

Jackendoff, Ray 2009 'Parallels and Nonparallels Between Language and Music', *Music Perception: An Interdisciplinary Journal* 26 (3), 195–204

Jay, Timothy, and Janschewitz, Kristin 2008 'The Pragmatics of Swearing', *Journal of Politeness Research. Language, Behaviour, Culture* 4 (2), 286 https://doi.org/10.1515/jplr.2008.013

Jay, Timothy, and Janschewitz, Kristin 2012 'The Science of Swearing', Association for Psychological Science, 25 April https://www.psychologicalscience.org/observer/the-science-of-swearing

Johnson, Stephen n.d. Brahms Violin Concerto, *Gramophone* https://www.gramophone.co.uk/reviews/review?slug=brahms-violin-concerto-0

Jolly, James 1998 Editorial, *Gramophone*, January

Jordan, John-Erik 2021 'The Science of Curse Words: Why The &@$! Do We Swear?' *Babbel Magazine*, 2 November https://www.babbel.com/en/magazine/why-do-we-swear

Jury, Louise 2011 'Nigel Kennedy on Bach, Bob and that Tory MP', *This Is London Magazine*, 5 August http://www.thisislondon.co.uk/music/article-23976025-nigel-kennedy-on-bach-bob-and-that-tory-mp.do

Kanter, Jake 2020 'BBC Scraps TV Channel Controller Roles in Major Streamng-Led Restructure', *Deadline*, 8 December https://deadline.com/2020/12/bbc-scraps-tv-channel-controller-roles-restructure-1234652035/

Kawabata, Maiko 2010 'How Gilles Apap's New Cadenza illuminates Mozart, via Bakhtin', *Echo* 12.1 https://echo.humspace.ucla.edu/issues/how-gilles-apaps-new-cadenza-illuminates-mozart-via-bakhtin/

Kelly, Henry 2002 '10 Classical Heroes 1992-2002', *Classic FM*, September

Kelly, Thomas Forrest 2000 *First Nights: Five Musical Premieres*, New Haven, CT: Yale University Press

Kennedy, Michael 1989 *Portrait of Walton*, Oxford: Oxford University Press

Kennedy, Michael 1999 Notes for EMI Great Recordings of the Century re-issue of Elgar/Menuhin, CD, EMI

Kennedy, Nigel 1984 *Nigel Kennedy Plays Jazz*, CD, Chandos

Kennedy, Nigel 1984(a) *Elgar Violin Concerto*, CD, EMI

Kennedy, Nigel 1986 *Music by Ellington and Bartók*, CD, EMI

Kennedy, Nigel 1987 *Walton Violin and Viola Concertos*, CD, EMI

Kennedy, Nigel 1989 *Vivaldi, The Four Seasons*, CD, EMI

Kennedy, Nigel 1991 *Always Playing*, London: Weidenfeld & Nicolson

Kennedy, Nigel 1991(a) *Brahms Violin Concerto*, CD, EMI

Kennedy, Nigel 1992 *Tchaikovsky and Sibelius Violin Concertos*, CD, EMI

Kennedy, Nigel 1992(a) *Beethoven Violin Concerto*, CD, EMI

Kennedy, Nigel 1996 *Kafka*, CD, EMI

Kennedy, Nigel 1996(a) 'The Great Kennedy Comeback', *Classic CD*, July

Kennedy, Nigel 1997 *Elgar Violin Concerto; Vaughan Williams The Lark Ascending*, CD, EMI

Kennedy, Nigel 1998 *Kreisler*, CD, EMI

Kennedy, Nigel 1999 'Fiddling with Hendrix', Interview with Neville Marten, *Guitarist*, 185

Kennedy, Nigel, and Harrell, Lynn 2000 *Duos for Violin and Cello*, CD, EMI

Kennedy, Nigel 2002 *Nigel Kennedy's Greatest Hits*. CD, EMI

Kennedy, Nigel 2002(a) Nigel Kennedy, Brighton Dome, April 10, *Argus*, 9 April https://www.theargus.co.uk/news/5133787.nigel-kennedy-brighton-dome-april-10/

Kennedy, Nigel 2003 *Vivaldi*, CD, EMI

Kennedy, Nigel 2005 *Inner Thoughts*, CD, EMI

Kennedy, Nigel 2005(a) *Nigel Kennedy Plays Bach*, DVD, EMI

Kennedy, Nigel 2006 *Blue Note Sessions*, CD, EMI

Kennedy, Nigel 2006(a) *Kennedy Live/Vivaldi Live à La Citadelle*, DVD, EMI

Kennedy, Nigel 2007 *Polish Spirit*, DVD, EMI

Kennedy, Nigel 2008 'Fiddler on the loose', *Radio Times*, 12-18 July

Kennedy, Nigel 2008(a) *A Very Nice Album*, CD, EMI

Kennedy, Nigel 2009 *Vivaldi, The Four Seasons*, 20th Anniversary Edition, CD & DVD, EMI

Kennedy, Nigel 2010 *SHHH!*, CD, EMI

Kennedy, Nigel 2012 Royal Philharmonic Orchestra Programme, 12 June

Kennedy, Nigel 2013 *The Four Elements*, CD, Sony

Kennedy, Nigel 2013(a) *Recital*, CD, Sony

Kennedy, Nigel 2015 *Vivaldi: The New Four Seasons*, CD, Sony

Kennedy, Nigel 2016 *My World*, CD, Neue Meister

Kennedy, Nigel 2017 'Nigel Kennedy talks about his devotion to Aston Villa F.C.', *The Strad*, 21 September https://www.thestrad.com/video/nigel-kennedy-talks-about-his-devotion-to-aston-villa-fc/7140.article

Kennedy, Nigel 2018 *Kennedy Meets Gershwin*, CD, Warner Classics

Kennedy, Nigel 2021 *Uncensored!*, Brimscombe: Fonthill Media

Kennedy, Nigel 2021(a) *Uncensored!*, CD, Warner Classics

Khomami, Nadia 2022 'Ruth Slenczynska: the pupil of Rachmaninov still releasing music at 97', 30 January https://www.theguardian.com/music/2022/jan/30/ruth-slenczynska-pupil-rachmanivov-still-releasing-music-age-97

Kimberley, Nick 1994 'Elements of the kitchen-sink drama', *Independent*, 5 February http://www.independent.co.uk/arts-entertainment/music/classical-music-elements-of-the-kitchen-sink-drama-when-composer-dave-heath-joined-the-scottish-1392169.html

Kipling, Rudyard 2015 *Stories and Poems*, Oxford, Oxford University Press

Klorman, Edward 2016 'String quartets were likened to refined conversation during the 18th and 19th centuries' *The Strad*, 1 August https://www.thestrad.com/playing-and-teaching/string-quartets-were-likened-to-refined-conversation-during-the-18th-and-19th-centuries/5161.article

Knights, Ben 2006 'The Future of Creative Writing within A-Level', *Writing in Education* 38

Kopatchinskaja, Patricia 2020 'Life Lessons', *The Strad*, 22 September https://www.thestrad.com/playing-hub/patricia-kopatchinskaja-life-lessons/11172.article

Kopatchinskaja, Patricia 2020(a) *What's Next Vivaldi?*, CD, Alpha Classics

Kramer, Lawrence 1990 *Music as Cultural Practice, 1800-1900* Berkeley, CA: University of California Press https://publishing.cdlib.org/ucpressebooks/view?docId=ft7j49p1r5&chunk.id=d0e3331&toc.id=&brand=ucpress

Kreps, Daniel 2021 'Roger Daltrey Drags the Rolling Stones', *Rolling Stone*, 14 November https://www.rollingstone.com/music/music-news/roger-daltrey-the-rolling-stones-mediocre-pub-band-1257719/

Lamperti, Francesco 1884 *The Art of Singing According to Ancient Tradition and Personal Experience. Technical Rules and Advice to Pupils and Artists*, Milan: G Ricordi & Co.

Lanz, Michelle 2017 'Rachel Barton Pine: Heavy metal and classical music have more in common than you think', *YourClassical*, 13 February https://www.yourclassical.org/story/2017/02/13/rachel-barton-pine-heavy-metal-and-classical-music-have-more-in-common-than-you-think

Larkin, Philip 1971 *The Whitsun Weddings*, London: Faber and Faber

Larkin, Philip 1974 *High Windows*, London: Faber and Faber

Larkin, Philip 1983 *Required Writing: Miscellaneous Pieces 1955-1982*, London: Faber and Faber

Larman, Alexander 2021 https://thecritic.co.uk/the-new-liberace-strikes-again/

Larson, Jeremy 2019 'Spirit of Eden: Talk Talk', *Pitchfork*, 13 January https://pitchfork.com/reviews/albums/talk-talk-spirit-of-eden/

Lawrence, DH 1972 *Selected Poems*, Harmondsworth: Penguin

Lawson, Mark 1993 'The importance of being Nigel', *BBC Music*, May 1993

Lazarus, Ben 2017 'The End Is Nige', *The Sun*, 21 September https://www.thesun.co.uk/news/4512129/nigel-name-babies-british/

Lazarus, Ben 2021 'Prince Charles is more socialist than the Labour Party': an interview with Nigel Kennedy, *Spectator*, 4 December https://www.spectator.co.uk/article/prince-charles-is-more-socialist-than-the-labour-party-an-interview-with-nigel-kennedy/

Lebrecht, Norman 1998 'Love Nige, love his dog', *Telegraph* http://www.telegraph.co.uk/culture/4714459/Love-Nige-love-his-dog.html (no longer accessible)

Lebrecht, Norman 2001 'Nigel Kennedy – Practice makes perfect', *LSM*, 9 May http://www.scena.org/columns/lebrecht/010509-NL-Kennedy.html

Lebrecht, Norman 2008 'Kennedy's hit and miss', *LSM*, 5 March http://www.scena.org/columns/lebrecht/080305-NL-Kennedy.html

Lebrecht, Norman 2016 'Nigel Kennedy ends 16-year American exile', Slippedisc, 4 May https://slippedisc.com/2016/05/nigel-kennedy-ends-18-year-american-exile/

Lebrecht, Norman 2016(a) 'In Defence of David Garrett', Slippedisc, 9 June https://slippedisc.com/2016/06/in-defence-of-david-garrett/

Lebrecht, Norman 2017 'Nigel Kennedy to David Garrett: "F... off"' Slippedisc, 3 April https://slippedisc.com/2017/04/nigel-kennedy-to-david-garrett-f-off/

Lee, Douglas 2002 *Masterworks of 20th-Century Music: The Modern Repertory of the Symphony Orchestra*, New York, NY: Routledge

Lennon, John 1980 'Neil and The Beatles', HyperRust http://hyperrust.org/Rust/TheBeatles.html

Lennox, Annie 2020 'Dido's Lament' https://www.youtube.com/watch?v=3yW-da4RJoOI; https://www.youtube.com/watch?v=f3DFaIovZxc

London, Jack 1956 *Jack London's Tales of Adventure*, ed. I Shepard, Garden City, NY: Doubelday (featuring Jack London quotation from *The Bulletin*, San Francisco, California, 2 December 2016)

Lord, Jon 2008 *Boom of the Tingling Strings*, CD, EMI

Loussier, Jacques 2000 *Toccata: Jacques Loussier Plays Bach*, CD, Camden (BMG)

Lowell, Robert 1970 *Notebook*, London: Faber and Faber

Lunden Jeff 2020 'Legendary Violinist Isaac Stern's Legacy Lives On After 100 Years', NPR, 19 July https://www.npr.org/sections/deceptivecadence/2020/07/19/892757782/legendary-violinist-isaac-sterns-legacy-lives-on-after-100-years

Ma, Yo-Yo 2020 Interview, CNBC on Assignment, Davos https://www.youtube.com/watch?v=nhy_vGow_lg

Ma, Yo-Yo 2022 'Cellist Yo-Yo Ma Recieves 2022 Birgit Nilsson Prize', The Violin Channel, 20 October https://theviolinchannel.com/cellist-yo-yo-ma-receives-2022-birgit-nilsson-prize/

Ma, Yo-Yo 2022(a) 'Birgit Nilsson Prize 2022 to Yo-Yo Ma', Birgit Nilsson Foundation, 17 May https://birgitnilsson.com/prize/en/home-birgit-nilsson-prize/

Maddocks, Fiona 2013 'Nigel Kennedy: Recital – Review', Guardian, 14 April https://www.theguardian.com/music/2013/apr/14/nigel-kennedy-recital-review

Maddocks, Fiona 2017 'Interview with Yoja Wang', Guardian, 9 April https://www.theguardian.com/music/2017/apr/09/yuja-wang-piano-interview-fiona-maddocks-royal-festival-hall

Maguire, Kate 2012 'Reflections on Practice as an Academic Adviser', ESCalate Themed Funding: Work Based Learning Grant Project Final Report http://escalate.ac.uk/downloads/8668.pdf

March, Ivan n.d. Vivaldi The Four Seasons review, Gramophone https://www.gramophone.co.uk/reviews/review?slug=vivaldi-the-four-seasons-27

Matthews, Brendan 2019 'On Kate Bush's Radical Interpretation of Wuthering Heights', Literary Hub, 13 February https://lithub.com/on-kate-bushs-radical-interpretation-of-wuthering-heights/

Max Planck Institute 2018 'Miles Davis is not Mozart: The brains of jazz and classical pianists work differently', 15 January https://www.cbs.mpg.de/brains-of-jazz-and-classical-pianists-work-differently

May, Rollo 1969 Love and Will, New York, NY: WW Norton & Co.

Maynes, Seymour n.d. 15 word sonnets, Jacket 2 https://jacket2.org/commentary/seymour-mayne-%E2%80%93-hail-15-word-sonnets

McCartney, Paul 2021 The Lyrics, London: Allen Lane

McDonald, Trevor 1994 Desert Island Discs, 11 December https://www.bbc.co.uk/sounds/play/p0093qpk

McPherson, Angus 2017 'If you're bullshitting it shows', Limelight magazine, 18 January http://www.limelightmagazine.com.au/features/"truth-fantastic-commodity"-says-nigel-kennedy

Media Wales 2008 'Kennedy 'prevented' from playing at Classical Brits', 8 May http://icwales.icnetwork.co.uk/whats-on/whats-on-news/2008/05/08/kennedy-prevented-from-playing-at-classical-brits-91466-20879024/ (no longer accessible)

Menuhin, Yehudi 1959 'In the violin world', New York Herald Tribune, 1 November

Menuhin, Yehudi 1996 Unfinished Journey, London: Methuen

Menuhin, Yehudi, and Hope, Christopher 1983 The King, the Cat and the Fiddle (illustrated by Angela Barrett), London: Ernest Benn

Menuhin's Children, 2000 BBC Two, 22 April. Promotional clip available at https://www.youtube.com/watch?v=2809HG3yVVI&t=85s

Millington, Barry 2012 'Paavo Berglund obituary', Guardian, 27 January https://www.theguardian.com/music/2012/jan/27/paavo-berglund?CMP=twt_gu

Mishra, James 2020 'The wall between record labels and streaming platforms is about to collapse', Click Track https://www.clicktrack.fm/p/the-wall-between-record-labels-and

Monson, Ingrid 1996 *Saying Something: Jazz Improvisation and Interaction*, Chicago, IL: University of Chicago Press

Morgan, Pete 1973 *The Grey Mare Being the Better Steed*, London: Secker & Warburg

Morris, RO 1935 *The Structure of Music*, London: Oxford University Press

Morrison, Richard 1997 'Mellower Kennedy hits high note on his return', *Times*, 11 April, 5

Morrison, Richard 2008 'Welcome back Nigel Kennedy', *Times*, 8 March https://www.thetimes.co.uk/article/welcome-back-nigel-kennedy-k73tbpz2t5n

Morrison, Richard 2013 'Abuse by music teachers? It can't be ignored, says Nigel Kennedy', *Times*, 5 August https://www.thetimes.co.uk/article/abuse-by-music-teachers-it-cant-be-ignored-says-nigel-kennedy-h95gdjh63qq

Morrison, Richard 2013(a) 'Proms 33 & 34 Review', *Times*, 10 August https://www.thetimes.co.uk/article/proms-33-and-34-nigel-kennedy-bavarian-rsojansons-albert-hall-sw7-jzj5366zqlf

Morrison, Richard 2015 'Nigel Kennedy: *The Four Seasons*', *Times*, 9 October https://www.thetimes.co.uk/article/nigel-kennedy-the-four-seasons-tcx-qthndjqr

Morrison, Richard 2021 'Nigel Kennedy *Uncensored!* review – plays like an angel, acts like a prat', *Times*, 18 December https://www.thetimes.co.uk/article/nigel-kennedy-uncensored-by-nigel-kennedy-review-jcmg8grnt

Moss, Stephen 1999 'Bach to the future', *Guardian*, 14 May https://www.theguardian.com/friday_review/story/0,,296686,00.html

Muldoon, Paul 1983 *Quoof*, London: Faber and Faber

Muldoon, Paul 2006 *The End of the Poem*, London: Faber and Faber

Munden, Paul 2015, 'Poetry by Heart', in G Harper (ed.) *Creative Writing and Education*, Bristol: Multilingual Matters

Munden, Paul, and Wade, Stephen 1999 *Reading the Applause: Reflections on performance poetry by various artists*, York: Talking Shop

Music Matters 2020 'Music in a changing world', BBC Radio 3, 2 July

Mutter, Anne-Sophie 2005 *Mozart: The Violin Concertos, Sinfonia Concertante*, CD, Deutsche Grammophon

Newman, Ernest 1906 *Elgar*, London: John Lane

Nickless, Stuart 1990 'Vivaldi's *Four Seasons*', *Classic CD*, May

Nida, Eugene 1964 *Towards a Science of Translating*, Leiden: EJ Brill

Nietzche, Friedrich 1996 [1879] *All Too Human* (Vol ii, Part One, no. 126, trans. RJ Hollingdale), Cambridge: Cambridge University Press

Nigel Kennedy's Greatest Hits 25th Anniversary Tour programme 2002

Nigel Kennedy at the BBC 2015, BBC Four, 2 January

Nigel Kennedy in Recital 2018 Tour programme

Nigel Kennedy plays Beethoven & Mozart Concertos 2008, film, dir. John Stanley, Ha Ha films https://www.youtube.com/watch?v=6aPlW9p1Tb4

'Nigel Kennedy's Polish Adventure' 2010 *Imagine*, BBC

Nigel Kennedy's Polish Weekend programme, 2010 London: Southbank Centre

'Nigel Kennedy & *The Four Seasons*' 2021 Episode of *Magic Moments of Music*, dir. Silvia Palmigiano, Isabel Hahn. ZDF/ARTE

Nigel Kennedy Quintet, *Live in Paris at the New Morning* 2007 DVD, Blue Note/EMI

Nigel Kennedy Tour Programme 2012

Niles, Laurie 2021 Interview with Vadim Gluzman, Violinist.com, 11 May https://www.violinist.com/blog/laurie/20215/28758/

Niles, Laurie 2021(a) 'Violinist Rachel Barton Pine to Perform Seated for the Fore-seeable Future', Violinist.com, 19 October https://www.violinist.com/blog/laurie/202110/28953/

Nogge, Haakon 2017 Viokinen-Legende vereisst David Garrett, *TZ*, 2 May https://www.tz.de/stars/violinen-legende-nigel-kennedy-verreisst-david-gar-rett-zr-8067436.html

Norris, David Owen 2021 Elgar's Violin Concerto, BBC Record Review Podcast, 31 October https://www.bbc.co.uk/sounds/play/p0b1gbf4

O'Brien, Lolly 2003 'A poem in the science lab', Princeton Alumni Weekly, 10 September https://www.princeton.edu/~paw/archive_new/PAW03-04/01-0910/features3.html

O'Hagan, Sean 1992 'Nigel Kennedy: Cat Whose Cream Went Sour', *Guardian*, 13 November https://www.rocksbackpages.com/Library/Article/nigel-kennedy-cat-whose-cream-went-sour

Ólafsson, Víkingur 2018 *Johann Sebastian Bach*, CD, Deutsche Grammophon

Olivas, Diego 2014 'Penguin Café Orchestra', Fond/Sound, 18 December https://www.fondsound.com/penguin-cafe-orchestra-the-sound-of-someone-you-love-whos-going-away-and-it-doesnt-matter-1976/

Owen, Nick, and Munden, Paul 2010, *Class Writing: A NAWE Research Report into the Writers-in-Schools Ecology*, York: NAWE

Patterson, Christina 2012 'Nigel Kennedy: Still pulling the strings', *Independent*, 31 August https://www.independent.co.uk/arts-entertainment/music/features/nigel-kennedy-still-pulling-the-strings-8095678.html

Paul, Catherine E 2016 *Fascist Directive: Ezra Pound and Italian Cultural National-ism*, Clemson, SC: Clemson University Press

Peacock, Kerenza n.d. https://www.kerenzapeacock.com/about

Pelé (with Robert L Fish) 1977 *My Life and the Beautiful Game: The Autobiography of Pelé*, New York, NY: Doubleday

Pentreath, Rosie 2020 'Sheku Kanneh-Mason', *Classic FM*, 2 September https://www.classicfm.com/artists/sheku-kanneh-mason/mother-kadia-tu-black-boys-state-school-music-instruments-interview/

Pettitt, Stephen 2008 'Nigel' Kennedy Is Back', *Sunday Times*, 6 April https://www.thetimes.co.uk/article/nigel-kennedy-is-back-hccwqtp93r5

Pierpoint, Claudia Roth 2010 'Black, Brown and Beige: Duke Ellington's music and race in America', *New Yorker*, 10 May https://www.newyorker.com/mag-azine/2010/05/17/black-brown-and-beige

Pinch, Trevor, and Trocco, Frank 2009 *Analog Days: The Invention and Impact of the Moog Synthesizer*, Cambridge, MA: Harvard University Press

Plant, Robert 1993 *Fate of Nations*, CD, Phonogram

Pochin, Juliette 2006 *Venezia*, CD, Sony

Poetry by Heart Handbook 2017

Potter, Tully 2020 'Book Review: Nigel Kennedy *Uncensored!*', *The Strad*, 22 June https://www.thestrad.com/reviews/book-review-nigel-kennedy-uncen-sored/14956.article

Pound, Ezra 1934 *Guide to Kulchur*, London: Faber and Faber

Pound, Ezra 1935 *Make It New*, New Haven, CT: Yale University Press

Pound, Jeremy 1997 'Kennedy Plays Live!' *Classic CD*, September

Powell, Robyn 2008 'Nigel Kennedy criticises "egocentric" conductors', *Telegraph*, 12 March

Powell, Stephanie 2016 'Chiara Quartet to Perform Bartok's Complete Cycle from Memory at Ravinia Festival', *Strings Magazine*, 23 August https://

stringsmagazine.com/chiara-quartet-to-perform-bartoks-complete-cycle-from-memory-at-ravinia-festival/

Powers, Ann 2000 'Critic's Notebook: A Haze As Ever Purple', *New York Times*, 13 October http://www.nytimes.com/2000/10/13/movies/critic-s-notebook-a-haze-as-ever-purple.html

Predota, Georg 2019 'Jacques Loussier (1934-2019)' *Interlude*, 23 April https://interlude.hk/jacques-loussier-1934-2019-combining-jazz-classical-music-creates-new-kind-energy/

Press Association 2016 'Sainsbury's apologises for ad seeking artist to revamp canteen for free', *Guardian*, 13 May https://www.theguardian.com/business/2016/may/13/sainsburys-apologises-ad-seeking-artist-revamp-canteen-for-free

Preston, John 2008 'I didn't want to be the Des O'Connor of the violin', *Telegraph*, 8 June https://www.telegraph.co.uk/culture/music/classicalmusic/3553974/Nigel-Kennedy-I-didnt-want-to-be-the-Des-OConnor-of-the-violin.html

Pritchard, FH (ed.) 1927 *Great Essays of All Nations*, London: George G Harrap & Co. Ltd

Pritchard, Stephen 2010 'Nigel Kennedy/Orchestra of Life', *Guardian*, 7 November https://www.theguardian.com/music/2010/nov/07/nigel-kennedy-orchestra-of-life

Quanrud, Ted 2011, 'Nigel Kennedy's *The Four Elements*', *Classical Music Guide*, 17 October http://www.classicalmusicguide.com/viewtopic.php?f=10&t=38552

Raffel, Burton 1964-65 'Music, Poetry, and Translation', *The Antioch Review* 24 (4) (Winter), 453-461

Raisin, Mark 2012 'Mark Raisin meets Dougal Butler – Keith Moon's Assistant', *Mod Culture*, 4 July https://www.modculture.co.uk/interview-mark-raison-meets-dougal-butler-keith-moons-right-hand-man/

Recomposed by Max Richter: Vivaldi, The Four Seasons, 2012 YouTube https://www.youtube.com/watch?v=qTapNp-31rU

Reid, Graham 2003 'Nigel Kennedy is back', *New Zealand Herald*, 7 November http://www.nzherald.co.nz/lifestyle/news/article.cfm?c_id=6&objectid=3533045

Reynolds, Matthew M 2011 *The poetry of translation from Chaucer & Petrarch to Homer & Logue*, Oxford: Oxford University Press

Richter, Max 2012 *Recomposed by Max Richter: Vivaldi, The Four Seasons*, CD, Deutsche Grammophon

Richter, Max 2022 *The New Four Seasons: Vivaldi Recomposed*, Deutsche Grammophon

Richter, Max 2022(a) 'Like seeing a sculpture from a different angle', *Guardian*, 10 June https://www.theguardian.com/music/2022/jun/10/like-seeing-a-sculpture-from-a-different-angle-max-richter-on-rewriting-the-four-seasons-for-the-second-time

Robbins Landon, HC (ed.) 1959 *The Collected Correspondence and London Notebooks of Joseph Haydn*, London: Barrie and Rockliff

Roberts, Christopher 2011 'How to Prevent or Even Cure a Violin Hickey', *Strings*, 1 February https://stringsmagazine.com/how-to-prevent-or-even-cure-a-violin-hickey/

Robinson, Andrew 2010 *Sudden Genius? The Gradual Path to Creative Breakthroughs*, Oxford: Oxford University Press

Robson, Catherine 2012 *Heart Beats: Everyday Life and the Memorized Poem*, Princeton, MA: Princeton University Press

Roff, Amanda Helen 2019 *Eurydice*, PhD thesis, La Trobe University, Melbourne

Romero Jr, Aldemaro 2012 'Ruth Slenczynska, the pianist who took her future in her hands', City University of New York https://academicworks.cuny.edu/cgi/viewcontent.cgi?article=1372&context=bb_pubs

Ross, Alex 2011 'Prince of Darkness: The Murders and Madrigals of Don Carlo Gesualdo', *New Yorker*, 12 December https://www.newyorker.com/magazine/2011/12/19/prince-of-darkness

Roth, Uli Jon n.d. https://www.ulijonroth.com/

Royal Festival Hall programme 1997, 10 April

Royal Philharmonic Orchestra programme 2012, 12 June

Sandall, Robert n.d. The Penguin Café Orchestra http://www.penguincafe.com/simon.htm

Sandved, Kjell B, 1957 *The World of Music: A Treasury for Listener and Viewer*, London: Waverley

Savage, Mark 2023 'Jeff Beck: British guitar legend dies aged 78' BBC News, 12 January https://www.bbc.co.uk/news/entertainment-arts-64228780

Scarlett, Liz 2021 'Roger Taylor admits...', *Classic Rock*, 28 December https://www.loudersound.com/news/roger-taylor-admits-that-queens-cultural-boycott-breaking-trip-to-apartheid-era-south-africa-was-a-mistake

Schiff, András 2015 András Schiff explains Bach https://www.youtube.com/watch?v=0SclAUqaj2Q

Schoen, Max 1922 'An experimental study of the pitch factor in artistic singing', *Psychological Monographs*, 31 (1), 230–259

Schulte, Rainer, and Biguenet, John (eds) 1992 *Theories of Translation: An Anthology of Essays from Dryden to Derrida*, Chicago, IL: University of Chicago Press

Schwalbe & Partners website, Emma Kirkby https://schwalbeandpartners.com/emma-kirkby-soprano

Schwarz, K Robert 2001, Isaac Stern, *Guardian*, 24 September https://www.theguardian.com/news/2001/sep/24/guardianobituaries

Searson, Charles 1992 'Nigel Kennedy', *Classic CD*, March

Seckerson, Edward 1996 'Nice one Nigel', *Independent*, 23 June http://www.independent.co.uk/news/nice-one-nigel-1338541.html

Service, Tom 2013 'Bach at Easter: take nothing for granted', *Guardian*, 29 March https://www.theguardian.com/music/tomserviceblog/2013/mar/29/bach-at-easter

Shave, Nick 2006 'Bowing to Jazz', *BBC Music Magazine*, November

Shipton, Alyn 2009 'Nigel Kennedy at the Cheltenham Festival', *Times*, 6 May https://www.thetimes.co.uk/article/nigel-kennedy-at-the-cheltenham-festival-vscsgpfclgz

Simeonov, Jenna 2014 'Encore?', Schmopera, 11 November https://www.schmopera.com/encore/

Simpson, Dave 2021 'Nigel Kennedy on his Classic FM fight', *Guardian*, 28 September https://www.theguardian.com/music/2021/sep/28/nigel-kennedy-classic-fm-fight-hendrix-beethoven-vivaldi-des-oconnor-duke-ellington

Singer, Isaac Bashevis 1979 [1960] *The Magician of Lublin*, Harmondsworth: Penguin

Singer, Jonny n.d. 'Facing the Music: Southampton's relationship with The Yehudi Menuhin School' https://thesetpieces.com/latest-posts/facing-music-southamptons-relationship-yehudi-menuhin-school/

Slenczynska, Ruth 1957 *Forbidden Childhood*, New York, NY: Doubleday

Smiley, Jane (ed.) 2003 *Writers on Writing, Volume II: More Collected Essays from the New York Times*, New York, NY: Henry Holt and Company

Smith, David 2003 'Kennedy reveals abuse at music school', *Guardian*, 28 September https://www.theguardian.com/uk/2003/sep/28/childprotection.schools

Smith, David 2014 Daniel Hope – Escape to Paradise (interview), *Presto Music*, 14 October https://www.prestomusic.com/classical/articles/1122--interview-daniel-hope-escape-to-paradise

Smith Start, Brix 2017, *The Rise, the Fall, and the Rise*, London: Faber and Faber

Snodgrass, WD 1980 'The Four Seasons', *Syracuse Scholar* 1: 2

Spanoudis, SL 2009 'Le Quattro Stagioni (The Four Seasons) by Antonio Vivaldi', *Poets' Corner* http://www.theotherpages.org/poems/part2/vivaldi01.html

St John, Lara 2003 *re: Bach*, CD, Sony

Stedman, Edmund Clarence (ed.) 1895 *A Victorian Anthology, 1837–1895*, Cambridge: Riverside Press

Steffen, Chris 2020 'The Story of the "Thunderbolt" That Led to Chick Corea Finally Appreciating Mozart', *AllMusic*, 19 May https://www.allmusic.com/blog/post/chick-corea-interview-premiere-mozart

Steinberg, Mark 2012 Gesualdo Madrigals (quintet arrangement), Program Note https://www.brentanoquartet.com/wp-content/uploads/2012/11/Gesualdo-Madrigals.pdf

Steinberg, Michael 2019 Program Notes: Elgar violin concerto, San Francisco Symphony Orchestra, May https://www.sfsymphony.org/Data/Event-Data/Program-Notes/E/Elgar-Concerto-for-Violin-in-B-minor,-Opus-61

Stephens, Richard 2017 'Think swearing isn't big or clever? Think again', *The Conversation*, 1 February https://theconversation.com/think-swearing-isnt-big-or-clever-think-again-71043

Steptoe, Andrew (ed.) 1998 *Genius and the Mind: Studies of Creativity and Temperament*, Oxford: Clarendon Press

Sterne, Laurence 1998 [1767] *The Life and Opinions of Tristram Shandy, Gentleman*, ed. IC Ross, Oxford: Oxford University Press

Strand, Barbara L 2015 'Studying the violin with Ivan Galamian, *The Strad*, 1 May https://www.thestrad.com/playing-hub/studying-the-violin-with-ivan-galamian/5194.article

Sullivan, Caroline 2012 'Freddie Mercury: the great enigma', *Guardian*, 27 September https://www.theguardian.com/music/2012/sep/27/freddie-mercury-great-enigma

Susam-Sarajeva, Şebnem 2014 'Translation and Music', *The Translator*, 14 (2), 187-200

Swafford, Jan 1997 *Johannes Brahms: a biography*, New York, NY: Alfred A Knopf

Sweeting, Adam 1998 'Elgar second time around', *Gramophone*, January

Sweeting, Adam 2010 'Nigel Kennedy's Polish Adventure', theartsdesk, 14 June https://theartsdesk.com/classical-music/nigel-kennedys-polish-adventure

Sweeting, Adam 2011 'Nigel Kennedy: My plan to put Vivaldi to an electro-beat', *Telegraph*, 1 September http://www.telegraph.co.uk/culture/music/classicalmusic/8734595/Nigel-Kennedy-My-plan-to-put-Vivaldi-to-an-electro-beat.html

Sweeting, Adam 2016 'Keith Emerson Obituary', *Guardian*, 13 March https://www.theguardian.com/music/2016/mar/13/keith-emerson-obituary

Szwed, John 2002 *So What: The Life of Miles Davis*, London: William Heinemann

Tango Song and Dance 2003 CD, Deutsche Grammophon

Taylor, Tom 2022 'John Lydon explains how Kate Bush is the Quaran of music', *Far Out*, 1 June https://faroutmagazine.co.uk/john-lydon-kate-bush-the-quran-of-music/

Tempesta, Erica 2015 '... what your dining habits say about your personality', *Mail online*, 30 September https://www.dailymail.co.uk/femail/article-3255208/Food-expert-reveals-dining-habits-say-personality.html

The Celtic 1997 inc. David Heath, *The Four Elements*, CD, Linn Records

The Listening Service (*TLS*), BBC podcasts https://www.bbc.co.uk/programmes/b078n25h/episodes/player

The Music Aficionado 2018 'Spirit of Eden, by Talk Talk', 13 September https://musicaficionado.blog/2018/09/13/spirit-of-eden-by-talk-talk/

The Open Ears Project https://www.npr.org/podcasts/759388255/the-open-ears-project?t=1570435071346

The School Run n.d. https://www.theschoolrun.com/what-does-gifted-and-talented-mean

Thompson, Graeme 2012 'Talk Talk: the band that disappeared from view', *Guardian*, 13 September https://www.theguardian.com/music/2012/sep/13/talk-talk-mark-hollis

Thorgerson, Storm 1998 Nigel Kennedy, Rockarchive https://www.rockarchive.com/prints/n/nigel-kennedy-kspi001st

Ticciati, Hugo 2016 'Vivaldi the baroque rock god', *Guardian,* 21 October https://www.theguardian.com/music/musicblog/2016/oct/21/hugo-ticciati-o-modernt-vivaldi-the-baroque-rock-god

Time Magazine 1996 'Capeman' Flops, 6 March http://content.time.com/time/nation/article/0,8599,10610,00.html

Time News 2022 '"Violins Not Violence": Nigel Kennedy plays for refugees', 22 March https://time.news/violins-not-violence-nigel-kennedy-plays-for-refugees-free-press/

Tommasini, Anthony 1998 'Elgar with a difference, as played by Kennedy', *New York Times*, 2 November https://www.nytimes.com/1998/11/02/arts/music-review-elgar-with-a-difference-as-played-by-kennedy.html

Tovey, Donald Francis 1936 *Essays in Musical Analysis*, Vol. III, London: Oxford University Press

Tsioulcas, Anastasia 2020 'Cellist Lynn Harrell Has Died', *NPR Music*, 28 April https://www.npr.org/2020/04/28/847462222/cellist-lynn-harrell-has-died-age-76

Tzuke, Judie 2001 *Wonderland*, CD, Sanctuary Records Group

Vaughan Williams, Ursula, 1964 *RVW: A Biography of Ralph Vaughan Williams*, Oxford: Oxford University Press

Venta Air Technologies Inc. https://www.venta-air.com/en_us/pianist-alfred-brendel-venta-family/

Violinists Support Ukraine http://violinistssupportukraine.com/

von Otter, Anne Sofie 2021 'Anne Sofie von Otter: Profile of the superlative Oktavian in Der Rosenkavalier', 5 May https://www.youtube.com/watch?v=8kc6UkRG-pwU

Wakeman, Rick 2008 *Grumpy Old Rock Star*, London: Preface

Wallace, Helen 2000 'They're only making plans for Nigel', *BBC Music Magazine*, March

Wallace, Helen 2006 'John Drummond Remembered', *BBC Music Magazine*, November

Wallace, Wyndham 2019 'Classic Album: Spirit of Eden – Talk Talk', *Classic Pop*, 26 February https://www.classicpopmag.com/2019/02/classic-album-spirit-of-eden-talk-talk/

Walters, John L 2010 'Kroke/Nigel Kennedy's Polish Weekend', *Guardian*, 2 June https://www.theguardian.com/music/2010/jun/01/kroke-nigel-kennedy-pol-ish-weekend-review

Walton, Chris 2014 *Lies and Epiphanies*, Rochester, NY: University of Rochester Press

Way, Darryl 2018 *Vivaldi's Four Seasons in Rock*, CD, The Right Honourable Recording Company Ltd

Way, Darryl 2021 *The Elements*, Youtube https://www.youtube.com/watch?v=71yk-fx5gP-4

Weingarten, Gene 2007, 'Pearls Before Breakfast', *Washington Post*, 8 April https://www.washingtonpost.com/lifestyle/magazine/pearls-before-breakfast-can-one-of-the-nations-great-musicians-cut-through-the-fog-of-a-dc-rush-hour-lets-find-out/2014/09/23/8a6d46da-4331-11e4-b47c-f5889e061e5f_story.html

White, Helen 2015 'Four and three-quarter seasons...', *Spinning Light*, 18 October https://spinningthelight.org/2015/10/18/new-four-seasons/

Wilde, Jon 2014 'Inside the head of Nigel Kennedy', *Daily Mail*, 26 April http://www.dailymail.co.uk/home/event/article-2611572/Nigel-Kennedy-Gary-Lineker-destroyed-half-crockery-kitchen-took-three-windows-nine-iron-Impressive.html

Wilkinson, Jessica 2014 *Suite for Percy Grainger*, Sydney: Vagabond Press

Wilkinson, Jessica 2019 *Music Made Visible: A Biography of George Balanchine*, Sydney: Vagabond Press

Williams, John 2015 Player Spotlight, Guitar Salon International, 1 April https://www.guitarsalon.com/blog/recording-artist-john-williams

Williams, Rita 2008 'The Eight Seasons', in Hong Kong Philharmonic Concert Program, 16/17 May 2014, 11–15 https://www.hkphil.org/f/concert/5689/20140516_TheEightSeasons_502.pdf

Williamson, Nigel 1998 'How to knit pop and the classics with four strings', *Times*, 10 June

Yoo, Hyesoo 2015 'Using Baroque Techniques to Teach Improvisation in Your Classroom', *Music Educators Journal* 102 (1), 92-96

Young, Graham 2016 'Nigel Kennedy at Symphony Hall...' *Birmingham Mail*, 29 January https://www.birminghammail.co.uk/whats-on/music-nightlife-news/nigel-kennedy-symphony-hall-talks-10755658

Young, Graham 2016(a) 'Nigel Kennedy praises Aston Villa star...' *Birmingham Mail*, 1 February https://www.birminghammail.co.uk/whats-on/music-night-life-news/nigel-kennedy-praises-aston-villa-10815880

Young, Graham 2017 'Fans walk out...' *Birmingham Mail*, 13 March https://www.birminghammail.co.uk/whats-on/music-nightlife-news/fans-walk-out-vio-linist-nigel-12731537

Young, Neil 1982 'Neil and The Beatles', HyperRust http://hyperrust.org/Rust/TheBeatles.html

Yule, Andrew 1989 *Fast fade: David Puttnam, Columbia Pictures, and the battle for Hollywood*, New York, NY: Delacorte Press

Index

A Note About the Varius Font

German designer André Maaßen used the contours of a violin's f-holes as the basis for his font family, Varius, used for the cover and headings for this book. The name of the font is an homage to the famous violin maker, Antonio Stradivarius. The unusual combination of chiselled and brushstroke lines represents a somewhat maverick typographical approach.